# Labour and Social Transformation in Central and Eastern Europe

Over a quarter of a century after the fall of the Berlin Wall and 10 years after their accession to the European Union (EU), Central and Eastern Europe Countries (CEECs) still show marked differences with the rest of Europe in the fields of labour, work and industrial relations. This book presents a detailed and original analysis of labour and social transformations in the CEECs.

By examining a wide range of countries in Central Europe, *Labour and Social Transformation in Central and Eastern Europe* offers a comprehensive and contrasting view of labour developments in Central and Eastern Europe. Chapters explore three related issues. The first deals with the understanding of the complex process of Europeanization applied in the sphere of labour, employment and industrial relations. The second issue refers to the attempt to link the Europeanization approach with an analysis mobilizing the theoretical concept of 'dependent capitalism(s)'. The third issue refers to the cumulative trends of labour weakening and labour awakening that has emerged, in particular in the aftermath of the crisis beginning in 2007–2008.

This book will be of interest to academics, policy makers and stakeholders at European and national level in the EU member states.

**Violaine Delteil** is Associate Professor at the Institute for European Studies, Paris University Sorbonne Nouvelle and member of the Research Centre ICEE (Integration and Cooperation in the European Space), France.

**Vassil Kirov**, PhD (Sciences Po) is Associate Professor at the Institute for the Study of Societies and Knowledge, Bulgarian Academy of Sciences (ISSK-BAS) and Associate researcher at the Centre Pierre Naville, University of Evry and at the European Trade Union Institute (ETUI), Belgium.

# Routledge Studies in the European Economy

# Labour and Social Transformation in Central and Eastern Europe

Europeanization and beyond

**Edited by Violaine Delteil and Vassil Kirov**

Routledge
Taylor & Francis Group

LONDON AND NEW YORK

First published 2017 by Routledge

2 Park Square, Milton Park, Abingdon, Oxfordshire OX14 4RN
52 Vanderbilt Avenue, New York, NY 10017

*Routledge is an imprint of the Taylor & Francis Group, an informa
business*

First issued in paperback 2020

*British Library Cataloguing in Publication Data*
A catalogue record for this book is available from the British Library

*Library of Congress Cataloging in Publication Data*
Names: Delteil, Violaine, editor. | Kirov, Vassil, 1971- editor.
Title: Labour and social transformation in Central and Eastern Europe :
Europeanization and beyond / edited by Violaine Delteil and Vassil Kirov.
Description: Abingdon, Oxon ; New York, NY : Routledge, 2016. | Includes
bibliographical references and index.
Identifiers: LCCN 2016007785| ISBN 9781138927995 (hardback) | ISBN
9781315682112 (ebook)
Subjects: LCSH: Labor—Europe, Central. | Labor—Europe, Eastern. |
Europe, Central—Social conditions—21st century. | Europe, Eastern—Social
conditions—21st century. | Regionalism—Europe. | European federation.
Classification: LCC HD8374 .L334 2016 | DDC 331.10943—dc23LC record
available at https://lccn.loc.gov/2016007785

ISBN: 978-1-138-92799-5 (hbk)
ISBN: 978-0-367-66822-8 (pbk)

Typeset in Times New Roman
by FiSH Books Ltd, Enfield

MIX
Paper from
responsible sources
FSC
www.fsc.org   FSC® C013985

Printed in the United Kingdom
by Henry Ling Limited

# Contents

# Illustrations

## Figures

## Tables

# Contributors

**François Bafoil** (Ph.D. from the Institut d'Etudes Politiques de Paris – IEP) is CNRS Senior Research Fellow at CERI – Science Po. He holds degrees in philosophy and in Polish (Langues'O). Before joining the CERI in 2003, he served as expert in charge of ex-ante assessment at the Ministry of Economy in Warsaw (2002–2003) and as a special advisor at the OECD for the Territorial Review Poland, (2008). He has taught at the universities of Köln and Frankfurt/Oder (Germany), Bilgui (Istanbul, Turkey), Fudan (Shanghai, China). In 2010 he was the leader of Coesionet, a research network supported by the French Spatial Planning Agency (DATAR) (www.sciencespo.fr/coesionet/) and now funded by EDF and La Caisse des Dépôts. This research network analyses different dimensions of energy transition and regional development policies in Europe and Asia. Among his last publication is the book *Emerging Capitalism in Central Europe and Southeast Asia: A Comparison of Political Economies*, 2014, Palgrave Macmillan.

**Amélie Bonnet** is a Doctor in Political science since 2014. Her research is focused on economic and social changes in Poland, women's situation, European social and employment policies, structural funds and the Europeanization of public policies. She works also on energy transition issues in Europe (governance and social dimension). She has contributed to the collective works *Accès à l'énergie en Europe. Les précaires invisibles* (ed. with François Bafoil, Dominique Le Roux and Ferenc Fodor, Paris: Presses de Sciences Po, 2014), to different French reviews (Regard sur l'Est, Grande Europe, Questions internationales) and to the review of the Bucharest University.

**Pepka Boyadjieva** is a Professor at the Institute for the Study of Societies and Knowledge at the Bulgarian Academy of Sciences and Honorary Professor of Sociology of Education, University of Nottingham. She is a member of the editorial boards of the ISA's Sage Studies in International Sociology Books, the International Journal of Lifelong Education and the Journal of Social Science Education. Her research areas are university models and social modernization, higher education and social justice, youth transitions, lifelong learning.

**Violaine Delteil** is socio-economist, Associate Professor in the Institute for European Studies at Paris University Sorbonne Nouvelle and member of the Research Centre ICEE (Integration and Cooperation in the European Space). Her main research agenda deals with industrial relations, labour market regulations and labor-management relations in Europe, and gives a particular focus to the Centre and Eastern European Countries and their integration process to the EU. She published in various national and european academic journals and recently co-edited two books: *Strategies of Multinational Corporations and Social Regulations: European and Asian Perspectives*, Violaine Delteil, Patrick Dieuaide, Xavier Richet (eds), Springer, 2014, and *Globalising Employment Relations? Multinational Corporations and Central and Eastern Europe Transitions*, Sylvie Contrepois, Violaine Delteil, Patrick Dieuaide, Steve Jefferys (eds), Palgrave Macmillan, 2011. She is currently involved in the *Balkint* European Research Program dealing with the EU integration process of the Balkan countries.

**Jan Drahokoupil** is a Senior Researcher at the European Trade Union Institute (ETUI) in Brussels. He published a number of books and journal articles on European and transition economies, welfare state, and multinational corporations. His book publications include *Transition Economies: Political Economy in Russia, Eastern Europe, and Central Asia* (with Martin Myant), Wiley-Blackwell, 2011, and *The outsourcing challenge: organizing workers across fragmented production networks* (edited), ETUI, 2015. Jan is an Associate Editor at *Competition and Change: The Journal of Global Business and Political Economy*.

**John Geary** is Professor of Industrial Relations and Human Resources at the College of Business, University College Dublin and Honorary Professor at the Marco Biagi Foundation, Università di Modena e Reggio Emilia, Italy. He holds a D.Phil (Sociology) from the University of Oxford (Nuffield College). In the past, John worked at Warwick Business School, held visiting professorships at the Università di Modena e Reggio Emilia and at the Department of Economics, University of Oslo. He was also Jean Monnet Fellow at the European University Institute (EUI), Florence. His areas of research interest include work and employment, employment practices and human resource management in multinational companies, employee voice, union organization and pay determination. He has published in the leading journals in the field of work and employment relations, including *Industrial Relations: A Journal of Economy and Society* (Berkeley); *The British Journal of Industrial Relations*; *Human Relations, Human Resource Management Journal*; *Work, Employment and Society*; *European Journal of Industrial Relations*; *Industrial Relations Journal*; *International Journal of Human Resource Management*; and *Economic and Industrial Democracy*. He is the author of the book *Partnership at Work: The Quest for Radical Organizational Change* (with Bill Roche), Oxford: Routledge, 2006.

**Ilona Hunek** is Assistant Professor at Kozminski University in Warsaw. She holds a PhD from the University College Dublin (College of Business). In years 2007–2008 she was an advisor to Irish Congress of Trade Unions on integration of migrant workers in Irish workplaces. Her research interests involve managing employment relations in multinational companies.

**Petya Ilieva-Trichkova** is Assistant at the Institute for the Study of Societies and Knowledge at the Bulgarian Academy of Sciences. In the period between 2010 and 2014, she was an early stage researcher in the FP7 Marie Curie ITN "EduWel". Her host institution was the Center for Public Policy Studies at Adam Mickiewicz University in Poznan, Poland, where she is currently a Ph.D. student in Philosophy. Her research interests are in the area of higher education, educational inequalities, social justice, and graduate employability.

**Miklós Illéssy** is a Researcher at the Institute of Sociology, Centre for Social Sciences of the Hungarian Academy of Sciences (Budapest). His research focuses on the various aspects of workplace innovation, organisational learning and sociology of work. In the past 15 years he was involved in numerous international projects, currently he is working on interrelations between innovation, job quality and employment in the framework of the QuInnE project (Quality of Jobs and Innovation Generated Employment Outcomes, Horizon 2020, 2015–2018, www. quinne.eu). Major recent publications: *Developing Dynamic Innovative Capabilities: The Growing Role of Innovation and Learning in the Development of Organisations and Skills in Developed and Emerging Nations of Europe*, (2015) *Journal of Entrepreneurship and Innovation in Emerging Economies*, Vol 1, Issue 1, January, SAGE publications, pp. 18–38. (co-authors: Mithchell, B., Makó, Cs.), *Organizational Innovation and Knowledge Use Practice: Cross Country Comparison* (Hungarian versus Slovak Business Service Sector), (2012) Tokyo: Maruzen Publishing Co., p. 296 (Co-authors: Makó, Cs., Iwasaki, I., Szanyi, M. and Csizmadia, P.).

**Mateusz Karolak** (1986) – PhD Candidate at the Institute of Sociology at the University of Wrocław. Between 2013–2016 Marie Curie Early Stage Researcher in the ITN "ChangingEmployment". He completed secondments at the University of Strathclyde in Glasgow and European Trade Union Institute in Brussels. Member of the editorial board of the *Praktyka Teoretyczna* journal.

**Vassil Kirov,** PhD (Sciences Po) is Associate Professor at the Institute for the Study of Societies and Knowledge, Bulgarian Academy of Sciences (ISSK-BAS) and Associate researcher at the Centre Pierre Naville, University of Evry and at the European Trade Union Institute (ETUI). His research interests are in the sociology of enterprise, work and organisations, employment relations, labour markets and Europeanisation. Vassil Kirov has been a researcher in large EU-funded research projects (SMALL, WORKS, WALQING) and has worked as an external expert for the European Commission, the International Labour Organisation, the European Foundation for Working and Living

Conditions, CEDEFOP, the Fundamental Rights Agency, the Swiss Development Agency, etc. Currently he is a lecturer at Sciences Po, France. He has published several books and articles in international scientific journals. Among his last publications are the co-edited book (with Holtgrewe, Ursula and Monique Ramioul) (2015), *Hard work in new jobs. The quality of work and life in European growth sectors*, Houndmills (Palgrave Macmillan) and *Trade unions strategies to address inclusion of vulnerable employees in 'anchored' services in Europe* (co-authored), *International Journal of Manpower* (2015).

**Agata Krasowska** (1975) – is a Lecturer at the Institute of Sociology, University of Wrocław, Poland. Her main research interests include theories of social change, social conflicts and sociology of knowledge. Her current research interests include precarisation issues and methodology of qualitative research.

**Csaba Makó** is specialized in organizational changes (innovations), in learning organizations and in their institutional (e.g. labour relations system, educational and training system, national innovation system etc.) contexts in an international perspective. He is a Scientific Advisor at the Institute of Sociology of the Hungarian Academy of Sciences and is involved in numerous national and international projects, the latest one: "Quality of Jobs and Innovation Generated Employment Outcomes – QuInnE, Horizon 2020, 2015–2018). He is a Prof.em.Dr. at Szent István University – Faculty of Economics and Social Sciences and at National Public Service University – Faculty of Public Administration. Major recent publications: *Developing Dynamic Innovative Capabilities: The Growing Role of Innovation and Learning in the Development of Organisations and Skills in Developed and Emerging Nations of Europe*, (2015) *Journal of Entrepreneurship and Innovation in Emerging Economies*, Vol 1, Issue 1, January, SAGE publications, pp. 18–38. (co-authors: Mithchell, B., Illéssy, M.), *Organizational Innovation and Knowledge Use Practice: Cross Country Comparison* (Hungarian versus Slovak Business Service Sector), (2012) Tokyo: Maruzen Publishing Co., p. 296 (Co-authors: Iwasaki, I., Szanyi, M., Csizmadia, P. and Illéssy, M.)

**Eugenia Markova** is Senior Lecturer in Economics at the Brighton Business School, University of Brighton, UK. She has an extensive research, consultancy and publication record on the economic and social aspects of labour migration. Her research has covered the UK, Greece, Bulgaria and Spain. Some of her recent publications include: E. Markova, A. Paraskevopoulou, A. Williams, G. Shaw (2013) *Migrant workers in small London hotels: employment, recruitment and distribution*, *European Urban and Regional Studies*, iFirst, 4 December 2013; McKay, S., E. Markova and A. Paraskevopoulou (2011) *Undocumented workers' transitions – legal status, migration and work in Europe*, London: Routledge. She holds a PhD in Economics from the Economics Department of the University of Athens. She has worked for the Faculty of Business and Law, and the Working Lives Research Institute at

London Metropolitan University; the Hellenic Observatory at the London School of Economics; the Sussex Centre for Migration Research at the University of Sussex; the University of Athens and the International Organisation for Migration – the Athens office.

**Guglielmo Meardi** is Professor of Industrial Relations and Director of the Industrial Relations Research Unit at the University of Warwick. He has published widely on the industrial relations dimension of EU enlargement, on foreign investment in Central Eastern Europe and on intra-EU migration.

**Adam Mrozowicki** (1978) – PhD in Social Sciences, lecturer at the Institute of Sociology, University of Wrocław, Poland. His academic interests lie in the areas of the sociology of work, comparative employment relations, and critical social realism. The chair of the Sociology of Work Section of the Polish Sociological Association (2013–2016) and the Vice-President for Communications of the ISA RC44 Labor Movements (2014–2018).

**Martin Myant** is head of the research unit on European Economic, Employment and Social Policy at the European Trade Union Institute in Brussels. He has been researching economic and political development and recent history of east-central Europe for many years with a primary focus on the Czech Republic. He has written or edited 12 books on economic and political developments in eastern and central Europe including *The Rise and Fall of Czech Capitalism: Economic Development in the Czech Republic Since 1989*, Cheltenham: Edward Elgar, 2003 and *Transition Economies: Political Economy in Russia, Eastern Europe, and Central Asia* (with Jan Drahokoupil), Wiley-Blackwell, 2011.

# Acknowledgements

This book project began with the International Conference on "Central and Eastern Europe: Work, Employment and Societies between Transition and Change", organised by the Centre Pierre Naville at the University of Evry (in France), in November 2013. The rich and stimulating debates provided a strong basis for analytical and theoretical ideas that subsequently developed into the book. We would like to thank Jean-Pierre Durand and Stephen Bouquin, of the Centre Pierre Naville, for their support with the conference and the book. Special thanks also go to Steve Jefferys who stimulated the editors to launch and pursue this book project. Thanks are also due to Christine Manigand, director of the ICEE research centre at the University Paris 3, for her constant support with the book project. We are also very thankful to François Bafoil and Rachel Guyet, of CERI, Sciences Po, who offered to organise an Editorial Symposium in Paris in September 2015, which hosted most of the contributors of the book and allowed for further rich debate on the issues covered in the book and its various contributions.

Our main acknowledgements are of course to the book's contributors, and for their active reading and commenting of texts by others. In this regard, we would like to thank especially François Bafoil, John Geary, Guglielmo Meardi, Adam Mrozowicki and Martin Myant for their feedback on the introductory chapter.

Our Routledge editors, Emily Kindleysides and her colleagues Laura Johnson and Elanor Best considerately and patiently guided us through the process of the book's production. Nicholas Sowels helped us with the proofreading of some of the chapters.

As always, the book results from an ongoing collective and participatory effort that extends well beyond our circle of authors, but the responsibility for any remaining errors is ours.

# 1 Introduction: revisiting the transition

## Labour markets, work and industrial relations in the new Europe

*Violaine Delteil and Vassil Kirov*

## Introduction

On 9 November 1989 the Berlin Wall fell and symbolically announced the beginning of what has often been called of post-communism; the period of political and economic transformation or "transition" in former communist states located in Central and Eastern Europe towards free market-oriented capitalist economies with some form of parliamentary democracy. For some observers this return to "normality" was expected to be a rapid process. But more than twenty five years after the fall of the Berlin Wall and ten years after the Central and Eastern Europe Countries (CEECs) acceded to the European Union (EU), they have still not lost their specificities and have not resolved all of the challenges they inherited or faced later in the transition and EU integration processes. This is particularly true in the field of labour markets, work and industrial relations, in which the CEECs still show original patterns which contribute to the socio-economic heterogeneity of the enlarged European Union. While the process of economic transformation is widely considered as having been relatively successful, especially since the beginning of the 2000s, the labour market and social regimes have indeed experienced much more problematic transition since from the start of the reforms and till present (Kohl, 2015). Key difficulties concern notably: low wages, precarious work, instrumentalized social dialogue and strong and continuous labour emigration (at least for some of the countries). Those difficulties have tended to provide some new support to the hypothesis of an "Eastern laboratory" of social regulations, in which the flexible use of employment has found new modalities.

In this complex dynamics of transformation, the processes of EU economic integration and EU regulation have been an ambivalent force for changes, increasingly playing against a "high road" convergence and Europeanization process. Semi-peripheric or peripheric integration of CEECs economic sector into European and international market and global value chain have played a decisive role in a context of competition between territories and institutional frameworks, to mitigate the convergence process. EU rules aimed at harmonizing labour and social norms, have also been largely inefficient to promote a "high road" Europeanization process, before downgrading its own ambition of a "European

Social Model". Echoing the very partial 'top-down' Europeanization, the 'bottom-up' Europeanization has remained contingent of vivid domestic resistances.

Echoing these specific dynamics, the main purpose of this book is to propose a renewed analysis of labour markets and social transformations in the CEECs. The book aims to address and articulate three related issues, whose theoretical and analytical backgrounds are discussed below. The first one deals with the understanding of the complex (multi-scalar, multi-actor) process of Europeanization applied here to the sphere of labour, employment and industrial relations. On this issue, the contributions discuss the more or less effective instruments promoting Europeanization, as well as the channels and obstacles that have contributed to mitigating significantly EU convergence, and which are revealed to be largely rooted in actors' strategies. The second issue refers to the attempt to articulate the Europeanization approach (which emerged in the 1990s) with an analysis mobilizing the theoretical concept of "dependent capitalism(s)" that gained ground in the academic agenda of the mid- and late 2000s. It aims at questioning the emergence or consolidation of external dependencies in the CEECs within the EU integration process, its various modalities and channels, as well as its consequences for actors' games, public policies and socio-economic performance. The third point refers to the ambivalent changes that affected the labour side, in this specific context marked by the "big transformation" of the rules of the game, a growing asymmetry among actors at the expense of the labour constituencies, but also and counterbalancing weakening labour, some forms of labour awakening. The latter are often interpreted as the "end of patience" (Beissinger and Sasse, 2014), which has emerged in particular in the aftermath of the crisis.

The theoretical ambition of the book includes attempts to discuss and re-evaluate the explanatory power of the theories that have driven the analysis of the "big transformation" of post-socialist countries, since its beginning. Explicitly or more implicitly, the chapters develop analytical tools and arguments that offer contributions and criticisms to the renewal of the theoretical and analytical frameworks in two main directions.

The first theoretical direction invites complementing the macro institutionalism centred on structural features and reforms, by drawing on micro-politics and micro-sociology. The focus is on the actors' strategies, their capacity to interpret the rules (foreign or domestic ones), to mitigate or oppose their implementation, as well as the modalities by which actors interplay and inter-relate together, form alliances and coalitions, and proceed to the cumulative definition of their roles. These appear to be very effective in analysing the dynamics of the trends. This approach also helps to reconsider, in a more micro and dynamic way, the "path-dependency theory" (Stark and Bruszt, 1998). The weight and structuring power of the past still appears as a key feature for understanding the peculiar roles endorsed by some groups and actors. These roles originated from their positions and relationships in the previous regimes, as illustrated by the trade unions for example. The latter were unable to efficiently represent and defend the interest of the employees, on many occasions while being cooperative in supporting governments in the changes.[1] Taking into account the permanent redefinition of these roles, which were rooted into the past but have been constantly reviewed according to the context and changing opportunities, helps in reconsidering the CEEC actors' inheritance and in dealing with present issues.

The second direction refers to the "Diversity of Capitalisms" (DoC) approach (see more in Bluhm, 2010; Amable, 2003), which appeared as a challenge to the "Variety of Capitalisms" (VoC) approach (based on the work of Hall and Soskice, 2001). The Diversity of Capitalisms approach has aimed at addressing the two main analytical pitfalls of the VoC: firstly its static stance, by calling for paying more attention to the dynamics of structures, institutions and the games of actors (see below); secondly, the VoC approach looks solely at the business side of capitalism, whereas the DoC literature seeks to enlarge the scene by considering a comprehensive interplay of actors, including domestic and external ones, incorporating coalitions and alliances of actors (be they explicit or not), as well as oppositions and political conflict.

In accordance with the above-mentioned theoretical purposes, the methodology of this book proposes to link macro analysis with a series of empirical findings at the micro level. This ambition is served by a multi-disciplinary approach mobilizing and in some cases bridging different academic fields: institutional economics (mainly under the banner of the DoC approach), the sociology of work, employment and industrial relations (forms of work organisation and employee representation) and political sciences including macro and micro politics (strategies of actors *vis-à-vis* the rules of the games).

The various contributions of the book cover a large range of countries from the region, with the ambition of offering a more comprehensive view of Central and Eastern Europe, and remedying the gaps of many recent contributions that have mostly exclusively focused on the Central European countries (Graziano *et al.*, 2013; Meardi 2012; Avdagic *et al.* 2011). This is particularly true for the discussion of the Europeanization process. Enlarging the panorama to the Balkan region in particular offers interesting insights that feed discussion and qualify "dependent capitalism" (and its regional variants).

Taken together the chapters of the book propose a wide range of illustrations of the Europeanization process and its limits, the building on and reinforcing the processes of external dependencies, as well as the reconfiguration, resistances and resilience of labour and social models in the CEECs. Among the variety of topics proposed in the book, the most original and rarely covered by the existing literature include the analysis of labour migration and migrants' remittances in the home countries (Markova, Chapter 6) and the role of "structural funds" in influencing public policy and the Europeanization process (Bonnet, Chapter 8). Other ground-breaking analysis concerns the development of new union strategies aimed at unionizing precarious workers (Mrozowicki *et al.*, Chapter 12), or aimed at using some external anchor like ILO intervention as a "positive" interference (or dependence) to opposing the domestic process of downgrading social and labour standards (Delteil and Kirov, Chapter 10).

## 1. Europeanization and beyond

We start by looking at what exactly Europeanization means in the context of the CEECs, how it plays out, how actors are impacted and what the impact Europeanization is. What are its instruments and channels? And what obstacles (internal, external) oppose the convergence of the CEECs on institutions and practices in the social and labour sphere? Finally, we ask how far the crisis has overhauled or contradicted the Europeanization project and may have implicitly laid the seeds for a "de-Europeanization" process that appears to be primarily grounded in the periphery of the EU.

The debate about the Europeanization process is not recent, but is ongoing. The general conclusion that emerges from the book echoes the view that concerning Europeanisation, "although acknowledging the EU was at times a motor of change, its power was limited to particular points in the accession process and varied significantly across policy areas" (Haughton 2007). In line with other scholars, the conclusions of the chapter converge on the claim that Europeanization has been a relative success in some spheres (e.g. the economic one) but with a mixed results and failures in the labour and social sphere.

Analytically speaking, the debate on the analysis of the Europeanization process reveals a number of distinctions. First, there are two cumulative processes, i.e. the "top-down" Europeanization monitored by the EU, and the "bottom-up" Europeanization, channelled by the strategies and practices of domestic actors, which are more or less connected to transnational networks. Second, there are various instruments and procedures supporting this process, ranging from the "hard *acquis*", "soft law" through to the downgrading of the EU itself in terms of social convergence. Third, there are phases or periods in the CEECs' institutional process of convergence, running from the preparation and rules' adjustment leading to EU membership, through to the public policy changes triggered by the last crisis.

### *1.1 Europeanization: channels and obstacles*

In the case of the CEECs, more obviously than for older member states, the structuring power of the "hard *acquis*" has been more limited and scrutinises the extent to which real standards and practices changed following EU accession, especially with respect to the myth of a socially cohesive Europe. As illustrated by Meardi (2012 and Chapter 7 in this volume), the limits to the enforcement process of social standards appear particularly relevant for the CEECs. The author shows how the transposition of the "hard *acquis*" remained somehow formal, and how its real impact has been often ambivalent: while the *acquis* has been able to uphold the reinforcement and upgrading of some labour and union rights, it has also had some reverse impacts. This conclusion echoes the analysis of Poland by Mrozowicki *et al.* (Chapter 12). These authors admit that on the one hand EU rules and recommendations contributed to the introduction of some worker-friendly policies, including non-discrimination principles, favourable formal regulations of temporary agency work and some new (not always effective) institutions of employment relations, such as works councils and European works councils (EWCs). However, while the EU directive has been used by some trade unions to impose the transformation of a civil contract to a labour contract, it also served the liberal forces for reforming the legislation on labour contracts and softened the conditions for using flexible, i.e. fixed-term contracts (see Mrozowicki *et al.*, Chapter 12). As summarized by Drahokoupil and Myant (2015: 332), the implementation of EU *acquis* was "slow and rather patchy" and intertwined with pressures from internal actors. Finally, with the distance of time it is clear that "the review of the accession period concerning social and employment issues reveals that specific choices by policy makers and employers actively constructed the enlargement as a social deregulation process, despite initially much talk of a 'European Social Model'. EU law has not had the proclaimed effect of preventing races-to-the-bottom" (Meardi, Chapter 7).

Less surprising, the soft *acquis* have played a much more limited structuring role, reflecting more obviously the weight of the dominant domestic actors, in using, interpreting and filtering EU rules and recommendations. "Top-down" Europeanization has been strongly mitigated by the strategies displayed by some groups of domestic actors, downplaying the enforcement of new institutional rules, and/or instrumentalizing EU recommendations for domestic purposes (i.e. the "use of Europe" as theorized by P. Graziano *et al.* 2013). This appears for instance in the Romanian context, in which the neoliberal government of Emil Boc overused the bail-out conditionalities to impose a profound overhaul of the Labour Code and the Social Dialogue Code, strongly dismantling labour and union rights (Delteil and Kirov, Chapter 10).

The influence of European Funds in the social and labour fields has been far less analysed in the recent literature, but is addressed by two contributions here stressing the structuring role of this incentive along two dimensions. The first one concerns domestic governance in the case of Poland, where it participated in the acceleration of decentralization, the partial retreat of the State in funding some social programs (that were replaced by the European Social Fund, ESF), and to the over-focusing of labour market policies towards some targets, which are not always adapted to specific local features and challenges (Bonnet, Chapter 8). The second dimension concerns the acculturation of trade unions within a cooperative partnership with employer organizations (Delteil and Kirov, Chapter 10). Yet, as cooperation among social partners is mainly directed towards employment policy (the fight against discrimination, informal labour etc.), which is generally an area of consensus and highly time-consuming, union efforts are diverted away from offensive industrial action.

Compared to "top-down" Europeanization, "bottom-up" Europeanization has revealed itself to be much more limited and random in the area of work. It is in particular conditioned to the limited advantages of business actors to harmonise (and upgrade) their labour norms, instead of playing the game of the territorial competition and taking advantage of the permissive institutional environment, counteracting or actually turning the transfer of practices of the multinationals upside down.

"Bottom-up" Europeanization has appeared however in a contrasted manner among sectors and firms, according to many factors. These relate to: commercial activities (export or domestic-led, transnational, productive activities and HR coordination), to the nationality and culture of the headquarters, to the permissiveness or resistance of the host country and affiliates (see for instance, Contrepois *et al.*, 2010).

Drahokoupil and Myant (Chapter 3), highlight the selective transfer of rules and practices within multinational companies (MNC), inducing only a partial upgrading of labour standards. In the banking sector, the domestic-led activity has seen top management dictate relatively low requirements for harmonizing the HR standards in the Eastern subsidiaries. As shown by Hunek and Geary (Chapter 4), the low convergence in the HR rules is also triggered by local management resistance to some harmonization requirements; Polish executives use their knowledge and good financial performances in order to negotiate more autonomy in the field of HR management.

On the labour side, "bottom-up" Europeanization has been largely limited by the lack of resources and transnational connections of local trade union organizations, in order to build effective cooperation with European counterparts throughout the global value chain (GVC) of MNCs. Recent research on European works councils confirms clearly the very constrained role of European social dialogue at firm level in boosting the high road convergence of labour rights. This conclusion that was first triggered by the EWCs, which are often "free zones of trade unionism" (Whittall and Kotthoff, 2011). But it results more generally from the difficulty of employee representatives in resisting the managerial instrumentation of EWCs, often used as a benchmark tool diffusing competition and pressure on HR standards among the different units of a MNC (Delteil and Dieuaide, 2010), even if more optimistic trends are also to be considered, as in the cases of General Motors and Volkswagen, which illustrated the resistance of labour unions to the national policy orientations triggered by the crisis and the emergence of new types of transnational labour protest (Pernicka *et al.*, 2015).

This remark recalls finally that the sense and amplitude of the Europeanization process is conditioned by the balance of power and the unequal capacity of the different actors to use the "EU anchor".

## 1.2 From Europeanization to de-Europeanization: neoliberal recipes prospering in times of crisis

The crisis period that started in 2008–2009 has confirmed many of the previous conclusions reached concerning the limits to EU convergence. But it also calls also for reviewing and reformulating the Europeanization debate.

This time of crisis has in the first place been marked by the vanishing of any ambition to upgrade the social models in the EU. This receding ambition illustrates the growing asymmetry in the EC in favour of the DG Ecofin at the expense of the DG Employment and Social Affairs, but it does not mean there is a decreasing influence of the EU on domestic social issues. During the crisis, the EU has not only reinforced the neoliberal shift in its agenda, but has also introduced new instruments to serve it, including some that are impacting more directly than before the social spheres.

Since 2011, a series of decisions by the EU institutions (the fiscal compact, "six packs", "two packs") have given shape to new economic governance within the framework of the "European Semester" (Lehndorff, 2015: 13). The "new governance" mechanisms have increased the EU pressure for fiscal austerity programs and "structural reforms for more competitiveness" (ibid.). Social policies, in the broadest sense, have today been designated and targeted as the European Monetary Union's (EMU) main adjustment variables (Pochet and Degryse, 2012: 217). More disrupting still has been the way this new EU governance permeates wage policies for the first time with the "European Semester" publishing bi-annual country-specific recommendations (CSR) on the nominal wage changes, with the target of preventing wage growth exceeding labour productivity trends (implicitly legitimizing the erosion of real wages due to inflation). Moreover there are recurrent demands for moderating minimum wage growth, even in countries (like Bulgaria) in which the ratios of minimum wages to median wages remain far below the 60 percent ratio recommended by a recent European Parliament resolution (2010/2039). This new EU scrutiny often replicates International Monetary Fund (IMF) and World Bank requirements conditioning the bail-out program, in favour of wage moderation or wage freezes, social and labour deregulation. Trade unions rights, more clearly presented by the EC as obstacles to the ongoing of reforms, are also more directly targeted to downward revision than before.

During the crisis, the EU has also gained voice and influence on domestic social issues through the conditions of its bail-out programs, and the cumulative pressures exerted by the IMF and the World Bank (as in Southern Europe, analysed for example by Meardi, 2014). This combined influence has been further reinforced by more explicit demands from foreign business (see below Section 3).

Finally, stronger demands have led to new governance arrangements concerning member states and have also offered new occasions for domestic actors to instrumentalize EU recommendations and demands. As illuminated by the case of Romania and outlined above, right-wing governments under the Emil Boc legislature over-stated the imperative dimension of conditionality, presented as non-negotiable, in order to gain external legitimacy to facilitate ongoing, unpopular neoliberal reforms in the labour and social spheres. In this particular case, the strong lobbying and expertise of the American chamber of commerce have revealed themselves to be decisive, as exemplified by the fact that the white paper released by the US chamber evidently served as a virtual draft of the new Labour Code (Delteil and Banarescu, 2013).

The second change of tack in the Europeanization process refers to the broadening of resistance to social Europeanization, which can be identified in the European Commission (EC) itself, and which complements the more traditional opposition to progressive social reform displayed by private multinational actors together with some domestic actors in the CEECs.

The DG Ecofin gave up not only promoting the "European social model" in the mid-2000s, in direct connection with the Eastward enlargement process, but also dropped the ambition of reducing the social fragmentation of the EU. The explicit request addressed by the EC to the Eastern (and Southern) Member States to deregulate labour markets and use the social regimes as the key lever for competitiveness lend to further consistency to this new stance. This shift has implicitly supported territorial competition, sometimes at high social cost, and could be interpreted as opposing the Europeanization process in the labour and social fields. This opposition complements the resistance initially orchestrated by domestic actors and/or multinational actors, and calls for considering the role of the EU as a potential driver of divergence, pressing implicitly towards "De-Europeanization". Incidentally, this reverse EU anchor helps in understanding the changing position and voice of more domestic actors, including some domestic employers, who are asking for state protection against neoliberal forces (see below Section 3).

Almost after a decade of crisis, the failure of the Europeanization project in CEECs appears to result from a conjunction of endogenous and exogenous obstacles. For the new member states, the shift from a "semi-peripheral integration" to "divisive integration" (Lehndorff, 2015) has had strong consequences, as has had the diffusion of neoliberal policies under the auspices of the new EU governance. It has resulted in a new distribution of the roles held by international organizations, with the EU becoming the main driver of austerity and deregulation, while the IMF and Organisation for Economic Co-operation and Development (OECD) have slightly reviewed their own discourse, calling for more awareness of the growth in inequalities and the need for some correcting measures to be taken (with warning being addressed to the EU in accordance).

## 2. "Dependant capitalism" under scrutiny

The CEECs' original dynamics and characteristics have undoubtedly challenged the "Varieties of Capitalism" approach (Hall & Soskice, 2001) which reveals itself to be too static to capture the "big transformation" that occurred in the post-socialist economies. The VoC approach is also too restricted – in its hypothesis and assumptions – for understanding the peculiarities of the mediations (beyond state and market) that have been emerging in these economies, and the interplay of forces (beyond business) that have been at work.

In a more or less tangential way to the VoC approach, and echoing the challenging "Diversity of Capitalism" approach (Amable, 2003), seminal contributions have proposed the notion of "dependent capitalism" (King, 2007; Myant and Drahokoupil, 2012), or "dependant liberal market economies" (Nölke and Vliegenhart, 2009), or "semi-peripheric capitalisms" (Bohle and Greskovitz, 2012). This notion stresses the distinctive features of the CEECs, and their incommensurability with the binary approach of the VoC literature which contrasts "liberal market" with "coordinated market" economies as the governing logics of Western capitalisms.

## 2.1 From dependency to dependencies

These contributions have undoubtedly opened up very promising routes for analysing the dynamics of change in a domestic context, surrounded and partially governed by globalization, through the analysis of the different sources, channels and dimensions of dependency.

Taken together, many analytical proposals and outcomes of the chapters in this book allow for an enlargement of the sources of dependency to be considered, going beyond the exclusive reference to the economic dependency organised through the hierarchical network of MNCs and their CEEC subsidiaries, as proposed in particular by Nölke and Vliegenhard (2009) (see also King, 2007).

In this respect, two main assumptions are considered, and illustrated by different chapters here. Firstly, economic dependency is not only driven by the hierarchical and pervasive power exerted by foreign capital, individually and/or collectively (represented by foreign Chambers of commerce or consulting agencies). Instead, it is first and foremost spread through international trade channels as stressed by Drahokoupil and Myant (2012), and Chapter 3 in this volume. It is also, and not marginally, structured by the transfer of migrant remittances that in South-Eastern Europe have sometimes exceeded FDI flows of capital, most notably in the Western Balkans (see Markova in this volume).

Secondly, part of the dependencies that affect and influence the domestic sphere are not only driven by economic forces but are also channelled institutionally, politically, and even culturally. These multi-faced dependencies, which are beyond the remit of this book, are also grounded (diversely) into the mid- to long term history of the countries, which experienced clear domination (by Comecon, the Austrian-Hungarian Empire, the Ottoman Empire or Russia), or more subtle dependencies that have originated from Western investments in the region.

Returning to more recent times, institutional and political dependencies have mainly been constructed by the intervention of supranational organisations and actors such as the EU (with its rules, recommendations, and distribution of structural funds), the international organizations (IMF, World Bank), and the commercial sections of some powerful foreign embassies (led by the US). As with economic dependency, institutional or political dependency (requirements from the bail-out organizations, or from EU labour directives) could be strategically used by domestic actors for their ends.

Dependency should then be analysed in terms of the respective ability of these different external forces to spread and shape normative rules and informal pressures on social regulations and practices, with the complicity or resistance of domestic forces. This approach complements the analysis inspired by the VoC approach that tends to overestimate the dependencies deriving from MNCs, and it questions the possible alternative or complementary powers and resistance to capital, driven by local alliances and coalitions of actors (labour, the state, some domestic businesses, etc.), or by integrating external forces (such as ILO experts, or international trade union federations).

Contributions of the book provide insightful analysis confirming (according to the approach and country considered) the dependency stemming from foreign markets, FDI or international institutions including the EU (see in particular Drahokoupil and Myant; Delteil and Kirov; Hunek and Geary, in this volume). The book also offers interesting elements for a comparison inside the "dependant capitalisms" in the CEE region, in particular by differentiating the Visegrad Group and the Balkan's countries.

## 2.2 *Variable dependencies paved by State models*

Taken together, analysis of the CEECs tends to confirm the heterogeneity of the countries that are more or less governed or trapped into external dependencies emanating from different sources. If the crisis introduced new dynamics capable of diffusing some dependencies and complicating the distinctions between countries, it does not really challenge, or only partially (Bluhm, 2014), the commonly used typology distinguishing Central Europe (Visegrad), Baltic Europe and South-Eastern Europe (Bohle and Greskovitz, 2012). Dependencies remain unequally distributed, reflecting the diverse performances and constraints of the economic models, as well as the uneven distribution of the power of negotiation and resources for resistance to labour deregulation.

The enlargement of the sources and channels of dependencies offers complementary assertions. Focusing on countries in which the State and labour have proved to be more resistant to the powers of normalization from outside, as illuminated by the case of the Czech Republic, calls for qualifying the assertion of "dependant capitalism". Features exemplified by the original trajectories of public policies in Czech Republic (Myant, Chapter 9) are also confirmed at micro-level. For Drahokoupil and Myant (Chapter 3), as for Hunek and Geary (Chapter 4), with local managers of subsidiaries manifesting significant power of negotiation in their dealing with MNC headquarters, as well as being able to resist the top-down standardization of local employment relations.

In comparison, this capacity of resistance appears far more limited in the Baltic or South-Eastern Europe (not to mention the Western Balkans that are more obviously trapped in external dependencies). This assertion, mirroring Bohle and Greskovits's typology and analysis (2012) seems to be strongly conditioned by the weakness of the State which characterizes those smaller, younger and/or more peripheral countries.

The "weak state" accumulates a scarcity of financial and cognitive resources, low capacity for filtering and opposing the exclusive demands or capture of private actors. Leaving large room for manoeuvre and opportunities to dominant actors in the design of public policies and reforms, the "weak state" has resulted in the postponement or imposition of reforms without domestic consent, in the "locking-in" of fragile economies into "low road" competitiveness policies, and (as shown more recently) has also led to varied deviations of domestic politics towards authoritarian, illiberal and post-democratic behaviour.

By threatening the viability of the economies (beyond the short term), the "weak state" has also participated actively in legitimating the recourse to foreign expertise that has multiplied the channels of dependencies and their cumulative forces in the domestic sphere (Delteil and Kirov, Chapter 10). Manipulating the "weak state", the dominant groups have also been able to position external dependency as a "beneficial constraint" in their own interests, reinforcing the external legitimacy imposed by international organisations and foreign economic actors.

Acting within "weak states" that have shown themselves unable to promote more balanced "social compromises", trade unions have found it hard to convert the relative organizational power they may have conserved (as in Romania and to a lesser extend in Bulgaria) into real political and veto power, capable of influencing the trajectory of public policies and economic models.

### 2.3 Ambivalent or sustainable dependencies

The great interference of external forces, as well as the dependencies they lead to, have undoubtedly had ambivalent impacts on the trajectories of the CEECs. It is worth mentioning, echoing some contributions of this volume (see in particular Bafoil; Drahokoupil and Myant; Mako and Illessy, in this volume) the decisive role played by FDI in the transformation process of the productive models, technological catching up, and the insertion into the international markets. Positive impacts in the economic sphere have however been declining over the last decade, leaving more room for ambivalent conclusions. The promises of investment vanished with the crisis, and the common practice of transferring the benefits from eastward subsidiaries to the headquarters has deprived the host countries of tax resources. Furthermore, these resources have been reduced by tax "rescripts" and other exonerations offered to foreign companies.

Moreover, FDI inflows have accentuated the inherited economic segmentations of the host countries in two cumulative ways. By concentrating in dynamic urban areas or industrial districts, FDI has been highly conducive of "agglomeration effects", i.e. spatial concentration of productive assets and wealth in well-endowed regions, at the expense of more peripheral and poorly-endowed areas (Bafoil, Chapter 2). This spatial divide has been reinforced by domestic policies, through the creation of "special economic zones" and technology-based "clusters" (dominated by foreign companies), special tax regimes and relevant public investment in infrastructure (co-financed by the European funds) aimed in some cases at facilitating the daily transport of employees, and first and foremost connecting companies to international production and sales networks.

Responding to a similar logic in the selection of resources, and accompanying their "high road" industrial strategies, FDI has been central in reinforcing the productive divide between high value added production which is strongly connected to international markets and more low cost and domestic-oriented activities. The anticipated "ripple effects" from the foreign industries to the domestic ones have not been as promising as expected, mitigating the catching-up mechanisms in most local productions. The productive divide between domestic and foreign business remains significant, with domestic firms mostly confined to the local market or integrated too peripherally with respect to global value chains to benefit from relevant technological and knowledge transfers. This productive divide is very clearly illustrated by the empirical analysis of Mako and Illessy (Chapter 5): based on the productive system, labour and training processes in Hungary, the authors conclude that there is a persistent segmentation of the Hungarian economy that goes hand-in-hand with the spatial divide and threatens the development perspectives of the country.

The ambivalence of the dependency is also to be found in the political sphere, according to the role played by foreign actors and organizations, and the way the external interventions are channelled and instrumentalized by domestic actors.

Foreign political prescriptions can act as an external anchor to discipline domestic actors in various ways. External controls may indirectly prevent some influential domestic actors from resorting to practices opposing the public inter- est: especially capturing public assets and corruption, but also the informalization of work, anti-union practices, etc. As stressed before, the EU and the ILO have proved to offer some tools (EU directives, European Social Charter, ILO conven- tions and technical memoranda) to support the protest and claims of domestic labour against dereglementation or for re-regulation (Mrozowcki *et al.*, Chapter 12; Delteil and Banarescu, 2013).

Even if very contestable in terms of its lack of clear arguments and transpar- ent criteria, the EU's carrot-and-stick approach, used in the Schengen negotiation process or in the delivery of Structural funds, has also been evaluated by domes- tic actors for its positive impact in the judicial and administrative sphere in Bulgaria and Romania. The approach incidentally explains the stable and diffuse pro-European position of political and societal actors in both countries.

Migration trends are also studied in the book and provide some further illus- tration of the ambivalent role of dependencies: offering decisive additional resources, potential cognitive resources (acquired abroad), and new transnational networks between the home and host economies as outlined by Markova (Chapter 6). If migration has played a key role in some regions in alleviating mass unem- ployment (especially among the young generation), it also appears as limiting the potential rise of social protest (with "exit" reducing "voice", as stressed by Meardi, 2012). Migration remittances also reveal their ambivalence in their capacity to fuel productive investment, as they are concentrated in the low value added domestic services sector.

## 3. From labour weakening to possible labour awakening: ambivalent trends ahead

The labour side in the CEECs has undoubtedly faced uncomfortable issues and incomparable challenges since the beginning of the transition. Despite being the sole organised force initially benefiting from high membership and resources (civil society being weak and fragmented), trade unions in the region rapidly lost legitimacy, capacity of mobilization, and influence over public policies.[2]

Quantitative explanations focusing on the dramatic decline of membership cover only a part of the process that mainly refers to the difficult repositioning of trade unions in a new role, turning away from their previous role as a "transmission belt" of political and management discipline, towards a role of representing, elaborating and articulating the claims of employees. The difficulty of this repositioning is not only due to "path-dependency". But it also calls for analysis of the changing patterns of constituencies and labour transformations within the interplay process in which labour has been confronted with the respective strategies of the two other main forces, i.e. business and political actors (and more recently social movements). In this respect, the atypical dimensions of unionism in the CEECs are very much related to the peculiar organisation of business forces (with are much more involved in lobbying than being keen to engage actively in the negotiation and the production of regulation), and the own strategies of the political actors. The latter are very often tempted to using social dialogue to gain legitimacy and share responsibilities for painful reforms.

A chronological analysis of labour power and weaknesses during the last twenty five years could follow a twofold track, in which the "labour acquiescence", passive cooperation and support of trade unions for the main reforms (as quoted by Crowley and Ost, 2001:1), has been challenged more recently by the "end of patience" (Beissinger and Sasse, 2014), and the awakening of new counter-movements. One prevalent economic view before the crisis was to link "labour quiescence" to economic decline associated with the transition, and the "end of patience" to the subsequent recovery (and a sharp decline of unemployment) preceding and accompanying EU membership. A political reading could explain the emergence of new expressions of discontent, triggered by "angry citizens" (Greskovits, 2015: 283), as the cumulative outcome of undelivered promises, the continuous degradation of employment conditions, and persistent poor economic prospects. Finally, a sociological analysis (like that proposed by Mrozowicki *et al.*, Chapter 12) shows that opportunities in terms of entrepreneurship or exit (migration) have gradually decreased, pushing labour in the CEECs to envisage collective action.

### 3.1 The "end of patience"

Trade unions in the CEECs have been challenged not only by their new role in the post-communist societies, but also by their changing constituencies. The tremendous economic restructuring in the CEECs, which started just after the political changes in 1989, challenged the trade unions' constituencies. Already in the 1990s most companies and jobs went to the private sector, and often to small and medium-sized enterprises (SMEs). The further developments of privatisation (Bafoil, Chapter 2), internationalization and segmentation of these economies put pressure on the labour side in the direction of external (labour markets) and internal (in-company) flexibilization (see Holtgrewe *et al.*, 2015). The different waves of the precarization of labour occurred in all the CEECs, even if specific patterns and momentum could be differentiated (Mrozowicki *et al.*, Chapter 12). In addition, recent research has definitively rejected the presumption about the progressive compression and disappearance of informal work in the CEECs (see Petkov, 2015). The rising inequalities and greater vulnerability of workers have affected not only the most vulnerable groups but also qualified individuals (Mrozowicki *et al.*, Chapter 12), including qualified young persons often facing high risks of precariousness and job mismatch (Ilieva-Trichkova and Boyadjieva, Chapter 11 in this volume). These processes of restructuring and precarization have impacted the trade union constituencies directly. As a result, large segments of the labour force and economic sectors have remained uncovered and unrepresented, even if during the last years some attempts to reverse this trend have been made (Mrozowcki *et al.*, Chapter 12). Undoubtedly, the weakness of the industrial relations institutions (especially at branch level) is not helping the trade unions to face their numerous challenges, which call for more state regulations to complement industrial relations where social partnership is weak (Holtgrewe *et al.*, 2015).

How can these new challenges facing labour be addressed? Is the "end of patience" likely to reverse the "labour quiescence" dynamics and fuel new labour protest and influence? Taken together, the contributions of the book offer a more cautious conclusion, drawing on different perspectives and complementary monographs. They suggest more that labour weakening and labour awakening have been unfolding as parallel processes since the beginning of the 2000s, following the initial transition phase.

Firstly, the "labour quiescence" thesis overestimates the passive acceptance of the trade unions. Labour quiescence was very much relative in many countries of the region, except in Poland where the authors have focused their analysis. It could manifest itself very differently in the Slovenian, the Czech, or even the Romanian cases. Myant's contribution on trade unionism in the Czech Republic (Chapter 9) recalls how trade unions were able to influence policies at least in some periods and domains, obtaining significant safeguards against excessive social costs since the beginning of the transition. Unions' ideational stance, supporting market-oriented reforms while voicing demands for social guarantees, their relative unity and their clear distance with the political parties facilitated their influence in the political sphere. These factors explain the relative resilience of Czech labour to the pressures of employment liberalization and social state retrenchment.

Secondly, if significant shifts in the power of labour are observed over time, this appears to be more fluctuating than solely suggested by the economic or institutional cycle (recovery and EU membership), and very contingent on the political cycle and the positioning of government. As dominant actor of this configuration, a government's orientation in favour of "voice" and offering channels to unions' demands appears to be decisive. So too is the context and pressure of external forces, both functioning as key vehicles of economic constraints and ideational arguments. The fact that the crisis has not been merely a period of union weakening, but a mix of ambivalent trends, including labour awakening, invites relativizing strongly economic explanations.

### 3.2 Towards a new tactical unionism in a more adversarial context

The crisis period since 2008–2009 has given stronger consistency to this ambivalence in the changes in the labour power, as detailed below. Methodologically speaking, the ambivalence calls for analysing labour empowerment and disempowerment, i.e. the influence of labour on public policies, by enlarging the lens and looking beyond the changes in the labour audience and mobilisation which have steadily become less sufficient in exercising political influence. It calls for analysing the roles, strategies and tools held by actors, in relation to the multi-actor game in which unions have been involved, as well as in reference to the constraints and opportunities of the context, illustrated in the first place by the "extraordinary politics" (Myant, Chapter 9) that characterized the years from the transition to the present crisis.

Regarding the trade unions, the change of tactics accelerated with the adversarial context that was largely shaped by the crisis, leading the unions to show a more active and strategic involvement in the political and social sphere. The unions have faced increasing adversarial forces, from the politics and business (the later reinforcing its power since 2000, with the support of external forces) but also new challenges, such as the need to reconnect with autonomous social movements, and to be much more offensive and expressive in social, environmental and political claims. As a result, trade unions have been pressed to review and enrich their strategies, in a more pro-active and expert-led way, in several directions. Unions have repositioned themselves in the aftermath of the crisis, re-evaluating their classical strategies and the tools mobilized. They have become more pro-active using more diversified modalities and tools, from expertise to innovative protest strategies.

Firstly, trade unions have tended to mobilize more expert resources, which is borne out in their more pro-active involvement in the public policy debate. In a process that has converged across many countries, unions have elaborated alternative "anti-crisis" packages linking many detailed measures. This "shift in expertise" has taken hold in two parallel trends: their participation in the various tripartite commissions that have been established at a variety of levels of administration in many countries; and unions' involvement, along with employer organizations, in monitoring European programs in social and employment policies issues. The expression of this union expertise has been translated in more institutional terms in countries marked by "weak state" and "weak government", where the lack of expertise in the State and the poor legitimacy of political actors has motivated the use of tripartism to negotiate the monitoring of the crisis (Delteil and Kirov, Chapter 10).

Secondly, trade unions have been engaged in a set of new organizational experiments, the development of new methods and tools, all mirroring the emergence of a more tactical unionism trying to overcome a more adversarial context, and the erosion of their classical instruments. Interestingly enough, while devaluing the classical channels of influence, like the tripartism reconsidered as "no more than one possible platform" (Myant, Chapter 9), many unions have engaged actively in building new alliances. This new strategy of alliances is directed on the one hand towards social movements, with the challenge of reconnecting unionism with citizen protest that has prospered with the crisis and the rise of precarious jobs (e.g. against "junk contracts" in Poland, see Mrozowicki *et al.*, Chapter 12). More illuminating in this regard is the alliance formed in Bulgaria between the two big union confederations and some social NGOs in 2014, following the release of a critical review of EU recommendations (European Semester and Country-specific recommendations), including one that pointed out that the minimum wage was too high in the country (Kirov, 2015).

On the other hand, and with more circumstantial coalition building, alliances' strategies are oriented towards political parties, and sometimes (and more surprisingly) have also been opened up to domestic business organisations. Common initiatives with domestic business have given rise to joint withdrawals from the tripartite councils, attempts to develop and obtain recognition of bipartism, and the sending of "joint-letters" to governments (Delteil and Kirov, Chapter 10).

Echoing the dynamics found elsewhere in the EU more closely, unions in the CEECs have also experimented with new mobilization strategies and seek to unionize precarious workers, as exemplified in the case of Poland, in relation to the huge importance of casual and precarious workers.

Finally, unions have appeared more keen and able to resort to supra-national anchors and tools to get support in their domestic battles. This "externalization of domestic conflicts" (Greskovits, 2015: 281) has been first and foremost directed towards the ILO, through claims for expertise and technical memorandums, aimed at publicising governments' violations of supra-national rules, be they ILO conventions or EU directives. The ILO has appeared as a legitimate body of mediation vis-à-vis governments (and the EC), when opposing the sharp dismantling of the Labour Code and Social Dialogue Code, as in Hungary (Toth, 2012), Romania (in Delteil and Kirov, Chapter 10; Trif, 2014), or Poland (Mrozowicki *et al.*, Chapter 12). If the unions have been confronted more and more with the implicit silence of the EC towards deregulation and labour code violations, they have continued (with variable successes) to make a strategic use of the EU's hard and soft laws, invoking directives to defend domestic labour and union rights, and also invoking European Parliament documents (e.g. the resolution on the minimum wage which supports the closing of the gap in minimum wage/median wage ratio, which has remained far below the Western norm, especially in Eastern Europe). However, the very relative success of unions' new tactics highlights the difficulties of their challenges.

### 3.3  *A dependent but uncertain future*

To conclude, if the crisis has generated new obstacles to union influence, it has also triggered new experiments that could consolidate union capacity to intervene in the political sphere. It remains difficult, however, to anticipate the translation of new union tactics in terms of labour power, because these are not generalised throughout the union movement, and because much interference still opposes the awakening and empowering of social forces. In some CEECs, such as Romania and Hungary, this includes union fragmentation and intra-union rivalries. The challenges unions also face relate to ideological clarification, as well as to their delicate repositioning vis-à-vis political actors, and their ability to acquire a role as constructive players holding a political veto (Gumbrell-McCormick and Hyman, 2013), while avoiding the risks of excessive politicization and political instrumentation.

Among the more recent, and somewhat unexpected opportunities to emerge, is the new strategic positioning of some domestic business organisations their willingness to form new alliances with trade unions, claiming more State protection of "national" businesses. If domestic forces have become more neoliberal in some particular contexts (Myant, Chapter 9), in others, they have turned to being more critical of the reinforcement of the competitive environment which is prepared to have favoured dominant economic actors (foreign multinationals ahead) over smaller indigenous enterprises.

Illuminating the new unexpected convergence of interest between domestic capital and labour, is the alliance that emerged in Bulgaria in summer 2015, between trade unions and business organizations, in order to combat the energy policy, and advocate for the State to reduce energy prices.

This re-positioning and new voicing of some segments of domestic businesses found in particular echoes in the most recent Hungarian and Polish context, in which domestic capital have expressed increasing criticism towards neoliberal measures adopted by governments, and moreover against the tax and industrial 'privileges' (incentives, tax remits, public facilities targeted to special MNC's needs, etc.) delivered by public authorities to foreign investors or the most influent of them.

Undoubtedly, this domestic business claims participated to the rise of a "selective economic nationalism" (Toth, 2015). Not exempt of political calculations, this selective state protection has served as tool of political clientelism and a vehicle of economic illiberalism.

This last remark may lead to reconsidering more seriously the largely-commented rise of populism or "political illiberalism", in particular through the re-evaluation of its socio-economic backgrounds, ie. the conjunction of social insecurities, economic instability, and external dependencies.

To end with the reflexions developed in this book, which take a 25-year perspective, it is important to stress the idiosyncrasies and internal diversities of the region, which echo and contributed to the heterogeneity of the European Union as a whole. Taken together, the various contributions also address and outline the complex set of forces that triggered changes in countries, through interplay of internal and external influences which have been more or less interconnected. In this respect, it validates the heuristic power of the "dependent capitalism" label, in its capacity to highlight the growing influence of external factors in the increasingly transnationalized and/or peripheralized economies, as most of the CEECs are. But it also calls for a consolidation of the analytical framework to apprehend better – upstream and downstream – the role played by internal forces in channelling, mitigating or opposing external influences. From this point of view, the future remains largely uncertain, not only because of unpredictable external forces, but also because of the new domestic experiments and strategies that trade unions and social movements are striving to develop.

## Acknowledgements

The research leading to these results has received funding from the European Union Seventh Framework Programme (FP7/2007–2013) under grant agreement No. 246556.

## Notes

1   Excluding Slovenia.
2   There are different interpretations of the changing role of trade union in the CEECs. It is worth mentioning that they have received some assistance from Western trade unions and the European Commission, but the results are limited. At the same time, they have lost many of their previous functions which have become obsolete or regulated by the market, such as management of housing, holidays, kindergartens, etc.

## References

Amable, B. (2003) *The Diversity of Modern Capitalism,* Oxford: Oxford University Press.
Avdagic, S., Rhodes, M. and Visser, J. (2011) *Social Pacts in Europe: Emergence, Evolution and Institutionalization*, Oxford: Oxford University Press, p. 322.
Beissinger, M. and Sasse, G. (2014) 'An end to 'patience'? The 2008 Global Financial Crisis and Political Protest in Eastern Europe', in Bermeo N. and Bartels, L. (eds), *Mass politics in tough times. Opinions, votes, and protest in the Great Recession*, Oxford: Oxford University Press, pp. 334–370.
Bernaciak, M. (2015) 'All roads lead to decentralization? Collective bargaining trends and prospects in Central and Eastern Europe', *Transfer*, 21(3) 373–381.
Bluhm, K. (2010) *Theories of Capitalism Put to the Test: Introduction to a Debate on Central and Eastern Europe,* HSR, 35(2): 197–217.
Bluhm, K. (2014) 'Capitalism theory in Central Eastern Europe. A critical review', www.emecon.eu/current-issue/1-2014/bluhm/ [accessed 1 April 2016].
Bohle, D. and Greskovits, B. (2012) *Capitalist Diversity on Europe's Periphery*, Ithaca and London: Cornell University Press.
Contrepois, S., Delteil, V., Dieuaide, P. and Jefferys, S. (2010) 'Globalising Employment Relations and Crisis: the role of Multinational Company transfers to Central and Eastern Europe', in S. Contrepois, Delteil, V., Dieuaide, P. and Jefferys, S. (eds) *Globalising Employment Relations*, London: Palgrave.
Crowley, S. and Ost, D. (eds) (2001) *Workers after workers' states: Labor and politics in postcommunist Eastern Europe*, Lanham, MD: Rowman & Littlefield.
Delteil, V. and Banarescu, M. (2013) 'Roumanie: Le modèle social sous la pression des bailleurs de fonds: les syndicats à la recherche de nouvelles tutelles', *Chroniques internationales de l'IRES,* n°143, novembre.
Delteil, V. and Dieuaide, P. (2010) 'Comités d'entreprise européens et européanisation des relations professionnelles dans l'UE élargie : résultats d'enquête auprès de huit firmes

multinationales françaises', *Travail et Emploi,* n°123: 39–51.

Drahokoupil, J. and Myant, M. (2015) Labour's legal resources after 2004: the role of the European Union, *Transfer*, 21(3): 327–341.

Graziano, P. R. *et al.* (2013) Usages et européanisation, De l'influence multiforme de l'Union européenne sur les réformes des systèmes nationaux de protection sociale, *Politique européenne,* 2(40): 94–118.

Greskovits, B. (2015) 'Ten years of enlargement and the forces of labour in Central and Eastern Europe', *Transfer*, 21(3): 269–284.

Gumbrell-McCormick, R. and Hyman, R. (2013) *Trade Unions in Western Europe: Hard times, hard choices*, Oxford: Oxford University Press, p. 242.

Hall, P.A. and Soskice, D. (2001) *Varieties of Capitalism: The Institutional Foundations of Comparative Advantage,* Oxford: Oxford University Press.

Haughton, T. (2007) 'When Does the EU Make a Difference? Conditionality and the Accession Process in Central and Eastern Europe'. *Political Studies Review*, 5(2): 233–246.

Holtgrewe, U., Kirov, V. and Ramioul, M. (eds) (2015) *Hard Work in New Jobs. The quality of work and life in European growth sectors*. Houndmills: Palgrave Macmillan.

King, L. P. (2007) 'Central European Capitalism in Comparative Perspective'. In B. Hancke, M. Rhodes and M. Thatcher (eds), *Beyond Varieties of Capitalism: Conflict, Contradiction and Complementarities in the European Economy*. Oxford: Oxford University Press, pp. 307–327.

Kirov, V. (2015) *Bulgaria: New alliance rejects European Commission recommendations*, EurWork online, available at: www.eurofound.europa.eu/observatories/eurwork/articles/labour-market-industrial-relations-social-policies/bulgaria-new-alliance-rejects-european-commission-recommendations [accessed 1 April 2016].

Kohl, H. (2015) Convergence and divergence – 10 years since EU enlargement, *Transfer*, European Review of Labour and Research, August 2015, 21(3): 285–311.

Lehndorff, S. (ed.), (2015) *Divisive integration. The triumph of failed ideas in Europe — revisited*, Brussels, ETUI.

Meardi, G. (2012) *Social Failures of EU Enlargement: a case of workers voting with their feet,* London: Routledge.

Meardi, G. (2014) Employment Relations under External Pressure: Italian and Spanish Reforms during the Great Recession, in Hauptmeier, M and Vidal, M. (eds) *The Comparative Political Economy of Work and Employment Relations,* London: Palgrave, pp. 332–350.

Meardi, G., Marginson, P., Fichter, M., Frybes, M., Stanojevic, M., and Toth, A. (2009) 'Varieties of Multinationals: Adapting Employment Practices in Central Eastern Europe', *Industrial Relations: A Journal of Economy and Society*, 48(3): 489–511.

Myant, M. and Drahokoupil, J. (2012) 'International Integration, Varieties of Capitalism and Resilience to Crisis in Transition Economies', *Europe-Asia Studies*, 64(1): 1–33.

Nölke, A. and Vliegenthart, A. (2009) 'Enlarging the Variety of Capitalism: the Emergence of Dependant Market Economies in East Central Europe', *World Politics*, 61(4): 670–702.

Pernicka, S., Glassner, V., Dittmar, N., Mrozowicki, A. and Maciejewska, M. (2015) 'When does solidarity end? Transnational labour cooperation during and after the crisis – the GM/Opel case revisited', *Economic and Industrial Democracy,* Published online before print May 7, 2015, doi: 10.1177/0143831X15577840.

Petkov, K. (2015) 'Les nouveaux mouvements syndicaux et sociaux en Europe de l'Est', *Les mondes du travail*, n 15: pp. 45–64.

Stark, D. and Bruszt, L. (1998) *Postsocialist Pathways: Transforming Politics and Property in East Central Europe,* Cambridge University Press.

Tóth, A. (2012) 'The New Hungarian Labour Code – Background, Conflicts, Compromises', *Working Paper*, Budapest: Friedrich Ebert Foundation.

Trif, A. (2014) *Austerity and collective bargaining in Romania. National Report: Romania*, Dublin City University and European Commission, November, p. 44.

# Part I

# Dependent capitalisms and labour changes

# 2 The limits of Europeanization in Central Europe

## A critical perspective on property rights, banking capital, and industrial relations

*François Bafoil*

A variety of theoretical frameworks from sociology and political science have shaped how scholars have analyzed the transformation of Central European economies and societies over the past twenty-five years. Two of them have proven to be especially influential – the "Europeanization" approach and the "Variety of Capitalisms" or VoC approach. Both frameworks employ the notion of "backward-ness" and focus on the various long-term "lags" in growth, social development, and territorial imbalances[1] accumulated by Central European countries, as well as on efforts to use these criteria to compare Central and Western Europe.

The "Europeanization" approach gained ground after EU membership became a priority for the leaders of the candidate-countries in the early 1990s. An institutionalist focus tended to dominate in these studies, some of which focused on "rational institutionalism," which investigates phenomena such as incentives, preferences, and the calculation of benefits, while others concentrated on "socio-logical institutionalism," which explores how collective experience is mobilized as well as people's abilities to select from available options (Cowles *et al.* 2001; Schimmelfennig and Sedelmeier, 2005). Both of these orientations have attempted to describe changes caused by direct and indirect EU pressures at ideal, institutional, and political levels, with a particular interest in how these changes have affected member-states' and their partners' deliberations and decision-making processes. Pressures were applied via a range of mechanisms intended to remedy certain asymmetries between the EU15 and EU membership candidates.

The VoC approach, which was founded by Hall and Soskice (2001), has yielded a significant body of scholarship regarding Central European economies (Bohle and Greskovits, 2006; Bohle and Greskovits, 2012). These studies critically appraise the institutional convergences between these countries and member-states in order to better understand their "catch-up processes" and, consequently, their dependency. The concept of "dependency" has been used to describe the extent to which these processes involve dependency on international markets and FDI. The old national institutions, territories, and unions of Central Europe were too weak to resist these forces by presenting a solid front or to break free of this long-standing condition of dependency. This institutional tendency towards weakness in turn made it possible for foreign investors to impose their own economic logic, thereby also controlling R&D centers and technological innovation. As this chapter will endeavor to demonstrate, however, these external forces also met with considerable resistance from central governments that were seeking to defend and protect their newfound sovereignty. Resistance was also encountered at the local level, where coalitions of stakeholders reinforced internal protectionist and corporatist measures inside companies. Finally, dependency on foreign capital appears to have exacerbated the polarity between centers concentrated in large cities and the Western portions of Central European countries and and not in peripheral and rural areas or in more Eastern regions.

These trends caused a consensus to develop that provides an illustration of the ways in which markets and companies exercise control – the focus of the VoC approach – and the fact that these tools were not applicable to countries that were in the midst of distancing themselves from Soviet-style institutions. Indeed, the real issue actually centered on how new regulations and institutions could best respond to the new demands of democracy and the market (Myant and Drahokoupil, 2012; Nölke and Vliegenthart, 2009). For companies, these questions guided decisions regarding property rights and how to address questions related to labor organizations and social benefits. Another central question involved the different governments' capacities to achieve a balance between providing a regulatory environment that could cope with the mass opening up of commercial exchanges within a globalized market while also defending their freshly acquired national sovereignty. For this reason, the study of property rights and industrial relations has the potential to enhance our understanding of the relationships between governments and the market during this period of deep systemic change in Central Europe.[2]

The concept of hybridization that these studies have highlighted describes a process of recombination (Stark, 1996) of each country's specific historical experience with the West's differentiated influence across different domains as they adapted to new market-based rules and to the *Acquis communautaire*. The frequently cited construct of "path dependency" has served to guide studies in economics (North, 1994) as well as sociology (Stark and Bruszt, 1998) to focus on continuity and rupture in the dynamics of recombining the legacies and creating new contexts for participation. The present chapter represents an effort to portray the transformation of property rights that dominated the first post-communist decade (I) as well as that of the systems of industrial relations (II). These two dynamics reveal the differential impacts of the forms of banking capital while also providing an empirical basis for the construct of hybridization (III). Combined together, these data provide a nuanced portrait of the full impact of Europeanization in the region (IV).

## The political economy of transforming state property

In Central Europe, the political leaders responsible for the process of transformation were apparently often motivated by a single over-riding concern – breaking the old worker coalitions to allow a new generation of labor organizations to develop. Shields echoes this perspective when he argues that "one of the principal tasks of the transition to capitalism has been to break the resistance of the working class" (Shields, 2004: 148). Analyzing the forms of privatization and changes in property ownership regulations, however, appears to suggest that this perspective does not encompass the entire picture, which has also been characterized by the development of "hybrid" solutions.

## The varieties of privatization

There a number of widespread common consequences of the failure of Soviet-style economies, chiefly a profound uncertainty among the countries' leaders about precisely what to do after they realized that they were responsible for simultaneously managing change, preserving the government's legitimacy, and maintaining law and order. Although the international organizations of the so-called "Washington consensus" (i.e., the World Bank and the IMF) attempted to apply the old recipes used in Latin America in the 1970s and 1980s, the massive effort required to transform Central European property rights partly explains why the process began slowly. It is worth noting too that the industrial park in need of transformation amounted to over 8,000 very large firms in Poland, and nearly the same number in Czechoslovakia. For this reason, the question was whether it was more important to restructure in order to privatize more effectively was more important, with governments assuming heritage debts,[3] or whether it was preferable to sell companies off to the highest bidder, a more direct path to privatization.[4] Considering the bankruptcy of the former economies, this question was framed in every country in more or less the same way: Should privatization take place right away, at the risk of losing control over the process and of being heavily dependent on foreign capital, or was it better to take more time, at the risk of increased deficits and foreign partners giving up?

The reasons for a common desire to "sequence" public actions varied from one case to the next, but the phases involved were similar among the various countries. The first reason was "small privatization." For government authorities, this involved rapidly divesting themselves of local units by transferring them to their managers. The goal was to make a new class of small owners assume responsibility for managing the transformation, with government assistance. These new owners were joined by groups of individuals who were converted to "private initiative" who had managed to acquire – at low cost – full ownership of their housing. Additional steps included privatizing large companies, where the working class had first developed as both the symbol and an important constituency of the former regimes. Although reducing privileges such as work guarantees had become necessary, the new authorities could not afford the risk of widespread social discontent or endangering the recent political consensus regarding national sovereignty by allowing general strikes to break out. In a sequence of events that was somewhat similar from one Central European country to the next – although not Romania and Bulgaria – the first step in transforming companies was to convert them to private law via "corporatization." This was then followed by opening them up to foreign capital, backed by reforms in the banking system, and finally by establishing stock exchanges. Instead of producing a sudden break, these phases were intended to be "gradualist," despite involving major changes. The use of the "path dependency" (Stark and Bruszt, 1998) approach, which calls attention to two comparable dynamics, was justified in both cases. On the one hand, this meant engaging in a process of reconstructing legacies in ways consistent with new market-based rules. On the other, it meant that some top company managers retained their positions because they were familiar with commercial circuits in sectors in the midst of radical transformation and with newly emerging networks, from which the new leadership itself had arisen and whose development they encouraged. Due to external pressures, this front line did not survive after 1995–1998, when the EU and international banks demanded closer conformity with the rules of the market rules. The adoption of the *Acquis Communautaire* beginning in 1997 and 1998 finally forced this issue into the open, an interesting topic that is beyond the scope of the present essay.

### The variety and "hybridity" of property rights

A complete lack of knowledge about privatization in Central Europe, including criteria for implementing it or for estimating company values, severely crippled efforts to liberalize property ownership rights (Bornstein, 1999). Most officials who had participated in the revolutionary movements of 1989 were also partisans of the protectionist wall surrounding their countries' freshly regained sovereignty. As a consequence, privatization was a major threat in the eyes of the region's new national governments. Powerful coalitions developed to confront the privatization threat, in some cases between political leaders seeking to preserve the nation and top managers and union leaders in large companies, united by the central issue of preserving economic stability. Czech policy was an excellent example of this kind of economic nationalism, which unfailingly backed company employees – "insiders" – while opposing inroads by foreign investors or "outsiders."[5] Skoda, the Czech Republic's largest industrial firm, was an illustration of this tendency because after being taken over by Volkswagen, it reproduced the German co-management model (*Mitbestimmung*). The case of Skoda was a successful exception, however, that justified the free-market approach later adopted by the Czech authorities. In reality a number of studies have shown that some negotiations with foreign investors failed because of direct pressure by the Czech authorities, who were attempting to avoid relinquishing control over industrial units that they perceived as critical to national sovereignty, even if it meant rehiring former company managers who were well known Communist Party members (Myant, 2003; Pavlinek *et al.*, 2009). The method of handing over government-owned firms to Czech (and some Slovakian) citizens through a voucher system, called "mass privatization," reflected the leadership's desire to create a class of smaller owners who would support the regime. The vouchers transferred company ownership based on estimates of companies' value, and they have remained in citizens' hands, although in reality they were later absorbed by investment funds whose stakeholders were in fact banks that had remained under government control (Lavigne, 1999). A similar process took place in Poland, where the labor union *Solidarnosc* advocated for public ownership instead of privatization, which they claimed would transfer companies to small fringe-groups of ostensibly "liberal" figures. Handing the nation's patrimony over to foreign investors was out of the question for leaders determined to revive a Nation inside recognized borders and united around a sovereign people. The great diversity of property ownership regulations produced by this sovereignist, protectionist stance reflects complex political dynamics that resulted in frequent political changes (Aghion and Blanchard, 1998).

In nearly every case, the solutions ultimately adopted led to "corporatizating" firms, first by converting them from government-owned entities with a legally murky status to publicly owned companies under the authority of the Treasury. They were then commercialized either through restructuring or liquidation after attempts to transfer ownership proved unsuccessful. Resistance by union organizations as well as the top management of large companies and foreign investors' initial timidity allowed insiders to dominate in most areas during the first post-Communist decade, slowing efforts to initiate a genuine transformation process. Keeping companies in previously protected sectors in their original positions, however temporary, cost unskilled workers dearly, however. In Poland, 20 percent of unskilled workers had been eliminated from labor markets by 2000 (Adamski *et al.*, 2000), and, as in Slovakia, vast numbers of "worker-peasants" were among the first employees to be the victims of mass layoffs. It is currently acknowledged that Poland only began to truly catch up economically in 1995 with the repeal of a September 1981 law that transferred power to self-management committees in large companies.[6] An additional 1995 law authorized the "commercialization" of government-owned firms without insider agreement and the privatization of several national banks (Bovin and Leven, 1996). The 1995 Hungarian budget crisis forced leaders to implement deep changes in the mechanisms that governed systemic transformations. The 1996 Czech crisis also ended questionable arrangements favoring the central government, along with the "Czech miracle." These changes also gave rise to a new government and a genuine privatization policy that was open to foreign investment. It took two additional years to overturn Meciar's protectionist, sovereignist policies in Slovakia. All of these changes paved the way for adoption of the *Acquis Communautaire* to be linked to national privatization policies in all four Central European countries, thus binding EU membership to major domestic economic reforms.

Ten years after these policies were initiated, companies that had been handed over to "insiders" remained very important, and even twenty-five years later, a relatively substantial number of companies remain government-controlled (see Table 2.1). It should also be noted high levels of public ownership continue to prevail in some countries – approaching 20 percent in Hungary and Poland in 2015 – as well as, as might be assumed, a number of persistent social compromises between various stakeholders, managers, and unions. As a consequence, a major

*Table 2.1* Company re-distribution according to method in Central Europe in 1997 (%)

| | Sale to foreign investors | Sale to domestic investors | Sale through vouchers | Sale to insiders | Other | Continued government ownership |
|---|---|---|---|---|---|---|
| Czech Republic | 10 | 10 | 40 | 5 | 5 | 30 |
| Hungary | 45 | 12 | – | 3 | 20 | 20 |
| Lithuania | 12 | 2 | 43 | 9 | – | 43 |
| Poland | 10 | – | 6 | – | 44 | 40 |
| Romania | 5 | 5 | 20 | 10 | – | 60 |
| Slovakia | 7 | 3 | 25 | 30 | 5 | 30 |
| Slovenia | 1 | 8 | 18 | 27 | 21 | 25 |

Source: S. Djankov (1998) *Ownership Structure and Enterprise Restructuring in Six Newly Independent States*. Washington, DC: World Bank, based on UNCTAD

divide exists between large industrial entities that are the heirs of government-owned companies that struggled to maintain high levels of legal protectionism, small and medium-sized firms without professional organizations, and companies left to foreign investors, some of which did attempt to sustain employee-management dialogue within their companies.

## The deregulation of industrial relations

To differing degrees, and depending on a range of factors, European leaders have sided with the interests of big business. This tendency has been reflected in certain performance indicators, such as profitability and rapid revenue yields, low wages, and labor market segmentation. Several deregulatory processes also resulted from this trend.

### *Wages, flexibility, and union membership*

The first step in deregulation related to wages, which were kept at low levels based on the idea that low labor costs appealed to foreign investors. In 1990, there was a 1 to 10 wage gap between Western Europe and Eastern Europe. This was cut in half by the time of EU entry in 2004. Average monthly private-sector wages at the time in Poland were 590€, 580€ in the Czech Republic, 540€ in Hungary, and 450€ in Slovakia (but 148€ in Bulgaria and 264€ in Romania) (Visser, 2008).

Flexibility also became the order of the day among labor unions and was applied to the forms of employment, as well as work time and management methods, most of which were authoritarian. From one region to another, very similar approaches for organizing labor were noted in companies that were under foreign management. (These approaches were often inspired by Japanese models, although without the concept of lifetime employment contracts). Having in reality been reduced to slogans such as "just-in-time" and "0 defect" that were lifted from the Kaizen method and other "honor boards" for recognizing deserving workers, they functioned as reminders of the techniques employed in Soviet-style companies (Bafoil, 1999). Another attribute shared with the former regime was labor contracts, and both regions make massive use of temporary workers (Drahokoupil, Martin and Domonkos, 2013).

Labor unions were granted formal guarantees to operate after the rapid adoption of ILO (International Labor Organization) guidelines, particularly with respect to the right to unionize encoded in Article 89. They nevertheless encountered a number of obstacles that sharply diminished their powers, and unionization rates quickly plummeted to extremely low levels, with membership rates far below average rates in developed economies (Clarke, 2006; Ost, 2000). Unions are also completely absent from small and medium-sized firms, where job growth was and continues to be highest. Unionization rates fell steadily between 2004 and 2014, reaching levels far lower than the European average, except for Slovenia, while the four Central European countries experienced the lowest levels of all (see Table 2.2).

*Table 2.2* Union membership rates and rate of coverage by collective bargaining agreement (% of employees covered) in 2004[1] and 2014[2]

|  | Union membership in 2004, % | Employers, % | Coverage of collective bargaining agreements, % | Works councils | Union membership in 2014, % |
|---|---|---|---|---|---|
| Slovenia | 42% | 50% | 98% | Yes (broad spectrum) | 27% |
| Slovakia | 35% | 50% | 48% | Yes (weak) | 17% |
| Hungary | 25% | 40% | 42% | Yes (average) | 12% |
| Czech Republic | 30% | 30% | 35% | Only in exceptional cases | 17% |
| Poland | 18% | 19% | 30% | Only in firms remaining under government ownership | 12% |
| Latvia | 19% | 30% | 20% | Still rare | 13% |
| Estonia | 15% | 30% | 20% | No | 10% |
| Lithuania | 14% | 20% | 13% | Anticipated | 10% |
| Total EU 2012 |  |  |  |  | 23% |

Notes:
1 Kohl 2005, pp. 57–58.
2 In http://fr.worker-participation.eu/Systemes-nationaux/En-Europe/Syndicats consulted on September 21, 2015.

## Industrial relations

The most striking feature of industrial relations in Central European, considered as a whole, is the near-total absence of strong branch-level systems of negotiation (Crowley and Ost, 2001; Gardawski *et al.*, 2010). Where such systems do exist, they are extremely weak and cover only a few employees (Myant, 2014). This was true in 1998, and it was even worse in 2014 – there are half as many as the EU average, again with the notable exception of Slovenia (see Table 2.3). One might have thought that solid social organizations would have spontaneously developed after end of communism in 1989, reflecting the enthusiastic social movements that brought communist domination to its knees in the first place. This was obviously not the case, for a number of reasons: 1. A desire to discredit the former labor unions; 2. The refusal of collective commitments after 1990; 3. An abrupt shift to an individualistic ideology, reinforced by massive decentralization of private management (Morjhe, 2003), and 4. A prolonged, two-decades-long economic crisis. This institutional vacuum fostered the rise of "tripartite" forums in which each party – the government, the unions, and

*Table 2.3* Collective bargaining agreements, 1998 and 2014[1]

|  | Collective bargaining agreements in 1998 | | Collective bargaining agreements in 2014 | |
|---|---|---|---|---|
|  | Number of multi-employer agreements | Percentage of workers covered | Percentage with agreements in 2014 | Primary level of agreements |
| Bulgaria | – | 20% | 30% | Firm |
| Czech Republic | 1998: 25 | – | 38% | Firm |
| Estonia | 2001: 10 sub-sectorial agreements | Fewer than 10% | 33% | Firm |
| Hungary | 1998: 48 1999: 52 | 11% (in 1999) | 33% | Firm |
| Latvia | | Fewer than 10% | 34% | Firm |
| Lithuania | – | Fewer than 10% | 15% | Firm |
| Poland | 2000: 136 | Fewer than 10% | 25% | Firm |
| Romania | – | – | 36% | Sector and firm |
| Slovakia | – | Up to 60% | 35% | Sector and firm |
| Slovenia | – | 100% | 90% | Sector |
| EU total | | | 62% | |

Note:
1  http://fr.worker-participation.eu/Systemes-nationaux/En-Europe/Negociations-collectives, consulted on September 21, 2015.

representatives of state-owned enterprises (SOEs) – successfully established social benefits, usually reduced to the basic minimum (Delteil and Kirov, Chapter 1). In a period of unending crisis, the advantage for unions of this form of partic-ipation was not only that they were able to play at least some social role, but also that it helped limit the negative social consequences of multi-level destructuring that that heavily impacted the former working classes (Plessz, 2010; Kideckel, 2001; Crowley, 2004; Gardawski *et al.* 2010). References were made to "instru-mentalized social dialogue," a reminder that labor-management interactions were being reformulated by management, i.e., foreign investors, in collusion with national authorities. This ensured them a significant influence on the extent to which they invested in social benefits (Contrepois *et al.*, 2010).

The need for foreign capital to recapitalize over-indebted firms and ultimately to dispose of everything missing from the Soviet-style economy – from market access to new technologies, and from training to employee careers – meant that public and private authorities did nothing to promote or strengthen the legal frameworks that governed social protections. Indeed, social benefits were drasti-cally reduced, and protections that could have embedded labor relations inside of branches or firms were eliminated. Other lost benefits included some tied to particular professions, such as exchange vouchers for miners and welders, but also such basic benefits as subsidized cafeterias, child day-care centers, and even group vacation centers. This internal coordination of social protections that allowed labor relations to encompass not only workers, but also their families, had remained untouched under communism amid extremely undiversified economic environments. In companies taken over by foreign investors, however, new technologies triggered the immediate, drastic elimination of skills that were previously critical to these industries, particularly the sorts of informal skills necessitated under economic conditions dominated by "shortages." The investors in charge of newly re-organized firms tended to recruit young people with no experience of collective action, terminating more experienced workers (Bafoil, 2009).

It is paradoxical, then, that after 1990, industrial relations in the region first began to develop in large firms taken over by multinationals. They were prima-rily due to the requirements of Western professional organizations, which had no intention of seeing Central Europe become a site for experimenting with "social dumping" within the EU. This was particularly true of German companies and labor organizations, which supported the establishment of powerful systems of industrial relations (Drahokoupil and Myant, Chapter 3). At the extreme opposite of this co-management approach (*Mitbestimmung*), some Asian investors (Kia or Hyundai, although not Toyota) reportedly installed uncooperative management that imposed rigorous work rules very similar to the South Korean model (Hunek and Geary, Chapter 4). A lack of respect for labor laws, long working hours and reduced break times, and infringements on the right to unionize have frequently been noted in these companies. These differences between investment types have been confirmed by studies of the networks to which German firms' investments belong, whether they are tied to a firm's industrial sector or to Chambers of

Commerce and Industry, embassies, or German cultural centers. These organizations have all helped spread the corporate culture, norms, and values of parent companies. These findings confirm the distinction made during the first post-communist decade between the "high road" to industrial development involving strong industrial relations for skilled individuals, primarily men working in sectors with a strong value-added, and the "low road" that is more typical of unskilled women working in sectors in decline (Neuman, 2000). The automotive industry has provided examples of both "roads," with high-end products and highly skilled workers versus temporary, short-term, low skilled or unskilled employees, poorly paid and not covered by collective bargaining agreements (Drahokoupil *et al.*, 2013).

## Foreign capital and developmental zones

Once property laws and the privileges of the large industrial groups had been modified or abolished, foreign capital had free reign to invest, particularly because top leaders perceived FDI as a clear path to stimulating development. Strategies to attract investors included tax incentives and social deregulation, i.e., the removal of any obstacle related to managerial autonomy. As noted earlier and noted by a number of studies, the foreign investors' takeovers of government-owned firms did not automatically result in the disappearance former regulations. Indeed, quite the contrary. Although a number of studies have demonstrated that FDI had a positive impact on job growth and increased service-based activities, other studies have established that local impact was far less clear, or at best highly uneven (Farkas, 2000). Foreign investors often arrived bringing with their own suppliers, leaving only the simplest local tasks to local employees. Regional value chains, (where they exist) thus became vulnerable due to volatile types of investments because investors could so quickly and easily abandon projects.

Banking capital long remained unprivatized, a lag primarily related to their strategic role among national leaders. An added factor was – and remains – the absence of a solution the preponderance of "legacy" debts that the region's leaders considered satisfactory. Another factor that slowed the transformation of the banking system was ultimately the difficulties governments experienced in privatizing their own banking offices. From the perspective of a government that plans to continue to preside over privatization processes, banks represent a major partner in the restructuring process; on the other hand, in the case of releasing companies to external partners, foreign investors play the role of principal.

The gradual transformation of banking systems paved the way for widespread, heavy dependence on Western banks throughout Central and Eastern Europe.[7] The Baltic banks were quickly handed over to Nordic, primarily Swedish, banks. In fact, not a single national bank remained by the late 1990s after Swedish buyers had acquired them; two Swedish banks, Hansapank and SEB, controlled 74.6 percent of Estonian banks until the 2008 crisis (Brixoa *et al.*, 2009). To a lesser extent than the Baltics, Central European countries also allowed their banks to be bought out by Austrian, Italian, French and German capital. Bulgaria and

Romania performed the same favor for German and Austrian banks. The 2008 crisis exacerbated the dependency created by the substantial integration of Western banking capital. What might have been perceived as a key to the successes of earlier years – there was even talk of "Baltic Tigers," a reference to the "Asian Tigers" of the 1990s – was revealed as the very reason for economic collapse after 2008. The case of Bulgaria provided dramatic evidence of this observation. Although Bulgarian monetary authorities' voluntary submission to a financial directorate dominated by the *Deutschmark* (DM in 1997) allowed spectacular improvements in the ensuing decade, it was later shown to a major contributor to Bulgaria's collapse ten years later in 2008. It was thought that the collapse was precipitated by the directorate's inflexibility and the country's leaders' inability to rapidly react to the *lev*'s devaluation.

Foreign capital was also implicated in creating the local conditions to attract FDI to "special economic zones." The success of these zones occurred at the expense of significant tax revenues because of generous tax concessions. The European Commission reduced so-called "State Aid" to avoid violating the rule of non-distortion of competition required on European territory and because of the influx of structural funds, which represented considerable aid to regions in crisis.[8] The fact remains that several special economic zones proved to be highly successful, although their success cannot be attributed exclusively to tax breaks granted to investors. It is no coincidence the greatest development activity was in zones with a long-standing industrial base, access to qualified labor, and rampant unemployment in the 1990s. The most successful of these zones were centered on a pentagon-shaped region defined by Katowice-Wroclaw, Prague, Bratislava, and Budapest and their immediate surroundings (Pavlinek, 2004; Domański and Guzik, 2009). This area represents the "heart" of Central Europe's automobile industry, where the large global automobile manufacturers and their suppliers are located. In-depth analysis would show that this economic concentration is closely linked to available transportation infrastructure that was primarily constructed using European funds and was intended to improve links between Central and Northern/Western Europe, although not necessarily to Eastern Europe or Russia (Lepesant, 2013). Regardless of their level of success, however, the special economic zones could be characterized as contributing to dependency, because most R&D centers continue to be located in the West. Very few of the automotive sector's research centers have been relocated, for example. There were 13 industrial research centers in Poland in 2009, and in the same year in Hungary, foreign investors accounted for 70 percent of R&D spending (Nölke and Vliegenthart, 2009). One explanation could be the uniformly weak level of public R&D spending in post-communist countries. Although the European Commission asked every member-state to allocate 3 percent of public spending to R&D, Western members (the EU15) scarcely reached 2 percent (2,8 percent in Sweden; 2,6 percent in Germany, and 2,3 percent in France), while except for the Czech Republic, Central European member-states (EU10) have not surpassed 1 percent and Poland devotes a mere 0,7 percent of its budget to R&D.

## The limits of Europeanization

The data presented above inform for two interpretative frames for analyzing the limitations of the Europeanization process. These two methods for analyzing decision-making emphasize either the evaluation of "consequences" (Börzel and Risse, 2000; Börzel and Risse, 2003) or the perception of "appropriateness" (Hall and Taylor, 1996) and grew out of efforts to describe economic patterns surrounding EU expansion in 2004 and 2007. The consequences-versus-appropriateness distinction stems from studies by March and Olsen (1989), who demonstrated that two types of logic guide deliberations and stakeholders' decision-making. The focus on consequences is based on a "rational institutionalism" approach and underscores the interest that joining the EU represents for candidate countries, meaning that the adjustment process is informed by cost-benefit analysis. The logic of appropriateness, on the other hand, is based on constructivism and on "sociological and historical institutionalism." This approach is interested in stake-holders' abilities to modify the limitations imposed by the EU so that they match their historical trajectories, the density of their institutions, and their abilities to counter organized interests. Joining the EU was a high priority for former Soviet countries, for which the most important goal was to preserve national sovereignty while guaranteeing economic development. Furthermore, there were consider-ably "lags" in these countries, which meant that candidate member-states had few tools with which they could resist EU regulatory pressures. In other words, they had few options but to embrace the rules imposed by the EU (i.e., the *Acquis communautaire*). The term "consequences" refers to the strict logic of adjusting to the expectations of the Western partners. A number of studies have neverthe-less demonstrated that this kind of "mechanism" was very rare in the adjustment sequence, and that a conflict-ridden adjustment process usually resulted. This tendency towards conflict occurred because of institutional densities that varied according to different industrial sectors and bureaucracies, the duration of the adjustment period, changes in preferences among Western stakeholders, and the many pressures applied by the EU. For these reasons, "appropriation" by various stakeholders ruled the day (Bafoil and Beichelt).

### Beyond the "logic of consequences" and "logic of appropriateness"

Neither the approach based on the "logic of consequences," which assumes strict adjustment to European regulations (Sedelmeier, 2003; Sedelmeier, 2005; Schimmelfennig, 2010), nor the "logic of appropriateness" approach, which emphasizes the ability to adapt to regulations as a function of the various kinds of heritages that stakeholders brought to the table (Börzel and Risse, 2006; Cowles *et al.*, 2001), is relevant to the field of industrial relations. The "consequences" approach appears to imply a top-down logic, in which the EU regulation is imposed on a domestic context that lacks resiliency because of the weakness of stakeholder institutions. The "appropriateness" approach is more about the reverse, i.e., a horizontal perspective in which cooperation between public, private, and associative stakeholders at different governance levels share similar representations, values, and interests and manage to cooperate with each other to create shared rules.

The first form of logic for action corresponded to EU expectations in terms of "compliance" and relied on a strict, rational calculation of ends and means under the weight of EU-imposed constraints. On one hand, the sectorial asymmetries between the EU15 and the candidate countries were so significant that only unconditional adjustment to European membership prerequisites would suffice. On the other hand, however, these countries shared few values or cultural aspects. As a result, benefits tied to membership and to subsequent revenues were judged to be vastly superior to the costs of adjustment, and rational decision-making led to strict conformity with EU expectations. This only transpired, however, in very limited segments of the adjustment process, in which Central European countries were unable to oppose strong interests with respect to adopting chapters of the *Acquis communautaire*. The fields of competition (Chapter 6) and financial control (Chapter 28) required little or no adaptation for the simple reason that they were not institutionalized. There was little or no heritage and no interest groups, and as a result, few conflicts. There was little resistance to Chapter 13, which relates to social policy, because it treats the social accompaniment of workers within the EU and focuses on the mobility of information procedures and employee consultation. It took only 18 months for Poland to conclude this chapter, 14 for Hungary and Slovakia, and 6 for Bulgaria and Romania. The short duration of these discussions is indicative of a low level of conflict and hence of the determination of interest groups to defend the acquis.

Clearly, this was not the case with Chapter 21, which focuses on regionalization. A large number of stakeholders made their views apparent, defending heritages that were inherently incompatible with each other and deeply charged in historical terms. The negotiations on regionalization therefore often lasted 35, or even 40 months in Poland. Numerous conflicts erupted on the regional boundaries regarding the skills of the various echelons and relations with the central government, against the backdrop of extremely varied historical experiences. This necessitated that the parties to the discussions, as well as those with highly institutionalized stakeholder groups prior to 1989 – the Church, miners and welders, and even certain groups of farmers (of very large farms)–find local compromises. These discussions and the resulting compromises reveal that Europeanization, and specifically the adoption of EU regulations, tends to become a conflictual process when long-standing heritages and the organization and structure of group, sectorial, and national interests are involved.

### *Neo-liberalism and national sovereignty as endogenous strategies*

The second limit refers to macro-level, neo-liberal dynamics implemented by the new leaders in the economic and social fields, layered with a strong dose of protectionism, such as the Czech elites under the leadership of Vaclav Klaus. When he argued in favor of a "market economy with no adjective" in the early

1990s, it was not to promote all-out liberalism, but instead to avoid German influence while marching in step with Thatcher-era neo-liberalism – concentrating central power, liquidating centralized union organizations, and imposing strict company-friendly agreements.

As mentioned earlier, one of the most remarkable characteristics of the transition during the first decade of the post-communist period was the widespread combination of a neo-liberal wave of foreign origin – exemplified by the desire to privatize the industrial bastions of the various governments – with the desire to maintain the national industrial patrimony under in order to protect and defend national sovereignty. Under certain circumstances, this helped strengthen several political coalitions that were alternately, and sometimes simultaneously, able to play according to two different tunes: Either aligning themselves with large foreign groups, or blocking these same large groups in order to gain the support of former top industrial managers, who were very well-attuned to internal circuits. While this was often the case in Bulgaria and Romania,[9] it should be noted that in the Czech Republic, Klaus was roundly criticized for sinking contracts that would have encouraged foreign capital investment (Pavlinek, 2002). In Poland, this meant maintaining Solidarnosc inside large companies at the same level as its ex-communist competitor, OPZZ. These union organizations – at least in the early stages – were closely tied to the political parties that typically negotiated company takeovers between foreign investors and company managers, who preferred to meet with them rather than organizations with no traditions or local connections.

This is an essential difference between the Central European "Big Transformation" and the transitions of ex-communist countries of Southeast Asia, where the complexities of opening the economies of such small countries as Cambodia to foreign trade resulted in extreme deregulation. This is why the concept of "developmentalism" applied so accurately to the Central European economies, which successfully negotiated with foreign partners to create industrial policies that built on existing industrial facilities as well as "special economic zones." And paradoxically, it is why the identical concept was so much less applicable in Southeast Asia, where the political leadership was able to create special economic zones, but only at enormous social cost and at the expense of any local development (Bafoil, 2014).

When the Central European special economic zones were first being created, the most important concern centered on jobs. During the first post-communist decade, these zones flourished in locations where unemployment rates were often double the national average, which were already very high, often in sectors such as heavy industry. During the second decade, some zones, including the one in Upper Silesia, around Katowice and Walbrzych, near Wroclaw, became drivers of development because local and regional officials found ways to build on a two-centuries-old industrial culture, a skilled labor pool, and training centers, as well as a well-articulated transportation network connected to the West and proximity to large German cities. In addition to these advantages, they also proved skillful in managing structural funds. True industrial clusters grew up in these zones that succeeded in linking regional and local authorities, investors, and firms, and also universities. There are hundreds of such "success stories" in the Central European quadrangle, proving that endogenous development has been a crucial determiner of successful Europeanization. It is therefore clear that the "logic of consequences" is not the optimal approach, but rather "appropriateness," which relies on the attentive "recombination" of collective experiences within the context of new regulatory structures.

## Conclusion

Since 1990, the growth rates posted by the countries examined in this chapter have been impressive, particularly between 2004 and 2008, and they continue to be significant in Poland, the only country that did not experience a recession and that boasted 3,1 percent growth in 2014 (Table 2.4).

These rates were nevertheless driven by exports, and they primarily involve – at least for some countries – foreign capital and, less often, endogenous productivity that would suggest the existence of value chains embedded in the territoires, the development of capital within companies, and the continuous establishment and funding of research centers. Other than a few highly developed urban areas in each region – Poland, for example, possesses an enormous comparative advantage due to its excellent urban links beyond Warsaw – significant fragility continues to characterize investments, which also lack interconnections. As argued earlier, a profound rift between the capitals and their surroundings has developed, as well as a further cleavage between the foursome at the heart of Central Europe and the more peripheral regions. This kind of conclusion should prompt a reevaluation of the already outdated "dependency" approach (Cardoso and Faletto, 1978; Peixoto, 1977; Hirschman, 1981) by corroborating the peripheralization of Central Europe relative to certain Western countries. This insight is supported by obvious differences between the various Central European countries, which do not share a common destiny, as might have been true fifteen years earlier, and because of differences between how respectively integrated these

*Table 2.4* Per capita GDP (in current dollars)

|  | 1990 | 2000 | 2012 | 2013 | 2013 (PPA) |
| --- | --- | --- | --- | --- | --- |
| Bulgaria | 2,377 | 1,579 | 6,978 | 7,498 | 15,731 |
| Czech Republic | 3,787 | 5,725 | 18,683 | 19,858 | 29,017 |
| Hungary | 3,186 | 4,543 | 12,531 | 13,485 | 23,334 |
| Romania | 1,651 | 1,651 | 9,036 | 9,490 | 18,974 |
| Slovenia | 8,699 | 10,045 | 22,000 | 23,295 | 28,858 |
| Poland | 1,694 | 4,454 | 12,708 | 13,653 | 23,689 |
| Ukraine | 1,570 | 636 | 3,867 | 3,900 | 8,790 |
| Germany | 22,219 | | | | 46,251 |
| France | 21,883 | | | | 42,560 |

Source: World Bank 2014.

countries are into regional economies as a function of country-specific factors. Finally, future studies could explore the connections between this insight and the ways in which the political scenes have evolved and developed: A quarter century after the fall of communism, regional politics continue to be volatile, with new political parties and strong protectionist tendencies, despite high levels of support for EU membership, at least in the Central European democracies. Future studies will further improve our understanding of what determines a "weak" vs a "strong" government by linking these concepts to the ability of countries to successfully manage the social environment despite the various challenges that these countries have faced.

## Notes

1    This notion of backwardness is quantitatively based on the observation that in 2004 at the time of integration of the 8 former Soviet-style countries, their average GDP was 40 percent of the EU average. Prior to EU enlargement, income differentials between individuals living in the top 10 percent of the richest areas in the Union and those living in the poorest 10 percent revealed a gap that was less than 1 to 3. After enlargement, this gap more than doubled to its current levels of 1 to 6. The poorest region after enlargement in 2007, Bulgaria and Romania, had a regional GDP of roughly 29 percent of the EU average, while the wealthiest region (Inner London) posted a GDP 334 percent of the EU average. (DG Regio 3rd report).
2    This chapter focuses principally on four Central European countries – Poland, the Czech Republic, Hungary, and Slovakia.
3    Company debt corresponded to 25 percent of the Polish government's budget in 1990.
4    This pathway for moving from a planned economy to a market economy was recommended by the economist Janos Kornai (2000).
5    Regarding these dynamics in the Eastern region, see Frydman *et al.* (1996).
6    At the *Solidarność* union's first meeting in September 1981, self-management, or *samorzad*, was proposed as the cornerstone of a new socio-political system. The Jaruzelski regime that took power following the December 13, 1981 *coup d'état* never questioned this proposal because he was trying to reach consensus with the working class, particularly technicians and skilled workers in large companies. After coming to power in 1990, the representatives of this self-management current proposed a program that would not privatize public industrial ownership if the policy reduced national sovereignty by introducing foreign capital into affected companies.
7    Percentage of foreign ownership in four strategic sectors:

| Country | Automotive sector | Manufacturing sector | Electronics | Banking sector |
| --- | --- | --- | --- | --- |
| Czech Republique | 93.1 | 52.6 | 74.8 | 85.8 |
| Hungary | 93.2 | 60.3 | 92.2 | 90.7 |
| Poland | 90.8 | 45.2 | 70.3 | 70.9 |
| Slovakia | 97.3 | 68.5 | 79.0 | 95.6 |

Source: Nölke Vliegenthart, 2009, p. 681

8    Between 2007 and 2013, these funds were considerable, rising to more than 60 bn euros in Poland, 14 bn the Czech Republic, 10 bn in Hungary, and 6 bn in Slovakia.
9    This is true in countries that have progressed more slowly, such as Bulgaria and Romania. See Gallagher (2009).

# References

Adamski, W., Martin, D. and Bunczak, J. (1999) *System Change and Modernisation: East-West in comparative perspective*, Warsaw: IFIS Publishers.

Aghion, P. and Blanchard, O. (1998) 'On privatization methods in Eastern Europe and their implications', *Economics of Transition*, May, 6 (1): 87–100.

Bafoil, F. (1999), Enquêtes dans les entreprises polonaises, unpublished report, Grenoble CERP IEP, p. 220.

Bafoil, F. and Beichelt, T. (2008) *L'européanisation d'Ouest en Est*, Paris: Harmattan.

Bafoil, F. (2009) *Central and Eastern Europe: Europeanisation and social change*, London: Palgrave Macmillan.

Bafoil, F. (2014) *Emerging Capitalism in Central Europe and Southeast Asia: A comparison of political economies*, London: Palgrave Macmillan.

Bohle, D. and Greskovits, B. (2006) 'Capitalism without Compromise: Strong Business and Weak Labor in Eastern Europe's New Transnational Industries', *Studies in Comparative International Development*, Spring, 41 (1): 3–25.

Bohle, D. and Greskovits, B. (2012) *Capitalist Diversity on Europe's Periphery*, Ithaca: Cornell University Press.

Bonin, J.P. and Leven B. (1996) 'Polish Bank Consolidation and Foreign Competition: Creating a Market – Oriented Banking Sector', *Journal of Comparative Economics*, 23: 52–72.

Bornstein, M. (1999) 'Framework Issues in the Privatization Strategies of the Czech Republic, Hungary and Poland', *Post-Communist Economies*, 11 (1): 47–77.

Börzel, T. and Risse, T. (2006) 'Europeanization: The Domestic Impact of European Union Politics' in Knud-Erik Jorgensen (ed.) *Handbook of European Union Politics*, London: Sage, pp. 482–504.

Börzel, T. and Risse, T. (2000) 'When Europe Hits Home: Europeanization and Domestic Change', *European Integration online Papers* 15 (4), http://eiop.or.at/eiop/texte/2000-015a.htm [Accessed 1 April 2016].

Börzel, T. and Risse, T. (2003) "Shaping and Taking EU Policies: Member State Responses to Europeanization." *Queen's Papers on Europeanization*, 2/2003. http://ideas.repec.org/p/erp/queens/p0035.html [Accessed 1 April 2016].

Brixiova, Z., Vartia, L. and Wörgotter, A. (2009) 'Capital inflows, household debt and the boom – bust cycle in Estonia economics', *Working Paper*, n° 965, OECD.

Cardoso, F.-H. and Faletto, E. (1978) *Dépendance et développement en Amérique latine*, Paris: Presses Universitaires de France.

Contrepois, S., Delteil, V., Dieuaide, P., and Jefferys, S. (2010) *Globalising Employment Relations: Multinational firms and Central and Eastern Europe transitions*, (ed.), London: Palgrave Macmillan.

Cowles, M., Caporaso, J. and Risse, T. (2001) *Transforming Europe: Europeanization and Domestic Change*. Ithaca, London: Cornell University Press.

Crowley, S. and Ost, D. (eds) (2001), *Workers after Workers' States. Labor and Politics in Postcommunist Eastern Europe,* Lanham, MD: Rowman & Littlefield Publishers, Inc.

Crowley, S. (2004) 'Explaining Labor Weakness in Post-Communist Europe: Historical Legacies and Comparative Perspective', *East European Politics and Societies*, 18 (3): 394–429.

Drahokoupil, J., Myant, M. and Domonkos, S. (2013) 'Managing flexibility: Responses of automotive MNCs to host country industrial relations in Central and Eastern Europe', Paper, International Conference 'Central and Eastern Europe: Work, Employment and

Societies between Transition and Change," Evry, France (Université d'Evry-Val-d'Essonne), 21–22 November 2013.

Farkas, P. (2000) 'The Effects of Foreign Direct Investments on R&D and Innovation in Hungary', *Working Paper* n°108, Budapest Institute for World Economics.

Frydman, R., Gray, C. and Rapaczynski, A. (1996) *Corporate Governance in Central Europe and Russia. Volume 2. Insiders and the State*. Budapest/London/New York: Central Europe University Press.

Gallagher, T. (2009) *Romania and the European Union. How the weak vanquished the strong*, Manchester: Manchester University Press.

Gardawski, J., Bartkowski, J., Męcina, J. and Czarzasrty, J. (2010) *Working Poles and the Crisis of Fordism*, Warsaw: Wydawnictwo Naukowe Scholar.

Hall, P.A. and Taylor, R. (1996) 'Political Science and the Three New Institutionalisms', *Political Studies*, 44 (5): 936–957.

Hall, P.A. and Soskice, D. (2001) *Varieties of Capitalism: The Institutional Foundations of Comparative Advantage*. Oxford: Oxford University Press.

Hirschman, A. (1981) *Essays in Trespassing: Economics to politics and beyond*, Cambridge: Cambridge University Press.

Howard, M.M. (2003) *The Weakness of Civil Society in Post-Communist Europe*, Cambridge: Cambridge University Press.

Kideckel, D.A. (2001) 'Winning the Battles, Losing the War: Contradictions of Romanian Labor in the Postcommunist Transformation', in Crowley, S. and Ost, D. (eds) *Workers after Workers' States. Labor and Politics in Post-communist Eastern Europe,* Lanham, MD: Rowman & Littlefield Publishers, Inc., pp. 97–112.

Kohl, H. (2005) 'Arbeitsbeziehungen in den neuen EU Mitgliedestländern und ihre Implikation für das europäische Sozialmodell', in Beichelt Tim and Wielgohs Jan, (eds), *Perspektiven der europäischen Integration nach der EU – Osterweiterung*, Dokumentation, FIUT, Viadrina, pp. 51–71.

Kornai, J. (2000) 'What the Change of System from Socialism to Capitalism Does and Does Not Mean', *Journal of Economic Perspectives*. Winter 2000, 14 (1): 27–42.

Lavigne, M. (1995) *The Economics of Transition. From Socialist Economy to Market Economy*, London: Macmillan.

Lepesant, G. (2013) 'Pologne: Vers un nouveau modèle de développement économique et territorial?', *Questions Internationales*, October, 1–7.

March, J.G. and Olsen, J.P. (1989) *Rediscovering Institutions: The Organizational Basis of Politics*. New York: Free Press.

Myant, M. (2003) *The Rise and Fall of Czech Capitalism: Economic Development in the Czech Republic since 1989*, Cheltenham: Edward Elgar.

Myant, M. and Drahokoupil, J. (2011) 'International Integration, Varieties of Capitalism, and Resilience to Crisis in Transition Economies', *Europe-Asia Studies*, May, 64 (1): 1–33.

Myant, M. (2014) 'Economies Undergoing Long Transition: Employment Relations in Central and Eastern Europe', in Wilkinson, A., Wood, G. and Deeg, R. *Oxford Handbook of Employment Relations: Comparative Employment Systems*, Oxford: Oxford University Press, pp. 359–384.

Neumann, L. (2000) 'Decentralized Collective Bargaining in Hungary', *International Journal of Comparative Labor Law and Industrial Relations*, n° 16: 113–128.

Nölke, A. and Vliegenthart, A. (2009) 'Enlarging the Varieties of Capitalism: The Emergence of Dependent Market Economies in East Central Europe', *World Politics*, 61 (4): 670–702.

North, D.C. (1994) 'Economic performance through time', *The American Economic Review*, 84 (3): 359–368.

OECD (2006) *Business clusters. Promoting enterprises in Central Europe*, LEED, www.oecd.org.

Ost, D. (2000), 'Illusory Corporatism in Eastern Europe: Neoliberal Tripartism and Post communist Class Identities," *Politics and Society*, 28 (4): 503–530.

Pavlinek, P. (2002) 'The Role of Foreign Direct Investment in the Privatisation and Restructuring of the Czech Motor Industry', *Post-Communist Economies*, 14 (3): 359–379.

Pavlinek, P. (2004) 'Regional Development Implications of Foreign Direct Investment in Central Europe', *European Urban and Regional Studies*, January, 11 (1): 47–70.

Pavlinek, P., Domański, B. and Guzik, R. (2009) 'Industrial Upgrading Through Foreign Direct Investment in Central European Automotive Manufacturing', *European Urban and Regional Studies*, 16 (1): 43–63.

Peixoto, A.C. (1977) 'La théorie de la dépendance: bilan critique', *Revue Française de Science Politique*, 27 (4): 601–629.

Plessz, M. (2010) 'Les ouvriers en Central Europe: la dissolution d'une catégorie sociale dans les statistiques', *Sociologie du travail*, 52 : 340–358.

Schimmelfennig, F. and Sedelmeier, U. (2005) *The Europeanization of Central and Eastern Europe*. Ithaca: Cornell University Press.

Schimmelfennig, F. (2010) 'Europeanisation beyond the member states', *Zeitschrift für Staats- und Europawissenschaften*, 8 (3): 319–339.

Sedelmeier, U. (2003) 'EU Enlargement, Identity and the Analysis of European Foreign Policy: Identity Formation Through Policy Practice', *RSC EUI Working Papers* 2003 (13), http://cadmus.eui.eu/bitstream/id/1646/03_13.pdf [accessed 1 April 2016].

Shields, S. (2004) 'Global Restructuring and the Polish State: Transition, Transformation or Internationalization?', *Review of International Political Economy*, February, 11 (1): pp. 132–154.

Stark, D. (1996) 'Recombinant Property in Eastern European Capitalism', *American Journal of Sociology*, 4: 993–1027.

Stark, D. and Bruszt L. (1998) *Postsocialist Pathways: Transforming Politics and Property in East Central Europe*. Cambridge: Cambridge University Press.

Visser, J. (2008) *The Institutional Characteristics of Trade Unions, Wage Setting, State Intervention and Social Pacts – ICTWSS database*, Amsterdam: Amsterdam Institute for Advanced Labour Studies.

# 3 Dependent capitalism and employment relations in East Central Europe

*Jan Drahokoupil and Martin Myant*

Central-East European Countries (CEECs)[1] have been integrated into the international economy to a great extent through inward investment by multinational companies (MNCs). This high level of foreign ownership and control over their economies has justified a claim that these countries have developed a form of dependent capitalism. There are reservations to the characterisation of economic dependency. The conventional understanding rightly emphasizes the dependence on outside knowhow and technology, but overstates the degree to which the economic structures are vulnerable, or unsustainable, and one-sidedly dependent on decisions taken in other countries.

Moreover, that leaves open the question of its possible relationship to institutional dependency. That can take several forms, but the focus here is on the extent to which MNCs, the agents of dependency in the economic field, have also been instrumental in the introduction of institutional forms or how far they have accepted those which previously existed, leaving them to evolve under a different set of influences. The chapter concentrates on employment relations both as a case for studying the role of MNCs in institutional evolution and as an arena in which labour's influence on that evolution is likely to have been significant.

We consider institutional dependence on two levels. On the macro-level, we investigate the role that MNCs played in shaping key institutional features. CEECs are characterized as 'segmented' political economies where MNCs play a central economic role, but prefer to accept the institutional and legal environments as given, with relatively minor direct pressures for change. In fact, somewhat paradoxically, their presence, by providing a home for organised labour, may have served as a force for preserving features that took shape in the early 1990s while domestic business and domestic politics were susceptible to more clearly neo-liberal thinking.

Even if they kept a low profile at the national political level, MNCs could be expected to have a more direct role in shaping employment relations and practices at the level of the enterprise. However, even there their strategies, home-country institutions and business systems have been mediated by the interaction with host country institutions and actors. We present evidence from empirical research on employment relations in the plants of multinational motor vehicle manufacturers to show how a process of negotiation and bargaining, often implicit as much as explicit, led to a continued significant role for organised labour. Practices of MNCs in their home countries did play some role, but always alongside other factors. It was never a matter of simple imposition of a pre-existing model as domestic actors also played a role in determining outcomes. We demonstrate this for a particular sector and therefore also for particular MNCs. We therefore cannot prove that the conclusions can be generalised. However, there is evidence in other cases of MNCs adapting to domestic practices, albeit in somewhat different ways, as shown with reference to banking in Poland in Chapter 4.

The chapter is structured to start with a critical discussion of classification of CEECs as dependent varieties of capitalism. The second section refines the dependent concept with a discussion of the limited influence of MNCs on the legal framework for employment relations which is decided by political processes. The third section discusses general thinking on the transfer of practices within MNCs. The fourth section follows the specific case of the transfer of employment relations systems in plants of MNCs producing motor vehicles, demonstrating the importance of labour's strength in determining outcomes. The fifth section illustrates the points with the specific case of labour flexibility regimes in these MNCs. The conclusion ties the sections together, summarising the strengths and limitations of the characterisation of CEECs as a dependent form of capitalism in the light of the role of domestic actors, especially in this case organised labour, in shaping the kind of capitalism that has emerged.

## Dependent market economies

By the mid to late 1990s, CEECs had established the essential defining characteristics of capitalism, meaning market exchange, broadly free price systems, a predominance of private ownership, private profit as the principal motivation for economic activity and integration into the world economy (Lane, 2007). However, they differed in important respects from the established capitalisms of Western Europe. These differences included economic levels and structures, forms of ownership and capital market operations and features of the links between business and political power. It has, as a result, continued to be difficult to fit CEECs into established modes of classification, notably the 'Varieties of Capitalism' typology, that linked specific institutional forms with different forms of innovation and international competitiveness (see Drahokoupil and Myant, 2015b).

Instead, it has been argued that a distinct variety of capitalism, a dependent market economy, has emerged in the four CEECs Poland, Hungary, Czechia and Slovakia (Nölke and Vliegenthart, 2009). Various reservations to this characterisation have been set out elsewhere, pointing to alternatives such as the more neutral characterisation as FDI-based economies (Myant and Drahokoupil, 2011), which retains the emphasis on the economic importance of foreign-owned MNCs. Competitiveness of these economic models depends not on indigenous innovations, as in the more advanced market economies (cf. Hall and Soskice, 2001), but on imported technology, relatively cheap labour and raw material endowments.

The defining characteristic is thus the high level of foreign ownership over key productive assets. OECD figures for FDI stocks relative to GDP in 2014 show levels of 42 percent for Poland (2013 figure), 53 percent for Slovakia, 54 percent for Czechia and 72 percent for Hungary.[2] These are not exceptional by Western European standards, but MNCs dominated key economic sectors in CEECs with very little balancing outward FDI.

While institutions have a key role in the standard theories of comparative capitalism, they are less prominent in the dependent capitalism model. To be attractive to inward investors the dependent economies need to have attractive institutional frameworks, meaning stable legal environments for business, employment relations systems ensuring a reasonably stable labour force and good international contacts. They do not need complex financial systems or the bases for domestic innovation as those come with the multinational companies. CEECs are therefore dependent on innovation and financial systems based elsewhere in the world.

Domestic institutions are only part of the explanation for MNCs choosing to locate in CEECs. Thus, they are attracted by reasonable levels of political, social and economic stability and by a reasonable degree of transparency in legal processes. However, apart from such strictly institutional points, they are attracted above all by labour costs considerably below western European levels, by economic heritages, meaning that reasonably skilled labour forces already existed, and by geographical locations. The CEECs provided a base with good transport links, close to the heart of Western Europe's industrial areas, and safely within the EU. With those preconditions met, MNCs are not too concerned over details of employment law, welfare provision and other features that could define a variety of capitalism. There is, then, considerable scope for flexibility as regards domestic institutions that would be compatible with attracting MNCs.

In the dependent market economy model, MNCs directly resolve problems of access to capital, skills, and know-how, effectively sidestepping domestic institutions. The 'dependent' label thus gives an accurate impression of dependence on outside knowhow and technology. At the same time, it should not be read to mean that development is necessarily vulnerable, or unsustainable, and dependent entirely on decisions taken in other countries. Foreign ownership of large-scale industry has been associated with quite rapid growth that gave rise to economic structures that have proven to be relatively resilient to economic shocks. Some firms have come and gone, but those in motor-vehicle manufacture both play important economic roles within CEECs – completed passenger car exports alone were equivalent to over 8 percent of GDP for Czechia and Hungary and almost 15 percent for Slovakia in 2014 – and appear to have committed themselves to long stays. It can thus be argued that the MNCs are as dependent on the favourable environment they find in CEECs as those countries are on them (cf. Pavlínek, 2015).

In fact, inward investment increased these countries' resilience to the effects of the 2008 economic crisis (Myant and Drahokoupil, 2012). CEECs were affected to varying degrees, with Hungary suffering particularly severely, but manufacturing industry was a stabilising factor in all CEECs. MNCs in these countries no longer engage in the rapid expansion of productive capacities, but have entered a consolidation stage of expanding profitable operations through reinvestment (Galgóczi *et al.*, 2015). The crisis thus had a more severe impact in the 'peripheral market economies' (Myant and Drahokoupil, 2011) in Southern Europe and the Baltic states, where foreign-controlled manufacturing sectors were much less developed.

The weak link between foreign ownership and dependence on external economic development can be further illustrated from developments in banking sectors. Capital inflows contributed to unsustainable growth patterns in the period up to 2008 not only in the 'peripheral economies', but also in some of the CEECs. However, foreign ownership of banks in fact led to a degree of stability and security. Difficulties in the finance sectors were not the result of foreign ownership (Myant and Drahokoupil, 2012). Slovakia and Czechia, with respectively 99 percent and 85 percent of bank assets owned abroad in 2007 (Myant and Drahokoupil, 2011: 262), were the least dependent on finance from outside, thanks to adequate domestic deposit levels to cover domestic credits. This, despite foreign ownership, ensured their relative stability during the crisis period.

## Industrial relations and segmented political economies

The voice of labour in CEECs was strong in the early period shortly after 1989 (Myant, 2014 and Chapter 9, below) when employment law frameworks were negotiated and initial changes made to welfare provision. The political background was a fear within the new elites of possible social protests as painful effects of economic reforms were felt. There were also at the time no significant private employers and therefore no significant voice to represent a specifically employers' interest. The voice of trade unions, as the only organised bodies with mass membership at the time, was therefore at its strongest.

Subsequent years saw a weakening of labour's influence, reflected in declining union membership – down from near universal membership to under 20 percent in all cases – lower bargaining coverage – under 50 percent in all CEECs – and the increasing importance of plant-level worker participation.[3] Reasons for the decline are discussed for Czechia in Chapter 9 and broadly apply across other CEECs too. This gradual weakening was accompanied by a marginalisation of formal employee representation – where tripartite structures remained they had purely advisory roles – and a trend towards liberalisation of employment law, albeit limited by continuing trade union strength at the political level (Drahokoupil and Myant, 2015a).

However, the reduction in trade union strength meant that those laws and protections that did exist were often breached, leaving employees at the mercy of market forces (Drahokoupil and Myant, 2015a). Even where protection for permanent employees was still strong, legal frameworks allowed for the growth of more precarious forms of employment that nullified the effectiveness of legal protections for much of the labour force.

This pointed to an imbalance between labour's weak influence in workplaces and the continuation of significant legal protections. The systems of employment relations that developed have been characterized as legalistic or 'statist' (Kohl and Platzer, 2007), reflecting the extensive dependence on the use of legal provisions and a larger role for politics than in Western European countries. Thus laws protect the lowest paid worker groups through minimum wages while labour code stipulations also largely determine the topics addressed in collective agreements and provide reasonable levels of protection. Trade union actions in turn focus to a large extent on defending the legal frameworks negotiated in the early 1990s and on ensuring that laws are applied.

It has been argued that the position of labour is weakened by the dependence on MNCs that can choose where they invest and possibly also relocate further to the east. Coming to the region to exploit lower wages for their assembly operations, MNCs 'will not accept factors such as high wages, high union density, comprehensive collective agreements, powerful worker representation or cumbersome procedures for layoffs' (Nölke and Vliegenthart, 2009: 648). At the same time, it is argued, MNCs appease workers in terms of working conditions negotiated in company-level collective agreements in order to retain skilled workers and prevent disruptions of integrated commodity chains.

However, despite the possible implications of the quote above, MNCs have not been driving forces for labour-market liberalisation: relative wage levels are low enough for them to take a tolerant attitude towards established employment practices. They prefer to keep out of partisan politics and to maintain as good relations as possible with all currents and interests. More frequently it is domestic business that appears to carry political weight belying its relative failures on the business front and this has provided a broad base for pressure for more substantial reductions in employee protection (cf Chapter 9 below for the Czech case).

This points to a paradox of segmented political economies in dependent capitalism. Domestically-owned firms in CEECs are not internationally competitive and are largely confined to non-tradable activities (see also Mako and Illessy, Chapter 5). Representation of business interests in politics might be expected to depend more on foreign than domestic firms, but this is generally not the case. Domestic business and higher-income groups have the desire and to some extent the capacity to influence politics. This has strengthened neo-liberal trends, to a greater extent than has been the case in western Europe. At the same time, only a few big MNCs have been able to influence particular policy issues that affect them directly, such as that of flexible work accounts referred to below. They have a significant indirect influence in that decisions clearly are taken to attract them. They gain access to the maximum permissible level of subsidies permitted under EU rules and benefit from favourable decisions on infrastructure investment. However, they do not appear as important players across political fields that do not affect their interests directly.

Nevertheless, even if not changing their institutional environment much through political processes, MNCs played a role in shaping the institutional features that are part of their own practices. Even here, key features were often left unchanged. They were not generally opposed to collective bargaining, but they have influenced the shape of that bargaining. Thus their frequent reluctance to join existing employers' associations – stemming from their lack of interest in a collective employers' voice in domestic politics – led many such organisations to fall into disuse, in turn ending effective sectoral-level bargaining. There have been exceptions. In Slovakia, there were cases of MNCs contributing to the continuity of sector-level social dialogue and its complementarity to plant-level bargaining (Kahancová, 2013). While generally accepting the employment law framework as a given, there were also cases of MNCs lobbying directly for changes to labour codes. For instance, as discussed below, flexible work accounts in Slovakia were introduced after Volkswagen had approached the government with a request for a change in the legislation. That was a change, but in no sense a fundamental overhaul of the existing employment law framework.[4]

## Institutional dependence and the transfer of practices in MNCs

Interpretations of MNC strategies at the enterprise level have been informed by three broad perspectives on dependency. The first theorizes the role of the systems of business, home country institutions and specific strategies of the incoming company. The second emphasizes the established institutional framework in the host country and the third allows for a possibility of more complex interaction, involving different sets of actors, between the first two.

The first is associated with a body of literature that sees firm strategies as determining practices in subsidiaries (Boxall and Purcell, 2011), or that attributes employment practices in affiliates to influences of the systems of business and other home-country institutions (Harzing, 1999; Whitley, 2001). However, the extent of transfer of practices varies with the particular field of activity. Technology is most likely to be centrally decided and closely integrated production systems require coordinated control. MNCs are less likely to integrate employment policies as these also depend on specific legal, institutional and historical circumstances (Cooke, 2007). Dependency may therefore be only partial.

A central theme in this literature has been the question of how far MNCs transfer their domestic employment-relations systems into the host country and difficulties they may face in so doing. This links to plausible conclusions that can be tested. Thus, the literature on home-country effects typically expects a stronger central control over employment practices among North-American MNCs. In contrast, employment practices linked to the participatory model of German employment relations are seen as difficult to transfer beyond the institutional milieu of the so-called coordinated capitalism. However, MNCs from those economies, it has been argued, can develop a distinct approach to employment relations in affiliates that is adapted to the constraints and opportunities of the host environment (Ferner, 1997; Ferner *et al.*, 2001).

This informed a controversy over whether German companies, representing the bulk of investors in Czechia and Slovakia, imported their models of employment practices and industrial relations, or acted strategically and took advantage of East European locations to evade social dialogue. Research provided evidence for either possibility (compare, e.g., Jürgens and Krzywdzinski, 2009; Meardi *et al.*, 2009), but these debates implicitly assumed that MNCs had considerable freedom to make their own choices rather than confronting established practices defended by interests that could offer serious resistance. Evidence on the importance of that element, crucial for assessing the role of MNCs as purveyors of institutional dependency, can only come from further empirical research.

The importance of domestic environments has received remarkably little direct attention, possibly reflecting a view that they represented a blank slate onto which MNCs could impose their chosen models. However, MNCs needed to cope with established systems of employee relations that had developed out of reforms from state socialism. These incorporated central specification of national minimum wage levels and holiday entitlements and national maximum permissible working hours and overtime levels. More favourable conditions for employees were permitted and could be negotiated by collective bargaining. Trade union representatives were given some legal protection and collective agreements, usually signed annually, were binding on both parties. Thus, this was not a picture of unconstrained flexibility and employers were required to negotiate with employee representatives over issues of irregular working hours.

This points to the value of our approach to dependency that seeks to take account both of MNC strategies and of domestic environments and actors. Dependency is thus not only partial, but also negotiated in the interaction, often involving conflict, between various actors within the MNC. This has much in common with actor-centred institutionalist approaches that have analysed employment practices as outcomes of micro-political struggles between actors within the MNC (Dörrenbächer and Geppert, 2011) with transfer of work practices seen as conditioned by how the practices transferred by the company affect existing interests of actors in the affiliate and by the capabilities and resources of these actors (Ferner *et al.*, 2012). The congruence of interests could lead to the implementation of a work practice even when it does not match host country regulations (which could be changed through lobbying or reinterpreted in the affiliate). When there is opposition, outcomes are conditioned by the resources individual actors can mobilize in the negotiation, with power resources available to labour playing a key role.

Thus, this approach accords a much bigger role to host country actors, which in employment relations issues will mean employees and their representatives, while still leaving the active role in pressing for change to the MNCs. Similarly to the lines of research referred to above, the approach here embodies the assumption that MNCs will not want to make some changes in host countries' practices. They may want to transfer at least some home practices. They may want to escape from them and apply a model without listening to the employees' voice. However, change in any direction can imply conflict with domestic actors which constrains the MNCs power.

## Labour's strength and the transfer of employment relations

Light can be shed on these open questions from evidence on transfer of employment relations and practices from our research on motor vehicle assembly. Developments were followed in 2012 and 2013 in a comparative study of nine plants in three countries, Czechia, Slovakia and Hungary (Drahokoupil *et al.*, 2015). The plants studied included those involved in the first wave of foreign investments in the early 1990s – i.e. Škoda Mladá Boleslav (Czechia), Volkswagen (VW) Bratislava (Slovakia), Suzuki Esztergom, and Audi Győr (both Hungary) – and the production plants established on greenfield sites after EU accession in 2004 – i.e. TPCA (Toyota Peugeot Citroën Automobile) Kolín (Czechia), Kia Žilina (Slovakia), PCA (Peugeot Citroën Slovakia) Trnava, Hyundai Nošovice (Czechia), and Daimler Kecskemét (Hungary).[5]

The study revealed the extent to which the MNC contexts shaped the actual role of trade unions in the individual plants and how the strength of labour affected MNCs' approaches to importing their established practices. The study focused on how the employers coped with the problem of labour flexibility, meaning how they could vary labour input in the face of inevitable fluctuations in demand while also retaining a secure and competent labour force. This proved to be a sensitive issue that required negotiation with employee representatives. In a number of other areas host-country actors offered no resistance to the transfer of practices from MNCs' home countries. That applied to much of payment and grading systems and to systems for employee participation in minor innovations and technical improvements. These therefore followed slightly different models depending on the MNC. However, in areas where domestic actors felt threatened, their strength proved crucial in determining outcomes.

The weak position of labour in domestically-owned private enterprises is not duplicated across all foreign-owned firms, especially in export-oriented manufacturing. These do appear more likely to play by rules that follow from the existing bodies of employment law and also often to concede better conditions than the legal minimum through collective bargaining. The motor-vehicle sector was one area of relative union strength. Collective bargaining functioned in almost all plants we investigated, albeit with the majority of the workforce unionised in only three of the nine cases.

There were differences between the countries reflecting historical and legal conditions. In the Czech and Slovak cases the trade union organisation was the main form of employee representation, typically signing annual collective agreements with managements at company level. Hungary differed by having adopted an adaptation of the German system of works councils and this greater affinity of German and Hungarian forms was reflected in some more direct involvement of German unions in developing the Hungarian industrial relations system. In the other countries, foreign unions were active only at the very general level of giving implicit support to collective bargaining.

Trade union strength, in the sense of ability to persuade management to concede to union demands, reflected five key influences. The first was the product market which affected both long-term company investment strategies and approaches to collective bargaining. Employee representatives consistently wanted higher investment, over which they had no significant direct influence, and also wanted security for those already employed. Companies had a choice over where to place new investment and over how to share out short-term output variations. This was a background consideration in all bargaining with unions aware, even if these points were rarely explicitly covered in collective agreements, that concessions to management on pay, conditions and flexibility could bring benefits in employment security.

The second influence was the position on the local labour market. Labour's power was enhanced and management became more willing to concede to demands when attractive conditions had to be offered to secure an adequate labour force. Thus, Hyundai, Kia, and Suzuki where in areas of high unemployment and had no difficulty recruiting. Škoda, VW Bratislava and TPCA were in areas where there was inadequate labour, which made them more likely to concede to union demands. Thus TPCA suffered from distressingly high labour turnover in its first months after opening in 2005, when demand for its products was high, and responded by providing permanent accommodation to attract workers from further afield – 851 flats were promised for core workers – and then by agreeing to improve pay and other conditions as demanded by union representatives. VW Bratislava found the local labour market tough and offered conditions to attract workers from a wider region (100 km distance).

The third influence was the historical legacies which were crucial in determining the size of union organisations. Workplaces carried through from state socialism started with universal union membership and it was much easier to keep a high level than to build it up from scratch. This factor gave the Škoda plants and Volkswagen in Bratislava the largest union densities at 70 percent of employees, followed by the Audi plant in Győr with 56 percent membership.

Contrasting cases are Hyundai, Kia and Suzuki (with density rates of 15 percent, 28 percent and 5 percent respectively), the first two relatively recent greenfield investments. Trade union representatives complained of initially strong hostility from management and of continuing extreme difficulties in operating within these plants. In Hyundai no union representative was released from work responsibilities, no union office was allowed on the premises, no union activity was allowed during working hours and the media reported periodic complaints of threats to union members, typically of reclassification into a lower bonus band (e.g. *Právo,* 11 February 2012). However, the particularly difficult union positions in these plants also depended on the fourth and fifth influences, covered below.

The fourth influence was the labour relations position in the parent MNCs. Investors came with different conceptions, both in terms of detailed employment practices and of the value they might attach to good relations with employee representatives. However, the transfer of any practices also depended on the fifth influence, the scope for employee international contacts, understood as including the ability to influence trade union, and more generally public, opinion in the MNCs home country.

This marked an important difference between Asian and European MNCs. German automotive MNCs are characterized by developed systems of co-determination with strong union presence (Haipeter *et al.*, 2012) and recognised trade unions in all cases investigated here. That was practically inevitable in Škoda in 1991 as the plant inherited near universal union membership. However, elsewhere it was a reflection of the power of local union organisations, in the sense of their ability to impose a heavy cost on MNCs that dragged their feet over recognition through bad publicity in local media and in the MNC's home country (Myant, Chapter 9).

This proved to be an important weapon in persuading them to choose a more conciliatory approach, but it had no further implications for precise forms of employee representation. It meant that they accepted the system of employee representation already developing in CEECs in which collective agreements were negotiated annually with union representatives. Indeed, these negotiations were conducted by local personnel managers, in many cases natives of the country concerned. Union representatives felt able to negotiate over almost any issue without their negotiating partners needing to refer to a higher authority, with the one clear exception of the total wage bill. It should be noted in this context that cases of local roots did not make personnel managers a source of resistance to the introduction of practices from the MNCs' home countries. They were part of the company hierarchy and career structure, often moving between countries and subsidiaries and there is no evidence of them challenging their own companies' general approaches. Union representatives did at times complain of local managers taking aggressively anti-union stands, but the outcome depended on the factors covered above rather than the nationality of individuals.

Thus, the general point here is not that German, French, Japanese or Korean companies automatically transferred practices from home. Nor was it necessarily their desire so to do. They might have wanted to transfer in total home-country practices, but that would need to be acceptable to host-country actors who in practice were capable of offering varying degrees of resistance. They might also have wanted to escape from home-country systems that they saw as constraining, but that too depended on overcoming varying levels of opposition from employees. In general, in the case of European companies, geographical proximity, ease of contact, legacies of past history and powerful enough unions in the home country ensured a practice of recognising and negotiating with employee representatives (Bluhm, 2007; Krzywdzinski, 2011). Where existing forms were very close, that could blend into transfer of home-country practices. There was more scope for this from Germany to Hungary, with its system of employee representation closer to that of Germany. In the case of Daimler the European Works Council and the works council of the main plant in Rastatt were heavily involved in helping to establish German-style institutions of employee representation.

Structures of social dialogue had an important role also in Toyota, the dominant parent of TPCA, and in PSA, the parent of PCA in Trnava (Delteil and Dieuaide, 2012). Those employers accepted from the start that they would be recognising and negotiating with union organisations. In contrast, Korean plants of Hyundai and Kia brought adversarial labour relations characterized by a pervasive distrust between management and strong unions (Lee and Kang, 2012). Union representatives in Czechia and Slovakia had minimal, and largely unproductive, contacts with their colleagues in Korea and could not threaten their employing company's image in its home country. Suzuki also practised adversarial industrial relations in its operations outside Japan and was effectively able to prevent unions from operating in the plant, resorting in 2006 and 2009 to what courts later confirmed to be two cases of unlawful dismissal of union organizers.[6]

Thus, the argument here is that employment relations developed not from the transfer of an outside system, but from a complex interaction between conceptions and aims of different actors coming from different institutional settings. Recognising trade unions as negotiating partners appeared to be fairly automatic for MNCs either coming from, or heavily committed in, western Europe. Their plants also tended to be in areas where labour markets were tighter and employee power was correspondingly greater. Trade union recognition was less automatic for Hyundai, Kia and Suzuki, coming as greenfield investments in areas of high unemployment, but proved unavoidable in the first two of these. Although accepting unions as partners in general terms, only in Daimler was there an attempt to recreate home-country (German) institutions of employee involvement. In general, incoming MNCs with European involvement, meaning German and French companies plus Toyota, were constrained from pressing any agenda that excluded union recognition by the bad publicity and negative reactions that they would receive. These points are substantiated and supported in more detail in the next section with reference to the conflicts over labour flexibility.

### Transfer of employment practices: flexibility regimes

Work-time flexibility is a crucial test case here as a prominent area in negotiations between employers and employee representatives and an area in which past practices and legal restrictions were important. This, then, was an area in which labour could set limits to institutional dependence.

Companies can react to demand fluctuations in several ways, depending on their severity and likely permanence. The most important are adjusting the total number of employees and varying working hours with the same total labour force. Both of these could conflict with the long-term aim of retaining a secure and reliable workforce and both could require negotiation with employee representatives.

To allow variation in total employment levels, all the MNCs used agency workers who were the first to be dismissed in times of falling demand, thereby cushioning the impact on a core workforce. Under an EU directive, agency workers should have comparable working conditions to core workers (cf. Schömann and Guedes, 2013), but their pay levels in CEECs are hardly ever set by collective bargaining and are not subject to effective outside scrutiny. Trade union representatives in practice accepted the presence of agency workers, rarely seriously questioning numbers and only infrequently taking up complaints they might be making. Numbers thus varied – from 5 percent of the labour force in Audi to 25 percent in Hyundai in 2013 – as employers used this source of labour to plug shortages where local recruitment was insufficient, to provide a cushion for times of falling demand and as a source of cheaper labour. Thus, to varying degrees, MNCs exploited leeway that had been created (or progressively included) in employment law to limit the application of protections established in the early 1990s to a core workforce alone.

Škoda was the only case of open conflict altering the status of agency workers after a complaint from the Polish Ombudsman in 2008, representing Polish agency workers in the Czech plant. Investigations by the Czech Ombudsman and the Czech Labour Inspectorate left no doubt that the law on equal pay for agency employees had been broken and that some were even being paid below the legal minimum wage. The management's reaction, in view of bad publicity and of the need for good relations with a stable core labour force and after negotiation with the union organisation, was to seek to regularise the conditions of agency workers, to consult with unions over employment conditions and to hire mostly Czech employees. As agency workers did gradually join the main union, so they could raise their complaints, the most frequent of which was that their pay had been inaccurately calculated or that they were entitled to only very limited holidays due to their short-term contracts. Thus in this case, where conditions were most favourable to labour, an MNC conceded ground in the interests of a good image and good employment relations.

Achieving numerical flexibility by varying the core labour force proved more difficult. This became an issue when demand had undergone substantial declines. Outcomes again reflected negotiation between employers and trade unions. The former were concerned to retain loyalty and stability from a core workforce. The latter were more determined on this than other issues, but had little by way of sanctions with which to threaten employers. Unions were therefore likely to make concessions on other flexibility policies and pay when faced with threats of lay-offs. Thus, VW Bratislava experienced a particularly severe drop in demand in 2008–2009 and, after dispensing with agency workers, it sought 700 voluntary redundancies from the core workforce. The unions later attributed their support for the *flexikonto* (explained below) implemented with their support from 2009, to their experience with the downturn. In contrast, Suzuki took a less accommodating approach to employees: with output in permanent and sharp decline in 2009, 1200 core workers had to leave, together with 400 agency workers, on an involuntary basis.

Work-time flexibility was a continual theme in negotiations and the source of some bitter conflicts. The inherited legal positions specified a minimum percentage of normal pay to be received during downtime and maximum permitted hours, plus requirements for employee acceptance, for overtime. Where unions were better placed, such as Škoda, TPCA, and VW Bratislava, both downtime and extra shifts were compensated well beyond legal minimums.

Here German MNCs were keen to introduce a specifically German form of flexible work account known as the *flexikonto*. The principal behind this is that the employer can cancel shifts when they are not needed and require employees to work extra shifts when they are needed, with the total over a period adding up to the contracted number of normal hours. This helps an employer to cope with short-term demand fluctuations by cutting costs of downtime and by ensuring an adequate turnout from regular employees for extra shifts. The alternative, paying a fixed proportion of regular pay during downtime and tempting volunteers into extra shifts by offering bonuses over stipulated overtime pay, would either be less reliable or more expensive. The *flexikonto* is therefore desirable for management, but not a necessity in countries where pay levels are considerably below those in Germany and where labour is a small share of total costs.[7] Any benefits depend on the time period over which plus and minus shifts are required to balance. This is always specified in such terms that, if extra shifts are not made available after a certain period, then the employer must pay compensation for down time. The employer therefore wants as long a time period for balancing as possible – ideally lasting over several years – while one of only a few months would be of little practical value.

German law allows for various forms of work accounts and German companies sought to introduce the same solution in Central Europe. This, then, was a case of MNCs actively trying to change a point of detail within its legal environment rather than just accepting what it had been given. It required changes to existing practices within employment relations, albeit not very large ones and, in some cases, changes to employment law, adding flexibility to existing rules for extra shifts. Volkswagen Bratislava negotiated a *flexikonto* in the second half of 2008 in the absence of a corresponding legal framework and then persuaded the government to change the legislation, allowing for flexible work accounts that could be evened out over a four-year period. In Hungary, Audi persuaded the government in 2009 to allow extensions beyond the existing 12-month accounting periods. In PSA, the parent of PCA, work-time accounts were negotiated after 2008 (Delteil and Dieuaide, 2012). In Slovakia, PCA implemented a *flexikonto* from 2009 and negotiated an extension of the accounting period to 30 months in 2013, in exchange for employment guarantees. In TPCA, without any explicit reference to the German model, there was a system for 203 shifts per year with some flexibility over when they would be required. In Škoda in the same period an effective *flexikonto* system was blocked by employee opposition – the agreement reached required shifts to balance out over a four-month period which is too short a period to be relevant to plausible demand fluctuations – despite strong pressure from management to adopt some version of the system being used in Europe across the Volkswagen group. The union was strong and well organised and production levels recovered quickly from the crisis conditions of early 2009, increasing employees' sense of security and hence willingness to oppose management plans that they did not like.

An opposing extreme is represented by Hyundai which relied in Korea on ad hoc solutions and long working hours (Lee and Kang, 2012). The same approach in Czechia led to open conflict shortly after the plant was opened in 2009. Following a failure to meet production targets, the company imposed continual extra overtime, running at two hours practically every day. Its own publicity confirmed that it was often not even giving two days' notice of overtime requirements, but refusing to work extra hours was treated as unexcused absence. Under Czech employment law compulsory extra overtime was permitted only for 'serious operational reasons'.

The response was a one-hour strike by 400 employees which started spontaneously without union involvement on 2 December. This was an extremely rare event in a country with hardly any strikes. The legal position was soon clarified as the local Labour Inspectorate found the company to be in serious breach of almost 50 laws and regulations.[8] For a time after that extra shifts were a matter for negotiation, but demand levels inevitably continued to fluctuate and the management found it difficult to abandon its inherited practices. Thus in late 2012 it decreed additional days of closure which would be unpaid. Although this would breach employment law, the union organisation, with only 15 percent of employees in its ranks and seeing no chance of calling a strike or even a protest meeting, felt unable to offer serious opposition.

Flexibility practices were thus outcomes of negotiations between management and unions and dependent on the overall power relations. We can set out two idealised extreme cases. In one there is full union recognition and prior consultation on all employment relations issues, general security of employment, restrictions and control over numbers of temporary or agency employees, full compensation for any time not worked and substantial extra pay for any extra shifts which are undertaken fully voluntarily. At the other extreme there is opposition or reluctance to recognise and consult with trade unions, a high level of employee instability and possibly a high share of clearly insecure temporary or agency workers. Variations in working hours are at best subject to the minimum of legal protection and laws may be circumvented or ignored.

These extremes are most loosely approximated on the one side by German multinationals and on the other by some Asian companies. The outcomes could be set on a scale with Suzuki at one end and Škoda at the other. The differentiating factors are the five influences on power resources set out in an earlier section, namely product market conditions, labour market conditions, historical legacies, labour relations in the parent MNC and employee international contacts.

## Conclusion

The types of capitalism that have emerged in CEECs have been characterised as dependent. This accurately captures the dependence on outside knowhow and technology, but economic dependence does not necessarily imply institutional dependence. There is clear evidence of ideas from outside influencing political and social development in CEECs, but receptivity to neoliberal ideas is more a consequence of the strengthening of a domestic high-income and business group, than of the direct influence of MNCs. We therefore postulate a notion of a segmented political economy in which the economically less successful domestic business sector has weight in internal politics while the economically successful foreign business sector is active only on a narrow range of issues.

The influence of MNCs on institutional forms by the setting of laws and by influence at the political level is not as important as their weight in economies would suggest. Influence is greater on institutional forms within the confines of their own companies, but even there they are often forced to compromise and adapt. This is followed here with the help of results from empirical research on employment relations in the plants of multinational motor vehicle manufacturers. Previous writing on this theme has often looked for MNCs succeeding in imposing home-country practice, failing to impose home-country practice or deliberately avoiding home-country practice so as to escape from constraints imposed by the need to compromise with employee representatives.

Our research points to more complex interactions in which different actors exercise varying degrees of strength which have clearly identifiable sources. Thus employment relations in MNCs took shape from a process of negotiation and bargaining, often implicit as much as explicit, which led to a continued significant role for organised labour. Practices of MNCs in their home countries did play some role, but always alongside other factors that determined outcomes on specific issues of dispute.

Strikingly, MNCs seemed more willing to accept existing legal frameworks and established practices than to press for major changes. There were several reasons for this, the most obvious being that they chose to invest precisely in countries that did provide acceptable environments. The preconditions they set also embodied large areas of flexibility. The most important requirement was the substantial difference in wage levels compared with western Europe. With this assured, they were less concerned by details of employment law or established practices. Any problems that arose from that could be resolved pragmatically. Indeed, when they did try to deviate significantly from what existed, they encountered resistance and the costs of pressing ahead outweighed any possible benefits. Thus this was an arena in which conditions and practices inherited from the first post-communist reforms of the early 1990s were likely to persist. It was also an arena that gave trade unions some continuity of existence that increased their potential political voice in general, as discussed for Czechia in Chapter 9.

Dependent capitalism, in the sense of domination of part of the economy by MNCs, held in check the neoliberal trend in the sphere of employment relations. Domestic capitalism was more likely to be associated with an actively neoliberal stance in domestic politics. In so far as that built from ideas developed elsewhere, that could be seen as a form of ideological dependence, but one linked to a degree of economic independence. Indeed, an important element of the institutional impact of large-scale manufacturing MNCs was that they had to compromise with domestic actors and in turn provided an environment for continuing trade union activity. The element of economic dependency therefore gave support to a role in society for labour which stood as a barrier to the unrestricted hegemony of neoliberal thinking.

# Notes

1 CEECs include Czechia, Hungary, Poland, and Slovakia.
2 OECD FDI in Figures, www.oecd.org/corporate/mne/statistics.htm.
3 See ICTWSS database, available at www.uva-aias.net/207. The figures for CEECs are, however, imprecise and probably over-estimate the actual unionization rate.
4 Direct lobbying by MNCs in support of labour market deregulation has been much more visible in Romania (see Delteil and Bănărescu, 2013; Trif, 2014). This case is not considered here. A number of factors, that are consistent with the argument presented in this chapter, could explain the difference including the nature of employment law in Romania at the time of post-crisis reforms, the opportunities provided to MNCs in the context of IMF-negotiated conditionality, the home countries of the major multinationals concerned, which included the USA and India, and the weaker trade union position owing to a smaller presence for large motor-vehicle assembly plants.
5 The research method included use of published sources and interviews with plant-level and national union leaders and, where possible, management.
6 *Origo.hu*, 16 March 2007, available from www.origo.hu/gazdasag/hirek/ 20070301visszahelyeztek.html; *HRportal.hu*, 16 June 2009, available from www.hrportal.hu/c/suzuki-birosaghoz-fordul-a-kirugott-szakszervezeti-vezeto-20090616.html.
7 Labour costs in Škoda amounted to only 7.7 percent of total production costs in 2012, *Výroční zpráva*, 2012, p. 98, http://new.skoda-auto.com/SiteCollectionDocuments/ company/investors/annual-reports/cs/skoda-auto-annual-report-2012.pdf.
8 See press release of the Labour Inspectorate in Opava, 22 February 2010, available from www.suip.cz/_files/suip-211979a3f39ac4c9fd40e39880226faf/kontrola_ hyundai_nosovice.pdf; *Deník Referendum*, 14 June 2010, available from www.denikreferendum.cz/clanek/4263-hyundai-porusovala-zakonik-prace-a-dostala-milionovou-pokutu.

# References

Bluhm, K. (2007) *Experimentierfeld Ostmitteleuropa? Deutsche Unternehmen in Polen und der Tschechischen Republik*. Wiesbaden: VS Verlag für Sozialwissenschaften.

Boxall, P. and Purcell, J. (2011) *Strategy and human resource management*. Houndmills, Basingstoke, Hampshire; New York: Palgrave Macmillan.

Cooke, W. (2007) Multinational companies and global human resource strategy. In: Boxall, P., Purcell J., and Wright, P.M. (eds) *The Oxford Handbook of Human Resource Management*, Oxford; New York: Oxford University Press, pp. 489–508.

Delteil, V. and Bănărescu, M. (2013) Roumanie : Le modèle social sous la pression des bailleurs de fonds : les syndicats à la recherche de nouvelles « tutelles ». *Chronique internationale de l'IRES* 143–144: 133–151.

Delteil, V. and Dieuaide, P. (2012) French multinational companies, new state regulations and changes in the employment relationship during the crisis the exemplary case of the automobile sector. *Transfer: European Review of Labour and Research* 18(4): 429–446.

Dörrenbächer, C. and Geppert, M. (eds) (2011) *Politics and Power in the Multinational Corporation: The Role of Institutions, Interests and Identities*. Cambridge: Cambridge University Press.

Drahokoupil, J. and Myant, M. (2015a) Labour's legal resources after 2004: the role of the European Union. *Transfer: European Review of Labour and Research* 21(3): 327–341.

Drahokoupil, J. and Myant, M. (2015b) Putting Comparative Capitalisms Research in its Place: Varieties of Capitalism in Transition Economies. In: Ebenau, M., Bruff, I., and May, C. (eds), *New Directions in Comparative Capitalisms Research: Critical and Global Perspectives*, Houndmills: Palgrave Macmillan.

Drahokoupil, J., Myant, M. and Domonkos, S. (2015) The politics of flexibility: Employment practices in automotive multinationals in Central and Eastern Europe. *European Journal of Industrial Relations* 21(3): 223–240.

Ferner, A. (1997) 'Country of origin effects and HRM in multinational companies', *Human Resource Management Journal* 7(1): 19–37.

Ferner, A., Quintanilla, J. and Varul, M. (2001) 'Country-of-origin effects, host-country effects, and the management of HR in multinationals: German companies in Britain and Spain', *Journal of World Business* 36(2): 107–127.

Ferner, A., Edwards, T. and Tempel, A. (2012) 'Power, institutions and the cross-national transfer of employment practices in multinationals', *Human Relations* 65(2): 163–187.

Galgóczi, B., Drahokoupil, J. and Bernaciak, M. (eds) (2015) *Post-crisis FDI trends and sectoral patterns*. Brussels: European Trade Union Institute.

Haipeter, T., Jürgens, U. and Wagner, K. (2012) 'Employment relations in the banking and automotive industries in Germany'. *The International Journal of Human Resource Management* 23(10): 2016–2033.

Hall, P. and Soskice, D. (eds) (2001) *Varieties of Capitalism: The Institutional Foundations of Comparative Advantage*. Oxford and New York: Oxford University Press.

Harzing, A-W. (1999) *Managing the Multinationals: an international study of control mechanisms*. Cheltenham, UK; Northampton, MA: E. Elgar.

Jürgens, U. and Krzywdzinski, M. (2009) 'Work models in the Central Eastern European car industry: towards the high road?', *Industrial Relations Journal, November,* 40(6): 471–490.

Kahancová, M. (2013) 'The demise of social partnership or a balanced recovery? The crisis and collective bargaining in Slovakia'. *Transfer: European Review of Labour and Research* 19(2): 171–183.

Kohl, H. and Platzer, H.-W. (2007) 'The role of the state in Central and Eastern European industrial relations: the case of minimum wages', *Industrial Relations Journal, November,* 38(6): 614–635.

Krzywdzinski, M. (2011) 'Exporting the German work model to Central and Eastern Europe'. In: Contrepois, S., Delteil, V., Dieuaide, P. *et al.* (eds), *Globalizing Employment Relations: Multinational Firms and Central and Eastern Europe Transitions*, Basingstoke: Palgrave, pp. 99–116.

Lane, D. (2007) Post-state socialism: A diversity of capitalisms. In: *Varieties of Capitalism in Post-Communist Countries*, Basingstoke: Palgrave, pp. 13–39.

Lee, B-H. and Kang, H-Y. (2012) 'Hybridisation of employment relations in the era of globalisation? A comparative case study of the automotive and banking industries in South Korea'. *The International Journal of Human Resource Management* 23(10): 2034–2050.

Meardi, G., Marginson, P. and Fichter, M. (2009) 'Varieties of Multinationals: Adapting Employment Practices in Central Eastern Europe'. *Industrial Relations: A Journal of Economy and Society* 48(3): 489–511.

Myant, M. (2014) 'Economies undergoing long transition: Employment relations in Central and Eastern Europe'. In: Wilkinson A, Wood G, and Deeg R (eds), *Oxford Handbook of Employment Relations: Comparative Employment Systems*, Oxford: Oxford University Press, pp. 359–384.

Myant, M. and Drahokoupil, J. (2011) *Transition economies: Political economy in Russia, Eastern Europe, and Central Asia.* Hoboken, NJ: Wiley-Blackwell.

Myant, M. and Drahokoupil, J. (2012) 'International Integration, Varieties of Capitalism, and Resilience to Crisis in Transition Economies', *Europe-Asia Studies* 64(1): 1–33.

Nölke, A. and Vliegenthart, A. (2009) 'Enlarging the varieties of capitalism: The emergence of dependent market economies in East Central Europe', *World Politics* 61(4): 670–702.

Pavlínek, P. (2015) 'Foreign direct investment and the development of the automotive industry in East-Central Europe'. In Galgóczi, B., Drahokoupil, J. and Bernaciak, M. (eds), *Foreign Investment in Eastern and Southern Europe after 2008. Still a Lever of Growth?*, edited by, 209–55. Brussels: European Trade Union Institute.

Schömann, I. and Guedes, C. (2013) Temporary agency work in the European Union: Implementation of Directive 2008/104/EC in the Member States. *ETUI Report* 125. Available from: www.etui.org/Publications2/Reports/Temporary-agency-work-in-the-European-Union [Accessed 3 April 2016].

Trif, A. (2014) *Austerity and collective bargaining in Romania, National report: Romania.* Dublin City University and European Commission. Available from: www.research.mbs.ac.uk/ewerc/Portals/0/Documents/SDDTEC/Romania%20Final.pdf [Accessed 3 April 2016].

Whitley, R. (2001) 'How and why are international firms different?: the consequences of cross-border managerial coordination for firm characteristics and behaviour'. In: Morgan, G., Kristensen, P.H. and Whitley, R. (eds) *The Multinational Firm: Organizing Across Institutional and National Divides*, Oxford: Oxford University Press, pp. 27–68.

# 4 Institutional transition, power relations and the development of employment practices in multinational companies operating in Central and Eastern Europe

*Ilona Hunek and John Geary*

## Introduction

This chapter examines the development of employment and HR practices in a Polish subsidiary of a German bank in the retail banking sector. The study aims to provide a better understanding of the role of multinational companies (MNCs) as a 'source of employment practice' in Central and Eastern European Countries (CEECs). It also contributes to the wider debate on the process of the Europeanization of employment relations, which is understood as a convergence of employment relations regimes, by providing an account of what is happening at firm level.

During the process of economic transition, CEECs became very dependent on foreign direct investment. Hence some scholars classified their emerging business systems as constituting a form of dependent market capitalism (Nölke and Vliegenthart, 2009; King, 2007). In turn, this dependence sparked an intense debate as to the role of MNCs in determining the shape of employment and HR practices in their host economies (Contrepois *et al.*, 2011). MNCs have been often perceived as being exporters of 'foreign best practices' through a process of the transfer of employment relations and human resource (HR) practices from the company's headquarters to their subsidiaries in the 'weak' or 'institutionally permissive' business systems of the CEECs.

A growing number of studies, however, present evidence that the transfer of employment practices, where it happens, is only partial and that the institutional transition process has had a significant effect on MNCs' practices (e.g. Meardi and Toth, 2006, Meardi *et al.*, 2009). This study seeks to add to this literature. It focuses on three areas of the company's employment policies: workforce adjustment, performance management and employee participation. We seek to answer the following questions: how might we explain the 'shape of' the employment and HR practices of a MNC from a mature developed economy in a transition economy? What is the nature of the influence of the transition environment on the development of these practices? And finally, how might such an influence vary across the three identified policy areas?

## Explaining the development of employment practices in MNCs in transition economies

Two major theoretical perspectives are identified in the literature as a means for explaining MNCs' employment and HR practices. These are the institutional perspective and the political perspective. The first concentrates on the influence of institutions, which are conceptualised as rules and assumptions that shape economic activity, and which structure the choices of organisational actors and create incentives for organisations to comply with institutional norms in the development of their policies and practices (Edwards *et al.*, 2007). It argues that companies' business and employment practices are rooted in the socio-political institutions of their country-of-origin. These are identified to equip firms with distinct sets of organisational capabilities that are then absorbed and transferred into the MNC's foreign operations (Whitley, 2001). This so called 'country-of-origin' effect is displayed as a nationally distinctive 'management style' or 'pattern of organisation' (Ferner, 1997). However, the 'strength' of the country-of-origin effect is not seen to be uniform across all national business systems or indeed across all business practices (Rosenzweig and Nohria, 1994). Thus, for example, some MNCs' practices are seen to be more embedded in their national business environment and require a battery of institutional supports for them to function properly. As a consequence, such practices may be more difficult to transfer to a company's foreign international operations (Whitley, 2001).

The institutional perspective also seeks to explain the extent to which, as well as the means by which, MNCs adapt to their host country environment. In order to be able to operate successfully in a foreign country, MNCs may be compelled to change their behaviour and adapt to the institutional environment of the host country. Kostova and Roth (2002), for example, have argued that MNCs need to do this in order to achieve legitimacy. Thus, for instance, it is suggested that if a MNC is dependent on local resources, it is likely to adapt its practices to local conditions (Rosenzweig and Nohria, 1994; Whitley, 2001). Key here, then, is the perceived 'institutional distance' between the institutions of the home and host country (Kostova and Roth, 2002) and, in particular, the institutional rigidity or strength of the latter (Whitley, 2001) in determining the shape of a MNC's practices.

The political perspective views MNCs as occupying 'transnational social spaces' which encompass firms' internal organisation as well as the multiple institutional contexts within which they operate. Transnational social spaces constitute arenas for political strategizing among organisational actors (Dörrenbächer and Geppert, 2006). The power resources and games 'played out' by actors in these arenas shape the development of organisational practices through processes that draw on institutional resources both at the macro-level of the host country and at the micro-level of the firm (Morgan, 2011; Ferner *et al.*, 2011). Corporate practices may be contested, circumvented or reinterpreted by local actors in a subsidiary, who use their knowledge of the local business context and other types of expertise to defend their interests. In other words, this perspective argues that organisational practices are the outcome of a bargained or contested process involving actors in the headquarters and in the subsidiaries, and are not solely determined by the rational prescriptions of corporate management.

The political perspective draws our attention to the resources that actors may mobilise in order to secure and advance their interests in the process of shaping employment practices in a MNC's subsidiaries. MNCs have huge resources to draw upon which might be used to force the subsidiary's workforce to adapt to corporate practices or resist the pressures for localisation coming from the host country institutions (Morgan, 2011). The power of MNC's headquarters derives not only from their 'material' resources, such as finance, investments, knowledge and expertise, but also from their formal authority to define decision-making structures and rules, and from their shaping of corporate cultures, codes of practices and the 'rhetoric' legitimating the introduction of a particular practice (Hardy, 2006; Ferner *et al.*, 2011).

On the other hand, the subsidiary's workforce may seek to draw upon the local sources of power available to them to deflect, avoid, negotiate or challenge what is proposed by the MNC's management (Ferner *et al.*, 2011). Ferner *et al.* (2011) argue that subsidiaries may derive power from their knowledge of the 'institutional complementarities' of the host business system which may be deployed to generate competitive advantage for the subsidiary (Dörrenbächer and Gammelgaard, 2011). A local subsidiary's power may also be sourced from the regulatory framework of the host country, such as its labour legislation or other regulatory institutions (Williams and Geppert, 2011). Further, local actors may also derive power from positioning themselves to act as skilled interpreters of the host country's institutional framework and in turn from their shaping of headquarters' management understanding of what is possible, and ultimately desirable (Ferner *et al.*, 2011: 174).

Increasingly, the political perspective is often found together with the institutional perspective, with recent studies attempting to understand the interaction of the two aforementioned influences. That is, they have sought to assess how actors embedded in particular institutional domains are able to draw upon specific institutional power resources to pursue and advance their interests (e.g. Morgan and Kristensen, 2006; Ferner *et al.*, 2011; Geary and Aguzzoli, forthcoming). With such integrated frameworks the emphasis is placed on understanding the interrelationships between institutions and the interests and power resources of the various actors.

We turn now to consider the influences emanating from transition economies. Transition economies are understood here as national business systems that are in the process of transformation from one socio-economic regime to another. Although they are considered in the literature as 'weak' and 'institutionally permissive' (Meardi *et al.*, 2009), they present a distinct set of challenges for incoming MNCs. At the outset, it is important to understand that there is considerable variation within the group of transition economies not only in terms of their size and economic performance, but most crucially in their 'paths' of transition and the 'varieties of capitalism' they assume (King, 2007). Here, however, we focus on broad, general 'patterns' that are shared by all transition economies and which may be said to distinguish them from mature advanced economies.

The first element is the continuity of the previous system; that is, the manner in which the 'institutional heritage' of the former centrally planned socialist economy influences the emerging business system. Transition –in part at least– is a path-dependent process, in the sense that long-established social mechanisms tend to reproduce themselves in changed circumstances. As such, the emerging institutional solutions are often embedded in the rationality of the pre-transition institutional arrangements (Stark, 1992). In times of uncertainty, the institutions of the previous systems may come to provide 'guidance' to actors' behaviour. As a consequence, the former institutions may survive the otherwise systemic change, at least to some degree and for some time (Kozminski, 1998).

The second feature is connected to the redistribution of power and influence during the process of transition. First, there is the strong presence of the national government in the economy. This is evident not only in its roles as the 'designer' and driver of major systemic and regulatory reforms (Offe, 1998), but also in its role as an actor which may directly seek to influence private firms' decisions (King, 2007). Second, the implementation of such reforms has often set in train complex political processes which have resulted in the creation of a new 'political capitalism' within which powerful elites – perhaps 'old' or 'new' – come to contest and seek to influence government decision-making (Staniszkis, 1991). Such a complex political environment poses enormous difficulties for incoming MNCs that are unfamiliar with such a political milieu and who inadvertently may threaten the interests of a particular powerful local actor.

The third element relates to the existence of so-called 'institutional imperfections or gaps', which are defined as areas of economic and business activity that are not regulated by institutions (Roth and Kostova, 2003). These imperfections are seen to have arisen from the quick collapse of the old institutional order and the relatively slow process of building new institutions (Newman, 2000). Where such institutional imperfections exist, they create additional uncertainty and ambiguity for actors, with the result that companies often seek, by means of their own resources, to 'correct' for such imperfections. One way in which this has been done is by 'looking out' and 'importing' norms and practices from outside the host country (Newman, 2000). The transfer of MNCs' corporate practices may thus be conceptualised as a way of 'filling in the gaps'.

## Research design and methodology

The objective of this chapter is to understand the influence of a transition economy on the development of employment and HR practices in the subsidiaries of a MNC originating from a mature Western economy. We undertook an in-depth case study analysis of a German MNC's subsidiary operations in Poland. We chose a German MNC as Germany represents a strong and highly regulated economy and whose MNCs are very numerous in CEECs.[1] The German business system places particular constraints on companies' freedom of action at home in areas such as collective bargaining, employee representation, training and employment security (Streeck, 2001). Such constraints tend to be more evident in unionised sectors, like banking. Further, its bank-based financial system typically provides firms with 'patient capital' affording them more time and space to invest in their businesses and in the development of their HR and employment practices. Studies of employment practices in German-based MNCs have identified that in their international operations they tend to demonstrate particular characteristics of their home-country business system, such as possessing a long-term orientation to employee development and training, representative-based workforce consultation, and an emphasis on skill-based functional forms of flexibility (e.g. Tuselmann *et al.*, 2003; Meardi *et al.*, 2009). Other studies, however, note that German MNCs might seek to abandon their home-country employment practices in their international operations and adopt practices characteristic of more liberal economic regimes (Dörrenbächer, 2004). One explanation is that 'German employment practices' rely heavily on the support of the institutional scaffolding of their home-country and, in the absence of similar institutional supports existing in the host country, are difficult to transfer. The MNC chosen for study is a large German bank that has extensive global operations particularly in the area of commercial and investment banking. However, it has relatively limited and recent experience of internationalising the retail banking arm of its business. The majority of the bank's retails operations continue to be located in Germany.

Poland was chosen as a case host country for a number of reasons. First, it is very dependent on foreign direct investment, particularly in the banking sector. Between 1994 and 2004 the level of foreign investments in Poland increased fivefold (Hardy, 2007), which represents the largest intake of foreign capital among the Visegrad countries. According to the National Bank of Poland, a total inflow of FDI into Poland in 2004 was €55 billion, in 2008 it was nearly €116 billion, and by 2013 it had risen to €160.5 billion. Second, of all the CEEC countries, Poland – along with Hungary – was at the forefront of political and economic liberalization. From the outset, economic reforms were cast along neo-liberal lines (Hardy, 2007). In subsequent years the Polish 'pattern' of transition was characterised by frequent changes of governments, which resulted in 'shifts' between neo-liberal and conservative policies representing different 'visions' of the development of institutions at a national level. Third, its weak labour markets, shortage of investment capital and a system of industrial relations that is highly decentralized granted employers considerable scope to pursue a variety of employment and HRM models, including ones informed by a non- or anti-union posture (Meardi *et al.*, 2009).

The choice of retail banking as a sector was informed by a number of criteria. First, it is of major strategic significance to a country's economic development and was thus expected to be subject to more government oversight and 'political gaming' than any other sector. Decisions in respect of the privatisation of Polish banks involving foreign investors, for example, were strongly influenced by different 'models' of privatisation proposed by different government elites (Bonin *et al.*, 2005). Second, the finance sector in Poland is characterised by a large inflow of FDI (Hryckiewicz and Kowalewski, 2008). In 2006, the share of foreign ownership in the banking sector was 73.6 per cent.[2] By 2008 the banking sector accounted for 20 per cent of the total inflow of FDIs into Poland. Third, employment in the finance sector grew substantially. According to the Central Statistical Office (2013), between 1995 and 2008 it doubled, and has remained relatively stable since then. In 2013, the sector employed 174,106 full-time employees (Central Statistical Office, 2014). Finally, the banking sector has been little studied. Much of our understanding of the employment and HR practices of MNCs comes from the manufacturing sector.

However, in pointing to the benefits of looking at the banking sector as a case study we need also point to its boundaries. First, banking is a multi-domestic industry and, unlike manufacturing, the dynamics of competition are very different. While back-office functions may be exposed to international competitive pressures of a form which permits international site competition (Sisson *et al.*, 2001), in front-office retailing banking, each national market is largely insulated from such pressures. As a consequence, country-dependent cost increases – in part at least – may be transferred onto customers (Meardi *et al.*, 2013). Competition is largely between different firms within a given country. Thus the axes of competition differ to those of more exposed sectors, such as the automotive sector. But such distinctions do not reduce the importance of understanding the manner in which employment practices are developed and implemented. Practices may still be transferred from a MNC's headquarters to its subsidiaries, although the logic and context may differ. Thus in retail banking it is likely to hinge less on the competitive performance of other subsidiaries within the MNC and more on the means by which such practices can be deployed to attain competitive advantage relative to other companies within the sector of a particular country.

In sum, this case is conceived of in the following terms. It is a study of a MNC from a strongly regulated, mature Western economy – Germany – with subsidiary operations in a major transition economy – Poland. Such a large MNC, from a strong economy, with extensive international experience[3] may be expected to seek to, and be able to, transfer its preferred management practices.

Three areas of employment and HR practices were chosen for analysis: employee participation, performance management and workforce adjustment. They were expected to set in train different sets of dynamics as well as patterns of adoption and adaptation. Practices in the area of employee participation are recognised in the literature as being shaped in large part by the system of industrial relations in the host country, especially with regard to collective bargaining (e.g. Rosenzweig and Nohria, 1994). On the other hand, performance management practices which are considered in the literature as being 'strategically important' to companies were expected to be formulated at a central level and transferred to the MNCs' international operations (e.g. Almond and Ferner, 2006). Workforce adjustment policies refer to practices related to forms of employment contract and employment numbers. Workforce adjustment employment practices are particularly important when a MNC develops its operations overseas through mergers and acquisitions. These practices are likely to be influenced both by the 'strategic needs' of the corporate headquarters and the local institutional environment (Rees and Edwards, 2009).

From our consideration of the debates in the literature and from our knowledge of the institutional and market context of the case study company together with the environment of the host country the following two hypotheses are derived.

### Hypothesis 1

We expected that as the case bank came from an institutionally rigid economy it would seek to transfer its employment practices to its Polish operation in a manner that would bear a distinct German imprint. However, we also anticipated that, in the absence of supporting German institutional scaffolding, the transfer of German practices would be partial and incomplete. However, we still expected that key elements of the bank's employment system, in particularly those that are less reliant on institutional supports, such as performance management, would be adopted.

### Hypothesis 2

However, we also expected that, as the case bank had no prior experience of operating in a transition economy, it may have been forced to staff key managerial positions with Polish nationals and rely on their expertise in navigating through the intricate complex of a transitioning business, political and employment context. In turn, we anticipated that this would give local management the space to influence and shape employment practices according to their interests.

The data was obtained from 12 in-depth semi-structured interviews, documentary sources and direct observation. Interviews were held at three different organisational levels: at a German corporate level, at a national level (Polish subsidiary management) and at branch workplace level (branch managers and employee representatives). Interviews at each level provided different perspectives on the HR and employment practices in the Polish subsidiary. Most of the data at the subsidiary level were collected between 2006 and 2010, with additional interviews conducted between 2012 and 2013. The long period of data collection allowed us to witness the development of practices over a 5 to 7 year period.

### The establishment of a German bank's subsidiary in Poland and the headquarters' control of operations

The German bank established its operations in Poland in the early 1990s by opening a representative office in Warsaw in order to provide financial services to its corporate clients. Until the late 1990s, the bank's activities remained concentrated on commercial banking. The bank's management intended to expand its retail operations by means of acquiring a large local bank. In the mid-1990s, the bank tried to become a strategic investor in one of the recently privatised Polish banks, but the attempt failed. As the last of the banks designated for privatisation was acquired by another investor in 1999, management decided to acquire a privately-owned Polish through a capital market acquisition. In order to gain permission to acquire more than 25 per cent of the shares in the acquisition target, the bank conceded to the National Bank of Poland's request to become a strategic investor in another small Polish private bank which was in danger of going bankrupt. The takeover attempt was, however, unsuccessful, and the German bank was left with the 'obligatory acquired' Polish bank in 1999. It was a small commercial bank with a branch network of 30 branches concentrated mostly in the south of Poland. Established during the period of liberalisation in the Polish banking sector, it experienced many of the problems which led to the banking crisis in the early 1990s. This included the financing of local businesses and local administrations without conducting proper risk assessments. This led to many 'bad debts', which, in turn, brought the bank to the verge of bankruptcy. Despite the dire financial state of the small Polish bank, the German bank decided to keep it, and, after modernising its structures, used it as a means for developing its Polish retail operations.

At the outset, the bank decided to maintain tight direct control over its Polish subsidiary by transferring a group of expatriate management and employment practices directly from Germany. At that time, however, the bank had not yet developed a cadre of international managers with the appropriate experience of managing operations in emerging markets. This lack of experience was exacerbated by a sense among some German managers that a secondment to Poland would not enhance their career development. According to the Polish branch managers who were interviewed, many German expatriates treated their assignment in Poland as an exile, and they were not interested in learning the specifics of the Polish banking system and its working culture. This was seen to create conflict between them and the Polish staff members. As a result, the German management found it difficult to meet the performance targets set for the Polish operations, which in turn led to a headquarters' decision to hire local managers and give them overall responsibility for managing and developing the subsidiary.

While the Polish managers were given some freedom in managing operations locally, they still had to adhere to centrally developed strategic plans, to follow corporate policies and procedures and to operate within tight budgetary constraints. The bank applied the 'pay as you go' method of financing investment in its subsidiaries. This meant that money for each investment was only sent from the headquarters once the short-term objectives of the investment schedule had been met. In addition, all decisions that involved changes in the strategic plan had to be approved by a headquarters' committee.

## Employment practices in the Polish subsidiary of the German bank

### *Employee participation and voice*

In Germany, the bank possessed structures for employee representation in the form of a well-established works council. Employees' representatives were also members of the banks' supervisory board. However, this system of co-determination was not transferred to the Polish operations and there was no evidence of headquarters' intention to transfer this practice. Neither did the Polish managers see the need for collective employee representation. The Polish director of sales, for instance, stated that he did not have a negative attitude towards collective employee representation in general, but he saw no need to treat the union seriously. Notwithstanding this, on the basis of an agreement between the bank's management and its works council, the Polish union was represented in the company's European Works Council (EWC). In practice, however, the Polish trade union leader conceded it afforded them 'little if any' influence. He perceived the Polish trade union as being too weak to be involved in transnational activities, and Polish issues were of no great interest to the other EWC representatives from the bank's subsidiaries in other countries. As a result, he stopped attending the meetings and delegated this task to another member of the union board.

There was only one trade union in the Polish subsidiary and it was only established in 1999 at the point when the bank was being taken over by the German MNC in an effort to protect staff from the likelihood of job losses. This was an independent enterprise–level union. It was established as such as, according to the trade union leader, the staff lacked trust in Poland's two large trade union confederations. These were seen to be 'too politically involved'. Union membership remained below 10 per cent of the subsidiary's employees – a legal threshold which is required to render a union 'representative' for the purposes of collective bargaining. The union leader explained the low membership by the lack of interest among employees in the trade union movement. Most were young and had little knowledge of the purpose of collective representation. In addition, both the union representative and the branch managers pointed out that, in a context of high demand for employees in the growing retail banking sector, employees were more likely to change jobs than to try to change aspects of their employment through a union within their workplace. As a result, the union's activities were largely confined to running the employees' savings and loans scheme and nominating the social labour inspector.[4] Contact between the union and the subsidiary's management was limited to meeting the MNC's statutory obligations, such as providing information about any planned employment measures.

There were two channels of individual employee voice in operation in the bank. They were an annual employee attitude survey and a corporate intranet. The latter invited employees to join different 'work groups'. The survey was conducted annually and was run globally through the bank's computer system. Its purpose was to measure staff commitment. The employees and branch managers admitted that they were not provided with feedback on the survey, and neither were they aware of any changes implemented as a result of the survey. As such they did not consider it a serious channel of communication or influence. The intranet was used frequently by the Polish employees, but mostly as a tool for accessing information about internal programmes within the bank, such as job advertisements. All managers admitted that they preferred direct communication with their employees. In summary, the development (or lack of) employee participation and employee voice practices was shaped on one hand by the weakness of the trade union and, on the other, by a lack of interest of management in the development of employee voice structures other than those which provided for direct communication.

### Workforce adjustment

In the course of the development of its retail operations in Poland the German bank made significant workforce adjustments in an effort to improve its efficiency and to develop the branch network. The employment structure and staff competences in the subsidiary were described by the Polish managing director as being 'tragic'. Both the Polish and the German managers pointed to the lack of staff competence, both in managing risk – which, they claimed, led to the financial difficulties of the bank – and in providing comprehensive customer service required of a modern retail bank. The acquired bank had also redundant and duplicate structures. All interviewees pointed to the bank's byzantine structures as being a manifestation of the power of the former branch directors, which, it was claimed, were characteristic of those evident during the former communist system. Moreover, there was a strong sense of 'job entitlement' among the bank's employees, especially those occupying more senior positions or specialist positions. In sum, the heritage of the previous system in the acquired subsidiary remained largely intact.

The employment restructuring process did not begin until 2001 when the acquired bank was incorporated into the German bank's structures. There is evidence that the German management tried to re-train the existing workforce before making them redundant. The interviewed managers, both Polish and German, agreed that the practice in the German bank's headquarters was to 'move an employee around' in an effort to avoid dismissing them. Many Polish employees, however, refused training and did not want to change their job roles or acquire new qualifications. Those employees were made redundant during the second wave of restructuring in 2003.

In an effort to expand the existing branch network, the German bank undertook a recruitment campaign. The strategy was to employ young graduates and train them in the German bank's sales indigenous procedures. Such an approach, though, did not allow the company to increase its workforce with haste. Then, shortly thereafter, the bank experienced a problem with employee retention. As the Polish retail banking sector began to grow fast in the early 2000s, the demand for skilled employees grew commensurately quickly. The practice of 'poaching' trained employees from other banks by offering them high salaries became common. The lack of familiarity with such 'poaching' practices among German management was recognised as one of the reasons for the failure of its staff retention practices.

Another reason why the restructuring of the Polish workforce and operations was difficult for the German management team, according to the German president of the supervisory board, was that the German managers tried to impose particular German practices (such as re-training) on the local workforce without any consultation. The trade union leader described the approach of management in the first years thus: 'this was the German order, which means we had to do what we were told'. Employees were not offered an explanation of why changes were being introduced. This generated resistance amongst the Polish staff and they were rejected as 'alien' practices, for example by employees' refusal to participate in training.

The second restructuring campaign was led by the newly appointed Polish management. It started with the closure of branches which were deemed to be uneconomic and unviable. This was followed by a wave of redundancies. The aim was to fire 'poor performers' and replace them with newly hired and appropriately qualified staff. By such means, 90 per cent of the 'original' branch managers and 70 per cent of the staff were dismissed. The newly-hired Polish director of sales, who was responsible for the restructuring of the branch network, was described as being 'ruthless' in his decisions and he side-stepped any obstacles in his way. For example, the process of employment reduction was organised in such a way that the number of people never exceeded legal quarterly limits, so consultation with the union was never formally required. Nor did the union engage in any active opposition. The trade union leader explained that they did not feel strong enough to resist management. He admitted that before each redundancy programme was initiated, he received the list of people who were going to be dismissed, but the union managed to protect only a few members' jobs.

The recruitment campaign that started almost at the same time as the employment reduction campaign was based in large part on two models, one on 'network-based recruitment', and the other on 'poaching' of employees from other banks. The network of personal connections of the Polish director of sales was an important source of recruiting qualified employees for managerial positions. Later, the newly-hired managers were encouraged to use their own personal networks as a source of further recruitment. The interviewed branch managers confirmed that they were recruited in this way. The same approach was used by branch managers in hiring employees for their branches. The branch manager from a newly opened branch in Warsaw described the process in this way:

> As in other banks, the German Bank has certain requirements for candidates for particular positions, but I can decide whom I recruit. When I was looking for people to employ in my branch, I first turned to those I knew from my previous employment. Then I 'complemented' my staff with people I found in other banks. My way of looking for potential employees is to go to another bank and pretend I am a customer. When I find a potential candidate I call this person and ask him or her for a meeting.

The 'Polish' restructuring strategy and the localisation of workforce adjustment practices brought the immediate expected results in terms of a rapid growth of the sales network and increased performance. The number of branches increased from 24 in 2004, to 82 in 2008, and to 164 in 2012. Two factors contributed to this. First, there was the experience and approach of the Polish management team who had a very pragmatic and business-oriented approach to recruitment and HR management. Second, in being under pressure from the headquarters to deliver quick results, Polish managers were able to draw on local resources, in particular use their personal and business networks, to recruit a suitably skilled workforce and achieve their business goals in a timely fashion.

It bears emphasis that the local workforce adjustment practices were implemented by the Polish senior managers in opposition to the corporate employment policies and procedures. The Polish managers explained that it was difficult for the HR management in headquarters to understand, at least initially, that the Polish subsidiary was too small to 'move people around and re-train them' as required by corporate policies. The way the Polish management 'solved' this problem was to ignore corporate policies and procedures and apply local practice. The Polish managing director described this process thus:

> We hired and fired without consulting with the headquarters and they gave us a good scolding afterwards.

There is evidence, however, that the reprimands had little real consequence for the Polish senior managers. The Polish director of sales admitted that 'the headquarters often turned a blind eye' to his actions as long as he was able to achieve prescribed financial performance goals. However, the consequences for the Polish HR manager were more complicated. He admitted that the avoidance of corporate policies created conflicts which were difficult for him to manage:

> I am in a hard spot, because I have to satisfy our top management who are appraised for business development and for generating revenue. In order to achieve their goal I have to do the recruitment my way, which is different than the guidelines I get from the headquarters. But the Polish managers are technically not my direct bosses – the HR people in the headquarters are. So I have to obey them in order to keep my position. My 'bosses' in Poland don't need to worry because they are difficult to get rid of. My position is not so comfortable.

Nonetheless, in practice, the Polish HR manager admitted that he sided with his Polish colleagues and applied local practices and later sought to justify this to corporate HR in his reports.

The avoidance of corporate HR and employment policies by local management was made possible ultimately by the improvement in the subsidiary's performance. While local management was under pressure to deliver financial performance and to comply with corporate HR and employment policies, in the end the former took precedence over the latter. As a consequence, Polish managers were able to 'get away' with evading corporate HR and employment policies.

## Performance management

The MNC introduced a performance management system in the early 2000s. It included a performance pay bonus element which was linked with an appraisal of the subsidiary's performance. Corporate management, however, were not wholehearted in their support of the scheme, or in the necessity that it be embraced by Polish management. Nonetheless, the local managers considered the scheme to be of utmost importance. They devised and implemented their own local version as early as they possibly could. It was based on individually-set targets with bonuses paid on a monthly-basis. There was also an internal sales competition.

According to the Polish managing director, the individualisation of performance management not only provided better motivation for employees, but it also provided management with a means for identifying underperforming individuals. An employee with a documented record of underperformance for three months in a row was dismissed. The same rule applied to the branch managers, but their performance was evaluated on the basis of the branch's performance. This 'rule' was strictly obeyed during the restructuring process, which was personally supervised by the Polish senior management. After the restructuring finished in 2004, these measures were less strictly applied.

The Polish managing director admitted that this way of 'correcting for poor performance' was not entirely approved by the headquarters' HR department:

> Of course HR in headquarters was giving me a hard time, saying that this was the wrong way to manage poor performance. They told me that I should offer those people some training, and it would be best if I sent them to Germany, but I could not do it. Training in Germany was too expensive and not adequate to our needs. And I did not have enough money and enough time. I had to show growing sales results.

When asked why the Polish management was so keen to have their own performance management system, the managers' answers indicated that they felt insecure in their own positions as executives of the Polish subsidiary. The Polish managing director, for example, explained that he was appraised annually on the basis of the financial results of the whole subsidiary, and he was never certain whether he would be able to keep his position or not. That's why, according to him, he often applied 'drastic' measures to achieve good performance:

> I worked as the managing director for ten years, but at that time I did not know, how long I was going to remain in this position. I had to show results immediately and that was the only thing I was evaluated for. Therefore I had to develop solutions 'on the go'. Had I known in advance, that I had ten years to develop the business, I would have probably made different decisions in managing my employees.

The local performance management practices were identified as giving rise to the expected benefits of increasing sales and profits. (In 2004, the subsidiary reported a loss of €1.37m, in 2006 it delivered an operating profit of €1.22m, in 2008 its profits reached €13m, and in 2012 were €49.8m.) The practices were introduced without any overt resistance from the employees. The union was too weak to provide any collective resistance. Neither did the Polish labour code provide any obstacles to dismissing employees for poor performance. Moreover, as other foreign banks operating in Poland also introduced similar performance management practices, it quickly became 'the norm' in the retail banking sector.

## Discussion

This study seeks to account for the shape of employment practices in the Polish subsidiary of a German MNC. We draw on the institutional and political perspectives to explain our findings. We found that at the outset, the bank did indeed attempt to 'control' for the uncertainty of the host institutional context by transferring home country practices. However the outcomes were not as originally hoped for. In the end, there is little evidence of a German influence on the practices developed in the Polish subsidiary. This is, in large part, explained by the assertive posture of the Polish managers who were able to avoid implementing the bank's corporate policies and to a degree by the absence of local co-ordinating institutional supports. Thus in regard to our first hypothesis, we find that the transfer of German practices – in a context where proximate or parallel home country's institutional scaffolding was absent – was partial and incomplete. Further, as anticipated, of the three HR policy areas examined, it was in the area of performance management – which was the least reliant on indigenous country supports – that a Polish accent on the development of local practices was most evident.

The study's findings also confirm hypothesis 2. The German bank's initial strategy of relying almost exclusively on expatriate staff rebounded on it, and the bank was forced to hire local managers and adopt local practices. The findings also confirmed that the interests and power of local managers played a key part in shaping the subsidiary's employment and HR practices. It is plain from the evidence that the Polish managers derived considerable power from their intimate knowledge of the Polish national business system, albeit it was still in formation. The Polish management's power was enhanced further by their ability to meet the financial targets set for them, which emboldened them to impress upon their German superiors that they were best placed to manage their operations and were best left to their own devices.

In conclusion, then, the political perspective helps a great deal in accounting for the findings of this study. Studying the interests and power of actors in the Polish subsidiary revealed a two-way dependency between headquarters and subsidiary management. With the perceived imperative to restructure the subsidiary in haste the headquarters was compelled to rely on the expertise of local managers. This, in turn, enhanced the influence and power of the latter to resist the transfer of German practices and shape employment relations and HR practices in the subsidiary in the way they saw fit. The power of local managers was enhanced further by the weakness of organised labour in the Polish subsidiary. Low union membership and lack of activism in the union led to its marginalisation by the subsidiary management, thus depriving the employees of an effective voice channel through which they could influence the development of the subsidiary's employment and HR practices.

## Conclusion

Finally, when we put our study into a wider context, the findings do not support the assumption evident in much of the relevant literature in regard to the control of MNCs' corporate headquarters in determining the development of employment practices in CEEs (Nölke and Vliegenthart, 2009; King, 2007). It rather suggests that employment practices are shaped, in significant part, by the interaction of the interests and power resources of actors at headquarters and subsidiary levels (see also Drahokoupil and Myant, Chapter 3). The present case study demonstrates how local managers were able to 'break' from the close supervision of the German headquarters by drawing on their power resources which were in turn derived from their intimate knowledge of the local business environment and their competence in delivering to the bottom-line. This suggests that the role of local management as an actor shaping employment relations in dependent capitalism, at least in multi-domestic sectors (as in retail banking), is more important than that understood or recognised to date. Where such diffusion of common policies and practices is limited, or at least circumscribed by particular contingencies (the nature of the service delivery systems, the extent and reach of transition, corporate management ignorance and local management competence) so as scholars of transition economies do we need to be wary of theories which espouse sweeping claims of transformation and convergence along parallel and common lines. Europeanisation (in terms of common HR models) is likely to be a faltering and partial accomplishment.

## Notes

1   According to the Polish Information and Foreign Investment Agency, at the end of 2013 Germany was the largest provider of FDI in Poland with €27.7 billion worth of investment.
2   Although the share of foreign capital decreased to 63.6 percent in 2012 (according to the Office of Financial Supervisory Commission), it remains very significant.
3   Although the internationalisation of the German Bank's retail operations was relatively recent, the bank was able to draw on the international experience of its investment and commercial operations.
4   This is an employee representative whose role is to control whether health and safety procedures are obeyed and employees' rights are not violated.

# References

Almond, P. and Ferner, A. (2006) *American Multinationals in Europe,* Oxford: Oxford University Press.

Bonin, J., Hasan, I. and Wachtel, P. (2005) 'Privatization matters: bank efficiency in transition countries'. *Journal of Banking and Finance,* 29, 2155–2178.

Central Statistical Office (2013) Employment by kinds of activity according to ISIC rev 4 classification. Warsaw: Central Statistical Office.

Central Statistical Office (2014) Monitoring of Banks 2013. Warsaw.

Contrepois, S., Delteil, V., Dieuaide, P. and Jefferys, S. (2011) 'Globalising Employment Relations and Crisis: the role of Multinational Company transfer to Central and Eastern Europe', In: Contrepois, S., Delteil, V., Dieuaide, P. and Jefferys, S. (eds) *Globalising Employment Relations.* London: Palgrave.

Dörrenbächer, C. (2004) 'Fleeing or Exporting the German Model? – the Internationalization of German Multinationals in the 1990s', *Competition & Change,* December, 8(4): 443–456.

Dörrenbächer, C. and Gammelgaard, J. (2011) 'Subsidiary power in multinational corporations: the subtle role of micro-political bargaining power', *Critical Perspectives on International Business,* 7(1): 30–47.

Dörrenbächer, C. and Geppert, M. (2006) 'Micro-politics and conflicts in multinational corporations: Current debates, re-framing, and contributions to the special issue', *Journal of International Management,* 12(3): 251–265.

Edwards, T., Colling, T. and Ferner, A. (2007) 'Conceptual approaches to the transfer of employment practices in multinational companies: an integrated approach', *Human Resource Management Journal,* 17(3): 201–217.

Ferner, A. (1997) 'Country of origin effects and HRM in multinational companies', *Human Resource Management Journal,* 7(1): 19–37.

Ferner, A., Edwards, T. and Tempel, A. (2012) 'Power, institututions and the cross-national transfer of employment practices in multinationals', *Human Relations,* February, 65(2): 163–187.

Geary, J. and Aguzzoli, R. (forthcoming) 'Miners, politics and institutional caryatids: accounting for the transfer of HRM practices in the Brazilian multinational enterprise', *Journal of International Business Studies.*

Hardy, J. (2006) 'Bending workplaces institutions in transforming economies: foreign investment in Poland'. *Review of International Political Economy,* 13(1): 129–151.

Hardy, J. (2007) 'The new competition and the new economy: Poland in the international division of labour', *Europe-Asia Studies,* 59(5): 761–777.

Hryckiewicz, A. and Kowalewski, O. (2008), The Economic Determinants and Engagement Modes of Foreign Banks in Central Europe. Warsaw: National Bank of Poland.

King, L. (2007) 'Central European Capitalism in Comparative Perspective'. In: Hancké, B., Rhodes, M. and Thatcher, M. (eds) *Beyond Varieties of Capitalism: Conflict, Contradiction and Complementarities in the European Economy.* Oxford: Oxford University Press.

Kostova, T. and Roth, K. (2002) 'Adoption of an Organizational Practice by Subsidiaries of Multinational Corporations: Instutitional and Relational Effects', *Academy of Management Journal,* 45(1): 215–233.

Koźmiński, A. (1998) *Odrabianie Zaleglosci,* Warszawa, Wydawnictwo Naukowe PWN.

Meardi, G., Marginson, P., Fichter, M., Frybes, M., Stanojevic, M. and Toth, A. (2009) 'Varieties of Multinationals: Adapting Employment Practices in Central Eastern Europe', *Industrial Relations: A Journal of Economy and Society,* 48(3): 489–511.

Meardi, G., Strohmer, S. and Traxler, F. (2013) 'Race to the East, race to the bottom? Multi-nationals and industrial relations in two sectors in the Czech Republic', *Work, Employment & Society,* 27(1): 39–55.

Meardi, G. and Toth, A. (2006) 'Who is Hybridising What? Insights on MNCs' employment practices in Central Europe', *In:* Ferner, A., Quintanilla, J., Sánchez-Runde, C. (eds) *Multinationals, Institutions and the Construction of Transnational Practices. Convergence and Diversity in the Global Economy.* Basingstoke: Palgrave.

Morgan, G. (2011) 'Reflections on the Macro-politics of Micro-politics'. *In:* Dörrenbächer, C. and Geppert, M. (eds) *Politics and Power in the Multinational Corporation.* Cambridge: Cambridge University Press, pp. 415–436.

Morgan, G. and Kristensen, P. (2006) 'The contested space of multinationals: varieties of institutionalism, varieties of capitalism', *Human Relations,* 59(11): 1467–1490.

Newman, K. (2000) 'Organizational transformation during institutional upheaval', *Academy of Management Review,* 25(3): 602–619.

Nölke, A. and Vliegenthart, A. (2009) 'Enlarging the Varieties of Capitalism: the Emergence of Dependent Market Capitalism in East Central Europe', *World Politics,* 61(4): 670–702.

Offe, C. (1998) 'Designing Institutions in East European Transitions'. In: Goodin, R. (ed.) *The Theory of Institutional Design.* Collegium Budapest/Institute for Advanced Study.

Rees, C. and Edwards, T. (2009) 'Management strategy and HR in international mergers: choice, constraint and pragmatism', *Human Resource Management Journal,* 19(1): 24–39.

Rosenzweig, P. and Nohria, N. (1994) 'Influences on Human Resource Management Practices in Multinational Corporations', *Journal of International Business Studies,* 25(2): 229–251.

Roth, K. and Kostova, T. (2003) 'Organizational coping with institutional upheaval in transition economies', *Journal of World Business,* 38(4): 314–330.

Sisson, K., Arrowsmith, J. and Marginson, P. (2001) 'All Benchmarkers Now? Benchmarking and the 'Europeanisation' of Industrial Relations', In: 41/02, W. P. (ed.) *ESRC "One Europe or Several?" Programme Working Papers.* Brighton: Sussex European Institute.

Staniszkis, J. (1991) *The Dynamics of Breakthrough in Eastern Europe: The Polish Experience,* University of California Press.

Stark, D. (1992) 'Path Dependence and Privatization. Strategies in East Central Europe'. *East European Politics and Societies,* 6(1): 17–54.

Streek, W. (2001) 'Introduction: Explorations into the Origins of Nonliberal Capitalism in Germany and Japan'. *In:* Streeck, W. and Yamamura, K. (eds) *The Origins of Nonliberal Capitalism.* Ithaca: Cornell University Press.

Tuselmann, H.-J., Mcdonald, F. and Heise, A. (2003) 'Employee Relations in German Multinationals in and Anglo-Saxon Setting: Toward a Germanic Version of the Anglo-Saxon Approach?', *European Journal of Industrial Relations,* 9(3): 327–349.

Whitley, R. (2001) 'How and Why are International Firms Different? The Consequences of Cross-Border Managerial Coordination for Firm Characteristics and Behaviour',. *In:* Morgan, G., Kristensen, P.H. and Whitley, R. (eds) *The Multinational Firm. Organising Across Institutional and National Divides.* Oxford: Oxford University Press, pp. 27–68.

Williams, K. and Geppert, M. (2011) 'Bargained globalization: employment relations providing robust "tool kits" for socio-political strategizing in MNCs in Germany', In: Dörrenbächer, C. and Geppert, M. (eds) *Politics and Power in the Multinational Corporation. The Role of Institutions, Interests and Identities.* Cambridge: Cambridge University Press.

# 5 Segmented capitalism in Hungary

## Diverging or converging development paths?

*Csaba Makó and Miklós Illéssy*

## Introduction[1]

The comparison of different economic systems has remained at the centre of economists' interests in the last decades as the source of the different roads of economic developments and inequalities when comparing individual economies or even geo-political "blocs" of countries. Earlier, the "comparative political economy" dealt with the differences between Command and Market Economies emphasizing the contrasting role of the state on one side and the liberal labour market institutions on the other. Although the comparison between the Post-Socialist economies can be a relevant topic itself, it is worth taking diversity within the national economies into consideration as well. That is, not only can a cross-country analysis be interpreted as a comparative research, but also, the comparison of sectors and different operating practices can be surveyed within a country. This approach is the so-called "Segmented Capitalism" theory first labelled by Martin (2008). According to this theory, firms are the main actors when it comes to shape the economic system in a country. This expression fits to the main thesis of the Varieties of Capitalism (VoC) literature, namely that firms and their needs should be at the centre of analyses of economic systems. It is justi-fied by the fact that firms are the main actors and stakeholders of market economies and these institutions characterize and specify the structure of the system and the resultant economic performance of the country in the global perspective.

The segmented capitalism approach is of particular relevance in the case of the CEEC region where one of the main drivers of the post-socialist economic devel-opment is the foreign direct investments (FDI) and multinational companies (MNCs). This is especially true for the Hungarian case because economic modernization in the first decade of the transformation process (i.e. until year 2000) was primarily based on massive privatization and FDI-inflows. As Eyal *et al.* rightly note 'no other country of comparable size has such massive foreign ownership, which seems to be responsible for substantial levels of economic growth. Poland and the Czech Republic are the closest to Hungary in this respect, with Slovenia, Slovakia, and the Baltic Republics following somewhat behind.' (Eyal *et al.*, 2003: 35) This process significantly slowed down after 2000 when

FDI was seeking for other destination countries such as Bulgaria, Estonia or Slovakia.[2] These firms not only brought lacking financial assets and newest technologies to the country but also important 'soft technologies' such as work organization design and leading edge managerial practices. Furthermore, these companies offer direct links to global markets through involvement into the Global Value Chains (GVCs).

It is a vital question, therefore, whether Hungarian-owned small and medium-sized enterprises have been able to build long-term supplier relationships with these MNCs. Foreign-owned companies play a crucial role in the economic modernization of the country by creating new development paths and avoiding path lock-in situations (Makó and Illéssy, 2007).

This chapter is built upon Martin's approach and aims to investigate the internal segmentation of the Hungarian economy. In order to better understand the extent to which organisational and business practices of different segments of the Hungarian economy differ from each other, with a special focus on foreign-owned companies. Building on the original ideas of Martin, we create our own segmentation based on firm-level data. In our analysis we omit the aspects of the relationships between politics and economy, although these are relevant both in Martin's and also Drahokoupil and Myant's theses (Chapter 3). Instead, we pay particular attention to organisational innovations and other business practices improving learning capabilities of enterprises which is of crucial importance under the current economic circumstances. Another important difference compared to the latter is that we do not limit the scope of our investigation to MNCs but aim to include all segments of the Hungarian economy. Our assumption is that smaller differences between the different segments of the economy in business and organisational practices, lead to greater integration and enhance the participation of domestic firms and especially SMEs in GVCs, thus making these economies less vulnerable and more sustainable.[3]

Our aim is to identify the current processes in Hungarian firms' practices using the results of the first Hungarian matched employer-employee survey on working and employment conditions in the last quarter of a century. This database provides a unique opportunity for empirical analysis from several points of view. First, contrary to other large European-wide surveys (e.g. European Working Conditions Survey), the size of the sample is big enough to differentiate special segments of the Hungarian economy. Second, this is a linked employer-employee survey which allows the analysis a wider set of variables. For instance, employee-level surveys provide detailed databases on the characteristics of the workplace, while employer-level surveys give us reliable information on ownership structure, market characteristics, inter-firm cooperation and so on. The strength of one type of survey is the weakness of the other. In contrast, matched surveys usually provide all of these data. These advantages also mean considerable limitations for the scope of the analysis. The lack of similar national surveys elsewhere, however, makes any international comparison impossible[4] but we can expect to observe similar trends of segmentation in other transformation economies.

We also aim to comprehend the motives behind the firms' behaviours in the knowledge-based economy to a greater extent. The reason for doing so is the increasing economic importance of comparative advantages created by knowledge-intensive activities and high value-added production (CEDEFOP 2010). These trends justify the relevance of analysing the organizational knowledge development and the training practices as well as the characteristics of work organization within firms. With a detailed understanding of the industry-sector and the firm- level knowledge development practices, it is possible to describe the main mechanisms of the economic systems led by firms within the specific economy.

The structure of this chapter is the following. The first section offers a brief theoretical background of the "Segmented Capitalism" approach and presents the methodological aspects of the cluster analysis. The second section outlines the most important features of the different segments of the Hungarian economy identified through the cluster analysis. The third section focuses on the differences in the characteristics of the labour process and in the training practices between the four main segments identified. The conclusion is summarized at the end of the chapter, where we argue that after 20 years of the beginning of the post-socialist transformation process significant differences can be observed between the individual segments of the Hungarian economy.

## 1. Theoretical and methodological remarks

During the 1980s and 1990s a new approach emerged with a theoretical framework mainly inspired by the French regulation school. Works under this approach showed significant differences in their field of investigation ranging from national innovation systems to social systems of production, but – as Hall and Soskice rightly observed – their analytical tools did not differ greatly: 'Responding to the reorganization of production in response to technological change, these works devote more attention to the behaviour of firms. Influenced by the French regulation school, they emphasize the movement of firms away from mass production toward new production regimes that depend on collective institutions at the regional, sectoral, or national level' (Hall and Soskice, 2001: 3). Another common element of these studies were that these authors put the enterprises at the heart of their analyses and investigated the ways through which different social institutions influence their learning capabilities.

This approach was later theorised by Hall and Soskice (2001) under the heading of 'Varieties of Capitalism' stream. The emergence and rise of this school also had significant influence on the scholars analysing post-socialist changes in the region of the Central and Eastern European Countries (CEEC). The VoC approach fitted well in the so-called transition versus transformation of that time. According to the former argument, 'transition process' can be interpreted as a once-and-for-all shift from a political–economic regime based on the logic of central planning to another regime based on the logic of the market. This view overestimated the level of institutional coherence or homogeneity of both the former socialist and the succeeding capitalist socio-economic regimes and neglects the diversity of regulations governing individual and collective actions (Grabher and Stark, 1997). Another, more evolutionary view recognised the role of 'path-dependence' in the emerging new market institutions (e.g. privatisation, creation of autonomous labour relations system, governance structures of the firms, implementation of 'leading-edge' management practices, etc.) and the variety of development trajectories in the post-socialist economies in the CEEC region (Makó and Illéssy, 2007).

The first attempt to apply the VoC approach in the analysis of the post-socialist transformation can be found with Eyal *et al.* (1998). In their article the authors focused on the main agents who led the transformation process and concluded that diversity in the composition of this leading elites produced diversity in the forms of capitalism they created. In Russia, Romania, Bulgaria, Serbia, Ukraine and Belarus, party bureaucrats successfully converted their political power into economic benefits and private property: 'They were less interested and, arguably, less capable of building capitalist institutions such as free markets in labour and capital. So, in these countries we find capitalists without capitalism: former communist officials amassed private fortunes in the course of the transition but now operate in the context of weak or non-functioning market institutions' (Eyal *et al.*, 2003: 15). In contrast, in countries such as Hungary, Poland, and the Czech Republic, the transformation process was led by a coalition of technocrats, former dissident intellectuals and well-educated managers of socialist companies. According to the authors, this coalition was unable to accumulate such private property as did party bureaucrats in the former group of countries. Instead, they were more engaged and capable of building market institutions. Lacking a domestic bourgeoisie, foreign-owned firms played a central role in the mass privatization process. In conclusion the authors argue: 'There is an absentee capitalist class in Central Europe, in the form of foreign ownership by multinational corporations, but its alliance is with domestic technocrats and managers who also control the state. Thus, we argue that the Central European transition produced capitalism without capitalists, since these countries developed market institutions quickly but no domestic propertied bourgeoisie' (Eyal *et al.*, 2003: 16).

Interestingly enough, the authors argue that the central role of foreign-owned companies and export-oriented industrial and economic development led to a 'dependent developmental trajectory'. Another implication of this characteristic is that the integration of foreign businesses into domestic markets and supply chains emerges as a problem to be solved.

The VoC approach does not represent a radically new trend amongst comparative studies (e.g. Esping-Andersen, 1990; Sapir, 2005; Composto 2008; Gallie 2007; Baumol *et al.* 2007; Greskovits 2010; etc.), but rather a change in the focus of the former comparative political economy approaches from the importance of the state and other formal institutions to the role of firms' and the coordination mechanisms within organizations.

In his literature review, Martin identified four main models interpreting the post-socialist transformation, complementing the VoC theoretical framework: the "liberal market model", the "coordinated market model", "associative capitalism" or "heterarchy" as a third one and the "old left model of neo-colonialism" (Martin, 2008: 133). The liberal market model put emphasis on competition and regarded on the post-socialist changes as a rather simple transition from socialism to the capitalism. The role of the state is limited to ensure fair competition and to guarantee contracts. As Martin rightly observed, while this model proved to be useful in analysing the early phase of transformation, it exaggerated the coherence of the new business model and underestimated 'the significance of the socialist inheritance' (Martin, 2008: 140) and the social, political and economic costs of the transformation.

The "coordinated market model" is the other archetype of the capitalist business systems in VoC approach. It is a corporatist model based upon coordination between the state, trade unions and employers' representatives at firm, sector and national levels in the form of collective agreements. Some elements of this system have been evolved in Slovenia, but generally speaking it had limited influence in the Central and Eastern European (CEE) region: 'corporatist institutions established in the region lacked the political and popular support required for the effective coordination of market' (Martin, 2008: 140).

The third model trying to interpret post-socialist changes was elaborated by Gernot Grabher and David Stark (Grabher and Stark, 1997). Analysing the privatization process in the region, they concluded that it did not lead to 'real' property redistribution, but was mainly a 'recombination of assets' with newly emerged networks of firms and their managers. They called this business system "heterarchy" where the economy is organized neither by hierarchies (i.e. relations of dependence), nor by markets (i.e. relations of independence). According to Grabher and Stark, in the post-socialist organizational heterogeneity hierarchies are blurring and hardly visible inter-organizational networks are the central element of the business system (Martin, 2008: 136). As Martin pointed out: 'The heterarchy model accurately depicted the fluidity and complexities of the organizational structures of the early post-socialist period, but exaggerated the extent of agency available to post-socialist managers' (Martin, 2008: 140).

The fourth stream of attempts aimed at interpreting post-socialist transformation inspired by the VoC theoretical framework, regarded the CEE region as an emerging (or "neo-colonial") capitalist periphery in Europe. The fiscal, social and economic policies of national governments are shaped by international organisations (such as IMF, World Bank or WTO), while the development of local economies depends largely on multinational corporations and foreign direct investments. As a result, a 'dual business system develops, with a small internationally oriented segment alongside a large, locally oriented segment' (Martin, 2008: 138).

While the VoC approach tries to differentiate country clusters according to the sole coordination mechanisms, Martin (2008) argues that it is possible to identify the differences not only between countries or country clusters but also within countries regarding such important features of the economic systems as asset-ownership, means of access to capital and markets, and the relative autonomy of economy compared to the sphere of polity. Considering these characteristics of each economy it is obvious that coherent, integrated patterns as well as segmented systems can be observed.[5] Martin's conception, which combines the VoC approach and business system theory,[6] is based on an aggregated analysis of macro-statistics that shows four different patterns in the Hungarian economy: state, privatized, de novo, and international. The segmentation dimensions, as we have mentioned above, are the following: (1) means of access to capital; (2) mode of access to local, national and international production systems and product markets; (3) the role of differentiation between polity and economy; and (4) asset ownership. According to this classification of firms, the four segments can be characterized in a visibly different way, and the developing path of each segment is also distinctive.

The statistical source of our research is provided by a nation-wide survey, titled *'Employment relations in the workplace – 2010'* (Neumann and Simonovits, 2010). This was the first and so far the only empirical nation-wide research survey on employment relations in Hungary, providing a unique opportunity for further detailed research due to the large sample size and the method of collecting data.[7] As a result of this research program, two different levels of data-base were created, depending upon the type of the respondents. One level of responses encompasses the employees' answers to the survey questions, and the other level includes the opinion of the employers, trade unions, and works councils. This data-base is representative for the population of Hungarian firms and offers a great opportunity to compare employees' opinions with employers' answers. The representativeness is provided by the following dimensions: sector, region and the number of employees.[8]

Considering the possibilities provided by the database and Martin's segmentation dimensions cited above, an enriched set of independent variables were used in order to achieve more robust groups in the Hungarian business sector. These additional variables include the regional location of the firm, the type of activity, the year of establishment and the number of employees. Finally, the following variables were used in the cluster analysis: ownership, size of the firm, age of the firm, type of activity (sector), market structure, and regional location.

In terms of the ownership dimension, the survey made distinctions between Hungarian-owned firms, mostly privately owned, mostly state owned Hungarian firms, international private firms, and mixed ownership (half-and-half Hungarian and foreign ownership ones). The size of the firm was measured by the number of employees as identified in the following categories: micro-firms (10–19 employees), small firms (20–49 employees), medium sized firms (50–249 employees), and large firms (250 or more employees). The type of business activity indicates the sector where the firms are operating. This variable had 8 different sectors with a wide scale of activities, so it was necessary to simplify. As a result, 3 component variables were created: basic activities (mining, electricity, gas and water supply), manufacturing and services. The geographical location is an essential dimension in Hungary due to the significant regional differences in economic development. In this analysis, Eastern, Central, and Western regions of the country were distinguished and investigated, Budapest being the wealthiest region followed by Western parts of the country, while Eastern regions are lagging behind. Finally, the market structure covers the type of customers and the main market where the firms sell their products and services. In terms of the customers the firms can provide services or products for the individual customers only; business to business solutions (B2B); half-and-half for individuals and for other businesses and internal services for themselves (internal clients within the firm).

In terms of market structure, access to a customer base is also a fundamental concern to ensure corporate sustainability over the long run. The firms' responses on the existing and targeted markets were categorized into the following markets where their products or services were sold: local; regional; domestic; international markets. As for the statistical method, the K-means cluster analysis was used for categorization of the firm's market reach.[9]

## 2. The segments of the Hungarian economy

After the cluster analysis, the following 4 clusters, or so-called target/market segments were identified: (1) Hungarian Manufacturing segment; (2) Hungarian Personal Service providers' segment; (3) Hungarian Business Service providers (B2B); (4) Foreign-owned Business Segment. In what follows, we will briefly present each of these four segments.

### 2.1 The Hungarian manufacturing sector: concentrated in the less developed regions

This cluster includes 234 firms from the industrial and manufacturing sector. Most of them, approximately 67 percent, operate in the industrial sector, with the remaining 33 percent belonging to basic activities (i.e. mining, electricity, gas and water supply market segments). In terms of the market structure the dominant market is within the bounds of the Hungarian domestic market, with approximately half of the firms competing in the national market, and only approximately 20 percent of the firms competing in international markets, the rest of the firms sell their products and services at local or regional markets. The main costumers are business to business partners (B2B), and in addition, a further 30 percent of the firms produce for or service business and individual customers, as well.

In relation to the regional locations of the firms surveyed, more than 50 percent of these B2B firms operate in the Eastern region, while only a small percentage of B2B firms can be found in the Western part of the country. It suggests that the most developed region (Central) does not represent itself in the B2B cluster, while the less developed one is over represented. Firms belonging to this cluster are mainly concentrated in the developing regions of Eastern Hungary. Regarding the sizes of the firms surveyed, half (50 percent) of the firms belong to the category of small or medium enterprises (SME) – and two-thirds of these SMEs employ less than 50 employees. Private ownership of SMEs dominates the Hungarian segment.

*Table 5.1* Characteristics of the sample: Hungarian manufacturing firms

| Dimension | Dominant pattern |
|---|---|
| Market structure | Dominance of domestic market (50%) |
| | Rather weak international market (20%) |
| Customers | Mostly B2B – business to business partners (40%) |
| | Mixed: B2B + individual costumer partners (30%) |
| Location | East-Hungarian region (67%) |
| Firms' size | Dominance of the small firms (50%) |
| Ownership | Hungarian ownership (90%) |

Source: Own compilation

## 2.2 Hungarian personal service providers: dominance of the low value added services

The Hungarian personal services sector consisted of 178 firms and was composed of the three following sub-sectors: (1) domestic personal service providers, (2) domestic business service segment and (3) international service providers. These companies satisfy the needs of the customers in local and regional (sub-national) level. Their activities constitute rather weak value added services. Following the categorization of Salter and Tether (2006), these activities can be considered as the traditional services. The local economic environment does not change as dynamically as the global market. Due to the characteristics of the low value added personal services, these activities do not require strong learning capacity of their employees, and the majority of jobs are low-skilled. In addition, some firms choose to stay small either due to a small local market or the inability to exploit innovative opportunities available to them. The personal service segment can be described by the following main characteristics: a high share of small businesses (67 percent), of which a significant amount is made up of Hungarian-owned companies (78 percent). When examining the regional distribution of the firms it is important to note that the great majority of them are located in the least developed region of Eastern Hungary (66 percent).

*Table 5.2* Characteristics of the sample: Hungarian personal service providers

| Dimension | Dominant pattern |
|---|---|
| Market structure | Local (48%) and regional market (36%) |
| Customers | The share of personal costumers is 91% |
| Location | East-Hungarian region (67%) |
| Firms' size | Rather small business (68%) |
| Ownership | Hungarian ownership (78%) |

Source: Own compilation

## 2.3  Hungarian business services: concentrated in Budapest and active on the national markets

Firms in this cluster represent the knowledge-intensive service segment that mainly provides services for business to (business) services (B2B) in the national market. The majority of this segment (N=264) is composed of small businesses (55 percent), employing fewer than 50 employees, and a noticeable proportion of them employ 20 or fewer workers (27 percent). These firms operate mainly in the economically well-developed Central-Hungarian region.

## 2.4  Foreign-owned business segment: dominance of medium sized firms and the importance of the international markets

The most important distinctive features of this cluster reside in the ownership structure, in targeted markets and in number of employees. As the name of the cluster suggests, the majority of the companies belonging into this group of firms are foreign-owned. More specifically two thirds of them are exclusively in foreign property, whilst a further 30 percent can be characterized by mixed ownership. The size of the firms is also larger than the sample's average: 45 percent of companies are medium and 10 percent of companies are large firms. What seems to be even more important, these companies are present almost exclusively in national and international markets (41–41 percent). This cluster represents a very important link through which the Hungarian economy can participate in the GVC. International markets are important not only because they represent the most lucrative businesses – selling high value-added products and services – but mainly because through the participation of the GVCs, firms gain the opportunity to compete with and learn from the leading edge economic actors worldwide. The foreign-owned business segment is composed of manufacturing as well as service provider companies. In this cluster, the main customers are other private and public enterprises, so no differences between public and private customers were identified. In terms of regional location, almost half of the companies operate in the Central Hungarian Region, including the capital city of Budapest, and one third of those also provide services in one of the most developed region – after the capital – in Western Hungary.

*Table 5.3* Characteristics of the sample: Hungarian business service providers

| Dimension | Dominant pattern |
|---|---|
| Market structure | National, regional and local market (50%, 22%, 14%) |
| Customers | Mainly B2B, mixed personal and business services (30%, 34%) |
| Location | Central-Hungarian region (80%) |
| Firms' size | Small firms (55%), further 27% fewer than 20 employees |
| Ownership | Hungarian-owned (98%) |

Source: Own compilation

*Table 5.4* Characteristics of the sample: foreign-owned business segment

| Dimension | Dominant pattern |
| --- | --- |
| Market structure | National and international market (41–41%) |
| Customers | 42% exclusively B2B, 20% B2B and B2C at the same weight |
| Location | Most developed regions: Central and Western Hungary  (48%, 34%) |
| Firms' size | Medium (45%) and large enterprises (10%) |
| Ownership | Foreign (67%) and mixed (30%) ownership |

Source: Own compilation

The next section of the chapter focuses on the characteristics of the labour process, patterns of work organization, knowledge use and practices, that differ according to the four clusters identified.

## 3.  Foreign-owned business segment is by far the most innovative: segmentation is relevant to labour process and training practices

The quality of employment and the High Performance Working System (HPSW) are particularly important sources of sustainable economic competitiveness and development, and firms play the key role in both the exploration and exploitation of these possibilities (Becker and Huselid 1998). The permanent and increasing competitive economic pressure and the paradigmatic changes in the international division of work, as well as the radical sector shift between manufacturing and services are shaping the Hungarian economy significantly. Both international and national experiences indicate that these structural changes in the post-socialist economy have led to polarization in working and employment conditions instead of a general deterioration or improvement of them. In the firm's practice, the characteristics of quality of work are generally identified by the following factors (Arundel *et al.* 2007): skills and competences development; creative and learning organizations of work; family and work balance; employment security.

Amongst these factors, this study concentrates on some of the key features of the work and knowledge development practices within the firm. The 'Employment relations in the workplace – 2010' research project, widely surveyed various aspects of the labour process and focused on the formal and informal (situated) learning processes, as well. The formal aspect of learning processes was measured by the workers' participation in formal education or training, while the informal one or 'situated learning' covered On the Job Training (OJT), team work, etc. The latter forms of knowledge developments are integrative parts of both individual and collective learning in the labour process (Makó *et al.* 2010).

We assume that that various features of work organizations (i.e. autonomy in work, quality management, etc.) and the existing competencies, as well as the knowledge developing processes, are different in the four segments. This assumption is justified by the fact that the share and the amount of the individual employee's inclusion into the knowledge intensive economy as well as the skills required by the firm's core activities are definitely distinctive according to different clusters. In our approach, the work organization is the key framework of knowledge improvement, therefore the analyses start with the presentation of the job characteristics. This dimension was measured by the following three items: autonomy in work, the quality supervision and organizational innovation in work. Several variables were tested, but these imply the most significant and most illustrative relations.[10]

Concerning employees' autonomy, there is a positive correlation between autonomy in work and innovative work organizations. Work autonomy plays an important role in creating learning and training opportunities. Similarly to the method used in the European Working Conditions Survey (EWCS – Eurofound), workplace autonomy of employees was measured by the extent to which they can decide upon the pace of their work, the working methods, the division of tasks, and the working time schedule. As concerning the autonomy in the pace of work, there is no significant difference observed between the manufacturing and the service sectors. This can be explained by the fact that the formalization in domestic small businesses in manufacturing clusters is lower than that in mass-production. In contrast, the level of autonomy in choosing the working methods is significantly different by the segments.[11] In 88 percent of Hungarian business service providers, the workers can decide on the applied methods, while this figure is only 56 percent in the case of foreign-owned business segment.

In relation with the autonomy in division of tasks, employees have less autonomy in the Hungarian manufacturing sector in comparison with the service providers especially with the 'personal service providers'. This can be attributed to the smaller degree of rationalization of work in the service sector. In the case of the autonomy in scheduling work, employees working in both Hungarian business service sector and the foreign-owned business segment dispose the greatest level of autonomy compared to their counterparts in Hungarian manufacturing and personal services sector.

*Table 5.5* Autonomy in work

|  | *Hungarian manufacturing sector (N=243)* | *Hungarian personal service providers (N=178)* | *Hungarian business services (N=264)* | *Foreign-owned business segment (N=171)* |
|---|---|---|---|---|
| Selecting methods | 26% | 60% | 88% | 56% |
| Pace of work | 41% | 45% | 55% | 43% |
| Division of tasks* | 43% | 60% | 58% | 47% |
| Schedule of work* | 12% | 18% | 26% | 29% |

Note: Variables signed by (*) show statistically significant differences between clusters.

Source: Own compilation

Beside the level of autonomy in work, this study emphasizes the importance of organizational innovations such as job rotation, multi-disciplinary team work and project work in knowledge development and sharing within the firms often transferred by MNCs to Hungarian-owned firms. In relation with the project-based work, it is necessary to note that this form of advanced collective knowledge transfer tool is less popular[12] in the Hungarian personal service providers where only 27 percent of firms utilize it in comparison with the foreign-owned business segment where it was found in approximately every second (45 percent) of firms. Another important feature of innovative work organizations is the presence of multidisciplinary teamwork. This organizational arrangement is also most prevalent in the foreign-owned business segment: it characterizes every second firm (52 percent). However, almost half (46 percent) of the Hungarian manufacturing enterprises also apply such kind of teamwork to their firm's working practices. The two Hungarian-owned service clusters lag behind significantly: only one quarter of personal service (26 percent), and one-third (33 percent) of business service providers use multidisciplinary teams. This type of working group is not only a new form of integration of existing competencies, but also offers a possibility of solving problems collectively, which enables individuals to contribute to potential solutions. A further form of workplace innovation is the job rotation which requires a similar level of skills. This form of organisational innovation primarily occurs in the Hungarian manufacturing (57 percent) and in the foreign-owned business segment (54 percent). However, it is popular in Hungarian business service providers group too, where more than two fifths (45 percent) of the firms use them. In this context, it is useful to take into consideration that the various tasks that require skills in exchange were not typical in our examined business segment.

Another source for continuous improvement in the modern work organization is the use of 'quality circles'. In the use of this kind of quality management system where supervision of the quality is made by autonomous groups of employees, the foreign-owned business cluster stands out with almost 1/3 of the firms (27 percent) utilizing such kind of problem solving working groups. In the

*Table 5.6* Selective forms of organizational innovation

| | Hungarian manufacturing sector (N=243) | Hungarian personal service providers (N=178) | Hungarian business services (N=264) | Foreign-owned business segment (N=171) |
|---|---|---|---|---|
| Multi-disciplinary team work | 46% | 26% | 33% | 52% |
| Job rotation | 57% | 39% | 45% | 54% |
| Project-based work | 37% | 27% | 36% | 45% |

Source: Own compilation

three other clusters examined, less than one-fifth of businesses apply this solution to their standard operations. This is a statistically significant difference between the clusters.

The quality management system is widely used in the Hungarian manufacturing sector: just over half (53 percent) of the Hungarian firms apply it, while the results show that the Hungarian business services cluster is the least prone to this with only a 40 percent utilization rate (this correlation is statistically significant.) Due to the strong quality management involvement, the quality standards are also quite important in the Hungarian manufacturing cluster with 67 percent usage rate, as well as in the foreign-owned business segment where 64 percent of the firms use quality standards. The Hungarian business and personal service providers follow similar patterns in connection with quality standards. (There is a significant correlation by cluster, showing that these leading edge management and working practices are most widespread in clusters having the most intensive relations with international markets.)

Beside the examination of the various forms of organizational innovation (i.e. various types of team work, quality management), the employment relations survey also provided information on both formal and informal learning and training practices. The formal training was measured by the number of employees involved in the formal training/educational schemes offered by the firm, while the 'on the job training' (OJT), team work, visiting workshops, professional and exhibitions, etc., represent the informal training or the situated learning. These forms of informal training have great impact on practical and experimental knowledge transfer, thanks to their contributions to individual and collective knowledge of workers.

In this relation it is worth calling attention to the fact that the mainstream knowledge management methods focus on the formal and codified (explicit) knowledge and underestimate the importance of experience-based and tacit knowledge. This bias is reflected in both the economic and the employment policies, as well as in the orientation and interests of international surveys (e.g. the

*Table 5.7* Quality management practices

| | Hungarian manufacturing sector (N=243) | Hungarian personal service providers (N=178) | Hungarian business services (N=264) | Foreign-owned business segment (N=171) |
|---|---|---|---|---|
| Quality management system | 53% | 44% | 40% | 55% |
| Strict quality standards | 67% | 51% | 55% | 64% |
| Quality circles | 14% | 11% | 19% | 27% |

Source: Own compilation

Innovation Score Board[13]). In his seminal work, Nielsen (2006:96) noticed, 'Creativity and knowledge absorptive capacity are central resources in an organization striving for product and service innovation. Skills and formal training are, needless to say, important as preconditions, but what really matters is the ability to deploy qualifications in the job situation. This makes competence an important concept especially when it relates to the qualities of social capital such as cooperation capacity and to communication skills internally between different functions, and externally towards various actors. What the learning organization requires is a triad of formal education, competence and social capital.'

The existing skills and competencies, training practices, and generally the employers' attitudes in connection with various forms of training differ in the four segments.[14] The duration of training time was measured by (1) the number of the days spent with initial trainings by a new employee and (2) the average number of days spent with training in the last year. The results show that trainings lasting for more than 10 days characterize the Hungarian manufacturing sector with 30 percent of these firms having an average training exceeding 10 working days. A long-term training does not characterize the other segments of firms. This can be partly explained by the fact that as we saw earlier in the case of organisational innovations and quality management practices, companies belonging to the Hungarian Manufacturing and the Foreign-owned Business segments prefer informal ways of training (e.g. learning by practicing, learning by doing etc.) and more often establish such organisational arrangements that enhance organisational learning capabilities.

There are no statistic based differences between clusters in connection with the existence of formal training: for example two-fifths of the Hungarian manufacturing, personal and business service cluster provided work related training in the last year, while every second foreign-owned business segment firm organized some sort of training.[15] The 'length of an average training' varies in every segment, although these differences are not significant.[16]

Another important aspect of the work-related training is the number of participants in formal training. The following training forms were surveyed: organized

*Table 5.8* The amount of participants in company trainings

|  | Hungarian manufacturing sector (N=243) | Hungarian personal service providers (N=178) | Hungarian business services (N=264) | Foreign-owned business segment (N=171) |
|---|---|---|---|---|
| Organized and financed by the firm | 16% | 32% | 36% | 23% |
| Chosen by the employee but financed by the firm | 7% | 15% | 19% | 15% |

*Source:* Own compilation

and financed by the firm; chosen by the employee but financed by the firm; paid by the employee and supported by only working time discount. Firms in the Hungarian service clusters are similar to each other concerning the rate of participants in firm-financed training: the participation rate is higher than the average shown in the last column. Firms in the manufacturing sector put little or no emphasis on these forms of firms or employees' financed formal training. However, a higher participation rate was observed in the case of courses chosen by workers and financed by the company.

As it was noticed earlier, besides the formal training, forms of informal knowledge development such as OJT, consultation with the staff or the managers, job rotation, team work, and the importance of professional events encourage the cooperation – and social capital development – between the members in the firm. The OJT was particularly important in the foreign-owned business segment, as most of the informal training possibilities have larger significance in this cluster than in Hungarian ones. In this relation it is worth noting that "The empirical studies made until now indicate that even though there is growing potential for the electronic delivery of graphic, numerical, and text-based information, no part of the knowledge intensive business service transactions can be carried out without local presence of face-to-face contact" (Toivonen, 2006: 9).

It is also necessary to note that the type of ownership and the specific market segments seem to be more important factors shaping the company knowledge use practice than the type of main activity (e.g. manufacturing versus services). Further important differences can be observed between two Hungarian service sectors, namely that the personal service providers give higher importance to informal training, except OJT.

## Conclusion

Martin's concept of Segmented Capitalism Theory combining Variety of Capitalism (VoC) approach and business system theories is definitely a solid foundation for our analysis. In his article, Martin analysed the segmentation of the Hungarian economy according to the functional differentiation between the spheres of polity and economy and identified four segments of the Hungarian economy: state segment, privatized segment, de novo segment and segment of international firms. Our approach, although inspired by Martin's original ideas, took a bit of a different starting point. Using the results of the first nation-wide Employment Relations in the Workplace Survey – 2010, we identified company clusters on the base of such structural factors as ownership structure, number of employees, age of the firm, type of activity (sector), market structure and geographical location. The main finding of our analysis is that the segmentation theory is relevant in the Hungarian economy and that both researchers as well as policy makers shouldn't dismiss the different operating patterns (e.g. a vastly different knowledge acquisition practice between the sectors) and the obviously distinct integration mechanisms found between the segments of the economy.

This chapter highlighted the heterogeneous character of the post-socialist economy, based on the example of Hungary. Four clusters were identified, namely: the Hungarian manufacturing sector, Hungarian personal service providers, the Hungarian business service sector, and foreign-owned business segment. These clusters are significantly different in terms of ownership, number of employees, regional location, costumers/markets and the type of the activity. The most important differences are the followings. The only cluster that reaches international markets is, not surprisingly, the foreign-owned business segment and to a much lesser extent the Hungarian manufacturing sector.[17] The Hungarian business service sector is active mainly on the national markets, whereas Hungarian personal service providers are restricted to regional and local markets. Medium and large enterprises can be found in great number only in the foreign-owned business segment, the other three sectors are dominated mainly by small firms. We can also observe some territorial segmentation between the clusters. While Hungarian manufacturing companies and Hungarian personal service providers are located in the least developed Eastern regions of the country, Hungarian business services are operating in Central Hungary, while companies belonging to the foreign-owned business segment cluster can be found also in the most developed central and western regions of Hungary.

Differences between segments were observed in connection with some characteristics of the labour process and training practices. In most of the analysed items, the foreign-owned business segment showed similar patterns to the Hungarian manufacturing firms, while the Hungarian business service provider segment resembles to a large extent to the Hungarian personal service providers. However, the degree of workplace level autonomy of employees is much greater in the case of the foreign-owned segment than in the case of Hungarian manufacturers and their training activity is also more extensive. Both service provider segments tend to ensure more autonomy than the two other clusters and are more likely to provide formal company trainings than informal or situated learning possibilities.

One of the most important questions regarding the different segments of the Hungarian economy is the level of their integration to the global value chains. Our data suggest that there are significant differences between the clusters in terms of access to international markets. Out of the four segments identified only two have access to international markets, namely the foreign-owned business enterprises and the Hungarian manufacturers, although this access is very limited in the case of the latter (20 percent). This is especially important in the case of such post-socialist countries as Hungary, where the aim of the economic transformation is to (re)connect the economy to the new international division of labour. It is widely accepted view among Hungarian social scientists that economic modernization of Hungary was mainly based on FDI. Due to the lack of internal financial resources this was true for the majority of the CEECs, although to different degrees. FDI and MNCs play a key role in the economic performance of the country (for example in terms of their contribution to the exports),[18] Hungary failed to integrate local SMEs into the global value chains represented by MNCs (see also: Gém *et al.*, 2011) partly because the latter trust more in the member companies of their existing supplier networks, partly because the Hungarian SMEs are unable to meet high quality standards MNCs require from them.[19] This lead to an asymmetric modernization process and a dual economic structure in which leading edge multinational companies co-exist with local SMEs with only weak cooperation (Makó and Illéssy, 2007).

Our results call, as advocated by Martin, for a more integrated business system in Hungary: Economic development dependent on FDI and MNCs will not lead to vulnerability and unsustainability, only if the country is able to maintain its attractiveness in the view of global investors and/or if it is able to connect a growing share of domestic firms to international markets. This latter can be achieved by, for example, promoting Hungarian SMEs to become suppliers of MNCs or by upgrading in the GVCs providing high value-added business functions (e.g. R&D). If the low level of business system integration proves to be long lasting and the access to international markets remains restricted to foreign-owned companies it will threaten the stability of the whole social and economic development of the country. This fragile position of the Hungarian economy was well reflected by the moderate pace of economic growth, even well before the global financial and economic crisis, when the country lost much of its attractiveness and the inward flow of FDI had considerably slowed down. This economic downturn was deepened only later by the crisis. In order to create new development path, economic policies would need to be reoriented and would need to target the SME sector to make them capable of connecting to GVCs.

In this relation, it is worth mentioning the key results of the latest national survey on the competitiveness of the Hungarian SMEs. The problems of competitiveness are not related – contrary to public opinion – to the under-financing or financial difficulties. Instead, the lack of language skills, low level of further training, absence of cooperation/networking and the low intensity of innovation are the main inhibitors to connecting them to the GVCs. It is implausible that government intervention could have visible impacts in eliminating these difficulties. Firms in the SME sector need a tailor-made individual government intervention to cease or diminish the above listed constraints of competitiveness (Szerb *et al.*, 2015).

In a dynamic perspective, the next step for these firms would be to move up in the GVCs attracting more value-added economic activities within a particular value chain and thus stabilizing their position for the longer term. This is one way not only the Hungarian economy but almost all post-socialist economies could break with their existing asymmetric status and could be integrated into a much higher level of the global division of labour.

In this chapter, we briefly presented different segments of the Hungarian economy by analysing firm level data. Although this gave us a unique opportunity to test Martin's hypothesis in practice, we also should have to deal with serious constraints as well. Most notably, the relations between the worlds of politics and economy, an important dimension of segmentation in Martin's approach, was lacking in our analysis. In this respect, it is worth mentioning the notion of 'selective economic nationalism' developed by Tóth (Tóth, 2015). This highly politically motivated state-protectionism applies only to some sectors (mainly excluding industry or private sector business services), including public utility companies, the retail trade, the banks and sectors dependent on government contracts (e.g. EU-funded construction projects). In these sectors, government tend to promote domestic firms whom owners are loyal to it. Economic protectionism seems also to have been the subject of increasing claims from domestic firms, contesting the tax privileges (and other incentives) offered by the State to the FDI, which resulted in strong political discourse and promises in that sense.

Beyond the discourse however, government priorities remains largely unchanged, and in much sectors follow up a neoliberal-leaning policy aimed to attract and support new FDI projects, as revealed by a series of recent strategic agreements with key investors. Part of this attractiveness policy, is the new labour code, aimed at creating the most competitive labour market regulation in Europe and making it easier for multinational companies to pursue 'flexible' forms of work and employment' (Tóth, 2015: 243).

As we can see, segmentation of the Hungarian economy in which there is a gulf between MNCs and Hungarian-owned enterprises in terms of their manpower and knowledge use, is accompanied by a segmented economic policy approach: in some important segments of the economy which are dependent on government contracts there is a strong state protectionism and direct political influence, while FDI and the activities of the MNCs are supported at the same time by (for example) a labour market deregulation and the creation of strategic partnerships with key international investors. This double segmentation will hardly favour to any integration processes among economic actors but will likely increase or at least maintain existing differences between Hungarian and foreign-owned enterprises.

## Notes

1    We owe more than we can express to Samuel Rogers for the linguistic revision of the English version of the manuscript, and to Éva Farkas, former PhD student at the PhD School of Faculty of Economics – Debrecen University for the statistical analysis of the nation-wide employment survey.
2    The volume of FDI-inflows in the 1990s and the level of FDI-intensity of CEECs' economies are presented in detail in Tables 5.9 and 5.10 in the Annex.
3    One may argue, on the other hand, that less integration might limit the risk to imported crisis from the global markets to the domestic economy, but this may hold true only in the case of those economies, if there is any, where the domestic demand is large enough and resistant to the global crises.
4    We may add to this point that it is easily conceivable that such an analysis would result in different clusters in other countries which would make such a comparison even more problematic.
5    According to Martin's research the latter characterizes the Post-Socialist countries.
6    Business system theory was originally developed by Richard Whitley who defined it as: 'Distinctive business systems ... are particular arrangements of hierarchy-market relations which become institutionalized and relatively successful in particular contexts. They combine preferences for particular kinds of activities and skills to be coordinated authoritatively with variations in the degree of discretion exercised by managers from property rights holders and in the ways in which activities are co-ordinated. They also

exhibit differences in extent and manner in which activities are co-ordinated between economic actors. Thus the nature of firms as quasi-autonomous economic actors, their internal structures and their interdependencies are all interrelated and differ significantly between institutional contexts. (Whitley, 1992: 10, cited by Foss, 1997: 8).

7  "This is a matched survey, which means that the interviews were made with the management and employers' and also labour unions' or work councils' (elected) representatives of the chosen 1000 workplaces with at least 10 employees. Overall we have collected data from 6329 employees in 922 firms. We have conducted 139 inter-views with representatives of the trade unions at the workplaces and further 106 with works councils" (Neumann and Simonovits, 2010: 13).

8  Representativeness is ensured by a weighting process by using the variables mentioned above. As concerning the size, the sample is representative for firms employing 10 or more employees.

9  Due to the different measurement levels of independent variables these were stan-dardized before the cluster analyses. The relevance of variables included was tested by ANOVA test.

10  The most of the variables were dummies and show the appearance or the lack of each working or training solution.

11  The differences were measured by Chi-square method, the confidence level is 95 percent in every case.

12  Although this result is not statistically significant.

13  Holm *et al.* (2010).

14  For the statistical analyses ANOVA, Crosstabs and Chi-square methods were used depending on the measuring level of the variables.

15  Comparing to other results: 49 percent of Hungarian enterprises provide a sort of formal or informal training (Mako *et al.* 2011).

16  Confidence level is 0,05.

17  We have no data on this issue, but presumably these trends are at least partly connected, in other words Hungarian manufacturing sector reach international markets via Hungarian subsidies of MNCs.

18  Koltay described Hungarian economic transformation as an export-led and FDI-based growth where 73 percent of the GDP is composed or realized by exports and where the share of MNCs in exporting activities reaches 70 percent (Koltay, 2010: 8).

19  It's not necessarily a question of technology or human resources. In the automotive industry, for example, the compliance with the sophisticated quality management systems implemented by the MNCs often requires heavy investments in measuring instruments accredited by the principal firm.

# References

Arundel, A., Lorenz, E., Lundvall, B. and Valeyre, A. (2007) 'How Europe's economies learn: a comparison of work organisations and innovation mode for the EU-15', *Industrial and Corporate Change* 16(6): 1175–1210.

Baumol, W. J., Litan, R. E. and Schramm, C. J. (2007) *Good Capitalism, Bad Capitalism, and the Economics of Growth and Prosperity.* New Haven and London: Yale University Press.

Becker, B. E. and Huselid, M. A. (1998) 'High Performance Work Systems and Firm Performance: A synthesis of research and managerial implications'. *Research in Personnel and Human Resource Management* 16: 53–101.

CEDEFOP (2010) *Jobs in Europe to become more knowledge and skills-intensive.* CEDEFOP Briefing Note, February 2010.

Composto, R. (2008) 'Welfare State Models in the Enlarged European Union: A Cluster Analysis', CRISS Working Paper. No. 27.

Esping-Andersen, G. (1990) *The Three Worlds of Welfare Capitalism*. Oxford University Press.

Eyal, G., Szelényi, I. and Townsley, E. (1998) *Making Capitalism Without Capitalists: The new ruling elites in Eastern Europe*. London: Verso.

Eyal, G., Szelényi, I. and Townsley, E. (2003) 'On Irony: An Invitation to Neoclassical Sociology', Thesis 11, May, 73(1), 5–41.

Foss, N. J. (1997) *Understanding Business Systems: An Essay on the Economics and Sociology of Economic Organization*, Department of Industrial Economics and Strategy Copenhagen Business School, WP 97–6.

Gallie, D. (2007) *Employment Regimes and the Quality of Work*. Oxford: Oxford University Press.

Gém, E., Mikesy, Á. and Szabó, Zs. (2011) *Beszállítói kapcsolatok: a méret a lényeg?* (Supplier relationships: Does the size matters?) Budapest: Hungarian Development Bank.

Grabher, G. and Stark, D. (1997) 'Organizing Diversity: Evolutionary Theory, Network Analysis, and Postsocialism', In: Grabher, G. and Stark, D. (eds). *Restructuring networks in post-socialism: Legacies, linkages and localities*. Oxford: Oxford University Press, pp. 1–32.

Greskovits, B. (2010) *Evolving Patterns of Democratic Capitalism in Central-Eastern Europe*. Habilitation Thesis. University of Debrecen, Faculty of Economics and Business Administration.

Holm, J.R., Lorenz, E., Lundvall, B.-Å. and Valeyre, A. (2010) 'Organisational Learning and Systems of Labour Market Regulation in Europe', *Industry and Corporate Change*, 19(4): 1141–1173.

Hunya, G. (2013) *Growth Engine Stutters*. wiiw FDI Report 2013 Central, East and Southeast Europe. Wien: The Vienna Institute for International Economic Studies.

Koltay, J. (2010) *Multinational Companies and Labour Relations in Hungary: Between Home Country – Host Country Effects and Global Tendencies*. Budapest: Institute of Economics, Hungarian Academy of Sciences.

Makó, Cs., Csizmadia, P. and Illéssy, M. (2010) 'A munkaszervezet, munkaidő-felhasználás, képzés és a munkával való elégedettség főbb jellemzői' (Main characteristics of work organization, working time, training and employee satisfaction) In: Neumann, L. and Simonovits, B. (eds) (2010): *Munkahelyi foglalkoztatás viszonyok – 2010* (Employment relations in the workplace – 2010). TÁMOP 2.5.2. Emóció Bt, Budapest.

Makó, Cs. and Illéssy, M. (2007) 'Economic Modernisation in Hungary: Between Path Dependency and Path Creation', *Soochow Journal of Sociology*, 21: 89–122.

Martin, R. (2008) 'Post-socialist segmented capitalism: The case of Hungary. Developing business systems theory'. *Human Relations*, 61(1): 131–159.

Neumann, L. and Simonovits, B. (eds) (2010) *Munkahelyi foglalkoztatás viszonyok – 2010* (Employment relations in the workplace – 2010). TÁMOP 2.5.2. Emóció Bt, Budapest.

Nielsen, P. (2006) *The Human Side of Innovation Systems: Innovation, New Organization Forms and Competence Building in a Learning Perspective*, Aalborg: Aalborg Unversitetsforlag.

Salter, A. and Tether, B. (2006) *Innovation in Services. (Through the Looking Glass of Innovation Studies)*. Advanced Institute of Management.

Sapir, A. (2005) Globalisation and the reform of European social models. Background document for the presentation at ECOFIN Informal Meeting in Manchester, 9 September 2005. Brussels: Bruegel.

Szelényi, I. and Wilk, K. (2010) 'Institutional transformation in European post-communist regimes'. in: Morgan, G., Campbell, J. L., Crouch, C., Pedersen, O. K. and Whitley, R.

(eds) *The Oxford Handbook of Comparative Institutional Analysis*. Oxford: Oxford University Press.

Szerb, L., Csapi, V., Deutsch, N. and Ulbert, J. (2015) *Mennyire versenyképesek a Magyar kisvállalatok? (A Magyar kisvállalatok (MKKV szektor) versenyképességének egyéni-vállalati szintű mérése és complex vizsgálata)* Hungarian Small Firms and Their Competitiveness Intensity (Measuring and Comprehensive Investigation of the individual-firm level competitiveness of the Hungarian SME Sector), Pécs: University of Pécs – Faculty of Economics, TÁMOP Project – 4.4.4.A 11/1/KONV-2012-0058, p. 31.

Toivonen, M. (2006) 'Future Prospects of Knowledge-Intensive Business Services (KIBS) and Implications to Regional Economies', *ICFAI Journal of Knowledge Management*, 4(3): 18–39.

Tóth, A. (2015) Coming to the end of the via dolorosa? The rise of selective economic nationalism in Hungary. In: Lehndorff, S. (eds) *Divisive integration The triumph of failed ideas in Europe – revisited*. Brussels: ETUI, pp. 233–252.

Whitley, R. (1992). *Business Systems in East Asia*, London: SAGE.

## ANNEX I: FDI-inflows and inward FDI stock in CEECs

*Table 5.9*  FDI-inflows in some CEE countries in the first phase of economic transformation (in million US dollars)

|                | 1990    | 1991 | 1992 | 1993 | 1994 | 1995 | 1996 | 1997 | 1998 |
|----------------|---------|------|------|------|------|------|------|------|------|
| Bulgaria       | 4       | 56   | 42   | 40   | 105  | 98   | 138  | 507  | 537  |
| Czech Republic | No data | 983  | 564  | 762  | 2531 | 1280 | 1259 | 3574 | 6219 |
| Hungary        | 311     | 1459 | 1471 | 2328 | 1097 | 4772 | 3335 | 3715 | 3070 |
| Poland         | 0       | 117  | 284  | 580  | 1846 | 3617 | 4445 | 4863 | 6049 |
| Romania        | −18     | 37   | 73   | 87   | 341  | 417  | 415  | 1267 | 2079 |
| Slovakia       | 24      | 82   | 100  | 106  | 236  | 194  | 199  | 84   | 373  |

Source: Szelényi – Wilk, 2010: 570–571.

*Table 5.10*  Inward FDI stock as a percentage of GDP

|                | 2004 | 2005 | 2006 | 2007 | 2008 | 2009 | 2010 | 2011 | 2012 |
|----------------|------|------|------|------|------|------|------|------|------|
| Bulgaria       | 36.4 | 50.6 | 67.3 | 83.7 | 89.4 | 97.8 | 98.0 | 95.0 | 95.3 |
| Czech Republic | 45.8 | 49.1 | 51.2 | 57.9 | 52.7 | 61.4 | 64.1 | 59.9 | 67.9 |
| Estonia        | 76.1 | 85.5 | 72.0 | 70.9 | 72.5 | 84.8 | 87.2 | 81.0 | 83.9 |
| Hungary        | 55.0 | 58.2 | 67.9 | 65.4 | 59.2 | 75.1 | 70.2 | 65.5 | 80.3 |
| Latvia         | 29.8 | 32.2 | 35.7 | 35.5 | 35.5 | 43.6 | 45.4 | 46.3 | 45.0 |
| Lithuania      | 25.7 | 33.0 | 34.8 | 35.8 | 28.4 | 34.5 | 36.3 | 35.8 | 36.3 |
| Poland         | 31.0 | 30.8 | 33.5 | 37.3 | 30.4 | 39.1 | 43.1 | 38.6 | 43.9 |
| Romania        | 24.6 | 27.4 | 35.3 | 34.3 | 34.9 | 42.3 | 42.3 | 42.0 | 42.7 |
| Slovakia       | 47.3 | 51.9 | 57.3 | 53.0 | 56.2 | 58.1 | 57.2 | 57.4 | 58.8 |
| Slovenia       | 20.5 | 21.3 | 22.0 | 28.2 | 30.2 | 29.6 | 30.4 | 32.3 | 33.2 |
| NMS-10         | 37.5 | 39.6 | 43.8 | 46.2 | 42.3 | 51.2 | 52.4 | 49.4 | 54.3 |

Source: Hunya, 2013: 41

# 6 Migration and remittances in the Central and East European countries

*Eugenia Markova*

## 1. Introduction

This chapter examines the role of migration and migrant remittances in the countries of Central and Eastern Europe (CEE). It discusses the evolution of emigration from the region following the fall of the Berlin Wall, providing an historical reference to the years of socialism; it surveys the effects of remittances on the origin areas taking into account the existence of 'reverse flows'; and, analyses remittance behaviour drawing on the empirical findings from a purposive quota sample of Bosnian-Herzegovinian and Ukrainian migrants in the United Kingdom (UK).

Definitions of remittances differ according to the fields of expertise of the scholars. Economists define them as individual personal transfers in cash and in kind to households back in the country of origin. Transfers sent through legal channels are captured in a country's Balance of Payments. Anthropologists and sociologists argue that remittances are more than economic transactions. They attempt to understand them in their complexity as practices, which are performed in the transnational space created between the origin and the host country. Such practices are part of Basch *et al.*'s (1994: 6) 'transnationalism', which they define as "the process by which immigrants forge and sustain multi-stranded social relations that link together their societies of origin and settlement" and Guarnizo's 'transnational living' (2003). Financial and in-kind remittances flow in the social spaces created between the origin and the host countries. Often intertwined with them, generated by them or entirely independently, are the social remittances (Levitt, 2001) that capture those difficult-to-measure flows of ideas, new skills, practices, identities, motivations and involvements in actions and initiatives for change.

In this chapter, I blend economics, sociology and anthropology to frame remittance flows and remittance behaviour as an integral part of migrant economic transnationalism (Levitt and Jaworsky, 2007), which involves, among other activities, financial and in-kind remittances sent to family or friends at home; collective remittances and philanthropic projects of different scale; and, invested remittances in business ventures, housing and financial markets. Savings – in the origin or in the host country – are the flip side of the same coin. Savings invested in high-interest rate accounts in the home country are also considered another strand of the remittance flows to the origin. The intangible dimension of social remittances is added to the analysis.

The second section provides an historical overview of the emigration trends in the region from the end of World War II (WWII) to recent times. The third section surveys the literature on the home country effects of remittances. Section Four presents the methods employed for the collection of primary data on remittance practices of Bosnian-Herzegovinian and Ukrainian migrants in the UK; the following section reports on the empirical findings. Section Six summarizes the main issues raised and their policy implications.

## 2. Overview of emigration trends in the region

A decade ago, the renowned economic demographer of CEE Marek Okolski and his economist colleague Pawel Kaczmarczyk raised the question whether CEE still constituted a uniform and homogeneous region in terms of migration mobility and if so, what were the common observable characteristics (Kaczmarczyk and Okolski, 2005). Answering this question might be a feasible task when analysing the socialist years while it is less so for the years afterwards. The new millennium exposed more differences and fewer similarities in the emigration patterns of the CEE countries.[1]

The end of WWII brought a fundamental change in the migratory processes and policies in the countries of the Warsaw Pact. A new era commenced for their ethnic minorities as well. A ban on the free movement of citizens was introduced through sophisticated border policing systems and restrictive systems for issuing passports. Labour emigration was entirely controlled by the states. Apart from the republics of the Soviet Union, migration between CEE countries was considered insignificant (Bijak and others, cited in Kaczmarczyk and Okolski, 2005). It was the citizens of Yugoslavia, under Tito's regime, who enjoyed freedom of movement for work and leisure beyond the Iron Curtain. Nonetheless, the state control on the movement of people in the region was applied in varying degrees of restrictiveness in different countries in the region. At one end of the spectrum were the migration regimes in the former Czechoslovakia, Poland, and Hungary, which were considered more relaxed, offering routes for some movements and emigration while at the opposite end there were the countries of Bulgaria and Romania, which did not permit any emigration.

The establishment of the communist regime triggered a wave of political emigration from the region. In Bulgaria, this happened especially since 1948 when the leftist opposition parties were dissolved. They formed part of the long-term movements directed to Western Europe and North America. The rest were people in relatively privileged positions in the ranks of the communist party, who were given access to foreign passports and tourist visas. Once abroad, they rarely returned thus contributing to the formation of the CEE Diaspora behind the Iron Curtain. The main 'push' factors were of political and economic nature. The CEE citizens were stating political reasons for emigration in the destination, which facilitated their smooth legalisation and integration in the host countries. In the communist era, Poland was described as a typical migrant-sending country because of the state – run scheme of issuing pseudo-tourist visas. All the would-be migrants would comply with the requirements. It is estimated that a total of over 4.2 million residents departed from Poland between 1971 and 1980; their numbers in the 1980s were assessed at between 1.1 and 1.3 million people (Kaczmarczyk and Okolski, 2005: 6). In the period 1980–1988, official United Nations' population statistics[2] point to a figure of long-term emigrants, which is slightly over quarter of a million from Poland, nearly 10,000 from Hungary and some 26,311 from the former Czechoslovakia (Table 6.1).

Ethnic migration was an important component of the population movements in several countries. It was considered to be particularly significant in Latvia, Lithuania and Estonia, and relatively negligible in Bulgaria, the former Czechoslovakia, Poland and Romania. Hundreds of thousands of ethnic Germans moved to Germany from the Soviet Union and Romania (Kaczmarczyk and Okolski, 2005). Additionally, by August 1989, it was estimated that about 360,000 of Bulgarian Turks had left for Turkey (Zhelyazkova, 1998). Their exodus was not voluntary but one triggered by state political decisions. In the spring of 1989, a few months before the fall of the Berlin Wall, there was a large outpouring of Bulgarian Turks leaving for Turkey, ironically called the 'big excursion', which, most political scientists in the country credited with having a major impact on shattering the communist regime (Guentcheva *et al.*, 2003: 14). It marked the dramatic culmination of years of tensions and resilience among the Turkish community, which accelerated with Bulgarian government's assimilation campaign in the winter of 1985, when a policy of 'Bulgarization' was attempted. It began with a ban on wearing traditional Turkish dress and speaking Turkish in

*Table 6.1* Long-term emigration from Hungary, Poland and the former Czechoslovakia, 1979–1988

| Year | Hungary | Poland | Former Czechoslovakia |
|------|---------|--------|------------------------|
| 1979 | 1356 | 34181 | 3375 |
| 1980 | 1538 | 22724 | 3155 |
| 1981 | 1313 | 23750 | 3733 |
| 1982 | 1120 | 32038 | 3625 |
| 1983 | 1234 | 26381 | 3404 |
| 1984 | 1309 | 17401 | 2992 |
| 1985 | 1153 | 26578 | 2399 |
| 1986 | 1134 | 29008 | 2425 |
| 1987 | 1157 | 36436 | 2337 |
| 1988 | .... | 36291 | 2241 |

Notes: Emigration data for the other CEE countries was not available (e.g., data on tourists, business affairs and others was available for the USSR and Bulgaria).

Source: Data derived from Table 26: departures to another country or area, by major categories: 1979–1988, in: United Nations (1991) *1989 United Nations Demographic Yearbook*, Forty-first issue, Department of International Economic and Social Affairs, Statistical Office, New York: pp. 519–30.

public places followed by the forceful name-changing campaign. The Turkish minority reacted with resistance, in the form of protests and demonstrations, many of which were quelled by troops. In May 1989, the Bulgarian authorities began to expel them (Poulton, 1993). More than a third would subsequently return to Bulgaria once the ban on their names had been revoked (Guentcheva *et al.*, 2003).

The fall of the Berlin Wall marked the beginning of the largest economic experiment at the time as the former communist countries of CEE implemented economic reform programmes designed to expedite transformation away from state involvement and towards a market-based system. The collapse of the central planning system in CEE also liberalised the system of movement, abolishing the exit visa requirements and providing its citizens with greater opportunities to emigrate abroad. The first migration waves in the early to mid-1990s largely stemmed from the preceding years of political and economic isolation while the following ones were more influenced by the growing economic and social insecurity. Western Europe responded with tightened entry rules, which appeared to only have a moderate impact among the CEE populations' willingness to emigrate there. By the mid-1990s, the numbers of CEE migrants had started to decline (OECD, 1996). The labour markets of the Southern European countries of Greece, Italy, Spain and Portugal, with their considerable shares of informal and semi-formal segments, played a 'buffer' role of absorbing large numbers of undocumented migrants from the CEE region. In some countries – for instance, the Czech Republic – the outflow of people had significantly decreased by the mid-1990s (Kaczmarczyk and Okolski, 2005); their net migration remained positive since the early 1990 similar to Hungary and Slovenia (Table 6.2). Conversely, the emigration – both documented and undocumented – from the countries of Poland, Ukraine, Romania and Bulgaria, remained significant throughout the 1990s and into the new millennium. The Poles, Romanians and Bulgarians managed to legalise their status following their countries' EU accessions in 2004 and 2007 respectively.

When the European enlargement took place in May 2004, only UK, Ireland and Sweden fully opened their labour markets to the citizens of the new member states in Central and Eastern Europe, albeit with restricted access to public funds and welfare provisions in the case of Britain and Northern Ireland. By this time, a large number of Poles had already been working in the UK, many of whom irregularly (Anderson *et al.*, 2006). The undocumented status of many CEE citizens from the new member-states who were residing in the UK, Ireland and Sweden was legalised 'overnight'. By the end of June 2004, some 24,000 nationals from the new member states of CEE had signed up for the Workers Registration Scheme[3] in the UK; some 14,000 of them were already residing in the country. More than 681,000 Poles were allocated a National Insurance Number (NINo) from the beginning of 2002 till March 2008; with reference to other A8[4] countries, almost 100,000 registrations were made by Slovakians and Lithuanians and less than 10,000 by Estonians and Slovenians (Drinkwater *et al.*, 2010: 77). The second European enlargement in 2007, albeit not immediately, had

*Table 6.2* Net migration in CEE in the 1990s and 2000s

| Country name | 1992 | 1997 | 2002 | 2007 | 2012 |
|---|---|---|---|---|---|
| Albania | −443212 | −179606 | −175406 | −252926 | −91750 |
| Bulgaria | −356464 | −106602 | −83002 | −83002 | −50000 |
| Central Europe and the Baltics | −1514119 | −1176975 | −593078 | −811784 | −770310 |
| Czech Republic | 29999 | 46002 | 47402 | 250889 | 29999 |
| Croatia | −143579 | −188129 | −2580 | −22532 | −20000 |
| Hungary | 96796 | 78562 | 66163 | 95789 | 29999 |
| Moldova | −131953 | −165309 | −12079 | −47911 | −9529 |
| Macedonia, FYR | −133498 | −4999 | −15272 | −4999 | −4999 |
| Montenegro | −20249 | −21588 | −7999 | −3108 | −2412 |
| Poland | −240502 | −243932 | 38050 | 5235 | −73809 |
| Romania | −520001 | −610000 | −490472 | −874406 | −437201 |
| Russian Federation | 2519717 | 2308220 | 1735324 | 2157349 | 1117884 |
| Serbia | 178348 | −546911 | −276331 | −38215 | .... |
| Slovak Republic | −15108 | −2964 | 1199 | 9597 | 1199 |
| Slovenia | −17461 | 1487 | 14998 | 49624 | 4324 |
| Ukraine | 74421 | −462264 | −165445 | 235195 | 195000 |

Note: Net migration is the net total of migrants during the period, that is, the total number of immigrants less the annual number of emigrants, including both citizens and noncitizens. Data are five-year estimates.

Source: World Development Indicators, United Nations Population Statistics.

also granted freedom of movement for Bulgarian and Romanian workers. The growing tendency towards temporary and seasonal migration rather than permanent settlement further expanded with some CEE countries' EU membership (Markova, 2010).

The citizens of the non-EU countries of CEE most notably, Ukraine, Albania, Kosovo, Moldova and Bosnia-Herzegovina, defined by EU legislation as third-country nationals, are faced with limited legal emigration routes while experiencing deteriorating economic conditions, political instability and even military conflict in the case of Ukraine.

In recent years, there has been a growing tendency towards temporary seasonal rather than permanent migration with the preferred destinations being Greece, Turkey, Italy, Spain, Germany, the Netherland and the UK. Temporary movements are severely constrained by immigration status. The rise in temporary or repeated migration is attributed to increased unemployment in certain regions within the CEE countries. Pockets of extreme poverty persist in Bulgaria, Romania, Ukraine and some countries of the former Yugoslavia, especially in rural and ethnically mixed regions (in the case of Bulgaria) (Markova, 2010).

The past quarter of a century has witnessed a growing divergence and hetero-geneity of the CEE countries in terms of their migration experiences. Geographical positions, the history of socialism, the subsequently chosen paths of transitions to market-economy, the EU vs. non-EU membership, the timing of the membership, political instability and conflict – past or current – have all been contributing factors. The outcome is differentiated impacts of emigration.

## 3. Review of the literature on the nexus between migration and remittances

The vast multidisciplinary literature on migrant remittances captures various dimensions of the phenomenon by looking at the very nature of what constitutes remittances and remittance practices, the decision to remit, the reasons for remit-ting, the factors impacting on the amounts remitted, and the use of remittances hence, their impact on the receiving households, the local communities and the wider society. It has been recognised that remitting behaviour can be a two-way process, with 'reverse' capital (Mazucato, 2011) flowing from the origin to the destination. The wider (macro) impact of remittances on the origin society and the economy has remained of main policy concern.

Migration impacts on a home country in a variety of ways depending upon the magnitudes, composition and nature of migration flows, as well as upon the specific context from which migrants are drawn (Markova, 2010).

From a home country perspective, remittances are generally considered to be one of the positive outcomes of the migration process. Economists examine the role of remittances and other backflow of migrants to their home countries as redistributing the net gains from migration between the countries involved (McConnell *et al.*, 2009). Most remittances are sent to family members in the origin of the migrants. The income distribution will depend upon the type of fami-lies that receive them – whether it is the poorer or the wealthier families that receive them (Markova, 2010). Lukas (2005) argues that the increased incomes as a result of remittances can in turn increase incomes for families who receive no remittances at all; this can be achieved through the multiplier effects of expanded spending – as migrant families increase their consumption, the addi-tional demand for goods and services creates jobs for other families that also spend and thus increase demand.

There has been an extensive discussion about the use of remittances beyond consumption and domestic investment, and for productive and innovative invest-ment. Along Lukas's (2005) lines of analysis, at macroeconomic level, the amount of remittances that generate national investment is dependent upon the returns that can be obtained from those whose incomes were increased as a result of the remittances. Remittances may increase upward pressures on prices through expansion in consumption much of which is satisfied by imported goods, thus leading to trade deficits and current account deficits. In addition, remittances may allow for a real appreciation of the exchange rate through the infusion of foreign exchange. For economies with high imports relative to foreign exchange reserves, or for heavily indebted economies, the increased foreign exchange availability can prove valuable (Katseli *et al.*, 2006).

Much of the policy debate has focused on a missing link between increased remittance flows and economic growth. There is little empirical evidence to support a positive relationship between increased personal transfers and economic development. Barajas *et al.* (2009) claim that the most persuasive argument for this finding is the lack of a single country's example of a remittance success. Clemens and McKenzie (2014) explain this by three main factors; first, enormous differences in measuring remittance flows and measurement errors lead to miscalculating the growth of remittances; second, statistical methods may not be powerful enough to detect effects on economic growth. This is related – the authors reckon – to limited remittances data, which does not allow for capturing any significant economic impact. And, third, irrespective of measurement errors and insufficient statistical methods, the authors claim that the effect on growth may be too small to be detected. The effect of remittances can even be negative, they argue. Financial transfers may flow into the origin countries but they may not be able to compensate for the human capital that has left. The outcome will depend on whether those who had emigrated were working or not working in the home economy prior to emigration.

Official remittances data is recorded in the Balance of Payments of the CEE countries. It is plausible to assume that it captures less than half of the total transfers.

Table 6.3, illustrates an example of remittance flows' high responsiveness to macroeconomic changes in the host countries, partly contradicting Constant's *et al.* (2012) argument that remittances, as an integral part of migration, remain resilient to economic recessions and the business cycle. It supports Vargas-Silva's and Huang's (2006) findings that remittances are more sensitive to macroeconomic

*Table 6.3* Annual remittance flows (in US $ mil) to selected CEE countries, 2006–2013*

| CEE Country | 2006 | 2007 | 2008 | 2009 | 2010 | 2011 | 2012 | 2013 |
|---|---|---|---|---|---|---|---|---|
| Bulgaria | 1717 | 1626 | 1920 | 1591 | 1334 | 1483 | 1449 | 1668 |
| Romania | 1166 | 1627 | 1703 | 683 | 642 | 694 | 733 | 736 |
| Slovenia | 274 | 315 | 348 | 298 | 317 | 455 | 608 | 593 |
| Albania | 1363 | 1468 | 1496 | 1320 | 1156 | 1127 | 1028 | 805 |
| Bosnia and Herzegovina | .... | 2680 | 2712 | 2124 | 1819 | 1956 | 1840 | 1889 |
| Czech Republic | 1688 | 1895 | 2044 | 2017 | 2015 | 2075 | 2026 | 2272 |
| Hungary | 2020 | 2252 | 2464 | 2090 | 2093 | 2222 | 2090 | 2211 |
| Macedonia, FYR | 267 | 345 | 407 | 381 | 388 | 434 | 394 | 376 |
| Moldova | 1176 | 1491 | 1888 | 1199 | 1351 | 1600 | 1793 | 1985 |
| Poland | 8486 | 10468 | 10408 | 8094 | 7575 | 7641 | 6935 | 6984 |
| Slovakia | 1083 | 1477 | 1968 | 1672 | 1592 | 1754 | 1927 | 2072 |
| Ukraine | 829 | 4503 | 5769 | 5073 | 5607 | 6716 | 7291 | 8313 |

*Author's own computations utilising quarterly and monthly remittances inflow data

Source: World Bank Data, compiled by Migration and Remittances Team, Development Prospects Group (available at: www.worldbank.org/prospects/migrationandremittances, accessed on 9 January 2016).

changes in the host country than to such changes in the home country. Remittance flows to the CEE countries have increased in the period 2006–2008, dropped during the austerity times in the years 2009–2010, and have been gradually picking up since then. This is a reflection of the cyclical economic changes in the OECD countries in the past two decades, characterised by a period of economic growth during the 1990s and the early 2000s, followed by years of economic decline as a result of the financial crisis since late 2007–early 2008, and a consecutive period of post-crisis recovery.

Drahokoupil and Myant (2015) group the CEE countries according to their distinctive features of prevalent capitalist type and the corresponding levels of international integration. A category of 'remittance – and aid-based economies' is applied to a number of low-income countries in the periphery of Eastern Europe, most notably Albania, Moldova and Bosnia-Herzegovina. The capitalist variety appears an important predictor of emigration and remittance transfers. Table 6.4 and Table 6.5, below, provide a compelling example in support of the authors' grouping of the CEE countries. In Bosnia-Herzegovina, Moldova and to a much lesser degree Albania, migrant remittances have remained important contributors to the countries' Gross Domestic Product (GDP) formation, outperforming the role of Foreign Direct Investment. For instance, in the year 2014, the registered remittances in Bosnia-Herzegovina comprised 11.2 percent of the country's GDP while the corresponding contribution of the foreign investment was only 2.7 percent. Moldova is a stark example of a remittance-dependent economy, with official remittances contributing 26.2 percent toward the country's national income compared with a foreign direct investment contribution of 4.4 percent.

*Table 6.4* Annual remittance flows to selected CEE countries (% of GDP)

| Country name | 1998 | 2006 | 2007 | 2008 | 2009 | 2010 | 2011 | 2012 | 2013 | 2014 |
|---|---|---|---|---|---|---|---|---|---|---|
| Albania | 18.6 | 15.1 | 13.7 | 11.6 | 10.9 | 9.7 | 8.7 | 8.3 | 8.6 | 8.6 |
| Bulgaria | 0.3 | 5.0 | 3.8 | 3.5 | 3.1 | 2.9 | 2.6 | 2.7 | 3.0 | 3.0 |
| Bosnia-Herzegovina | 49.7 | 17.1 | 17.4 | 14.5 | 12.3 | 10.8 | 10.7 | 10.9 | 10.9 | 11.4 |
| Czech Republic | 0.5 | 1.1 | 1.0 | 0.5 | 0.6 | 0.6 | 0.6 | 0.7 | 0.8 | 0.9 |
| Croatia | 2.5 | 3.2 | 3.1 | 2.9 | 3.0 | 3.2 | 3.4 | 3.7 | 3.8 | 3.8 |
| Hungary | 0.5 | 1.8 | 1.7 | 1.6 | 1.3 | 1.6 | 2.0 | 2.8 | 3.4 | 3.4 |
| Moldova | 7.6 | 34.5 | 33.9 | 31.2 | 22.0 | 23.3 | 25.8 | 27.3 | 27.4 | 26.2 |
| Macedonia, FYR | 1.8 | 3.9 | 4.1 | 4.1 | 4.1 | 4.1 | 4.1 | 4.0 | 3.5 | 3.2 |
| Montenegro | N/A | N/A | 5.4 | 6.6 | 7.3 | 7.3 | 7.6 | 8.1 | 9.5 | 9.4 |
| Romania | 0.1 | 5.4 | 4.9 | 4.5 | 2.9 | 2.3 | 2.1 | 2.1 | 1.8 | 1.7 |
| Serbia | | | 9.3 | 7.2 | 10.9 | 10.4 | 8.5 | 8.7 | 8.8 | 8.4 |
| Slovak Republic | 0.1 | 1.5 | 1.7 | 2.0 | 1.9 | 1.8 | 1.8 | 2.1 | 2.1 | 2.4 |
| Slovenia | 1.0 | 0.7 | 0.7 | 0.7 | 0.7 | 0.7 | 1.0 | 1.4 | 1.5 | 1.5 |
| Ukraine | 0.0 | 2.9 | 3.7 | 3.8 | 5.1 | 4.8 | 4.8 | 4.8 | 5.3 | 5.6 |

Source: World Bank Data (available at: www.worldbank.org/prospects/migrationandremittances, accessed on 9 January 2016).

*Table 6.5* Annual foreign direct investment flows to selected CEE countries (% of GDP)

| Country name | 1998 | 2006 | 2007 | 2008 | 2009 | 2010 | 2011 | 2012 | 2013 | 2014 |
|---|---|---|---|---|---|---|---|---|---|---|
| Albania | 1.7 | 3.6 | 6.1 | 9.6 | 11.2 | 9.1 | 8.1 | 7.5 | 9.8 | 8.7 |
| Bulgaria | 3.7 | 23.0 | 31.0 | 18.8 | 7.5 | 2.5 | 3.7 | 3.3 | 3.6 | 3.5 |
| Bosnia-Herzegovina | 1.6 | 6.7 | 11.9 | 5.4 | 0.8 | 2.6 | 2.6 | 2.3 | 1.9 | 2.7 |
| Czech Republic | 5.6 | 3.6 | 5.6 | 3.7 | 2.6 | 4.9 | 1.8 | 4.6 | 3.5 | 2.4 |
| Croatia | 3.7 | 6.5 | 7.6 | 7.4 | 5.1 | 2.4 | 2.3 | 2.6 | 1.6 | 6.9 |
| Hungary | 6.9 | 16.3 | 50.8 | 47.8 | -2.3 | -16.1 | 7.5 | 8.3 | -2.9 | 9.0 |
| Moldova | 4.6 | 7.6 | 12.2 | 12.0 | 2.5 | 3.6 | 5.0 | 3.9 | 3.6 | 4.4 |
| Montenegro | N/A | 0.0 | 25.6 | 21.6 | 37.4 | 18.3 | 12.3 | 15.1 | 10.0 | 10.8 |
| Poland | 3.7 | 6.3 | 5.8 | 2.7 | 3.2 | 3.8 | 3.5 | 1.5 | 0.2 | 3.2 |
| Romania | 4.8 | 9.3 | 6.0 | 6.7 | 2.9 | 1.9 | 1.4 | 1.5 | 2.0 | 1.9 |
| Serbia | 0.6 | 16.2 | 11.0 | 8.2 | 6.9 | 4.3 | 10.6 | 3.1 | 4.5 | 4.6 |
| Slovak Republic | 1.9 | 5.8 | 4.5 | 4.1 | 1.8 | 2.4 | 3.7 | 1.6 | 1.0 | 0.1 |
| Slovenia | 1.0 | 1.7 | 3.9 | 1.9 | -0.7 | 0.7 | 1.7 | 0.1 | 0.2 | 2.1 |
| Ukraine | 1.8 | 5.2 | 7.1 | 5.9 | 4.1 | 4.7 | 4.4 | 4.7 | 2.5 | 0.6 |

Source: World Bank Data (available at: http://data.worldbank.org/indicator/
    BX.KLT.DINV.WD.GD.ZS, accessed on 9 January 2016).

Remittances are conceptualised as one of the defining characteristics and/or an outcome of the different varieties of capitalism that have developed in the CEE countries in the past quarter of a century. They can offer a financial route to a country's international integration and are thus incorporated as one of the 'explanatory variables' that can predict variations in the countries' levels of integration into the world economy (the 'dependent variable') (Drahokoupil and Myant, 2015). Along these lines of analysis, it is plausible to assume that migrant transfers are a relatively accurate reflection of a country's emigration rates. The CEE home country's adopted capitalist model, characterised by a myriad of distinctive features such as state capacity and institutional framework, the rule of law, the stability of the financial system, the degree of separation between politics and business, among others, determines the most prominent aspects of the 'push' factors for its population emigration.

There is a broad consensus in the academic literature and among policy makers that remittances as well as the circular and temporary labour migration have the potential to generate development effects on the sending countries. They both, it is argued, contribute to the allocation of resources from the core (the high-income host countries) to the periphery (low-income origin). The development potential of the circularity of labour can be maximised subject to its being well-managed and governed (Hugo, 2013). This requires a concept of circularity that clarifies the rights and duties of migrants. The pre-accession years of the 1990s and the early 2000s have witnessed a surge in the legal routes for temporary employment of CEE citizens in the EU area, in sectors such as the agriculture, care provision and hospitality. The EU enlargements of the past decade have contributed to a greater integration of the labour markets therefore promoting the increased recruitment of migrant labour on temporary basis (McLoughlin *et al.*, 2011). The continued policy interest in temporary as opposed to more permanent migration is embedded in the perceived benefits for both the sending and receiving countries. For the latter, temporary or seasonal migrant labour could be the flexible pool of workers that the country can draw on to fill gaps in the labour market and close when there is no demand for it. This flexibility almost excludes the requirement for full integration. For the former countries, it has the potential to replace 'brain drain' with 'brain gain'. It also includes the option of transnational activities by members of Europe's established diasporas to return to their (or their parents') country of origin for limited periods and engage in economic activities or civil society projects. In a well-integrated and functioning system of European labour markets, the circularity of labour can be seen as a remedy to unemployment and a way to enhance migrant welfare (ibid). Temporary and circulating migrants, some of whom may be undocumented in the host country, are expected to retain stronger connections with their origin-based family members given the greater degree of uncertainty that attaches both to their legal status and their employment. The impact effect for migrant legal status suggests that, on average and *ceteris paribus,* a Bulgarian migrant with legal status to remain and work in Spain remits almost 1,220 less in Euros per year than someone without this status (Markova and Reilly, 2007). This is resonant with findings by Markova and Sarris (2002) for Bulgarians in Athens. Those without legal status are more likely to have close family members based in Bulgaria, with whom they retain stronger connections given the uncertainty that attaches to their status. Similarly, most of the earned income is expected to be remitted to or saved in Bulgaria.

People move across borders and remit for a variety of reasons. Some have more opportunities to do so than others. Yet, all move in relation to households, and even those who do not remit make decisions that impact the households and the communities left behind (Grasmuck and Pessar, cited in Cohen, 2011). Stark (1991, Ch. 15) interprets remittances as the outcome of a migrant family's implicit contractual arrangement. Decisions to migrate are motivated by a concern to minimise the risks attached to household income variability and the private transfer of income from the migrant worker to the household constitutes an integral part of the migration decision. Initially, the sending household insures the migrant against the early uncertainties associated with finding work in the host market but subsequently, the migrant adopts the role of insurer to allow the household to engage in more risk-increasing activities. Although altruistic motives could explain why migrants comply with such arrangements, self-interested factors are likely to be important. Remittance practices change over the course of migrant life. Even if the migrant is well-established in the host labour market, such markets are not immune to cyclical fluctuations and retaining contact with the household in the origin can be important. This relationship is particularly relevant if the migrant does not possess a regular legal status in the host country. The family co-insurance model could also be viewed as an exchange model, with the service provided in the early stages by the household (insurer) repaid by the migrant (insurant) in the form of insurance premiums through the transfer of remittances. The repayments could give rise to an inverted U-shape with respect to time spent in the host country and thus consistent with notions inherent in the remittance decay hypothesis (Brown, 1997, cited in Markova and Reilly, 1997: 56).

The empirical analyses on the impact of remittances in the CEE region are predominantly at macroeconomic level. The impact of remittances on growth and income distribution has attracted a great deal of attention. Giannetti *et al.* (2009) utilise the EU-SILC (European Union Statistics on Income and Living Conditions) 2005 dataset to study the received inter-household cash transfers in Slovenia, Poland, the Czech Republic and Hungary. Their results showed that remittances were statistically significant determinants in terms of poverty reduction even though their effects were generally smaller than those of welfare transfers. Remittances impacts differed across the countries examined. The study strengthens the empirical evidence on the relative importance of the country's institutions and socio-economic conditions in optimising the effects of remittances in reducing inequality and social exclusion. Falzoni and Soldano (2013) use a panel data set on 15 East European countries to study how income inequality is affected by remittances, among other factors. Their preliminary results showed only a negligible effect of remittances in explaining inequality in the selected countries from the region. Macroeconomists have modelled the impact of invested remittances showing that external shocks such as an increase in migrant income in the host country is likely to lead to an increase in the amount of invested remittances per migrant (Naiditch and Vranceanu, 2010). Leon-Ledesma and Piracha (2004) have shown that remittances in the CEE region have a positive impact on productivity and employment through its effect on investment. The next section discusses the methodology applied for collecting micro survey data on the remitting behaviour of Bosnians-Herzegovinians and Ukrainians in the UK.

## 4. Methodology of data collection and analysis

The data utilised for the analysis in this chapter is subtracted from a large data set of over 300 migrant interviews in the UK, Austria, Spain and Italy who originated from Bosnia-Herzegovina, the Philippines, India, Ukraine and Morocco. The data was compiled in the period June 2014–April 2015 as part of the European project ITHACA: Integration, Transnational Mobility and Human, Social and Economic Capital Transfers.[5]

Primary data was collected through a combination of a questionnaire survey of respondents from the five groups and stakeholder interviews. The questionnaire contained both closed questions to allow for some profiling of the sample, and open questions where respondents provide insights into their experiences of transnationalism and integration in the UK, including their remittance practices.

A topic guide with open questions and prompts was developed for interviewing stakeholders.

The analysis in this chapter draws on a small-scale questionnaire survey of 11 Ukrainians, including one returnee and 13 Bosnians-Herzegovinians in the UK. The sample is broadly stratified by gender. Additional stratification aimed at ensuring representation of different national sub-groups was attempted. This was not entirely achieved due to limited resources and lack of availability of respondents. In the Bosnian sample, the strategy aimed to balance the inclusion of Bosnian Serbs and Muslims; with regards to the Ukrainian sample, the objective was to include proportionate representation of respondents from Eastern Ukraine (the war zone) and the rest of the country. Four stakeholders were interviewed to acquire a better understanding of the studied communities. The stakeholders provided useful initial contacts within the respective groups under study. We interviewed representatives of the British Red Cross, the Ukrainian Migrants Network, and the Bosnian Embassy in London, the Migrant Rights Network, and the Balkan "Magaza" shop. The Migrants Resource Centre, even though not included in the list of interviewed stakeholders, provided important entry points in to the communities under study.

The overall sample is severely skewed towards high levels of education, with almost 90 percent of all respondents possessing University and a post-graduate qualification, often obtained in both the UK and the origin country or in a third country. Half of the Ukrainian sample is post-graduates and the other half holds University diploma with only one respondent with vocational training; nine of the Bosnians hold either university or a post-graduate diploma. A large number of Ukrainian high-skilled respondents (university lecturers, researchers, business people and bankers) had entered the UK in the mid-2000s, through the Highly Skilled Migration Programme (HSMP) route or had benefited from the post-studies employment options.

The skewed educational distribution of the sample is partly explained by the definition of economic transnationalism that was deployed by the survey. Higher education as a signifier of certain wealth emerges as an important determinant of transnational economic behaviour. This, in turn, suggests that higher educated, higher skilled individuals are more open to direct contact; they are more likely to be found in University and business settings. They are more likely to respond positively to a request for a participation in a survey, being part of the 'new cast of characters' of cosmopolitanism (Robins, 1998: 1). Low skilled Ukrainians are mainly on forged Polish or Hungarian passports therefore avoiding trips to the origin and more reluctant to participate in surveys. Four of the Ukrainian respondents were born and still had families in the war zone of Crimea. Respondents from today's Bosnia-Herzegovina and Ukraine, in their 30s and 40s, reported being born in the former Yugoslavia or the former USSR respectively.[6] One Bosnian respondent held a dual Slovenian-Bosnian citizenship while two others were Australian – Bosnian. The Bosnian respondents, who had arrived as asylum seekers in the UK in the early 1990s, all held British passports as was the case for Ukrainians who arrived in the UK in the 1990s and the early 2000s.

## 5. Remittance practices: empirical findings on the case of Bosnians-Herzegovinians and Ukrainians in the UK

Migrant remittances have assumed increased significance over the last two decades for most countries in CEE. Earlier it was discussed that private transfers from abroad have the potential to play an important role in preventing households from falling into poverty and in stimulating economic development through investment (Markova and Reilly, 1997). In spite of the importance of migrant remittances for the CEE countries at macroeconomic level, there is little understanding of their determinants at micro-level. This section will attempt to provide some additional understanding on remittance practices drawing on migrant interviews with Ukrainian and Bosnian-Herzegovinian respondents residing in the UK, and relevant stakeholders.

### *Typologies of remittance/investment practices*

Respondents seem to alternate their remittance behaviour at different stages of their lives. A Ukrainian respondent was visiting family and friends in the first years of migration to the UK, taking cash to her mother back in Kiev; with increased duration of residence in the destination and capital accumulation, she and her husband became economically active; they developed contacts in both countries and, invested in a tea trade business in Kiev; corruption at the Polish-Ukrainian border closed the business a few years later and they returned to their initial activity of visiting family and friends back home, and taking cash and gifts during visits.

Any typology of remittance/investment practices appears transient and 'liquid' (Bauman, 2003), with often overlapping characteristics pointing to its complex nature. Its durability is frail and easily changeable throughout the life-cycle and under the burden of politico-economic changes in the destination and at home (the ongoing conflict in Ukraine and the traumas of the war in the former Yugoslavia). An attempt was made to typologise remittance practices embedded in different transnational guises, drawing on a variety of theories and scholars.

The most difficult-to-achieve profile was of the *remitters – transnational entrepreneurs –* defined by Drori *et al.* (2009: 1001) as "social actors who enact networks, ideas, information, and practices for the purpose of seeking business opportunities or maintaining businesses within dual social fields, which in turn force them to engage in varied strategies of action to promote their entrepreneurial activities". It was met by two Bosnian respondents in the sample, father and son who, following the outbreak of the war in the former Yugoslavia had arrived in the UK in the mid-1990s. The son came with his mother as minor – asylum seeker while the father followed a few years later as a dependent family member. They would make frequent travels to the republics of the former Yugoslavia and invest in purchasing supplies for their food store in London. On some trips they would bring cash or gifts to family members. Their collection of goods from across the former Yugoslavia illuminates a profound act of reconciliation and reconsideration of history pointing to the intangible flows of social remittances (Levitt and Lamba-Nieves 2011, cited in Isaakyan, 2015). This is reaffirmed in the father's passionate insistence that the food store in London is not Bosnian, it is Balkan.

*Transnational (economic) activists – remitters* – whom we defined as those involved in sending remittances for individual relief projects and collective transfers for wider community initiatives. Examples include the 'collective remittances' of Bosnian migrants in support of those affected by the floods last summer. For Isaakyan (2015), they are *political transnationalists*. The ongoing efforts of the Ukrainian people in the UK collecting clothes, money and medicines for soldiers (driving vans across Europe to deliver them themselves) is another example. A Bosnian activist shared her experiences of transnational activism.

> Last year when we had the financial crisis first in February then the natural disaster of the floods in May, I and other Bosnian people organised a Bosnian solidarity group in Brighton. We organised events in London and at Brighton University – connecting via Skype with NGOs on the front line in Bosnia – to spread the word of what people were going through there, to organise collective support with clothes, medicines but most importantly, to create this platform of researchers, practitioners in the UK and Bosnia-Herzegovina, to make sense of the events, to mobilise help. It was also a way to bring the insiders' (c.f. those left back in Bosnia-Herzegovina) perspective and raise awareness of how people can help.

Isaakyan (2015: 19) discerns 'rich social scripts' in this type of political trasnationalism. The related social remittances of being public activists are particularly important, she claims, for the Bosnian migrants affected by reconciliation policies or the Ukrainians currently forced in the war conditions.

Philanthropic activities were registered towards both countries. A Ukrainian couple was supporting a religious organisation in Ukraine (they had been members of it since their student days). A Bosnian respondent is involved in a collective imitative of 12 people who are supporting 12 families in Sarajevo covering their monthly shopping expenses (each member of the initiative buys the shopping for one month in the year). The same respondent had raised money to build a house for an elderly couple. Last year he raised £1,500 for the floods in Bosnia. *I take the money myself to go where they are meant to go; the corruption is too high to risk it,* he said.

*'Transnational business class' remitters* – It is argued that this category of remitting migrants shares some similarities with Sklair's (2001) 'transnational capitalist class', who are described by Yeoh and Huang (2011) as 'sojourners in London' or 'club class migrant(s)' by Knowles (2003). Among the Ukrainian interviewees in the sample, they were Masters of Business Administration (MBA) graduates, with professional, technical or managerial skills, in their late 30s to early 40s, often 'headhunted' for corporate jobs in the City of London. Most

arrived in the UK during the early 2000s when immigration rules were more lax, making use of the legal route offered by the HSMP Programme (subsequently scrapped by the Conservative government). Others came for post-graduate studies and subsequently remained in the UK for work, facilitated and encouraged by state post-studies programmes at the time. Their studies were usually financed by bank loans or parents' savings indicating a 'reverse' flow of money from the origin areas. Later on, high remuneration jobs would generate frequent travel and remittances back home, often through property investment. This model of transnational mobility and, remitting and investing at home changes adversely for women when they start a family. A distinct feature of the 'club class migrant' is their limited socio-cultural integration in the host environment; they are enclaved in professional clubs, schools and leisure centres. Several Ukrainian respondents in the sample employed in financial jobs in the City of London spoke of social and family life intertwined with and determined by professional commitments.

*Socio-cultural transnationalists – remitters –* most respondents with children in the UK (except the Ukrainians from the war zone who would be unable to travel there for safety considerations) would return to their origin countries for an extended period during the summer holidays, when they would bring children to visit relatives, taking them cash or gifts, travel to new areas in the country and for everybody to 'consolidate' and 're-connect' with their roots. They would also be remitting money mainly for subsistence needs. A mother lamented the summers when her young sons would spend in Bosnia.

> They would play on the streets all day long; they would have so many kids to play with, some would be their cousins; they would feel freedom and connection they had never experienced in London. I recall how tough and sad it was for them when we had to travel back; they would feel so lonely in London without the extended family, they would cry not wanting to leave (c.f. their grown-up children now travel independently to Bosnia-Herzegovina, forging ties and nourishing connections between the places).

Most remittances are sent to family members in the home country of the migrant. The income distribution across families will depend upon the type of remittance-receiving families – whether it is the poorer or wealthier families that receive them. There has been much discussion of using remittances beyond consumption and for investment; spending on education, housing and land acquisition are recognised forms of investment.

*'Reverse remittances'* were also identified in the narratives of the respondents. Family support and assistance during the travel between the UK and the origin country is an important facilitator of transnational mobility. Parents have financed the post-graduate studies of many Ukrainian respondents, including support with travel to visit home during the holidays. Once the children are in work in the UK, and that work is matching their qualifications, family support is restricted to home visits. Cultural specificities define different modalities of family support.

The interviews revealed different forms of family support that facilitate migrants' travelling back home. These include childcare, looking after properties and helping with investments; the provision of accommodation and transport during visits.

Many interviewees spoke of the significant emotional support provided by parents and family. A Bosnian woman was very proud of her mother' involvement in her transnational projects. *My mum provides accommodation when I go back but she is also the master-mind of all my projects.* Often nostalgia and strong feelings of belonging to the home area generate a specific type of cultural 'reverse remittances'. A Ukrainian woman would always bring to London Russian books and music, Russian and Ukrainian songs.

> Because my heart cries for Ukraine. This feeling will never come out of me. I had spent 29 years of my life there. I know the country and I love it for what it is. It is like loving your child. You may feel embarrassed by some of its actions but you love it. I feel very upset and angry if someone tries to offend my country especially now when it is so vulnerable.

### The mechanisms of maintaining ties with home and remittance behaviour

For many respondents in the sample, one of the important goals of settling in the UK was to obtain British citizenship or a permanent residence status that would pave the way for their transnational mobility. This involved not only travel to the home country but also the freedom to go anywhere in the world. Physical mobility makes transnational engagement much more feasible. It enables people to follow up on their philanthropic projects, financial investments, as well as to travel to give lectures and share their expertise. Mobility was particularly important for remitting as most respondents spoke of bringing money to relatives in the origin area rather than using other channels for transferring private funds. Others would send money through friends. A Bosnian academic spoke of giving the money to her friends to take it to her mum. *I like my mum to meet with my friends; it is also a social event for her.* A few people were using online services; banks were avoided as they were still charging high transaction fees.

The study shows that the conditions of arrival and the ensuing adaptation to life in the host country are likely to determine to a great degree the remitting behaviour.

For the Bosnians who had arrived during the war period, there was evidence that they had formed wide transnational fields, with commitments dominated by care for elderly parents and relatives in Bosnia and elsewhere. Unlike the other respondents in the sample, their initial adaptation to life in the UK was state-organised and supported by international refugee organisations. Their primary goal after arriving was to gain the right to remain. It was a period of unintended integration, garnered with hopes for going back soon to 'what was left behind before the war' and attendance of English language classes. The war took several years. The realization that there was more permanence to their stay in the UK than initially thought of, transformed their integration experience into a more intended settlement, with varying outcomes dependent on the age of arrival in the UK, class, economic and educational backgrounds. Their frequency of home visits was also determined by the regions in Bosnia they were coming from. A young Bosnian woman born in the UK, who has been spending every summer in Bosnia since she was a baby, explained:

> A lot of Bosnians lived in the city (Prijdor) before the war but they were forced out of their homes; if these people are now in the UK they can't go back as they have nowhere to go; (Serbs) have taken their homes; they were forced to go to other places; they are also reluctant to go back as some of the people who now live in the city are the ones who had killed members of their family or friends.

The younger generation who came to the UK as minors or who were born in the host country, maintain family and cultural ties with Bosnia, under the strong influence of their parents. They have never remitted money but since adolescence they have been sending gifts and presents, independently visiting their parents' origin places. The older generation who still have parents and siblings in the origin would still send money for subsistence, medical emergencies and education. They would still contemplate a return, even if in retirement years. Two Bosnians arrived to the UK with Australian passports (where they/their families were resettled during the war), and using the HSMP entry channel in the mid-2000s. Their transnational practices, determined by a higher position on the UK labour market, go beyond the commitments to family (as there would be no immediate family left in Bosnia-Herzegovina) – mobilizing resources for home country reforms and for relief from natural disasters and financial crisis (refer to examples earlier in the chapter).

Less than half of the Ukrainian respondents in the sample entered the UK on student visas, followed by an equal share of those who came on a 'family of a settled person visa' or on employment permit. Most of the Ukrainian respondents were classified as Managers/Technical professionals; the remaining were academics. Their successful professional integration in the host country is contingent on transnational activities related to property and business investments in both countries.

### *Investment and home country economic and political environment*

The ongoing conflict in the Ukraine appears to be a significant impediment on the frequency and duration of travel to the region, particularly of respondents from eastern Ukraine (the war zone).

A couple of respondents from Donetsk shared increasing concerns about their property investments, which had been abandoned as people were losing their jobs and not being able to pay rents/bills. Ten days before the interview, a missile destroyed the family home of one of the respondents; she had to relocate her parents to the capital Kiev. Those with children have stopped travelling to the area. Other respondents talked about shorter durations of stay there as, *it has turned into such a sad place; people talk only about the war; it does not matter where in the country you are, East or West, you are massively affected by the ongoing conflict; families and friends are divided.*

The war in the former Yugoslavia dates back over 20 years. Nonetheless, interviewees revealed an overarching impact on their physical mobility and their levels of engagement in the area. Some suggested deliberate segregation whereby people would sell properties in their previous places of residence to relocate to other places with higher concentration of Muslims/Serbs respectively. A Serbian respondent has not been back to his origin area since the start of the war when the family relocated to the Republic of Serbia.[7] *Sadly, I cannot see myself recovering to such a degree that would give me the strength to go back to Bosnia (c.f., in the exchange area), where we left a house and land with orchards.*

The struggling economy of Ukraine – months of turmoil have taken their toll – discourages investment and business activities, significantly affecting any transnational behaviour.

Others commented on Bosnia-Herzegovina as a difficult place for investment, following the 1995 Dayton Peace Agreement. Respondents argued that the increased administrative burden in the country has caused economic stagnation (the list of examples included, among others, the collection of many administrative fees; the lack of low cost carriers travelling to the country; the lengthy and expensive procedures for starting up a business; high social insurance contributions; irregular employment and, a burgeoning informal economy). One of the respondents attempted to produce his clothing designs in Bosnia but because of costly production and shipping, he went to Bulgaria. *It is difficult to be more involved in Bosnia, to grow my business there. I would not find a small, reliable factory there to produce my designs. It is not EU, which makes it expensive for shipping.*

## 6. Concluding remarks

This chapter sought to contribute to our understanding of the multidisciplinary and multi-layered nature of remittances and remittance practices, which are performed in the transnational spaces between the host countries in Western Europe and the home countries of Central and East Europe. This task was challenged by the marked divergence and heterogeneity of the CEE countries, which has been growing since the fall of the Berlin Wall, over a quarter of a century ago. The differentiated impacts of emigration and remittances intertwined with geography, socialist history and the adopted models of transitions to a market economy. We borrowed an analytical tool developed by Drahokoupil and Myant (2015) – grouping the CEE countries according to their distinctive features of prevalent capitalism – to steer the focus towards the 'remittance-based' economies of Moldova, Albania, Ukraine and Bosnia-Herzegovina. In 2014,

Moldova headed the list with a remittance figure of 26.2 percent of the country's Gross Domestic Product while the corresponding figure for Bosnia-Herzegovina was 11.4 percent and for Albania – 8.6 percent, all suggesting cases of external dependency.

Nevertheless, this chapter singled out the case of Ukraine and Bosnia-Herzegovina to account for the traumatic experiences of war – past and present – and their impact on remittance practices and engagement with home. The former belonged to the high risk investment countries while the latter was still paralysed by bureaucracy, corruption and clientelism. This added to the uniqueness of their migration and remittances experience which, despite the myriad of structural difficulties and insecurity, generated commendable initiatives of political activism and, philanthropic and entrepreneurial transnationalism, which translated into acts of reconciliation, poverty alleviation and support for change.

The impact and outreach of these acts of individual and collective efforts, however, is often marred by the acute need for policy changes. The same actors, namely established non-governmental organisations at home, repeatedly receive larger shares of diasporic donations. Similarly, specific diasporic fractions in the host countries get access to funding while others remain unfunded. It identifies the need for philanthropists and donors to be more attentive to transparency and outreach so that smaller organisations and individuals could benefit as well. The home states have a role to play in adopting a more sectoral approach to their provision of information to diasporic communities about political structures and administrative processes in the country of origin. The media's representation of returnees and diasporic communities abroad is often fraught with elitist discourses, which portray the image of 'the other'. More sensitive media policies have the potential to create dialogue platforms between diasporic communities, locals that stayed behind and returnees. A question emerges whether the home state or the European Union, or the country of destination could act as facilitator. The former designs and implements the integration framework for the immigrant communities. Integration policies are often problematic with regards to transnational practices and engagement with the origin as they implicitly assume settlement and weakening ties with home. Such policies, therefore, may need to be re-designed so as to allow for more mobility and the nourishment of multiple ties. Nevertheless, the academics still lack knowledge of the intergenerational differences in transnational engagement, and the understanding of concrete transnational practices triggered by past or current conflict, which could underpin tailored government strategies in the origin and the destination.[8] Any potential remittance contributions that may result from the ongoing conflict in the Ukraine and Bosnia-Herzegovina's struggles to reconcile with its past are yet to be seen.

## Notes

1   It is beyond the scope of this chapter to discuss immigration flows, including the unprecedented rise in the numbers of asylum seekers through the region since the summer of 2015.

2    During the Cold War period, the emigration category only existed in the population statistics of Hungary, Poland and the former Czechoslovakia.
3    One of the specific arrangements of the UK government imposed in 2004 referred to the establishment of a formal way of registering A8 migrants in employment – the Workers Registration Scheme (WRS). The scheme closed in April 2011.
4    The A8 countries were eight of the ten countries that joined the European Union in 2004, namely: Czech Republic, Estonia, Hungary, Latvia, Lithuania, Poland, Slovakia, Slovenia.
5    ITHACA was co-funded by DG Home of the European Commission.
6    Union of the Socialist Soviet Republics (USSR).
7    1995 Dayton Agreement divided Bosnia into two entities, Bosnian Federation where most Muslims were relocated and Republic of Serbia, with an estimated 95 percent Serbian population.
8    This paragraph largely draws on the recorded Minutes from the plenary discussions at the ITHACA workshop, held on 25th September 2015 in Brighton, the UK. It brought together Bosnian-Herzegovinians and Ukrainians from the UK sample, and those residing in Austria as well as experts and relevant stakeholders based in the home countries of Bosnia-Herzegovina and Ukraine. The minutes were prepared by the research teams at the International Centre for Migration Policy Development (ICMPD), Alexandra Konig and Katharina Schaur, and London Metropolitan University, the author of this chapter, Eugenia Markova.

# References

Anderson, B., Ruhs, M., Rogaly, B. and Spencer, S. (2006) *Fair enough? Central and East European migrants in low-wage employment in the UK.* York: Joseph Rowntree Foundation.
Barajas, A., Chami, R., Fullenkamp, C., Gapen, M. and Montiel, P. (2009) 'Do Workers' Remittances Promote Economic Growth?', *IMF Working Paper, WP/09/153.*
Basch, L., Schiller, N.G. and Blanc, C.S. (1994) *Nations Unbound: Transnational Projects, Postcolonial Predicaments, and Deterritorialized Nation-States.* Amsterdam: Gordon and Breach.
Bauman, Z. (2003) *Liquid Love.* Cambridge: Polity Press.
Cheah, P. and Robins, B. (1998) *Cosmopolitics: Thinking and Feeling beyond the Nation.* Minnesota: Minnesota University Press.
Clemens, M. and McKenzie, D. (2014) 'Why Don't Remittances Appear to Affect Growth?', *Policy Research Working Paper* 6856, The World Bank, Development Research Group, May 2014.
Cohen, J.H. (2011) 'Migration, Remittances and Household Strategies', *Annual Review of Anthropology,* 40: 103–114.
Constant, A.F., Nottmeyer, O. and Zimmermann, K.F. (2012) 'The Economics of Circular Migration', *Discussion Paper Series,* IZA DP No. 6940.
Drahokoupil, J. and Myant, M. (2015) 'Putting comparative capitalism research in its place: Variaties of capitalism in transition economies', forthcoming Chapter in: Ebenau, M, I. Bruff and C. May (eds) *New Directions in Critical Comparative Capitalisms Research.* London: Palgrave Macmillan.
Drinkwater, S., Eade, J. and Garapich, M. (2010) 'What's behind the figures? An investigation into recent Polish migration to the UK', in: Black, R., Engbersen, G., Okolski, M. and Pantiru, C. (eds) *A Continent Moving West? EU Enlargement and Labour Migration from Central and Eastern Europe*, IMISCOE Research: Amsterdam University Press, pp. 73–88.

Drori, I., Honig, B. and Wright, M. (2009) 'Transnational Entrepreneurship: An Emergent Field of Study', *Entrepreneurship Theory and Practice*, September, 33(5): 1001–1022.

Falzoni, A.M. and Soldano, K. (2013) 'Remittances and inequality in Eastern European countries', very preliminary results, 14 November 2013, University of Bergamo and University of Milan.

Giannetti, M., Federici, D. and Raitano, M. (2009) 'Migrant remittances and inequality in Central-Eastern Europe', *International Review of Applied Economics*, 23(3): 289–307.

Guarnizo, L.E. (2003) 'The Economics of Transnational Living', *International Migration Review*, 37(3): 666–99.

Guencheva, R., Kabakchieva, P. and Kolarski, P. (2003) *Bulgaria: The social impact of seasonal migration*. IOM & European Commission Project. Vienna: IOM.

Hugo, G. (2013) 'What We Know about Circular Migration and Enhanced Mobility', *Policy Brief* No 7 September 2013, Migration Policy Institute.

Isaakyan, I. (2015) 'Capital Transfers and Social Remittances of Transnational Migrants in the EU', ITHACA Research Report N. 6/2015, European University Institute.

Kaczmarczyk, P. and Okólski, M. (2005) *International Migration in Central and Eastern Europe – Current and Future Trends,* United Nations Expert Group Meeting on International Migration and Development, New York, 6–8 July, 2005.

Katseli, L., Lucas, R. and Xenogiani, T. (2006) 'Policies for Migration and Development: A European Perspective', OECD Development Centre Policy Brief 30, OECD Publishing.

Knowles, C. (2003) *Race and Social Analysis*. London: SAGE Publications Ltd.

Leon-Ledesma, M. and Piracha, M. (2004) 'International Migration and the Role of Remittances in Eastern Europe', *International Migration,* 42(4): 65–83.

Levitt, P. (2001) *The Transnational Villagers*. California: University of California Press.

Levitt, P. and Jaworsky, B.N. (2007) 'Transnational Migration Studies: Past Development and Future Trends', *Annual Review of Sociology,* 33: 129–156.

Lukas, R.E.B. (2005) *International Migration and Economic Development: Lessons from Low-Income Countries*. Cheltenham: Edward Elgar Publishing Ltd.

Markova, E. (2010) 'Effects of migration on sending countries: lessons from Bulgaria', *Hellenic Observatory Papers on Greece and Southeast Europe,* May, GreeSE Paper No 35.

Markova, E. and Sarris, A.H. (2002) 'Remitting and Saving Behaviour of Bulgarian Immigrants in Greece', Discussion Paper No 2002/34, Faculty of Economics, University of Athens.

Markova, E. and Reilly, B. (2007) 'Bulgarian Migrant Remittances and Legal Status: Some Micro-level Evidence from Madrid', *South-Eastern Europe Journal of Economics,* 5(1): 55–69.

Mazzucato, V. (2011) 'Reverse Remittances in Migration – Development Nexus: two-way flows between Ghana and the Netherlands', *Population, Space and Place,* 17(5): 454–468.

McConnell, C., Brue, S. and Flynn, S. (2009) *Microeconomics: Principles, Problems, and Policies*. New York: McGraw-Hill/Irwin.

McLoughlin, S., Munz, R., Bunte, R., Hulton, G., Muller, W. and Skeldon, R. (2011) 'Temporary and circular migration: opportunities and challenges', Working Paper No 35, European Policy Centre, ISSN-1782-2424.

Naiditch, C. and Vranceanu, R. (2010) 'Equilibrium migration and invested remittances: The EECA evidence', *European Journal of Political Economy,* 26(4): 454–474.

Poulton, H. (1993) *The Balkans: Minorities and States in Conflict*. London: Minority Rights Publications.

Sklair, L. (2001) *The Transnational Capitalist Class.* Oxford: Blackwell.

Stark, O. (1991) *The Migration of Labor.* Massachusetts: Blackwell Publishers.

Vargas-Silva, C. and Huang, P. (2006) 'Macroeconomic Determinants of Workers' Remittances: Host vs. Home Country's Economic Conditions', *Journal of International Trade and Economic Development,* 15: 81–99.

Yeoh, B. and Huang, S. (eds) (2011) 'In and out of Asia: the cultural politics of talented migration', *Journal of Migration and Ethnic Studies,* 37(5): 681–690.

Zhelyazkova, A. (1998) 'The Social and Cultural Adaptation of Bulgarian Immigrants in Turkey' (Available at: www.omda.bg/public/imir/studies/nostalgia_1.html [Accessed 3 April 2016).

**Part II**

# Formal dependencies and informal resistances to the Europeanization of labour and industrial relations models

# 7 The fate of the 'hard' and 'soft' *acquis communautaires* in the new member states

*Guglielmo Meardi*

## Introduction

The EU eastern enlargement of 2004–07 is predominantly described as a success, at least in comparison with the economic and political troubles that the EU has encountered since then on other fronts (the Eurozone crisis, difficult neighbourhood policies on the East and the South, fall of consent). This assessment is largely based on a conception of the EU enlargement as merely an institutional and economic undertaking. But while it is true that the project was primarily concerned with economic benefits and institutional stabilization, social considerations were also very important in the process that led to the enlargement, and should be included in the analysis of its outcomes.

In the applicant countries, aspirations to approach western social standards, not only in consumption levels but overall economically, were very important in public opinion, if often in a confused manner (as understandable in societies going through deep socio-economic transitions). In the referendum campaigns that took place in the applicant countries in 2003, governments often turned to social reassurances and promises when faced with the risk of very low, and therefore not legitimizing, turn-outs. For instance, the ruling party in Poland focused its campaign on four social topics (education, work, opportunity and equality).

Even more important were social reassurances on the Western side, where public opinion was lukewarm and fears of mass immigration, budget costs and unfair competition often emerged. Therefore, in the run-up to the enlargement EU institutions increased their attention to social issues and issued a number of reassuring reports and studies. Three policy reports were particularly important in shaping and presenting the European Commission's stance. In 1999, the Amato Report downplayed fears about the socio-economic gap between EU15 and applicant countries and that sustained growth enabled by EU accession would have fostered convergence (Amato, 1999). The argument that there was little actual poverty in CEE was based on the curious observation that 'when asked how often they had to go without food, heating and electricity, and clothes they really needed, most people [in applicant countries] reported they never or rarely went without' (30). Placing the poverty line at the starvation level may be suited to developing countries, but is at odds with any idea of a 'European Social Model' and with the established definitions of poverty in developed countries (whether as relative poverty, or in the EC's own definition of 'people living in poverty if their income and resources are so inadequate as to preclude them from having a standard of living considered acceptable in the society in which they live' (EC, 2004)). The report also embraced a particularly optimistic view on market-driven economic convergence, neglecting the existence of historical counterfactuals.

Soon afterwards, the Boeri-Brücker report on migration presented a similarly optimistic approach, concluding that no migration wave was to be expected, on the ground that little movement had occurred after the accession of Greece, Spain and Portugal in the 1980s (Boeri and Brücker, 2001) – in fact, in the five years after accession, migration from first wave of new member states (NMS) was at least twice the size forecast by the report (two millions rather than one). Finally, the Kok report of 2003 stated that on social dumping 'fears are overstated. Part of joining the EU is the adoption of a process of social dialogue and measures of social regulation' ... 'policy at both the EU and national level should encourage [wage] growth in the new member states' (Kok, 2003: 41).

This chapter questions that optimistic promise that EU policies would have been sufficient to foster convergence between new and old member states. It addresses, in sequence, the two main kinds of EU policies that constitute the 'acquis communautaire' of regulations the acceding countries had to adopt: 'hard' regulations through supranational legislation (Directives) and the increasingly used 'soft' regulations through benchmarks, targets and non-binding recommendations. The chapter focuses on the first five years of accession (2004–09) and primarily on the first wave of accession from Central Eastern Europe (CEE), with some additional notes on Romania and Bulgaria. It examines therefore the effects of EU policies in the best, fair-weather scenario of years of growth, before the financial and Eurocrisis added new problems and new policy responses.[1]

### The 'hard' acquis

At the time of the enlargement, many looked at the EU for hope with regard to social progress. Mailand and Due (2004) noted that the status of industrial relations in the NMS was so dismal that it could only be improved through a massive effort from the EU side. A similar argument, but in a more pessimistic tone, was made by Vaughan-Whitehead (2003). Hence most observers had major expectations from the transposition of EU social regulations, the so-called 'hard' law.

The 'hard' *acquis communautaire*, despite covering only a relatively narrow set of social and labour issues, was particularly apt to affect countries with a rather legalistic, top-down approach to these issues. In fact, policy makers in the NMS generally considered the European Social Model as nothing more than a series of EU directives (Neumann, 2007; Keune 2009; Bluhm 2006).

EU Directives on employment relations cover five fields: information and consultation of employees (including the European Works Councils), restructuring, health & safety (including working time), equal opportunities, and integration of weak categories into the labour market. How, and with what effects, were these regulations transferred to the NMS?

The NMS could be expected to perfectly fulfil all requirements and miraculously attain all social targets by simply passing new regulations – the old member states themselves are far from complying with all of them. But it is legitimate to check whether the process of implementation has moved at all, and in what direction: improvement or worsening of the hitherto existing social standards.

The 'hard' social *acquis communautaire* was imposed rather smoothly and quickly on the candidate countries during the pre-accession negotiations, in spite of some resistance from local employers, who requested some 'transitional periods' before being forced to adapt to EU standards (Meardi 2002). The result is that in terms of formal transposition, all NMS actually performed better than many old ones (Falkner and Treib, 2008). The problem is not the transposition, but its form and the actual compliance with it: the experience of the first years after accession is that if the NMS are blameless in terms of literal transposition, theirs is just a 'compliance of dead letters' (*ibidem*), where transposition occurs in a minimalist way, or is not followed by effective monitoring and sanctioning.

### Health and safety and working conditions

Social actors in the NMS are widely sceptical about EU regulations on health and safety (H&S), used as they are to more legalistic (precise professional standards rather than broader preventive principles) regulations in the field. In particular, in Poland there are fears that EU rules, rather than improving standards, could jeopardize the established role of the Polish Labour Inspectorate, which is still perceived as the main pillar of monitoring on H&S, even if they are themselves affected by a number of shortcomings (it is reported that they often deliberately 'spare' companies in economic difficulties). Even less promising has been EU accession for Slovakia, where the centre-right government, in the name of free market and EMU convergence, reduced the number of labour inspectors (Falkner and Treib, 2008).

It is difficult to evaluate whether the effects of EU regulations have improved workplace safety in the NMS, as statistics in this field are notoriously unreliable, distorted by under-reporting, and incomparable due to different collection methods. As acknowledged by the European Foundation for the Improvement of Working and Living Conditions – 'gentlemen agreements' among member states open the way to cosmetic improvements of official data (EWCO, 2008) – therefore, the same institution's impression that the gap in working conditions between East and West may be narrowing (Peña-Casas and Pochet, 2009) is only provisional. A proposed EU Regulation on statistics on H&S, which might have paved the way to better data, has been proposed but not agreed upon: while the EU is keen on comparing and monitoring macro-economic indicators and public budgets, it considers fatalities and accidents at work not important enough to deserve attention and statistical rigor.

In the 'worst scenario' of the Baltic states, the European H&S regulations' inadequacy, because of their 'softness' (Woolfson, 2006), has been well-documented by a number of studies, and notably the Baltic Working Environment and Labor survey (Woolfson and Calite, 2008; Woolfson *et al.*, 2008). In the years around EU accession (before the collapse of 2008), the Baltic states experienced very high, mostly double-digit economic growth, but at the cost of unchecked work intensification with damaging H&S outcomes. The gloom situation in the Baltic states is, of course, not EU-originated, but is common to all post-Soviet Union republics. Survey data indicate that work intensification has slowed down after 2004 in comparison to the late 1990s-2002, but this might be because an 'effort ceiling' is being reached (Woolfson *et al.*, 2008: 319). It is nonetheless apparent that EU integration has not managed to improve working conditions, or to correct a form of socially unregulated, and eventually unsustainable, economic development that contrasts with the 'European Social Model'. Data on mortality have remained nearly the same as in 1990 – although at least they have not worsened as has happened in Russia over the same period. In Lithuania, between 2004 and 2006 the number of Labor Inspectorate inspections fell by 1.5 times, and no reported case of H&S violations led to criminal proceedings, something that even concerned the ILO (Woolfson and Calite, 2008).

The most important point made by Woolfson (2006: 199) with regard to the gap between eastern and western members of the EU is that, according to Eurostat data on fatal accidents at work, while the *acquis communautaire* was being introduced (1998–2002) occupational safety was improving more slowly in the NMS (–5 percent) than in the old (–25 percent), and in some NMS (Hungary, Lithuania, Latvia) it was even worsening in real terms. The gap, accordingly, was widening, rather than narrowing. After 2004, this divergent trend appears to have stopped, but neither has it inverted into any sign of convergence. Eurostat data show better-than-average improvements in some NMS (Hungary, Czech Republic, Slovakia, Estonia) for 2004–06, and overall the same change in old and new member states (although they were still worsening in still-to-join Romania and Bulgaria). At that time, interestingly, the worst changes were in Sweden (+29 percent between 2006 and 2003) and UK (+16 percent), countries with high number of new migrants or contract workers from the NMS, especially in construction (Ireland, in a similar situation, shows unusually highly volatile figures between 2003 and 2006, that do not allow to detect a clear trend). It may then be that the safety problem has been 'exported' rather than solved.

The impact of the Working Time (WT) Directive on local debates and regulations is more visible, and it is puzzling. The Hungarian case is particularly telling. The WT Directive was implemented in 2001, but Hungarian trade unions, rather than welcoming it as an example of 'Social Europe', opposed it and defined it as a unilateral governmental concession to the demands of employers, and especially multinational companies (Neumann 2007). The main measure introduced was the extension of the reference period for working time measurement, which translates into more working time flexibility unilaterally managed by management, associated with easy collective and individual opt-outs. While the introduction of annualized working hours, in theory, could contribute to 'German-style' co-determination in the workplace, this is unlikely to happen in countries where industrial relations are so different. The Hungarian case is not isolated in this regard. Similar transpositions, worsening rather than improving employees' prerogatives, took place in most of the NMS, meeting particular trade union opposition and employer enthusiasm in Estonia (Eamets and Philips, 2004) and Lithuania (Blažiene, 2007). In Poland, the WTD implementation was the opportunity, in 2002, for reducing minimum overtime payments from 100 percent to 50 percent, as well as extending the reference period for working time calculation. It is true that, as highlighted by Leiber (2007), employers complained about the Directive because of the new rules on daily rests, but there is no evidence that those regulations actually made working time any less flexible. In Slovakia, it led to 'opening clauses' allowing employers to negotiate flexible working time with their employees without union involvement (Falkner and Treib, 2008). The non-detriment clauses of European H&S regulations therefore proved unfit for the purpose of preventing national arguments to autonomously reduce pre-existing provisions. Employee-friendly implementations occurred only in the Czech Republic and Slovenia (Falkner and Treib, 2008), two countries that at the time of the enlargement were ruled by genuine centre-left governments (the Czech social-democrats and Slovenian centre-left coalition were not renamed former Soviet-bloc parties, such as those that had the occasion to rule Poland, Hungary or Bulgaria, but quickly moved from the old eastern orthodoxy to the new western one).

Working time therefore remains a problematic feature in the region: according to the 2005 European Working Condition Survey, in the NMS, in comparison to the EU-15, working hours are longer, shift work is more frequent, employees have less autonomy over working time and their health is more affected by it (Parent-Thirion *et al.*, 2007; Morley and Sanoussi, 2009). Moreover, there is no evidence of convergence between western and eastern member states (Morley and Sanoussi, 2009). In terms of regulations, not only have all NMS taken advantage of the opt-out, but they also (with the exceptions of Slovakia and Bulgaria) allow workers to combine more employment contracts and thereby work over the limits: a legalized form of 'moonlighting'. And even the regulations that have been passed are met with huge problems of application and enforcement – something inherited from the previous situation, but which the EU failed to address. Falkner and Treib (2008) report that often employees voluntarily work longer hours than allowed by the law because they need the extra-pay – a recurrent finding also in my fieldwork research. They add that the litigation system is very slow, with labour law courts being very slow (14 months in Slovakia, 1–2 years in Hungary, up to three years in the Czech Republic, against the one year average in Western Europe), no effective information campaigns were conducted, and the Labour Inspectorate are not only under-resourced, but specialized in technical H&S issues only and they therefore neglect working time issues. In the worst case of Lithuania, where 53 percent of employees declare working over-time, 42 percent of them add that overtime hours are unpaid (Woolfson and Calite, 2008).

There are also domino-effects on Western Europe, such as concession bargaining on working time in companies threatening relocation, reforms of the 35-hour week in France and, above all, the shelving of the planned revision of the WT Directive.

If EU regulations do not seem to have positively affected statutory substantive conditions, they might at least have fostered procedural changes, in the direction of stronger involvement of social dialogue: a process which arguably could provide positive results in the medium-long term. A defining feature of the EU Occupational H&S strategy is that in its aim of creating a high level of 'risk awareness', it foresees a crucial role for employee representatives and thereby employee 'voice'. But this is a dimension that has not been pushed through the local barriers that obstruct it. Procedures for involving trade unions and civic society in monitoring and judicial proceedings have remained minimalist in most NMS (Falkner and Treib, 2008). In the Czech Republic, the Chamber of Commerce filed a complaint with the Constitutional Court claiming that the Czech transposition law of the WT Directive is unconstitutional for giving trade unions rights over H&S matters (Hala, 2007). In the Baltic States, the ineffectiveness of the foreseen participation and voice mechanisms on H&S has been documented most vividly: even if formal compliance with the regulations seems good, in Lithuania 78 percent of employees do not know of any H&S reps in their workplace (Woolfson *et al.*, 2008). Moreover, a large majority of employers (91 percent in Estonia, 71 percent in Latvia, 60 percent in Lithuania) is opposed to the creation of H&S reps (ibid.). The weakness of trade unions and employee workplace representation is reproduced, with damaging effects, in the area of H&S.

## *Information and consultation of employees*

The most important directive in industrial relations, in theory, should have been the one on Information and Consultation (I&C) of Employees (2002/14/EC), officially meant to set a minimum floor of rights for employees in the EU. The Directive was expected to affect the new post-communist member states more than the old ones, as in the majority of them (the exceptions being Hungary and Slovenia) trade unions were the only channel of employee representation, which might now be replaced by a dual channel. However, such transfer has not occurred, at least not in a way that makes the NMS more similar to the German model.

Promoters of the transfer of the dual channel into the NMS (e.g. Tholen, 2007) may be neglecting that works councils have historically been an effective channel for employee voice only in countries where they have been preceded and supported by a strong labour movement as in Germany. In post-communist countries (including in East Germany, where works councils undermine unions more often than in West Germany), the context is rather negative, as private employers are already reluctant to negotiate with trade unions and the weakness or inexistence of multi-employer collective bargaining means that trade unions could be deemed redundant if they lost their workplace role. Even in the 'best case'

Hungary, where the dual system had been introduced 'endogenously' in the 1990s, works councils failed to play the expected role wherever unions were absent (Tóth and Neumann, 2004a). In Poland, interestingly, the pre-existing works councils, which in the 1980s had often played important functions against nomenklatura management, had been abandoned soon after 1989 at the initiative of Solidarity (Weinstein, 2000) and without any particular resistance: given this history of dismissal, it is naïve to expect positive developments from the I&C Directive.

While the Directive was officially meant to set a minimum floor of rights for employees in the EU, as happened with the WT Directive, several NMS governments have been quick at exploiting the opportunity to undermine, rather than reinforce, employee prerogatives. Governments' initial proposals tried to replace the single channel with a dual-channel system in which the establishment of a works council could have easily made the unions disposable. The specific proposed laws allowing works councils to replace the prerogatives of existing unions were particularly dangerous, as they would have opened an avenue for union-avoidance techniques and 'yellow', or at least ineffective, works councils. Although other possible transpositions introducing works councils *while* strengthening unions were available, for instance along the Italian *Rappresentanze Sindacali Unitarie* or the South African Workplace Forums examples, both guaranteeing union presence in the works councils, this option was not considered. Union-threatening legislative proposals were pushed by governments in Poland, Slovakia and Estonia. Only after strong union opposition (which in the case of Estonia, where the proposed law restricted the prerogatives of trade unions, also required the solidarity intervention of international unions) were such proposals amended and replaced by 'residual' works councils systems, which give priority to unions as employee representatives (of all employees, not just union members) in workplaces (Carley and Hall, 2008). Only Bulgaria and Estonia introduced a dual channel that guarantees union presence but still raises some union concerns. The Czech Republic is exceptional for two reasons. Firstly, an agreement between Social-democratic government and trade unions occurred early on an implementation system (works councils only where there are no trade unions) that would provide minimal change to the existing system (this arrangement was eventually adopted by Estonia, Poland and Slovakia too, after more anti-union plans were defeated). Secondly, an additional Czech specificity is that it is unique in the EU for defining 'consultation' as 'negotiation': however, this little sign of hope for employee voice remains futile given that basically no works councils were introduced in the country.

The legal framework has since been changed in some countries by interventions from the Constitutional Courts, reintroducing threats for trade unions. In the Czech Republic, in March 2008 the Constitutional Court decided that a works council can be established at an employer's business and can also operate alongside a trade union, which raised preoccupation from the trade unions. In Poland, in July 2008 the Constitutional Court took a similar decision. Thereby, a dual channel has been introduced by the back door. In the short term, experts expect no major change (trade unions are likely to keep their dominance of the already established works councils), but for the future the option for non-union representation and the undermining of independent employee organization is now open: if German trade unions struggle to fend off 'yellow' rivals and conservative reforms, the task will be even more difficult for their weaker counterparts in the NMS. However, not all Courts decisions have been in this direction. An earlier Polish ruling increased the scope of information and consultation rights, which initial legislation had established in a very vague form.

The implementation of the new I&C bodies seems to be proceeding slowly. In the Baltic states, it is reported that employees lack the assertiveness and information to take action demanding I&C rights (Woolfson *et al.*, 2008). In Slovakia and Poland few companies have introduced innovations (Gładoch, 2008). In Poland, according to data from the State Labor Inspectorate, about 2,000 I&C bodies (out of at least 17,000 companies covered by the legislation, i.e. with over 50 employees) have been constituted, but 90 percent of them are simply ratifications of previously existing union bodies. Moreover, the remaining 10 percent appear to be weaker and less active than union bodies (Surdykowska, 2008). Gardawski (2009b) reports some gradual positive developments in the I&C bodies, but again, mainly when they are dominated by one strong pre-existing trade union. Research on employee participation rights in MNCs in the Czech Republic, carried out in 2007–08, found no effect of the Directive at all (Meardi *et al.*, 2013). In February 2008, a review of the Directive's implementation by the European Commission (EC, 2008a) reported no, or problematic, impact in Bulgaria, Czech Republic, Estonia, Lithuania, Poland and Romania – and the positive impact reported in Latvia, Hungary and Slovakia was so generic to be possibly due only to national rose-tinted glasses (governments have an interest in reporting success rather than lack of it). The Directive's failure to produce any tangible improvement in workplace employee participation rights is therefore plain.

Analogous problems are encountered by other, more specific pieces of EU regulations involving employment relations: in Hungary, for instance, the transposition of the Transfer of Undertaking Directive contains no clear definition of information of employees, making the norms rather hollow (Neumann, 2007). By contrast, EU deregulation policies appear more incisive and disruptive of employee rights: in Hungary, a new company Act was passed in 2006 reducing the role of board-level employee representatives, in the name of the freedom of investment.

In a similarly distorted way, the Charter of Fundamental Rights of the EU, which in the West is often portrayed as strengthening social rights including the right to strike, in the NMS is mentioned to limit it (e.g. the proposed restriction of the right to secondary action in Estonia) and to support the introduction of a different right to industrial action – that of lockout (in Poland and Lithuania). The feebleness of EU social rights protection is confirmed by the fact that in 2007 the populist government of Poland joined the UK in refusing (with a protocol) the Charter altogether, although for reasons of disagreement on the civil rather than social rights – a decision confirmed by the following liberal government).

A more promising field for advances in employee consultations and informa-tion exists for that small minority of workforce who are employed by multinational companies covered by the European Works Council Directive. However, the European Works Councils appear to have effects only where employee initiatives manage to go beyond the narrow field of the Directive, and there are no spill-over effects to the broader systems of industrial relations.

Overall, then, the I&C Directive has remained entirely inadequate to improv-ing employee representation standards in the enlarged EU (Donaghey *et al.*, 2013). In the meanwhile, not only union membership, but also the perception of union rights keeps falling. In 2007, the Polish survey 'Working Poles' found that only 41.4percent of employees believed that the right of unionizing is respected – a fall of 18.3 points in comparison to the same survey two years earlier (Męcina, 2009a: 280).

*Equal opportunities*

On equal opportunities, EU legislations and policies are indeed contributing to shaping debates on these issues, especially on sexual harassment, indirect discrimination and on sexual orientations. Equal opportunities may remain excep-tional as a 'success story' of EU social policy only because of its nature as "cheap", relatively innocuous, even high-sounding platform for demonstrating the EC's commitment to social progress' (Ellis, 1998). It has to be reminded that CEE has a different history on gender, made of formal equality and full (but not necessarily voluntary) female employment under communism followed by capi-talist restructuring that hit women employment and living conditions disproportionately (Pollert, 2003). Such a combination is not easily conducive to equal opportunities policies, which face the negative similarities with communist-time slogans as well as serious current socio-economic obstacles, and, in the most Catholic and Orthodox countries such as Poland, Slovakia and Romania, tradi-tionalist cultural opposition in large parts of the population.

In the case of the Employment Framework Directive (2000/78/EC), introduc-ing non-discrimination principles on age, religion, sexual orientation and disability, only Hungary and Slovenia extended its scope beyond the required minimum, the area of employment. In the Baltic States, Czech Republic, Slovakia and Poland there was strong resistance from the Christian-Democrats and the Christian Right, especially on sexual orientations (Falkner and Treib, 2008). In the Czech Republic, the opposition from the Senate and from the President Vaclav Klaus impeded the adoption of a new bill, and transposition only occurred though a complex arrangement of individual provisions, that, according to Falkner and Treib (2008, 302), 'are marked by several shortcomings if compared to the European standards', given that the country 'failed to create a proper Equal Treatment Body, which is meant to provide assistance to victims, conduct its own surveys and publish independent reports about equality issues'. Vaclav Klaus opposition to the Directive is resolute: in May 2008, he vetoed the new bill required by the EU as 'poor, counter-productive and unnecessary', and as a product of the Soviet mentality forcing equality of outcomes and social engineering. In the Czech Republic, particular opposition meets the idea of non-discrimination of the Roma minority.

In the other member states the situation is not necessarily better. Opposition to ethnic minorities or homosexuals affects large parts of local societies, and the Equal Treatment Bodies, even where introduced, lack visibility (Falkner and Treib, 2008). Latvia in 2006 omitted sexual orientations from its implementation of the Framework Anti-discrimination directive. In Poland, the new rules' ineffectiveness is proved by the fact that senior Polish ministers can repeatedly call for a ban of homosexuals in occupations such as teaching, and that the country altogether 'opted out' (through a protocol limiting its scope) from the Charter of Fundamental Rights of the EU, seeing it as excessive protection for homosexuals. In Lithuania, the parliament went even further by approving a 'censorship' law (vetoed by the president) forbidding any public demonstrations and any reference to homosexuality on TV before night time. Overall, a realistic assessment is that EU influence on gender equality is conditional: local compliance depends less on EU commitment (or rather, lack thereof), and more on mobilization of women's movements and reactionary forces within each member state (Avdeyeva, 2009).

It is, as on health and safety, the application and enforcement that are particularly lacking: according to Falkner and Treib's account, enforcement bodies' resources and actual performance have lagged behind their formal competences (Falkner and Treib, 2008). Sissenich confirms the same on Hungary and Poland (although Hungary has done a little more than Poland): on equal opportunities like on labour law, the 'adoption of the *social acquis* has focused on approximating secondary legislation, with behavioural adoption lagging far behind' (Sissenich, 2005: 157).

Besides the non-discrimination regulations, EU rules on sex equality include the Directive on pregnant workers, which provides for a minimum of fourteen weeks maternity leave. In Poland, the transposition of the Directive in 2002 involved the *reduction* of maternity leave from 24 to 16 weeks (Leiber, 2007). Again, like with the WT Directive, the non-retrogression principle of EU labour law was ineffective. Moreover, the Directive did not manage to affect the Polish system's 'protectionist', rather than equality-oriented, approach: Poland maintained its list of work prohibitions (e.g. night work) for pregnant workers, which is potentially discriminatory for the European Commission, rather than adopting the EU principle of individual risk assessments. The regulation of pregnancy is, by nature, a complex and potentially double-edged sword in terms of sex equality, but Poland managed not to improve women treatments on either side: protection was reduced in terms of maternity leave, and discrimination risks were maintained in terms of work prohibitions.

As with health and safety and working time, there are knock-on effects on the EU as a whole, with a slowing down of initiatives in this field and even risks of political shifts. A telling sign was the election, in 2004, to chair of the European Parliament's Committee on Women's Rights and Gender Equality (historically, an major instrumental body for promoting gender equality in the EU) of Slovak

Christian democrat Anna Záborská, a traditionalist personality in striking contrast to her feminist predecessors (in 2009, the post went back to a leftwing MEP).

## The 'soft' acquis

The results of the 'soft' social *acquis* appear as disappointing as those of the 'hard' one, despite the EU apparent numerous efforts at supporting social dialogue in the NMS, especially through the European Employment Strategy (EES), and the promotion of social pacts in the process of convergence into the European Monetary Union (EMU), as well as through involvement in inter-sector and sectoral European social dialogue.

### European Employment Strategy

The European Employment Strategy, despite its original aims when it was launched in 1997 and its formal promotion of social dialogue, has not favoured social negotiations and regulation of the labour market in the NMS. Even worse: since its redefinition in 2000 under the 'Lisbon Agenda' umbrella and the stress on 'competitiveness', it has had a deregulatory function, rather than a social one. Such role is much more visible in the NMS. The Polish Forum of the Lisbon Strategy, created in 2003 and promoted by the Ministry of the Economy, has as its core the neoliberal Market Economy Research Institute, whose Director, Jan Szomburg, openly advocates an 'Americanization' role for Poland in the EU (Kowalik, 2009). At its Conference on employment policy of 2005, the Forum recommended limiting trade union influence on the labour market and a reduction for the already very narrow scope for sector collective agreements (Sztanderska, 2005).

The role of the EES has been increasingly marked by its focus being on the Danish-inspired 'flexicurity', seen as a relevant solution for the weak labour markets of the NMS (Cazes and Nesperova, 2007). The European Commission, in its 2006 'Employment in Europe Report' devoted to flexicurity, argued that 'progress on flexibility and security, together with the resources needed to implement comprehensive activation and lifelong learning policies, requires a well-developed tripartite social dialogue' (EC, 2006: 110). The argument was based on the need of avoiding 'political difficulties' and 'social turmoil', and drew on the examples of Denmark and the Netherlands. While recognising that corporatist structures are not present in all countries, the EC argued in that report that the crucial point is broadening the bargaining agenda to include employment, which is seen as a positive-sum game – something that all member states, in theory, can do. The NMS entered the EU with weaker labour markets and, in particular, low employment rates: Hungary and Poland, together with Malta, took over from Italy the title of worst performers. So, in the NMS there should be a particularly wide scope for change promoted by the EES.

Yet flexicurity leaves little space for union interest: the stress in the NMS is on the 'flexibility' side, while the 'security' one is hampered by structural long-term unemployment and budget constraints. The general doubts on flexicurity that have been expressed in the West (e.g. Funk, 2008) acquire a more dramatic dimension in those CEE countries (Poland, Slovakia, Hungary) where unemployment is higher and the public budget smaller. In such situations, the Danish model of high unemployment benefits – developed in a country with high public expenditure and, even at its peak, low unemployment – is simply unrealistic, and as a matter of fact it has not been taken seriously. In Poland, for instance, unemployment benefits' replacement and coverage rate have kept falling since their introduction by Labour Minister Jacek Kuroń in 1990: by 2007, only 14 percent of Polish jobseekers received benefits, and these amounted to a meagre 20 percent of the average wage (Spieser, 2009). With EU accession, things have kept going in the wrong direction: unemployment benefits, now labelled as 'passive' policies, lost legitimacy, and the same happened to other benefits, which have often played a substitutive role to unemployment insurance: incapacity benefits were cut in Slovakia in 2004 (causing street protests in the East of the country), and early retirement was strictly limited in Poland in 2008 (despite large union protests). On the flexibility side of flexicurity, the NMS are characterized by high flexibility even when, formally, employment protection law remains apparently strict: as shown by the ILO (Cazes and Nesperova, 2007), these countries already suffer from excessive, rather than insufficient, flexibility. If the flexicurity recipe could be judged as 'not balanced' in the West (Keune and Jepsen, 2007), the unbalance is even more striking in the East. In the extreme case of the hyper-liberal Baltic states, there is an entrenched insecurity system, as indicated by the very few ILO conventions that have been ratified, and both numerical flexibility and pay flexibility meet little institutional constraints (Eamets, 2009).

As a 'soft policy', the EES affects member states through peer pressure and through resources – rather than financial, it is the case of 'symbolic' resources, which can be used strategically by national players. Mailand (2008) has detected that the EES has had more effect on Poland (and Spain) than the UK and Denmark. This would suggest that, somehow, the EES is succeeding in narrowing the gap between old and new members. But his analysis needs more careful investigation. The main reason of the bigger impact in Poland is simply the worse starting point in terms of compliance and performance: changes are more visible. But are really these changes significant, and are they likely to continue in the direction of convergence? Mailand reports positive effects on public employment services, but fails to give any real example. His analysis is just a secondary report of other observers' opinions: it is more a rumour than an empirical test.

It is true that, thanks to the EES and funding through the European Social Fund, funding for active labour market policies increased in comparison to that for 'passive' policies. In Poland, for instance, expenditure for active labour market policies jumped from 20 percent to 50 percent of total Labour Fund expenditures between 2003 and 2006; however, much of these policies are ways to artificially, and temporarily, 'delete' jobless people from unemployment statistics, and the impact for such policies for recipients' employability has remained 'very limited' (Portet and Sztandar-Sztanderska, 2008: 156). Even in the 'best scenario' of the Czech Republic (low unemployment, relatively strong welfare state and little competition from undeclared work) the results of 'flexicurity' are dubious: the number of people benefiting from Active Labour Market programs has nearly doubled between 2002 and 2007, but the total expenditure has hardly increased and the outcomes are indistinct, inducing strong union criticism (Janicko and Sirucek, 2009). The NMS figure particularly badly on a core measure of the EES and the Lisbon Strategy, i.e. lifelong learning: they are not only the countries with the smallest share of adult workers in training (4.4 percent in 2006, against the EU average close to 10 percent); they are also those with the slowest progress (a mere 0.1 percent in four years, against a two percentage point increase in the EU) (EC, 2008b).

If we analyse the NMS' National Reform Programmes (NRP, the documents member states have to elaborate every three years to comply with the Commission's 'Integrated Guidelines for Growth and Jobs'), we find regular ritual mentions to social dialogue (a requirement), but we struggle to detect any meaningful outcome from it. In 2005 Poland failed to even mention any consultation in its NRP.

In 2005, The Commission's Guideline 22 explicitly recommended collective bargaining as a tool for employment-friendly wage policy. Despite it, the Czech Republic and Poland failed to address the issue at all, not mentioning trade unions or collective bargaining in their NRPs. In the other countries, plans remained extremely vague (administrative support, information, promotion through small European Social Fund projects). The only exception in 2005 was the elaborated Hungarian programme, which had some effects in creating sector social dialogue committees and leading to the first private-sector collective agreement in construction; Romania and Bulgaria, that joined the process in 2007, also presented more specific programmes. Moreover, where they mention collective bargaining, governments betray that they are concerned, rather than with its promotion as an autonomous process, with its control from a monetaristic perspective. This is most clear in the Estonian case, which introduced a limit to minimum wage increases (contrary to the social inclusion aim claimed by the EES), which is hardly surprising given the overall Commission's and European Central Bank's predicament.

At the round of NRPs that followed in 2008, social dialogue was further diluted into more generic consultations that neglected the centrality of negotiations with employer associations and trade unions, as representatives of the core productive forces in a capitalist economy. Despite two Commission Guidelines (nr 21 and 22) calling, if vaguely, for social dialogue, the Estonian and Polish programmes do not mention either of the social partners, nor any social dialogue initiative besides a generic broad consultation. Slovenia, Hungary, Bulgaria and Romania remained the only countries to include meaningful social dialogue negotiations. In the extreme case of the Czech Republic, the unions had to express and register their formal disagreement on the 2008 National Reform Programme. It is worth citing the Czech National Reform programme's point on social dialogue for its typical top-down, monetarist-biased interpretation of social dialogue: 'Czech

Republic intends to provide quality information and analysis, which will allow for the social partners to become convinced of the need for moderate growth of salaries' (Czech Republic, 2008: 23).

## Social pacts: between façade and distortions

National-level social dialogue was not a distinctive feature of Central-Eastern Europe before EU accession: tripartite institutions had been established everywhere in the early 1990s, but their actual functioning attracted dismissive definitions such as 'illusory corporatism' (Ost, 2000), aimed at pre-empting possible union opposition. However, EU accession had been seen as an opportunity to strengthen social dialogue, part of the 'soft' *acquis communautaire*, and more specifically to promote the practice of 'social pacts'.

Social pacts are tripartite (state – unions –employer associations) agreements on income policies and the welfare state. They have been popular in Western Europe in the 1990s, especially in relation to the introduction of the EMU, and have been achieved in countries like Italy, Spain, Portugal, Ireland and Finland, They are not formally required by the EU: many old Member States have done without them. Yet, they appear to have been frequently recommended during 'peer reviews' at multiple levels, mostly by the ILO (e.g. Ghellab and Vaughan-Whitehead, 2003: 28) but also by the EU. A comparative study by the European Foundation for the Improvement of Working and Living Conditions in 2004 promoted the idea that social pacts would be the most socially acceptable way to meet the Maastricht criteria (Tóth and Neumann, 2004b), an opinion which is also expressed by academic observers (Donaghey and Teague, 2005).

The argument in such promotion was that EMU reforms (notably, meeting the 'Maastricht criteria' on inflation and public deficit) are socially costly and require some co-ordination and restraint on wages: in order to avoid social protest or uncontrolled wage demands by groups of workers (so-called 'leapfrogging', continuous wage increases prompted by workers' fears, in each company, to receive lower wage increases than their neighbours), it is best to involve the social partners in centralized, national level negotiations in the name of national competitiveness. These are particularly necessary in those countries where trade unions are dominated by the protected public sector, rather than the exposed manufacturing and export ones – and therefore, are not 'disciplined' by the market – which is exactly the case of the NMS.

These arguments have not convinced many local policy makers. In the Baltic states, macroeconomic convergence was not as compelling an issue because these young nations have not inherited high debt. In those countries, the Maastricht criteria were practically already met (Lithuania had expected to enter the EMU in 2007), apart from inflation which, in pre-credit crunch times, was not perceived as a warning sign of the underlying economic unsustainability. At the time, there was no social pact because, they said, there was no social problem, as an Estonian officer explained to me at a conference in 2007. When the Baltic bubble (caused by low-interest credit in foreign currency, dumped on the countries by foreign-owned banks thanks to the freedom of movement of capitals) eventually burst in 2008, governments started to need social pacts very much, to face protest and unpopularity, and negotiate the drastic reforms requested by the International Monetary Fund and the EU – Latvia, in the summer of 2009, cut state-sector wages by 15–27 percent, and shut down 10 percent of state schools (Rekacewicz and Rucevska, 2009). Social pacts were signed in the three Baltic states in 2009, in a situation of emergency and despite protests. But, not having made any effort to build the necessary organizational capacities and dialogue culture before, these social pacts were characterized by very poor governability capacity: cross-sector agreements that were not respected by sector-level employers and trade unions; therefore, in the public sectors hit by cuts protests and strikes went on, while in the private sector wages were not controlled. The 2009 social pacts were no more than concession bargaining, but in an ineffective way: they did not provide unions with any guarantees that concessions would be sufficient, and governments soon started planning even harsher reforms and cuts. Given such poor governability, a political crisis accompanied the economic one. Riots occurred in Riga and Vilnius, the Lithuanian government lost the elections in October 2008 (although, paradoxically, to a more pro-EU and neoliberal coalition), the Latvian one fell in February 2009.

In the Visegrád countries (Poland, Czech and Slovak Republics, and Hungary), by contrast, public debt (and to a lesser extent inflation) is an open problem, but governments have opted, rather than for social pacts, for two opposite strategies: unilateral enforcement of macroeconomic convergence, at the cost of electoral defeat (Slovakia, Poland and Czech Republic) or a Maastricht-ignoring Euro deferral in order to ensure political survival (Hungary). Even more than in the West, then, EMU entry and socio-political stability are mutually irreconcilable: you cannot satisfy at the same time the electorate on one side, and international financial institutions on the other – unless you have an instrument to involve society in the reforms, and make the latter acceptable. This is what social pacts were meant to offer, and why governments should have looked for support from the social partners. However, this has not happened. Social pacts did not occur, or they occurred in one-sided, ineffective ways.

Among the Visegrád countries, at the EU accession, only in Hungary did the government prioritize social consent to Maastricht. The socialist-liberal coalition that narrowly won the 2002 elections engaged in populist concessions and especially wage increases in the public sector, disregarding the financial implication: unilateral concessions were the main strategy for political support (which was no different from the practice of the previous rightwing government). It also experimented, in November 2005, with a sort of tripartite social pact, including a three-year minimum wage agreement and pay policy guidelines (Tóth and Neumann, 2006a). However, this pact responded to internal political considerations only (the imminent elections and the agreement between the MSzOSz union and the ruling Socialist Party) rather than EMU constraints. As a result, the government did, with an exceptional recovery of popularity, manage to win the elections of April 2006, but immediately after, it was punished by the international markets for the excessive budget deficit (7 percent) and a financial crisis followed, with the Fiorint's value falling. A few months later, when, under direct international and EU financial pressure, the same government had to introduce a real economic program of monetary convergence, social dialogue was promptly abandoned. The unions were left to protest against the government's unilateral and hard proposals, the employers considered terminating the 2005 agreement, and the president referred the draft laws on social dialogue to the Constitutional Court with the aim of setting policy free from corporatist constraints. Violent riots accompanied the 2006–07 period. A new national wage agreement was concluded in January 2007 only with much difficulty after the trade unions were threatened with the end of national negotiations. In 2008, public sector strikes hit the country and the opposition called and won a 'social referendum' against some of the reforms. Hungary's curve in the EU was symptomatic of the instability that bypassing social dialogue involves: from populism, to futile electoral success, to financial crisis, to social anger.

Slovakia's path was the opposite of the Hungarian, and shows symmetric consequences of the lack of social dialogue. EU accession was immediately followed by the deterioration of social dialogue: the conservative Dzurinda government in November 2004 repealed the Act on tripartism and replaced the Council for Economic and Social Concertation with a watered-down, consultation-only Economic and Social Partnership Council (Mansfeldová, 2007). Socio-economic reforms pleased Brussels and foreign investors, the Slovak 'flat tax' of 19 percent for VAT, income tax and capital tax became the flagship of liberal reformers across the whole region, and the country met the Maastricht criteria allowing it to enter the EMU in 2009. However, those reforms, involving drastic cuts to social expenditure, caused social discontent, from riots in 2004 to healthcare strikes in 2006, that led to Dzurinda's defeat in the 2006 elections (Bohle and Greskovits, 2010), when a coalition of populist parties from the Right and the Left came to power. The path was, then, from financial orthodoxy, to EMU success, to social discontent, to populism.

The fact that in the EMU macroeconomic social dialogue (in spite of having been mentioned in the so-called 'Cologne Process' in 1999) remains no more than a disposable, optional extra is confirmed by the fact that in the only NMS where social dialogue flourished in the 1990s and continued until 2004, it has been subsequently weakened. In Slovenia, a social pact on the EMU had been signed already in 2003, but the new right-wing government elected in 2004, while making EMU accession an urgent priority (the country became the 13th EMU member in 2007), disposed of social dialogue in favour of unilateral neoliberal and monetarist proposals. The EU had a direct impact on the deregulation of the previously corporatist Slovenia by requiring the separation of the Employer Confederation from the all-encompassing Chambers of Commerce and challenging state control on large firms, undermining in this way two important pillars of the Slovenian social model. Increased competition for foreign investment in the single market achieved the rest. The Slovenian unions were left with no other option than protesting, organizing the largest demonstration since independence in December 2005 and successfully opposing the introduction of a 'flat tax' in

2006. A new social pact was signed after EMU accession, in 2007, but under a strict subordination of social aims to the Maastricht criteria and international competitiveness considerations (especially inflation), unlike the pre-2004 social pacts that contained pay-off for labour as well (notably, generous pension reforms) (Stanojević 2010). Interestingly, the one-sided pact of 2007 (unlike those of the 1990s) was not enough for the government to avoid electoral defeat the year after. With the arrival of the crisis, and a new Centre-Left government, Slovenian social partners negotiated hard over a new social pact in 2009, but the negotiations broke down and the employers left in protest the Economic and Social Council. Europeanization may have meant the end of the Slovenian brand of corporatism.

The real EMU effects are on wage growth and public expenditure controls. Their implementation through social dialogue may have been a reasonable strategy for Western unions with large loyalty reserves, but it is dangerous for unions in NMS, which would risk losing the little popularity they have – also because the euro has lost much of its attractiveness in the meanwhile.

The point of a negative EU effect can be proved even more strongly through an *a contrario* argument. If EU regulations and policies had a positive effect, these effects should be most visible where governments are EU-committed and compliant, and least visible under EU-sceptic governments. However, the opposite is clearly the case. In Poland and Slovakia, the EU- and EMU-devoted governments were replaced, after the accession, by Euro-sceptic parties. In Poland, a coalition of chauvinistic conservatives (Law and Justice, led by the Kaczyński twins), anti-EU agrarian populists and fundamentalist extreme right (publicly naming the EU as an organization led by sodomites and paedophiles) came to power in 2005, while in Slovakia, a coalition of New Left, extreme right and nationalists (who when in power until 1998 had kept the country at the fringes of the EU integration process) formed a new government in 2006. The revulsion these governments provoked abroad has overshadowed their labour policies. The winners in the elections were supported by the largest trade unions (Solidarity and KOZ respectively) thanks to their pro-labour manifestos: the 2005 elections in Poland were portrayed as a 'solidaristic Poland versus liberal Poland' contest. While being explicitly Euro-sceptic and even refusing to subscribe to the Charter of Fundamental Rights of the EU, the Kaczyński twins showed an unusual consideration for labor rights. Even the post-communist trade union OPZZ (my interview, 2009), which cannot be suspected of any sympathy for Law and Justice, appreciates the Jarosław Kaczyński's electoral commitment never to liberalize the Labour Code, a commitment he kept and that distinguishes his governments from all previous and later ones. After coming into power, while cold-footed on EU policies, Law and Justice stopped some anti-labour proposals from the previous governments (e.g. the flat tax) and introduced more progressive measures in spite of business opposition. In Poland, these include a new Labour Code with more protection for atypical workers, more restrictive working time regulations (increased overtime bonus, limits to Sunday working), a union-friendly Information and Consultation Directive implementation, and the abandonment of the previous (EU-friendly and social-democratic) government's proposal to introduce a right to lockouts. In Slovakia, they include a steep minimum wage increase, employee-friendly working time and health and safety regulations, a reformed Labour Inspectorate, and a new bill on tripartism to advance social dialogue; moreover, a social pact on income policies and public expenditure was signed in February 2008 (Bohle and Greskovits, 2010). In both countries, measures deemed unattainable when proposed by the EU were now easily implemented by local governments responding to internal social demands.

As Hassel (2009) has argued, when comparing social pacts in Central-Eastern and in Western Europe, governments and trade unions had an interest in tripartism only in the initial phase of post-communist transformation, when they both needed legitimacy. Soon after, the strengthening of governments (allied with powerful international institutions such as EU and IMF), and the emergence of employers as a new assertive actor, have quickly marginalized social dialogue. Symbolic tripartism has allowed unions to survive as organizations, but nothing more. EU accession – and Europeanization in general in the whole of the EU – may have fostered the 'expressive' functions of concertation, and thereby guaranteed the survival of tripartism despite its apparent lack of results (Traxler, 2010). But this has happened at the cost of concertation's instrumental functions in the actual regulation of labour, and therefore the content is increasingly nebulous. In this way, while tripartite social dialogue may have contributed to limit the 'legitimation crisis' (Traxler, 2010) of the state in the region, this has happened at the cost of deepening the 'legitimation crisis' of trade unions: increasingly associated to obscure central negotiation with the elites and thereby perceived as far away from the workplaces. Social dialogue after EU accession, in this way, has reinforced the power unbalance as a structural problem to social dialogue.

The Polish case, with its instability, illustrates the point particularly clearly. Poland has been considered as the worst performer in terms of social pacts among the Visegrad countries (Avdagic, 2006). What is interesting, however, is that in Poland there had been some genuine political initiatives in terms of social pacts, by two eminent labour ministers who were keen supporters of corporatism (Jacek Kuroń and Jerzy Hausner), there was a historical tradition of national social agreements (in 1980 and 1989), and there was a clear demand for consensus over difficult labour market and welfare state reforms. However, the Polish Tripartite Commission established in 1994 has achieved no meaningful social pact (Gardawski and Meardi, 2010).

### The weakest link: multi-employer bargaining

The inclusion into existing European-level social dialogue structure is reported to have had substantial effects in promoting social partners' capacities, especially at the sector level (Kusznir and Pleines, 2008). Yet there is little evidence of any spill-over effect: the sector remains the weakest level of collective bargaining in nearly all NMS.

At least as far as wages are concerned, a precondition of co-ordinated social dialogue is the existence of multi-employer collective bargaining, which in western Europe tends to occur at the sector level. In the NMS, with the exception of Slovenia, it has been long noticed that this important prerequisite is nonexistent (Slovakia has a relatively large number of sector agreements, but of very little incidence). On the eve of EU enlargement, ILO experts had labelled sectoral social dialogue in the region as 'the weakest link, and pointed at the meager content, low coverage and poor enforcement of collective agreement (Ghellab and Vaughan-Whitehead, 2003). As explanations for this dire situation, the weakness of the social partners, the ambiguous role of the state (at the same time too interventionist and too little facilitating) and the economic environment were mentioned (*ibidem*, 15ff).

As far as the social partners are concerned, it is employer organizations that constitute the crucial pillar of multi-employer bargaining: in some western countries such as Germany, it is the strength of employer organizations that allows sectoral level collective bargaining to survive in spite of rapid weakening of trade unions. In the NMS, until recently the weakness of employer organizations was blamed on, more generically, employers' organizational weakness due to their recent (post-1989) emergence as autonomous economic actors. For instance, in her study of Polish employer organization, Kozek argues that Polish business was not strongly organized because it was still 'in a developmental state', 'fighting for survival', faced with 'the challenges of the European market and globalization', still in search of its 'ethos', and 'social identity' (Kozek, 1999: 102). Such an interpretation requires a fundamental revision: business in the NMS is not weak at all and its disorganization is not a fate, but a choice.

As Offe and Wiesenthal (1985) have argued, collective organization is actually simpler for employers than for employees. And in the NMS, it is not the weakest employers, as small and medium enterprises, who hold back organization: it is, from the beginning (as mentioned by Ghellab and Vaughan-Whitehead among others), the multinational companies, who are neither weak nor unused to employer organizations. Moreover, employer organizations actually exist, and are highly efficient in other activities than social dialogue, and especially in political lobbying – as in the case of the Polish Private Employers' Confederation (Behrens, 2004).

The point is therefore not the capacity of employers to organize, but their choice of not doing it – and the failure of the EU to set up any incentive in the opposite direction. Collective bargaining in the NMS has actually declined with EU accession, at company as well as at sector level. In Poland, for instance, the decline in registered company-level agreements has been constant: from 1,389 in 1996, to 405 in 2004, to 199 in 2008 (data from the State Labour Inspectorate). Moreover, according to the State Labour Inspectorate, there is a tendency towards the reduction of provisions that are advantageous to employees, and an increase in detrimental provisions, which have been allowed by the liberalization of the Labour Code (Państwowa Inspekcja Pracy, 2008). The decline is associated with the privatization of the economy, something the EU has encouraged without setting any safeguard for employee rights. In the same way, sector-level bargaining has declined with the retrenchment of state-controlled sectors: in 2000, in Poland there still were six significant (i.e., without including small sub-sectors) sector-level agreements in the private sector. By 2008, half of them had disappeared due to employer withdrawal: road transport, cereal processing, and steel – all sectors where major privatization took place. Only one case followed the opposite trend: previously state-owned railway workers managed to keep a sector-level agreement despite privatization. As a result all four surviving private sector agreements have their roots in the public one: railways, energy, mining, military industry.

Private employers' active disinterest in co-ordinated bargaining is clear. In Poland, employer organization representatives from the private sector explicitly exclude relations with the trade unions from their functions, and some business organizations have gone as far as to forbid agreements with trade unions (Anacik *et al.*, 2009). Gardawski (2009b: 487–8) reports the telling cases of Polish foundry, automotive and retail sectors, in which, despite union pressure and advanced negotiations, eventually employers decided to withdraw or even, to avoid any risk of having to sign anything, to dissolve the employer associations themselves. It was not the lack of organization, but the explicit choice to disorganize that prevented collective agreements.

Why, in spite of some institutional pre-condition through the discussion of minimum wages in tripartite institutions (Hassel, 2009), is collective bargaining rejected by employer organizations? Certainly, the EU has not helped: industry-wide wage negotiations were not seen as a part of the European social model but as an infringement on entrepreneurial freedom, as for example by the Klaus government in the Czech Republic from 1992 to 1997 (Bluhm, 2006; Stark and Bruszt, 1998).

Multinational companies, thanks to their 'systemic power' (Bohle and Greskovits, 2007), have been the main actors behind this decision to avoid sector-level collective bargaining. Those operating in the export sectors, in particular, set their wage references cross-nationally and they are largely uninterested in national developments. But even in the sheltered sectors, such as services, competition on wages is, rather than avoided, actively promoted by private companies – which betrays a focus on short-term predatory profit opportunities, rather than on long-term sustainable investment and competition on the basis of quality and efficiency.

If we look inside the companies, the rejection of co-ordinated social relations and social dialogue actually goes even further and has even deeper roots. For not only is wage setting decentralized towards the enterprise, but also very often towards the individual, especially in the extreme case of the Baltic states. Woolfson *et al.* (2008: 328) describe the informal individualistic approach to salary issues in Estonia, Latvia and Lithuania, which leads to a drastic re-appraisal of the real impact of collective bargaining even in those companies where it occurs. The widespread practice of 'envelop wages', constitutes a barrier against formal negotiations of wages (Williams, 2009). Wage secrecy is a very common company policy, even if it meets resistance on the employee side. The competition from the large informal sector is a major obstacle to effective formal collective bargaining. According to the most trustworthy estimates, in 2004, the informal sector accounted for between 17 percent (Slovakia) and 39 percent (Latvia) of the economy, all above the OECD High Income average of 15 percent (Schneider and Buehn, 2007). There is little evidence that this has declined: actually, according to Schneider and Buehn, if there is a trend at all, it is towards increasing informality. In Poland, the Central Statistical Office estimates that the number of workers in the informal sector has increased from 900,000 to 1.2m between 2002 and 2008, with a further increase expected for 2009 due to the economic slowdown in the formal economy (data: GUS). In Romania, a link has also been noted between emigration and informality, as circular migrants have a strengthened preference for short, informal jobs and tend to develop a 'culture of evasion' (Parlevliet and Xenogiani, 2008).

## Conclusion

The review of the accession period on social and employment issues reveals that specific choices by policy makers and employers actively constructed the enlargement as a social deregulation process, despite much talk of a European Social Model. EU law has not had the proclaimed effect of preventing races to the bottom. On some issues, as with the WT Directive, increased competition has led to more work intensification regardless of the new regulations, and in extreme cases, the new regulations have been used against their aims, with no concern with the non-retrogression clause. Overall, the disappointing effects of the 'hard' social *acquis* reveal that the problem is not simply one of 'compliance' by the NMS, but involves the easily distortable nature of the regulations itself. The enlargement test has revealed that EU regulations on working conditions are so 'soft' that they can be bent into the opposite direction. As a result, instead of convergence towards western European standards, the new member states have experiences instances of divergence (Meardi, 2012) or, later, of convergence towards the standards of Southern European countries in crisis (Kohl, 2015).

So, the race has not been towards the top, as the official story of the European common market tells. To the contrary, the enlargement has stopped social initiatives at community levels. The period starting in 2004 has obtained the definition of 'quasi-collapse' of social Europe (Barbier, 2008). The enlargement coincided with the beginning of the new, neoliberal-oriented, Barroso Commission. The two facts have been so simultaneous to be analytically inseparable: there would have been no Barroso without the NMS, and the NMS would have experienced different EU policies without Barroso.

The 'quasi-collapse' of social Europe is evident in the lack of new meaningful EU social legislation since 2004, after the twelve years of legislative activism that followed the social protocol of Maastricht of 1991 (European Works Councils, non-discrimination, part-time, temporary work, information & consultation...). No new social directives have been ratified between 2004 and 2008 – with the exception of the directives on seafarers and on workers in cross-border railways of 2005. Some long-awaited acts, such as the Directive on work-related musculoskeletal disorders, were stalled.

The increasingly adopted method of 'soft' regulation has not helped either. The EES has had a negligible impact and has been watered down and distorted concomitantly with, and in connection to, the enlargement. Social pacts have been by-passed or used very selectively. Of course, the state of social dialogue in the NMS cannot be blamed on the EU: it has deeper roots relating to the communist period and the transition phase. But the EU has not reversed the trend in any perceivable way. As a result, social dialogue in the NMS, when implemented as tripartism, has depleted trade unions of their own, fragile, legitimation. The frequently heard criticism of trade unions in the region as excessively political is therefore misplaced: the problem is not that trade unions use politics (if anything, they should have used it more, given the magnitude of the political decisions that have been made), but that politics has used trade unions – to then dispose of them. The double paradox is that while EU 'hard' policies are actually very 'soft', the 'soft' policies have accompanied very 'hard' decisions: the single market and liberalization, the road to the EMU and the Maastricht criteria, the competition for Foreign Direct Investment.

This chapter only covers the foundational period of the enlarged EU, 2004–09. Later years have revealed some divergence amongst countries in the region (Bohle and Greskovits, 2012) and presented new macro problems, from the financial crisis to the Euro crisis to the Eastern neighbourhood crisis. Yet it broadly confirms the trend. Popular disappointment with social and living conditions, despite a certain economic success, keeps emigration at very high levels, and results in Eurosceptical victories in countries once seen as the best transition performers (Hungary in 2010 and 2014, Poland in 2015). The extreme case of the Baltic countries have become even more extreme and is now presented as a 'model' to other parts of Europe, despite its very high social costs (Sommers and Woolfson, 2014). While Poland has taken over from Spain the record of highest share of temporary employment, it is no longer the CEE labour markets that become extremely precarious, but the foundations of a united Europe themselves.

## Note

1    The chapter is largely based on Chapters 1 and 2 of Meardi (2012).

## References

Amato, G. (1999) *The Long-Term Implications of EU Enlargement: The Nature of the New Border*. Florence: European University Institute.

Anacik, A., Krupink, S., Otręba, A., Skrzyńska, J., Szklarczyk, D. and Uhi, H. (2009) *Diagnoza stanu rozwoju sektorowego dialogu społecznego w skali ogólnopolskiej*. Krakow: Wyższa Szkoła Europejska im. ks. Józefa Tischnera.

Avdagic, S. (2006) *One Path or Several? Understanding the Varied Development of Tripartism in New European Capitalisms*. Cologne: MPFIfG Discussion Paper 06/5.

Avdeyeva, O. (2009) 'Enlarging the Club: When Do Candidate States Enforce Gender Equality Laws?' *Comparative European Politics*, 7(1): 158–177.

Barbier, J.-C. (2008) *La longue marche vers l'Europe sociale*. Paris: Presses Universitaires de France.

Behrens, M. (2004) 'New Forms of Employers' Collective Interest Representation' *Industrielle Beziehungen*, 11(1–2): 77–91.

Blažiene, I. (2007) *Unions Protest over Low Pay and Plan to Extend Working Hours*. www.eurofound.europa.eu/eiro/2006/11/articles/lt0611029i.htm [Accessed 4 April 2016].

Bluhm, K. (2006) 'Auflösung des Liberalisierungsdilemmas – Arbeitsbeziehungen Mittelosteuropas im Kontext des EU-Beitritts', *Berliner Journal für Soziologie,* 16(2): 171–186.

Boeri, T. and Brücker, H. (2001) Eastern Enlargement and EU-Labour Markets: Perceptions, Challenges and Opportunities. IZA Discussion Paper 256.

Bohle, D. and Greskovits, B. (2012) *Capitalist Diversity on Europe's Periphery*. Cornell: Cornell University Press.

Bohle, D. and Greskovits, B. (2007) 'Neoliberalism, Embedded Neoliberalism and Neocorporatism: Towards Transnational Capitalism in Central-Eastern Europe', *West European Politics*, 30(3): 443–466.

Bohle, D. and Greskovits, B. (2010) 'Slovakia and Hungary: Successful and Failed Euro Entry without Social Pacts.' In *After the Euro and the Enlargement: Social Pacts in the European Union*, edited by Pochet, P., Keune, M. and Natali, D., pp. 345–370. Brussels: European Trade Union Institute.

Carley, M. and Hall, M. (2008) *Impact of the information and consultation directive on industrial relations* www.eurofound.europa.eu/eiro/studies/tn0710029s/tn0710029s.htm [Accessed 4 April 2016].

Cazes, S. and Nesporova, A. (eds) (2007) *Flexicurity: A relevant approach in Central and Eastern Europe*. Geneva: International Labour Organization.

Czech Republic (2008) *National Reform Programme of the Czech Republic* http://ec.europa.eu/archives/growthandjobs_2009/pdf/member-states-2008-2010-reports/czech_republic_nrp_2008_en.pdf [Accessed 4 April 2016].

Donaghey, J., Carley, M., Hall, M., Purcell, J. (2013) *National practices of information and consultation in Europe*. Report: EF1329. Dublin: Eurofound.

Donaghey, J. and Teague, P. (2005) 'The Persistence of Social Pacts in Europe', *Industrial Relations Journal* 36(6): 478–493.

Eamets, R. (2009) 'Flexicurity specificities in small and open transition economies – The Baltic States.' In *Reconciling Labour Flexibility with Social Cohesion. The Experiences and Specificities of Central and Eastern Europe*, edited by Council of Europe, pp. 103–133. Strasbourg: Council of Europe Publications.

Eamets, R. and Philips, K. (2004) *Working Time Legislation to be Amended*. www.eurofound.europa.eu/eiro/2004/06/feature/ee0406102f.htm [Accessed 4 April 2016].

EC (2006) *Employment in Europe Report 2006*. Brussels.

EC (2008a) *Communication on the Review of the Application of Directive 2002/14/EC in the EU*. Brussels.

EC (2008b) *Employment in Europe Report 2008*. Brussels.

EC (2014) *Joint Report on Social Inclusion 2004*. Brussels.

Ellis, E. (1998) *EC Sex Equality Law*. Oxford: Oxford University Press.

EWCO (2008) *Annual Review of Working Conditions in the EU 2007–2008*. Dublin: European Foundation for the Improvement of Working and Living Conditions.

Falkner, G. and Treib, O. (2008) 'Three Worlds of Compliance or Four? The EU-15 Compared to New Member States', *Journal of Common Market Studies* 46(2): 293–313.

Funk, L. (2008) 'European Flexicurity Policies: A Critical Assessment' *International Journal of Comparative Labour Law and Industrial Relations*, 24(3): 349–384.

Gardawski, J. (2009a) 'Ewolucja polskich związków zawodowych.' In *Polacy pracujący a kryzys fordyzmu*, edited by J. Gardawski, pp. 459–532. Warsaw: Scholar.

Gardawski, J. (ed.) (2009b) 'Wstęp. Omówienie wyników badań.' In *Polacy pracujący a kryzys fordyzmu*, edited by J. Gardawski, pp. 15–50. Warsaw: Scholar.

Gardawski, J. and Meardi, G. (2010) 'Keep Trying? Polish Failures and Half-successes in Social Pacting.' In *After the Euro and the Enlargement: Social Pacts in the European Union*, edited by Pochet, P., Keune, M. and Natali, D., pp. 371–394. Brussels: European Trade Union Institute.

Ghellab, Y. and Vaughan-Whitehead, D. (eds) (2003) *Sectoral Social Dialogue in Future EU Member States: The Weakest Link*. Geneva: International Labour Office.

Gładoch, M. (2008) 'Meandry partycypacji pracowniczej w Polsce', *Dialog. Pismo dialogu społecznego*, 2: 59–64.

Hala, J. (2007) *Controversy over New Workplace Health and Safety Legislation*. www.eurofound.europa.eu/eiro/2006/11/articles/cz0611039i.htm [Accessed 4 April 2016].

Hassel, A. (2009) 'Policies and Politics in Social Pacts in Europe', *European Journal of Industrial Relations*, 15(1): 7–26.

Janicko, P. and Sirucek, P. (2009) 'Three pillars of flexicurity: the case of the Czech Republic', *Transfer*, 15(3–4): 596–603.

Keune, M. (2009) 'EU Enlargement and Social Standards: Exporting the European Social Model?' In *The European Union and the Social Dimension of Globalization. How the EU Influences the World*, edited by Orbie, J. and Tortell, L. pp. 45–61. London: Routledge.

Keune, M., and Jepsen, M. (2007) 'Not balanced and hardly new: the European Commission's quest for flexicurity', *ETUI Working Paper* 2007/01.

Kohl, H. (2015) 'Convergence and Divergence – 10 Years Since EU Enlargement', *Transfer*, 21(3): 285–311.

Kok, W. (2003) *Enlarging the European Union*. Florence: European University Institute.

Kowalik, T. (2009) *Polska transformacja*. Warsaw: Muza.

Kozek, W. (1999) 'Społeczne organizacje biznesu i jego związki w Polsce', in *Społeczne organizacje biznesu w Polsce a stosunki pracy*, edited by W. Kozek, pp. 13–102. Warsaw: Wydawnictwo B-P.

Kusznir, J. and Pleines, H. (eds) (2008) *Trade Unions from Post-Socialist Member States in EU Governance: 5 Changing Europe*. Stuttgart: Ibidem Verlag.

Leiber, S. (2007) 'Implementation of EU Social Policy in Poland: Is There a Different "Eastern World of Compliance"?' *Journal of European Social Policy* 17(4): 349–360.

Mailand, M. (2008) 'The Uneven Impact of the European Employment Strategy on Member States' Employment Policies: A Comparative Analysis.' *Journal of European Social Policy* 18(4): 353–365.

Mailand, M. and Due, J. (2004), 'Social Dialogue in Central and Eastern Europe: Present State and Future Development', *European Journal of Industrial Relations* 10(2): 179–197.

Mansfeldová, Z. (2007) *Trade Union and Employers' Associations on the Way to Multi-level Social Dialogue – Comparison between Czech Republic, Slovakia and Slovenia*. EUSA Conference, Montreal.

Meardi, G. (2012) *Social Failures of EU Enlargement*. London: Routledge.

Meardi, G. Strohmer, S. and Traxler, F. (2013) Race to the East, Race to the Bottom? Multinationals and Industrial Relations in Two Sectors in the Czech Republic. *Work, Employment And Society,* 27(1): 39–55.

Męcina, J. (2009a) 'Prawo pracy w przebudowie – kierunki i cechy ewolucji zmian w prawie pracy.' In *Polacy pracujący a kryzys fordyzmu*, edited by Gardawski, J., pp. 258–306. Warsaw: Scholar.

Morley, J. and Sanoussi, F. (2009) *Comparative Analysis of Working Time in the European Union*. Dublin: European Foundation for the Improvement of Working and Living Conditions.

Neumann, L. (2007) 'European Labour Standards' Impacts on Accession Countries: The Hungarian Case.' In *Industrial Relations in the New Europe: Enlargement, Integration and Reform,* edited by Leisink, P., Steijn, B. and Veersma, U., pp. 63–80. Cheltenham: Edward Elgar.

Offe, C. and Wiesenthal, H. (1985) 'Two Logics of Collective Action.' In *Disorganized Capitalism,* edited by Offe, C. pp. 170–220. Cambridge, MA: Polity Press.

Ost, D. (2000) 'Illusory corporatism in Eastern Europe: Neoliberal Tripartism and Postcommunist Class Identities', *Politics and Society*, December, 28(4): 503–530.

Parent-Thirion, A., Fernández Macías, E., Hurley, J. and Vermeylen, G. (2007) *Fourth European Working Conditions Survey*. Dublin: European Foundation for the Improvement of Living and Working Conditions.

Parlevliet, J. and Xenogiani, T. (2008) *Report on Informal Employment in Romania*. Paris: OECD Development Centre, Working Paper 271.

Peña-Casas, R. and Pochet, P. (2009) *Convergence and Divergence of Working Conditions in Europe: 1990–2005*. Dublin: European Foundation for the Improvement of Living and Working Conditions.

Pollert, A. (2003) 'Women, Work and Equal Opportunities in Post-Communist Transition', *Work, Employment and Society*, 17(2): 331–357.

Portet, S. and Sztandar-Sztanderska, K. (2008) 'Pologne. Indeminisation du chômage: le spectre de l'illégitimité', *Chronique Internationale de l'IRES*, 115, 147–60.

Rekacewicz, P. and Rucevska, I. (2009) 'La crise vue de Léttonie', *Le Monde diplomatique*, 666, September.

Schneider, F. and Buehn, A. (2007) 'Shadow Economies and Corruption All Over the World: Revised Estimates for 120 Countries', *Economics: The Open-Access, Open-Assessment E-Journal*, 1.

Sissenich, B. (2005) 'The Transfer of EU Social Policy to Poland and Hungary.' In *The Europeanization of Central and Eastern Europe*, edited by Schimmelfennig, F. and Sedelmeier, U., pp. 156–77. Ithaca: Cornell University Press.

Sommers, J. and Woolfson, C. (eds) (2014) *The Contradictions of Austerity: The socio-economic costs of the neoliberal Baltic model*. London: Routledge.

Spieser, C. (2009) *Institutionalising Market Society in Times of Systemic Change: The Construction and Reform of Social and Labour Market Policies in Poland in a Comparative Perspective (1989–2004)*. Florence: PhD Thesis, European University Institute.

Stanojević, M. (2010) 'Social pacts in Slovenia.' In *Social Pacts in the European Union*, by Pochet, P., Keune, M. and Natali, D. (eds), pp. 317–344. Brussels: European Trade Union Institute.

Stark, D. and Bruszt, L. (1998) *Postsocialist Pathways: Transforming Politics and Property in East Central Europe*. Cambridge: Cambridge University Press.

Surdykowska, B. (2008) 'Prześwietlanie rad pracowniczych', *Dialog. Pismo Dialogu Społecznego*, 2, 14–21.

Sztanderska, U. (2005) *Efektywna polityka zatrudnienia*. Presentation at the Conference on the National Lisbon Strategy, Warsaw, 19 December.

Tholen, J. (2007) *Labour Relations in Central Europe. The Impact of Multinationals' Money*. Aldershot: Ashgate.

Tóth, A. and Neumann, L. (2004a) *Works Councils Examined*. www.eurofound.europa.eu/ eiro/2004/01/feature/hu0401106f.htm [Accessed 4 April 2016].

Tóth, A. and Neumann, L. (2006a) *Three-year Central Agreement Reached on Minimum Wage Rises and Pay Policy Guidelines*.

Tóth, A. and Neumann, L. (2004b) *National-level Tripartism and EMU in the New EUMember States and Candidate Countries*. Dublin, European Foundation for the Improvement of Living and Working Conditions.

Traxler, F. (2010) 'Corporatism(s) and pacts: changing functions and structures under rising economic liberalism and declining liberal democracy.' In *After the euro and enlargement: social pacts in the European Union*, edited by Pochet, P., Keune, M. and Natali, D. Brussels: European Trade Union Institute, pp. 45–82.

Vaughan-Whitehead, D. (2003) *EU Enlargement versus Social Europe? The Uncertain Future of the European Social Model*. Cheltenham: Edward Elgar.

Weinstein, M. (2000) 'Solidarity's Abandonment of Worker Councils: Redefining Employee Stakeholder Rights in Post-socialist Poland', *British Journal of Industrial Relations*, 38(1): 49–73.

Williams, C. (2009) 'Illegitimate Wage Practices in Central and Eastern Europe: A Study of the Prevalence and Impacts of "Envelope Wages', *Debatte: Journal of Contemporary Central and Eastern Europe*, 17(1): 65–83.

Woolfson, C. (2006) 'Working Environment and "Soft Law" in the Post-Communist New Member States', *Journal of Common Market Studies*, March, 44(1): 195–215.

Woolfson, C. and Calite, D. (2008) 'Working Environment in the New EU Member State of Lithuania: Examining a 'Worst Case' Example', *Policy and Practice in Health and Safety*, 1: 3–29.

Woolfson, C., Calite, D. and Kallaste, E. (2008) 'Employee 'Voice' and Working Environment in Post-communist New Member States: An Empirical Analysis of Estonia, Latvia and Lithuania', *Industrial Relations Journal*, 39(4): 314–334.

# 8　The European Social Fund in Poland

## A tool for Europeanization and the redistribution of power between domestic actors

*Amélie Bonnet*

## Introduction

Since 2007, Poland has been the first recipient of structural funds among all European countries, receiving more than €67 billion in the 2007–2013 programming period, and €77 billion in the current programming period (2014–2020). The European Social Fund (ESF) accounted for €10 billion and €13 billion respectively. This represents the highest shares of all EU countries and is much higher than for any other Central and Eastern European country (CEEC) [see Table 8.1]. By the end of 2013, Poland was one of the leading CEECs in absorbing EU funds: the country had absorbed 93.3 percent of the Union's structural funds allocated to it: among CEECs, only Estonia and Lithuania achieved a higher, 95 percent absorption rate, while the average absorption rate in the EU reached 85.3 percent.

The ESF in Poland has two main roles: the first one is to help improve the labour market in favouring access to all categories of population, and to further social and territorial cohesion. The second role of the ESF is to adapt Polish employment policy to EU recommendations; in other words, to further the Europeanization process in Poland's employment sphere. While Polish GDP per capita has steadily improved since 2004, it still remains well below the EU average.[1] Social indicators like average employment, unemployment and poverty rates have also shown undeniable progress since accession.[2] But they do not reflect the profound disparities that have persisted as a historical legacy throughout the territory. The country is characterized in particular by two main territorial cleavages, one separating Western and Eastern Poland (commonly named "Poland A" and "Poland B"), another dividing urban and rural areas, which are the subject of this chapter. Rural inhabitants still represent more than one third of the Polish population and agriculture still accounts for around 16 percent of employment, according to Polish statistics.[3] The unemployment rate in rural areas in Poland (9.5 percent in 2014) is apparently close to the urban rate (8.7 percent in 2014).[4] But national and regional figures do not reflect the specificities of rural areas in this field, especially hidden unemployment – which is strongly prevalent in Eastern Poland – or high levels of unemployment that have characterized some districts of Western Poland since the closing of State farms.[5] At the same time, official employment rates in Polish rural areas (50.9 percent in 2014)[6] do not take into account undeclared work which has proliferated since the 1990's. Lastly and generally speaking, the fall of communism led to the emergence of new kinds of inequalities during the 1990's, according to age, sex, education level, handicap, etc., and to the rise of job insecurity (see Mrozowicki *et al.*, Chapter 12). Inequalities seem to be well entrenched now in Polish society, and are reflected in employment and social statistics.[7] In terms of reducing all kinds of cleavages and inequalities, the challenge for the ESF remains considerable.

The intervention of the ESF is framed by the European employment policy, which is a soft law policy. Employment policies remain a national competency in the EU, but the ESF in Member States is strongly regulated and controlled at the EU level. Consequently, and because the ESF has become the main tool of employment policy in Poland – especially as regards the development of active labour market programmes (ALMPs) – the pressure to adopt EU norms and principles regarding employment in this country may be particularly high.

This chapter questions the process of Europeanization in employment policy in Poland under the effect of the ESF, with a focus on its implementation. It is a contribution to the study of Europeanization dynamics in CEECs, but the special contribution of this chapter lies in an original approach centred on subnational levels of governance, where various types of ESF projects are organized for the local population, and on actors who implement ESF projects. Most studies dealing with structural funds in CEECs have been dedicated to institutional adaptation, multi-level governance and regionalization processes in these countries before their accession to the EU (Aïssaoui, 2005; Bailey and De Propris, 2002; Czerniekewska *et al.*, 2004; Ferry 2004; Hughes *et al.* 2004; Szlachta 2001). A few studies have dealt with the implementation of the European Regional Development Fund (ERDF) in Poland since accession, highlighting "the multifaceted nature" of the impact of EU Cohesion policy at subnational levels (Dąbrowski, 2012: 742). In the sphere of employment and social issues, however, studies have remained focused on the national level, looking at changes in national strategies, documentation or legislation (De la Rosa, 2005; Mailand, 2008; Sissenich, 2005), at domestic actors' reactions – namely national policy-makers, political parties' leaders or social partners (Gwiazda, 2011; Sissenich, 2005). But these studies tend to leave out the role of subnational actors and the potential impact of the European Social Fund. Such studies provide a limited picture of the adaptation process to EU rules and norms regarding employment in the CEECs (especially in Poland), supporting the vision of top-down Europeanization stopping at national levels. This chapter provides a brief overview of the changes produced at the micro level in Poland under the effect of the ESF.[8] In this way, it highlights the profound limits of the Europeanization process.

The first part of the chapter deals with the theoretical framework of Europeanization and the analytical grid used in this study (the "3I" approach).

The second part exposes the norms and rules of the EU in the sphere of employment, which have to be relayed by the ESF in each country. The third part provides data concerning the relevance and use of the ESF in Poland since 2004. Lastly, the fourth part presents some results from empirical studies which were conducted in 2010–2011 in three Polish regions (the Subcarpathian, West Pomeranian and Łódź regions) and were focused on rural areas. Using the "3I" approach, we analyse in particular the changes and continuities observed in public labour offices situated at the level of the districts.

## 1. The Europeanization of public policy

The theoretical framework of this chapter is the Europeanization of public policy. We use here the definition provided by B. Palier and Y. Surel (2007: 39),[9] according to which Europeanization refers to "the whole processes of institutional, strategic and normative adjustments resulting from European construction". Interactions between the different decision-levels are at the heart of the concept, and actors are considered as being able to react and influence policy in return at the EU level.

Palier and Surel's definition suggests applying the "3I" approach in order to analyse adjustment mechanisms in EU countries. This approach helps to understand in detail the transformation of public policies – in our case, under the influence of the EU – drawing on the prism of institutions, interests and ideas. It derives from the works of Peter Hall (1986, 1997) and Hugh Heclo (1994) and the three neo-institutionalisms (rational choice, sociological, historical). "Institutions" refer to resources and/or constraints allocated to domestic actors in one country at one policy level, which have been eventually produced by the institutionalization of EU decisions and tools; "interests" refer to new kinds of collective action, interactions and motivations that could be stimulated by EU rules and regulations; lastly, "ideas" refer to the diffusion of EU ideas and norms and the extent to which this diffusion affects domestic behaviour. The 3I approach is a dynamic alternative to those models which have conceived Europeanization either in a top-down way (Cowles *et al.* 2011; Börzel and Risse, 2000), or with a bottom-up point of view (Radaelli and Pasquier, 2006). The 3I approach combines both logics, considering Europeanization as a set of permanent interactions, exchanges and adjustments between the different levels of governance.

The 3I approach offers a new perspective of the Europeanization process in the CEECs, while some scholars (Schimmelfennig and Sedelmeier, 2004 and 2005) have argued that Europeanization in these countries had followed a top-down model during the pre-accession period, between 1997–1998 and 2004.[10] This followed the conditionality surrounding the *acquis communautaire*. However, Europeanization did not implement a simple top-down logic in the CEECs before they entered the EU. In Poland, employment and social policy, equality policy as well as regionalization policy, have all been shaped both by domestic legacies and actors and by the EU (Bonnet, 2014), proving that the influence of the EU on domestic structures may be challenged by alternative sources of change in the

CEECs, including the legacies of communism and post-communism. Therefore, in addition to the Europeanization theory, this chapter relies on the concept of *path dependence* (Pierson, 1993 and 2000), which highlights continuities in public policies' trajectories due to past choices and institutional contexts that frame the decisions, conceptions, resources and even actors' capacities to mobilize.

This chapter focuses on one part of the Europeanization process of employment policy in Poland, which is understood as an interaction process between the different levels of governance. We consider that the 3I approach is the most relevant analytical model to describe and explain the changes occurring in such a policy under the influence of the EU, so that our analysis will use the prism of institutions, interests and ideas, without neglecting the role of historical legacies. The next part of the chapter deals with the EU's ideas, positions and goals regarding employment policy, and which have been carried on by the ESF in Poland since 2004.

## 2. The European Social Fund and the European Employment Policy

The intervention of the ESF in Europe has much evolved since the Fund was created in 1957 with the Treaty of Rome. Three main trends have characterized this evolution: first, the amount of funds which have been dedicated to employment and social issues under the ESF has increased substantially, further raising the number of ESF projects; second, the measures and targets supported by the ESF have adapted to the neoliberal ideology, which started to shape public policies in the Western world during the 1980's (Jobert, 1994); lastly, actors who implement employment measures with the support of the ESF have grown in number and have diversified in profile, in line with decentralization policies and the move toward neoliberalism in public action. In particular, the implementation of employment and social policy has been opened to private actors, challenging the role and functions of traditional Public Employment Services (PES) in all EU countries.

The growth of ESF funds has been concomitant with rising needs in EU countries in the social sphere since the 1970's crisis, the accession of new member states to the European Community, and the expansion of the regional or Cohesion policy, which has been included in the ESF since 1986 and the European Single Act. From then on, the general budget of structural funds has constantly increased,[11] as have ESF allocations.[12] ESF financing amounts to €10 billion per year.

The ESF has relayed the precepts of the European employment policy created after the Treaty of Amsterdam in 1997, taking the form of the European Employment Strategy (EES) at first, and of the Lisbon Strategy from 2000 onwards, and is now attached to the Europe 2020 strategy. Based on the Open Method of Coordination (OMC), the EES is supposed to be more open, flexible and respectful of the diversity of member states than top-down policies. It relies on the participation and cooperation of various actors within the policy process (EU institutions, national states, public authorities, civil society, social partners, etc.) at different governance levels, especially at decentralized levels. Through its general guidelines and the recommendations that EU countries are supposed to follow, the EES defines "the nature of the debate" in the employment sphere (Mosher and Trubek, 2003: 70) and may shape the discourse at the domestic level, furthering processes of *social learning*.

The EES has exemplified the shift from "managing unemployment" toward "promoting employment" that has characterized Western employment policies since the end of the 1980's. Active Labour Market Policies (ALMPs) have been encouraged, through life-long learning, business creation, making-work pay policies, selection of target groups and the use of personalized services for job seekers. Flexibility has been promoted in combination with security and quality of jobs. From 2000 onwards, the Lisbon Strategy has framed EU employment policy as well as the use of the ESF. The Lisbon Strategy aimed to make the EU "the most competitive and dynamic knowledge-based economy in the world" and has set common goals for the whole EU until 2010.[13] Since 2014, the ESF has operated under the framework of the Europe 2020 strategy. It finances projects dedicated to training, education, entrepreneurship, social inclusion and the improvement of public administration.

The last trend that has characterized the evolution of the European Social Fund is the growing number and diversity of actors who take part in its implementation. Implementation of ESF projects is opened to a wide range of institutions and organizations, be they private, public, non-governmental organizations, self-government units, etc. This opening up has resulted from decentralization processes which have been introduced in Western Europe from the late 1980's, as well as territorialisation movements in public policies. Subnational levels have emerged as key stakeholders of public action. The role and scope of public employment services and the intervention of the States have been challenged by the inflow of external operators in policies' implementation.

All the changes carried on by the ESF concerning financial support, policy content and the governance system in the sphere of employment have affected Poland as well, upsetting actors' behaviours and relations to each other. The next part presents the organization and operations of the ESF in Poland since 2004.

## 3. The ESF in Poland from 2004 to 2013

Between 2004 and 2006, the intervention of the ESF in Poland was framed by the Sectoral Operational Programme Human Resources Development (SPO RZL).[14] This program was financed by the ESF at more than €1.27 billion. The SPO RZL was divided into three main priorities, including focus on active employment policies and professional and social integration. Actions especially targeted the young, long-term unemployed and persons at-risk-of-social-exclusion, as well as women. Most of the program was managed by the Ministry of Labour in Warsaw, only 27 percent being under regional responsibility.[15] Since 2007, the ESF has been implemented under the Human Capital Operational Program (POKL), the total allocation for Poland reaching €10 billion.

*Table 8.1* Structural funds and ESF in Poland and the CEECs

|  | BG | HR | CZ | EE | HU | LV |
|---|---|---|---|---|---|---|
| Population (million) in 2015 | 7.202 | 4.225 | 10.538 | 1.313 | 9.849 | 1.986 |
| Annual GDP (EUR billion) in 2013 | 39.940 | 43.128 | 149.491 | 18.613 | 103.216 | 23.372 |
| GDP per capita (EUR) in 2013 | 5,500 | 10,100 | 14,200 | 13,900 | 9,900 | 11,600 |
| EU funds allocations 2007–2013 (EUR billion)[1] | 6.673 | – | 26.526 | 3.403 | 24.921 | 4.530 |
| ESF allocations 2007–2013 (EUR billion) | 1.185 | – | 3.787 | 0.391 | 3.627 | 0.583 |
| EU funds absorption rates 2007–2013 (%) | 80.2% | – | 80.6% | 95% | 80.6% | 92.8% |
| EU funds allocations 2014–2020 (EUR billion) | 7.588 | 8.609 | 21.982 | 3.590 | 21.906 | 4.512 |
| ESF allocations 2014–2020 (EUR billion) | 1.521 | 1.516 | 3.430 | 0.587 | 4.712 | 0.638 |

|  | LT | PL | RO | SK | SI | EU-28 |
|---|---|---|---|---|---|---|
| Population (million) in 2015 | 2.921 | 38.006 | 19.861 | 5.421 | 2.063 | 508.191 |
| Annual GDP (EUR billion) in 2013 | 34.631 | 389.695 | 142.245 | 72.134 | 35.275 | 13 068.600 |
| GDP per capita (EUR) in 2013 | 11,700 | 10,100 | 7,100 | 13,300 | 17,100 | 25,700 |
| EU funds allocations 2007–2013 (EUR billion) | 6.775 | 67.186 | 19.213 | 11.498 | 4.101 | 347 |
| ESF allocations 2007–2013 (EUR billion) | 1.028 | 10.007 | 3.684 | 1.498 | 0.756 | 76 |
| EU funds absorption rates 2007–2013 (%) | 95% | 93.3% | 63.8% | 71.8% | 91.3% | 85.3% |
| EU funds allocations 2014–2020 (EUR billion)[2] | 6.823 | 77.567 | 22.993 | 13.992 | 3.075 | 340.226 |
| ESF allocations 2014–2020 (EUR billion) | 1.127 | 13.192 | 4.774 | 2.167 | 0.717 | 86.412 |

Notes:
1 European Regional Development Fund (ERDF), European Social Fund (ESF), Cohesion Fund.
2 ERDF, ESF, Cohesion Fund, Youth Employment Initiative.

Source: Website of the European Commission (last access on 24 September 2015), Eurostat 2015.

The POKL is divided into ten priorities, with most measures (60 percent) and funds being managed at the regional level. Priorities managed by the regions include actions for unemployed people and for people receiving social assistance (priorities 6 and 7). In this context, the ESF finances projects offering training, counselling, support and funds to start a business, psychological assistance, etc. These projects vary depending on their duration and the number of beneficiaries. Between 2008 and the end of 2013, almost 39,500 contracts were signed in Poland for implementing an ESF project within regional priorities. These contracts represented more than €7.3 billion, of which €6,4 billion came from the ESF.[16]

In 2013, municipal public institutions (including social assistance centres) were the most numerous group of actors at the ESF implementation level (25.8 percent of all project organizers). They were followed by associations and social organizations (16.3 percent), individual entrepreneurs (11.1 percent), firms (10.4 percent), district public institutions – including district labour offices – (9.5 percent), foundations (6.8 percent) and higher education institutions (4.8 percent).[17] When project organizers were not district labour offices or social assistance centres, they receive ESF funds at the end of a competition process, the amount of funds depending on the type and scope of the project submitted and on the decision of the managing authority (the regional labour office). The POKL has also designated specific target groups which should be favoured in ESF projects and competitions: women (especially women returning to the labour market after a maternity leave), young people, people aged more than 50 years old, people having a low educational background, long-term unemployed people and disabled people. In addition, the needs of rural areas in professional and social support have been recognized, and specific types of projects have been designed for local communities.

## 4. The impact of the ESF: employment governance and policy at the local level

*Applying the 3I approach: general outcomes from the empirical study*

This section evaluates the influence of the EU (through the ESF) on employment policy in Poland at the stage of implementation, where concrete measures are produced (ESF projects). As mentioned before, implementation is realized by various kinds of actors who form the sub-regional employment system. Their changes and reactions under the ESF may be analysed thanks to the 3I approach. On the basis of empirical studies conducted in 2010–2011 in three Polish regions (the Sub Carpathian, West Pomeranian and Łódź regions), and focused on rural areas, I argue that EU's impact on Polish employment policy at the implementation level does not affect local institutions, interests and ideas to the same extent. The main impact of the ESF is felt on "institutions", because for local actors the ESF means – first of all – new resources and constraints. Resources and constraints produced by the ESF, by interacting with actors' own logics and concerns, frame their scope of actions and then the outputs of employment policy. In addition, because ESF funds have been attributed to a wider range of actors since 2008, resources and constraints produced by the ESF redistribute power in employment governance. The impact of the ESF on governance relations is

observed at the level of the regions and among sub-regional actors, in their relation with the State. The role of the regions has been reinforced during the second
programming period, because they have received a higher amount of funds to
manage and have acquired wider responsibilities in terms of distribution and
monitoring. However, if the regionalization process of employment policy has
accelerated under the ESF, the regions still lack experience in developing their
own regional employment policies. Regional employment policies are mostly
declinations of the national document, the National action plan for employment
(Bonnet, 2014). The effects and limits of the ESF on the decentralization process
are also well illustrated by the case of labour offices situated in mainly rural
districts, as shown below: the dependency of labour offices toward the State has
been reinforced under ESF funds and rules.

"Ideas" are the second dimension of the Europeanization process, if we look at
changes produced by the ESF among local actors. The diffusion of EU ideas and
norms regarding employment policy is unequal however: some of them are
already well entrenched among ESF project organizers (in particular the principles of activation and entrepreneurship). But this may be explained by the
political choices that were made by Polish governments at the beginning of the
1990's (the wish to adopt neoliberal rules) and during the post-communist
decade, and not only by the intervention of the ESF. Besides, other EU norms
regarding employment are not accepted locally and seem impossible to realize in
practice in Poland, due to the specific characteristics of the labour market, in rural
areas in particular. The diffusion and realization of EU ideas is therefore hindered
by local legacies (representations and realities of the labour market). Once again,
district labour offices are the most emblematic example of the limits of the ESF
in the field of ideas, as shown below.

Lastly, "interests" are the least impacted dimension of Europeanization, especially in rural areas. Although many new actors (firms, associations, higher
education institutions etc.) have intervened in the employment sphere at the sub-
regional level since 2008, interactions between them are almost inexistent. The
intervention of the ESF takes the form of multiple, disparate and short-term
actions, which do not favour cooperation among actors on the long-term.
Relations between actors, when they exist, are of a hierarchical nature (between
project organizers and regional or State authorities), or consist in an exchange of
information or advertising. As for official partnerships between project organizers, they formally exist and seem to increase in number, especially as partnership
is considered as a strategic criterion by regional authorities when they select projects and attribute ESF funds (therefore, a project based on a partnership has a
higher probability of winning the competition). However, in many cases, partnerships are concluded rather to win the competition and funds than to establish real
collaborations. Cooperation between ESF projects' organizers and external actors
like trade unions or local employers is very limited also. Trade unions are largely
absent in rural areas in particular (Bafoil, Chapter 2), and local employers are not
systematically involved in ESF projects. In addition, actions implemented in rural
areas within the operational program of the ESF (the POKL) are not coordinated

with measures dedicated to human resources which are co-financed by the European Agricultural Fund for Rural Development (EAFRD), while EAFRD and ESF projects are sometimes very similar.[18]

The next paragraph illustrates the process and limits of Europeanization induced by the ESF with the example of labour offices situated in rural districts. We focus here on the two main dimensions of Europeanization: "institutions" (resources and constraints modifying governance relations) and "ideas" (the diffusion and realization of EU ideas and norms regarding employment policy).

## The case of district labour offices (PUP)

*ESF resources and constraints: the weakened position of the PUP in the local governance*

Since the second wave of the decentralization process in 1998–1999, public labour offices are situated at the regional and at the *powiat* (district) level.[19] According to the 2004 Employment Promotion and Labour Market Institutions Act, regional labour offices (*Wojewódzkie Urzędy Pracy,* WUPs) are responsible for drawing, defining and coordinating a regional employment policy, given national guidelines, and for distributing funds from the Labour Fund[20] and from the ESF. District labour offices (*Powiatowe Urzędy Pracy*, PUP) are responsible for designing employment programs in their territory and executing active and passive measures. Since 2004, a share of active measures in the PUPs has been co-financed by the ESF. From 2008 onwards, they have been realized in the framework of systemic projects for which labour offices have received ESF funds each year. PUPs were also allowed to apply for other ESF funds from the regional authority (the WUP) through the competitive process. Lastly, labour offices could benefit from ESF funds to modernize and improve their functioning, under specific projects dedicated to institutional capacities.

There is no doubt that the ESF has had a positive impact on these institutions until now, especially as regards financial means, equipment and staff in offices. During the first years of the programming period, ESF funds compensated the lack of financial resources in which labour offices had been confined since the reduction of State subsidies in 2004.[21] Simultaneously, labour offices could implement more active measures, and in that way they could better comply with national orientations and with the law. Lastly, offices could acquire new equipment and supplies thanks to the ESF, and hire new employees.

However, the new actors that have entered the employment sphere challenge the capacity of the PUP to implement active measures for employment. The district labour office remains the only institution which allocates unemployment benefits, and so it remains a reference for the local unemployed population. However, active measures in labour offices are much more limited in scope, access and length than in many other organizations implementing ESF projects (like firms). Due to the high number of registered unemployed, especially in rural or isolated districts, access to active measures by PUPs is limited. Training programs last only a few days per year per person and subsidies to start a business are lower than those attributed in other ESF projects. Conversely, the implementation of many other ESF projects out of the PUP increases the possibility for the population to benefit from – and even multiply – training and counselling and to receive subsidies. In addition, a share of these projects takes place closer to the local population, in small towns or even in villages. They are implemented by social assistance centres, local associations or firms located in the capital city of the region. Projects implemented out of the PUP may also attract groups of populations who are "excluded" from public services, like the "hidden unemployed" in rural areas: small farmers who own just over two hectares of land and hence do not have the right to register as unemployed in labour offices.[22] Such people can benefit from projects organized in rural towns or villages by local associations or local action groups, who adapt activities to the constraints of farm work. Lastly, projects organized out of the district labour offices may address specific local problems, like the sudden rise of unemployment due to the closure of a former State factory.[23] Contrary to non-public organizations, the PUPs do not have the possibility of reacting to such changes in the very local labour market. If the ESF has been profitable for district labour offices, it also raises questions about their efficiency and their legitimacy among the local population, highlighting the deficiencies of their actions. Generally speaking, these district institutions are very criticized by other organizations (firms, associations) and by local beneficiaries.

In addition, the ESF has been used by the State to reinforce control over district labour offices, while weakening them at the same time. Between 2010 and 2011, ESF funds allocated to the PUPs were reduced by almost two thirds. These cuts have placed many offices in uncertain positions. By the end of 2011, directors of some PUPs in the region of Łódź were worried about the future of their office, the possibility of maintaining staff and of fulfilling the missions that PUPs are supposed to carry out:

> Last year we spent around 10 million [zlotys] on active measures to fight unemployment, and this year, three. It is the same with the ESF, less funds. We had 30 percent of previous years. [...] Therefore, the situation on the labour market is getting worse, unfortunately. We see it, in particular, where few jobs are created. In areas like ours.[24]

Simultaneously, new requirements have been imposed by regional authorities on labour offices regarding ESF actions. They have concerned target groups on which labour offices should focus (disabled people, people over 50 years old etc.), and projects' efficiency, namely the percentage of people who found a job after benefitting from an ESF project. These targets and objectives have been more or less the same in the other Polish regions, indicating the primacy of State decisions over regional initiatives. In district labour offices, such targets and criteria have been experienced as new burdens imposed by the State, increasing their difficulty of performing active measures and being disconnected from local possibilities. In this way, PUPs have felt inhibited and threatened by State decisions. This feeling has been reinforced by the (still) excessively bureaucratic procedures surrounding ESF projects, although labour offices have learnt to manage them.

The huge amount of funds that were allocated to Poland through the ESF for the period 2007–2013 has resulted in the implementation of a considerable number of projects throughout the territory. And because the POKL is mainly regionalized, the majority of ESF projects are carried out at decentralized levels, and not from the State, as was the case during the former programming period. In this sense, the ESF has accelerated the decentralization process in Polish employment policy. However, the case of district labour offices highlights the limits of this process and the persistence of a centralization trend in employment policy. This trend is even reinforced by the ESF, as it is used by the State to maintain control over labour offices, and to a lesser extent, over other projects' organizers. Consequently, while the ESF has initiated an Europeanization process in Polish employment policy in terms of governance, this process remains limited and is hindered by the legacies of centralization.

*The unequal adoption of EU ideas and norms in employment policy*

The adoption of EU ideas and norms regarding employment policy in Polish district labour offices is unequal. On the one hand, directors of PUPs are all convinced of the role of active measures and entrepreneurship in the fight against unemployment. Both ideas are widespread in directors' discourses, and the use of the ESF seems to reinforce their convictions:

> We are talking about the ESF in general, that it's a greater chance for people to acquire new skills, to get grants to start their own business, according to their own ideas […]. All this, in general, furthers development. Activation and development of entrepreneurship, before everything else.[25]

In the discourse of PUP directors, activation and entrepreneurship refer to the image of a proactive individual, who is responsible of his/her own destiny, who takes initiatives and does not rely on State support (as had been the case under communism). Such a vision of individuals has been encouraged since the early 1990's by Polish governments, who wanted to adopt the neoliberal paradigm in public policies and disengage the State from social issues in particular. However, this consensus was not translated immediately into real active employment policies, due to the extent of unemployment and poverty. These phenomena have required the setting up of emergency and compensation measures that have persisted over time – in both the areas of employment and social assistance – although activation measures were introduced in employment policy from 1994 onwards, and were then consolidated by the 2004 Employment and Labour Market Institutions Act. They were also included in national employment strategies from 2000, in accordance with EU principles. Since its creation, the Labour

Fund – which finances the traditional labour market programs in labour offices (apart from the ESF) – has been mostly dedicated to passive measures, namely to providing unemployment and early retirement benefits. However, due to the intervention of the European Social Fund, active measures have predominated in overall labour market expenditures in Poland since 2008.[26]

The rhetoric surrounding activation and entrepreneurship in district labour offices is complementary to the way beneficiaries are perceived. In the directors' discourses, registered unemployed are divided into those "who really want" (to work, to search for a job, to receive training, etc.) and those "who do not want". The former are considered as legitimate beneficiaries, because they are interested in activation measures implemented by PUPs, which in turn means that PUPs can carry out their active employment policies. The latter are viewed as illegitimate and are perceived as a burden on labour offices, because they register with a PUP only to receive benefits and health protection and not to find work.[27] Consequently, they prevent PUPs from fully meeting their active obligations. According to PUP directors, some of these "passive" people work illegally.[28]

While activation and entrepreneurship are well entrenched in local discourses, the realization of these principles is hindered by local specificities like illegal work, or sometimes by State rules, like the targets and efficiency rates which have been imposed on PUPs from 2011. These norms attest to the fact that Polish employment policy has moved even closer to EU requirements, but they are not accepted by local actors. Targets are considered as excessive, especially in some rural districts. Simultaneously, the impossibility for farmers who own just over two hectares of land to register as unemployed in labour offices – these people being "hidden unemployed" because in practice, they do not earn any revenue from their farm work – is perceived in rural districts as an unjustified rule, which prevents PUPs from helping part of the population in need. Such disconnections between official targets and rules and local specificities reflect the disconnection between the State and the other governance levels in policy-making, and the persistence of a top-down approach to public policies. As Kalužná has stressed:

> Voivodships and poviats are formally consulted when drafting and amending legislation but they do not have a significant role in policy-making. […] The view that labour offices (can) hardly do more than mechanically implement the instruments defined in law has frequently been expressed in reports, as well as by staff interviewed in labour offices.
>
> (Kalužná, 2009: 20)

Efficiency rates are also a source of concern for labour offices: first, because they have difficulty implementing active measures (unemployment remains high and as stressed above, a part of the registered population is a passive population, according to PUP directors); secondly, because the absorption capacity of the labour market in rural areas is very low. Most firms are very small or are even family firms, with no capacity to hire.[29] The productive fabric of small businesses and other workplaces like public institutions are not sufficient to absorb the whole unemployed population in rural areas. In addition, a share of jobs available in rural areas is only seasonal, especially in tourism, agriculture, building, woodworking, or for example in the small sewing workshops that have proliferated since the 1990's in the Łódź region. The seasonality of employment is sometimes combined with informality. Given the specificities of the rural labour market, which no one is able to predict nor influence at the local level, district labour offices see efficiency rates as unfair rules for which the State is responsible:

> In these European projects, [efficiency] is often imposed from above. And this year the demand for efficiency is definitely very high. It is about 80 percent. It will be difficult to achieve. [...] I think that 80 percent it's too high, and it is, as we say, a little bit "too much thought up" by our ministry.[30]

Despite the difficulty of achieving targets and efficiency rates in practice, such rules oblige district labour offices to consider the real effects of their actions. But in most cases, efficiency is based on the number of beneficiaries who have found a job in the three months following the project. Beyond these three months, what happens to beneficiaries on the labour market is not measured. In addition, ESF projects are considered as efficient if the jobs obtained are based on an employment contract, a civil contract, intermittent work, or if the former beneficiary is on a probation period. All these situations in the labour market result from the "destandardization" of employment which occurred during the 1990's in Poland (in particular, and to a lesser extent in many other Central and Eastern European countries; Vaughan-Whitehead, 2005), and its continuous casualization (Mrozowicki *et al.*, Chapter 12), but they cover many different realities in terms of working conditions. If flexibility of working relations has become a norm in Poland, it has developed in combination with flexibility of working times. The latter takes the form of atypical hours (evening work, night work, weekend work), usually without any financial compensation, or it takes the form of shift work. Contrary to EU ambitions, flexibility on the Polish labour market is not combined with security and quality of jobs.[31] Yet such issues are not taken into account in the evaluation reports of the ESF.

The case of district labour offices shows the limits of the Europeanization process as an idea relating to employment. Local actors seem to be converted to the principles of activation and entrepreneurship, but activation of registered unemployed may be difficult to achieve in public labour offices, and other norms like targeting policies and efficiency rates are considered as inappropriate, due to the characteristics of the labour market (high unemployment, hidden unemployment, informal work, seasonal work etc.). Lastly, some priorities promoted at the EU level – flexibility, new forms of work organization – have completely deviated in Poland, from their original form set out by the EU. But the ESF has no impact on them. While EU ideas and targets are formally existent in ESF documentation in Poland, their execution is hindered by domestic specificities, so that cognitive Europeanization in the employment sphere is still limited.

## Conclusion

This chapter has aimed to evaluate the process of Europeanization of employment policy in Poland under the influence of the European Social Fund (ESF). The study has focused on subnational actors in rural areas, especially on district labour offices, which implement ESF projects for the local (unemployed) population. On the basis of empirical studies and using the 3I approach, we have concluded that the ESF participated in the Europeanization process of Polish employment policy through the diffusion of cognitive and institutional rules (governance relations and policy targets in the sphere of employment). However, with the example of district labour offices, this chapter has also highlighted the limits of EU influence in employment policy in Poland, when it encounters centralization practices and specific characteristics of the rural labour market. In this way, this chapter completes Mailand's conclusions (2008), which argued that Poland was among the most permeable countries to the Europeanization process in the employment sphere, because it cumulated the following characteristics: non-compliance with the European Employment Strategy before accession to the EU; a relatively weak labour market; a lack of consensus among the main actors of the employment sphere; and a strong economic (and political) dependence on the EU, especially through structural funds (Mailand, 2008: 361–363). If Polish employment policy has been permeable to the Europeanization process since 2004, this process is still hindered by domestic peculiarities that are visible only at the local level.

The conclusions here call for a more systematic analysis of Europeanization in CEECs which would be based on local experiences, especially in the employment field, when considering the common trends that characterize the CEECs, namely: lower employment rates of young people and seniors, diversified unemployment rates within the countries, high long-term unemployment, the exclusion of some categories of population from the labour market (women, the disabled, etc.). The CEECs also share a common experience concerning the transformation of employment that occurred during the 1990's, with the development of atypical employment (temporary contracts, self-employment, and shift work), which is often synonymous with hard working conditions (especially long working hours), low wages, unpaid overtime etc. As we have seen in the Polish case, the precepts of the European Employment policy may be inappropriate to local contexts and unable to answer the needs of both local institutions and populations. Moreover, the European Social Fund has no impact on the forms of employment and of work organizations that have developed in Poland. The quality of jobs obtained thanks to the ESF remains an unexplored issue at the national and European levels, so that indirectly, the intervention of the ESF helps to maintain the *status quo*. It may be supposed that EU's influence exerted through the European Social Fund is also limited in other CEECs, despite the importance of structural funds and the needs for more social and territorial cohesion in these countries.

# Notes

1   The GDP per capita in Poland represented 68 percent of EU average in 2014 (Eurostat, 1 June 2015).
2   The average employment rate in Poland reached 57.3 percent in 2004 and 64.7 percent in 2012, compared with 67.4 percent and 68.5 percent at the EU level; average unemployment rates were 19.4 percent and 10.2 percent in Poland in 2004 and 2012 respectively, compared with 9.4 percent and 10.8 percent in the EU; the average at-risk-of-poverty rate in Poland was 45.3 percent in 2005 and 26.7 percent in 2012, while the EU average was 21.5 percent and 23.2 percent those same years (Eurostat).
3   Author's calculation on the basis of Central Statistical Office of Poland (GUS 2014a, 122).
4   Central Statistical Office of Poland (GUS), Local Data Bank.
5   In the West Pomeranian region, where State farms were massively established after the Second World War, the unemployment rate in 2012 still exceeded 25 percent in 11 of the 21 existing districts (GUS, Local Data Bank).
6   Central Statistical Office of Poland (GUS), Local Data Bank.
7   For example, the female and male employment rates in 2013 reached respectively 43.4 percent and 58.5 percent, the unemployment rate reaching 10.5 percent and 9.1 percent. In the last quarter of 2013, 51.5 percent of women aged more than 15 years old were inactive, contrary to 35.6 percent of men (Central Statistical Office of Poland (GUS 2014b, 4, 6, 12).
8   This chapter is based on the author's PhD, concluded in 2014, about the implementation of the European Social Fund in Poland and its impact on women in rural areas. The PhD contains the results of empirical studies, composed of 152 interviews and conducted in the Subcarpathian, the West Pomeranian and the Łódź region in 2010–2011 (situated respectively in the South-East, the North-West and the centre of the country) (Bonnet, 2014).
9   In 2000, C.Radaelli defined Europeanization as "processes of (a) construction (b) diffusion and (c) institutionalization of formal and informal rules, procedures, policy paradigms, styles, 'ways of doing things' and shared beliefs and norms which are first defined and consolidated in the making of EU public policy and politics and then incorporated in the logic of domestic discourse, identities, political structures and public policies" (Radaelli, 2000: 4).
10   The date of 1997–1998 is considered as the beginning of the Europeanization process in the CEECs which were candidates for EU membership.
11   Namely the ERDF, the ESF, the European Agricultural Guidance and Guarantee Fund (EAGGF) until 2007, the European Agricultural Fund for Rural Development (EAFRD) since 2007. Budget of structural funds increased from Ecu 69 billion in 1989–1993 to Ecu 351.8 billion Euros for the current programming period (2014–2020) (European Commission, 2008).
12   More than €76 billion between 2007 and 2013, €86 billion for the new programming period.
13   Among others, the average employment rate at the EU level should have reached 70 percent in 2010, exceeded 60 percent in the case of women and reached 50 percent for people aged more than 50.
14   Available on: www.funduszeeuropejskie.2007–2013.gov.pl/OrganizacjaFunduszy Europejskich/Documents/SPORZL_2004_2006.pdf
15   Regions, through regional labour offices (WUPs), have managed actions dedicated to young people and the long-term unemployed. Actions targeting other groups like women have been implemented by the national ministry.
16   Ministry of Infrastructure and Development, 2014, 22.
17   Ministry of Infrastructure and Development, 2014, 23. These figures concern the whole regional priorities of the POKL, including priorities for workers and firms in

transformation and education measures (prioritiesy 8 and 9). Note that social partners do not take part in the implementation of ESF projects.

18   Projects of the EAFRD are organized for farmers (contrary to ESF projects) and consist in training courses and support for entrepreneurship in sectors derived from agriculture, like agri-tourism, which is also often encouraged in ESF projects in rural areas.

19   16 voivodships were recreated by the Act of 24 July 1998, as well as 315 rural *powiaty* (districts) and 65 cities having a *powiat* status. The municipal level (2489 municipalities or *gminy*) had been recognized by the 1990 Act, and this was the first wave of the decentralization process in Poland.

20   The Labour Fund (*Fundusz Pracy*) was created in 1989 to finance all the measures implemented by public employment services. It relies on the contributions of employers, the self-employed and the European funds, but is managed by the State.

21   This situation was due to the disengagement of the State from the funding of public labour offices that occurred in 2004.

22   The number of hidden unemployed in Poland in 2007 was estimated at 300,000 (Ministry of Regional Development 2007, 19).

23   See the examples of the lace factory in Brzozów (Subcarpathian region) and the textile factory in Zelów (region of Łódź) (Bonnet 2014, 652–653).

24   PUP of Poddębice, region of Łódź, November 14th, 2011. The ministry in question is the Ministry of Regional Development, which became the Ministry of Infrastructure and Development in November 2013.

25   PUP of Piotrków Trybunalski, region of Łódź, November 24, 2011.

26   Active measures represented 28 percent of total expenditures on employment policy in 2005, then 52 percent in 2008, 46 percent in 2011 and 49 percent in 2013. The rates concern passive measures and reached 67 percent, 39 percent, 42 percent and 42 percent respectively (the rest of expenditures being dedicated to labour market services) (Eurostat Database, consulted on Octobre 30, 2015).

27   In the rural districts of Sieradz and Wieluń (region of Łódź) in 2011, PUP directors estimated that 30 percent to 40 percent of their beneficiaries were not interested in finding a job through the labour office. In the Subcarpathian region, the inverse proportion was given by PUP directors interviewed in Brzozów, Krosno and Lesko in 2010: only 30 percent to 40 percent of registered unemployed were searching for a job (Bonnet 2014, 621–622).

28   Illegal work in Poland concerned 732,000 people in September 2010, according to estimations (GUS 2011, 15).

29   In 2014 in Poland, 96 percent of firms situated in rural areas hired less than ten employees, and only 3.5 percent of firms had between 10 and 49 employees (National Statistical Office (GUS), Local Data Bank, consulted on November 2, 2015).

30   PUP of Poddębice, region of Łódź, November 14, 2011. The ministry in question is the Ministry of Regional Development, which became the Ministry of Infrastructure and Development in November 2013.

31   See some examples in the retail trade sector and in production plants in the Łódź region (Bonnet, 2014, 717–718).

# References

Aïssaoui, H. (2005) 'L'élargissement européen au prisme des fonds structurels: vers une européanisation de la gestion publique du territoire en Pologne?', *Politique européenne*, 15: 61–84.

Bafoil, F. and Surel, Y. (2008) 'L'européanisation plurielle', in Bafoil, F., Beichelt, T. (dir.). *L'européanisation d'Ouest en Est*, Paris: L'Harmattan, pp. 299–328.

Bailey, D. and De Propris, L. (2002). 'EU structural funds, regional capabilities and enlargement: towards multi-level governance?', *Journal of European Integration,* 24(4): 303–324.

Bonnet, A. (2014). *Les effets des programmes du Fonds Social Européen pour les femmes dans le milieu rural polonais,* PhD Thesis, Paris: Université Panthéon-Assas.

Börzel, T. and Risse, T. (2000) 'When Europe hits home: Europeanization and domestic change', *European Integration online Papers* (EIoP), 4(15): http://eiop.or.at/eiop/texte/2000-015a.htm [Accessed 4 April 2016].

Cowles, M., Caporaso, J. and Risse, T. (2001). *Transforming Europe: Europeanization and Domestic Change,* Ithaca: Cornell University Press.

Czernielewska, M., Paraskevopoulos, C.J. and Szlachta, J. (2004) 'The regionalization process in Poland: an example of 'Shallow' Europeanization?', *Regional & Federal Studies,* 14(3): 461–495.

Dąbrowski, M. (2012) 'Shallow or deep Europeanization? The uneven impact of EU cohesion policy on the regional and local authorities in Poland', *Environment and Planning C: Government and Policy,* 30(4): 730–745.

De la Rosa, S. (2005) 'La méthode ouverte de coordination dans les nouveaux Etats membres. Les perspectives d'utilisation d'un outil de soft law', in Snyder, F. (dir.). *Enlargement and the new Europe after 2004,* Brussels: Bruylant, pp. 141–168.

Ferry, M. (2004) 'Regional policy in Poland on the eve of EU membership: regional empowerment or central control?', *European Policies Research Centre* No.53.

Gwiazda, A. (2011) 'The Europeanization of flexicurity: the Lisbon Strategy's impact on employment policies in Italy and Poland', *Journal of European Public Policy,* 18(4): 546–565.

Hall, P.A. (1986) *Governing the Economy: The Politics of State Intervention in Britain and France,* Cambridge: Polity Press.

Hall, P.A. (1997) 'The role of Interests, Institutions, and Ideas in the comparative political economy of the industrialized nations', in Lichbach, M.I. and Zuckerman, A.S. *Comparative Politics: Rationality, culture and structure,* Cambridge: Cambridge University Press, pp. 174–207.

Heclo, H. (1994) 'Ideas, Interests and Institutions', in Dodd, L.C., and Jillson, C.C. *The Dynamics of American Politics: Approaches and interpretations,* Boulder: Westview, 1994, pp. 366–392.

Hughes, J.R., Sasse, G., Gordon, C.E. (2004) 'Conditionality and compliance in the EU's Eastward enlargement: regional policy and the reform of sub-national government', *Journal of Common Market Studies,* 42(3): 523–551.

Jobert, B. (1994) *Le tournant néoliberal en Europe: idées et recettes dans les pratiques gouvernementales,* Paris: L'Harmattan.

Kalužná, D. (2009) 'Main features of the Public Employment service in Poland', *OECD Social, Employment and Migration Working Papers,* OECD Publishing No.80.

Mailand, M. (2008) 'The uneven impact of the European Employment Strategy on member states' employment policies: a comparative analysis', *Journal of European Social Policy,* 18(4): 353–365.

Mosher, J.S. and Trubek, D.M. (2003) 'Alternative approaches to governance in the EU: EU social policy and the European employment strategy', *Journal of Common Market Studies,* 41(1): 63–88.

Palier, B. and Surel, Y. (2007) *L'Europe en action: l'européanisation dans une perspective comparée,* Paris: L'Harmattan.

Paraskevopoulos, C.J. and Leonardi, R. (2004) 'Introduction: adaptational pressures and social learning in European regional policy – cohesion (Greece, Ireland and Portugal) vs. CEE (Hungary, Poland) countries', *Regional & Federal Studies*, 14(3): 315–354.

Pierson, P. (1993) 'When effect becomes cause. Policy feedback and political change', *World Politics*, 45(4): 595–628.

Pierson, P. (2000) 'Increasing returns, path dependence, and the study of politics', *The American Political Science Review*, 94(2): 251–267.

Radaelli, C. (2000) 'Whither Europeanization? Concept Stretching and Substantive Change', *European Integration Online Papers (EIoP)*, 4(8): http://eiop.or.at/eiop/texte/2000-008.htm [Accessed 4 April 2016].

Radaelli, C. and Pasquier, R. (2006) 'Chapter 3. Conceptual issues', in Graziano, P. and Vink, M.P. (eds), *Europeanization: new research agendas*, Basingstone: Palgrave Macmillan, pp. 35–45.

Schimmelfennig, F. and Sedelmeier, U. (2004) 'Governance by conditionality: EU rule transfer to the candidate countries of Central and Eastern Europe', *Journal of European Public Policy*, 11(4): 661–679.

Schimmelfennig, F. and Sedelmeier, U. (2005) 'Conclusions: the Impact of the EU on the Accession Countries', in Schimmelfennig, F. and Sedelmeier, U. (eds). *The Europeanization of Central and Eastern Europe*, New York: Cornell University Press, pp. 210–228.

Sissenich, B. (2005) 'The transfer of EU social policy to Poland and Hungary', in Schimmelfennig, F. and Sedelmeier, U. (eds). *The Europeanization of Central and Eastern Europe*, New York: Cornell University Press, pp.156–177.

Szlachta, J. (2001) 'Polityka regionalna Polski w perspektywie intergracji z Unią Europejską' [The regional policy of Poland in view of integration to the EU], *Studia regionalne I lokalne*, 1(5): 25–40.

Vaughan-Whitehead, D. (2005) *Working and employment conditions in new EU member states. Convergence or diversity?* International Labour Organization.

### Documentary sources

Central Statistical Office of Poland (GUS) (2011) *Praca nierejestrowana w Polsce w 2010 r.* [Undeclared work in Poland in 2010], Warsaw.

Central Statistical Office of Poland (GUS) (2014a) *Mały Rocznik Statystyczny Polski* [Concise Statistical yearbook of Poland], Warsaw.

Central Statistical Office of Poland (GUS) (2014b) *Kobiety i mężczyźni na rynku pracy* [Women and men on the labour market], Warsaw.

European Commission, Directorate-General for Regional Policy (2008) 'EU Cohesion Policy 1988–2008: Investing in People's future', Inforegio Panorama, No.26.

Ministry of Infrastructure and Development (2014) *Sprawozdanie z wdrażania Programu Operacyjnego Kapitał Ludzki 2007–2013 w 2013 roku* [Report about the implementation of the operational program Human Capital 2007–2013 in 2013], Warsaw.

Ministry of Regional Development (2007) *Program Operacyjny Kapitał Ludzki, Narodowe Strategiczne Ramy Odniesienia 2007–2013* [Operational Program Human Capital, National Strategic Framework 2007–2013], Warsaw.

Official website of the European Commission.

# 9 Trade union influence in Eastern and Central Europe, the example of the Czech Republic

*Martin Myant*

## Introduction

Analysing the position of trade unions in the societies that emerged out of state socialism requires addressing both the influence they had on the changes that took place and how they were influenced and shaped by those social changes. Both are processes of continual change. As argued in Chapter 3, there are difficulties with application of a concept of dependent capitalism to these countries. Inward investment from multinational companies has meant dependence on imported technology, but its impact on employment relations practices has been a matter of adaptation and negotiation with internal actors. Domestic business and the emergence of higher-income groups have been more important in driving politics in a neo-liberal direction. Somewhat paradoxically, economic dependence, in the form of multinational companies, has created an environment in which organised labour can retain some influence. It may therefore be indirectly helping to hold back a neo-liberal tide. This is consistent with the view of Bohle and Greskovits (2012) who, in seeking to identify and explain differences between former state socialist countries, point to relatively high levels of welfare provision in central European countries as evidence of stronger resistance to a pure and free market than, for example, in the Baltic Republics.

However, the precise influence of trade unions on the broad directions of political, social and economic development is very difficult to verify. In fact, much of the literature on unions points rather to their surprisingly low level of visibility, apparently weak and conciliatory responses to policies they could be expected to oppose and, above all, dramatic and steady declines in membership (e.g. Crowley and Ost, 2001; Myant, 2014). This contrasts with an apparently excellent position after 1989, often as the only organised force with substantial membership and resources. As the editors of one major comparative study argued, the real question seemed to be 'Why has labor been so acquiescent in postcommunist Europe?' (Ost and Crowley, 2001: 1).

For present purposes, that question should be reformulated. Despite the appearance of relative acquiescence, have trade unions been able to influence policies in identifiable ways, at least in some time periods? Have they been a part, or even an important part, of a countervailing force to a neo-liberal trend? These questions could be addressed by comparisons between countries (those with numerically stronger trade unions might be expected to have adopted different policy measures) and over time (declining membership could be associated with a strengthening neo-liberal trend). However, neither of these approaches would be adequate when development was always very complex with many possible causal factors and directions of causation. The method here is to analyse trade union influence at a more detailed level, following their ability to influence individual institutional structures and individual policies. A full comparative study of CEECs is beyond the scope of this chapter which looks specifically at the case of the Czech Republic. It differed to some extent in the degree of continuity of industrial enterprises, which helped to stabilise trade union organisation. It differed from Poland and a number of other countries in that trade unions enjoyed total organisational continuity from the state socialist past and eschewed any exclusive links with a political party or any direct involvement in politics. This gave them a strong position in 1990, helping ensure a favourable set of employment law changes at the time. Thanks also to political developments, which frequently led to governments either with minimal majorities or broadly sympathetic to the trade unions' thinking, these factors helped ensure that tripartite structures became permanent, even if not particularly influential on much of the policy agenda.

The overall effect of these differences was to give Czech unions a somewhat stronger position for influencing policies in some specific spheres. Indeed, despite steadily declining membership, their ability to wield some influence on some policy spheres remained fairly similar through the period after 1990 although the methods used had evolved and the policy challenges had changed over time.

Explaining these trends, and the apparent lack of exact harmony between influence and membership, requires two lines of analysis. The following section provides an overview of trade union organisation followed by explanations for declining membership setting out some of the key features of Czech trade unionism. That is followed by more precise analyses of influence on policy areas.

## Sources of trade union weakness

The bulk of Czech union members have been organised in unions affiliated to the Czech-Moravian Confederation of Trade Unions (Českomoravská konfederace odborových svazů – ČMKOS) which developed from transformation of the official unions of the communist period, inheriting substantial property and almost universal membership among employees. Numbers fell steadily to probably under 10 percent of the employed labour force by 2010 (Myant, 2010b: 45), a low figure relative to Western Europe, with some further decline in the following years. Bargaining coverage remained higher than this, probably falling from 80 percent in 1991–1993 – albeit with reservations as to the content of agreements referred to below – to somewhat over 30 percent of the employed labour force in 2010. Strikes were almost unknown apart from short stoppages, with well below universal participation, linked to political protests or to pay demands in the public sector. Bargaining probably was effective in securing somewhat better pay and conditions, although that is difficult to confirm from available data.[1] Union density remained highest in some branches of large-scale industry (mining, steel, motor vehicles), in public transport and in major public sector activities such as health and education. Even in these cases, membership above 50 percent in a workplace was very rare. The union presence was minimal, if not non-existent, in much of the newer service sector. This was very similar to the picture across other CEECs with differences largely reflecting the extent to which established industrial enterprises survived.

Possible general explanations for this numerical decline are set out below under four headings in the context of comparisons with other countries in Central and Eastern Europe.

## 1. The communist past

A frequent starting point (Crowley and Ost, 2001; Crowley, 2004; Kubicek, 2004; Ost, 2005), and almost self-evidently a central issue in view of the generality of decline across all former state socialist countries, is the heritage left by communism in popular thinking. At the simplest level, ideas associated with the left were discredited and denigrated and trade unionism found itself tarred with the same brush. That has been a very common theme among trade union officials and activists, but it cannot be the whole explanation. Unions that took explicitly anti-communist stands fared no better, and often significantly worse, than those that emerged from the official structures of the past.

Moreover, Czech survey data shows an increase in trust for trade unions from 28 percent in 1991 (IVVM 1995) to figures that fluctuate around 40 percent in later years, quite a good result when compared with that for other institutions (e.g. CVVM, quoted in *MFdnes* 30 October 2013). A general public perception does not seem to explain either decline or the low membership level reached.

Nevertheless, the argument here is that the heritage of state socialism is the most important factor in explaining trade unions' relative weakness, but primarily by stifling the collective representation role typically assumed by trade unions, leaving a gap of 40 years or more in which traditions of organised conflict, representation and negotiation were lost. Instead, union activity centred on social and recreational activities and benefits for individual employees (Myant, 2014). This heritage affected how unions were perceived in society and limited the numbers who could come with an understanding of, or a strong commitment to, the general ideas of trade unionism. The new activists after 1989 had to learn from scratch how to negotiate or lead protests and the post-1989 environment proved unfavourable to the emergence of a new generation of shop-floor activists. Thus the starting point for the newly reformed unions was a preference for avoiding conflict and there was very little spontaneous pressure of action from below to alter this.

## 2. Structural changes in economies

These were unfavourable to trade unionism, shifting from large-scale industry towards smaller units and service-sector activities and this has been presented as a major factor in trade union decline (e.g. Bohle and Greskovits, 2006). Detailed evidence from the Czech Republic is fully consistent with this. Where workplaces disappeared, union members disappeared with them. It is also significant that unions retained the most strength where there was the most organisational continuity. That was the case in much of the Czech engineering, steel-making and mining sectors and in public-sector activities. Indeed, the continuation of a number of large enterprises – notably the Škoda car manufacturer taken over by Volkswagen from 1991 – was arguably of disproportionate importance in the consolidation of effective collective bargaining and in the continuation of some political influence.

However, an explanation for difficulties based on changes in economic structure begs the question of why membership so signally failed to materialise in the newer sectors, why forming a union organisation in new workplaces was generally so precarious and why decline was so general, even when not obviously helped on its way by structural changes. The weakness of trade union traditions, meaning that there were few individuals willing to step forward to initiate new organisations, or often to maintain existing ones, is a background factor that interacts with structural change.

## 3. Union strategies

Tactical and strategic choices made by unions could have contributed to decline. As far as broad strategies are concerned, the top levels of Czech trade unions probably made the best choices available. International comparisons suggest that those unions that identified closely with a political party faced difficulties (Myant, 2014). Those that actively opposed market-oriented reform seemed to isolate themselves from public opinion and lose influence. Those that identified themselves most clearly with support for market-oriented reform faced serious internal difficulties. The best course, in terms of retaining membership, was to keep clear of close identification with any particular party, to keep clear of too much involvement over economic reform and to keep the main focus on employment and social policies and on more narrowly defined trade-union activities, albeit with political involvement where it related closely to issues linked to those activities.

Czech trade unions were clearly cautious towards political involvement from the start. The first aim of the emerging leadership was to break from the organisations' past as a transmission belt from the party leadership. Instead, they set a new objective of a western European model in which they would undertake collective bargaining at enterprise and sectoral levels, negotiate with government and employers at the national level through tripartite structures, but eschew any specific commitment to any one political party. There was anyway little choice at first when new parties were yet to take definite shape.

Despite this ČMKOS thinking on political issues clearly was close in later years to that of the Social Democrats (for a 'European' social model, with protection in employment and public services), albeit with some occasional differences on specific policy issues (Myant, 2010b: 27–8). Some leading figures have represented that party in parliament, but others have deliberately avoided declaring any open political affiliation. Indeed, that is often seen among members and activists as a sign of greater trustworthiness, as a sign that criticisms of a government are not based on outside political influences. Closeness to the Social Democrats is also a very common argument used by union organisations outside ČMKOS to justify their reluctance to affiliate, or their decision to disaffiliate. ČMKOS involvement in parliamentary elections therefore amounts to demonstrating parties' positions on their policy demands. It is self-evident that there is much more agreement with parties of the left, but no advice is given on how members should vote.

### 4. Union organisational structures

These have been suggested as a source of strength or weakness in comparisons across countries (Avdagic, 2005). United unions, under one centre, could be expected to have the most influence on politics. This need not be the case. Fragmentation at the top for Slovenian unions did not prevent them from clearly wielding more political influence than any others in Central or Eastern Europe (Stanojevic, 2007). Czech unions appeared well-placed in this respect with only two union confederations, ČMKOS and ASO (Asosiace samostatných odborů, Association of Independent Trade Unions). The former emerged from the pre-1989 unions. It is much the larger and it alone can provide significant expertise, outside contacts and lobbying power. ASO was formed in 1999 by unions that split from ČMKOS (Myant, 2010b: 37–8).

The continuation of union centres masks a strong tendency towards decentralisation. The need for any substantial central organisation was questioned from the start as all lower levels, aiming for the maximum distance from the centralisation of the past, sought guarantees of the greatest possible independence. As a result the new union centre lost all its previous powers over affiliates. Immediately in 1990 basic organisations asserted their independence, taking up to 80 percent of the membership dues.

A structure in which basic organisations jealously guard their autonomy, often even preventing a central union record of members, was not a structure geared towards activity and involvement, or towards ensuring members are well- and quickly informed. Nor was it a structure that facilitated concentrating resources for building organisations in new sectors and workplaces. It was a structure best suited to inertia and decline. Strikingly, it has hardly ever been questioned by union leaderships who are aware of the negative reaction proposals for centralisation of membership would receive. The model of members joining a union first and then being allocated to a basic organisation has been applied in only one, relatively small, ČMKOS affiliate.

The years since 1990 have seen as much fragmentation as merging of unions (Myant, 2010b: 25–42), with a few organisations choosing to go it alone, with a few new unions forming and a few unions leaving confederations. Behind this lies a lack of commitment to, or belief in the importance of, large and united union organisations. An 'instrumental' approach remains very strong, with unions seen primarily as bodies that provide benefits in return for dues rather than primarily bodies that provide the most powerful possible collective voice. The former task is adequately pursued in a small organisation, continuing the past emphasis on social and recreational activities. The latter is best pursued in larger organisations able to formulate and implement strategies to maximise influence.

The resulting structure is characterised by a large number of small, or very small, unions (19 of the 31 affiliates to ČMKOS in 2010 had under 10,000 members), some affiliated to one of the centres but many completely independent and existing often as single workplace organisations. There is no record of the exact number of unions, but 397 organisations were registered in 2010 with titles that included the term 'trade union' (Myant, 2010b: 56), although many of these were of trivial importance, if not completely inactive. Basic organisations were also often small, averaging over 100 members in only a couple of unions. At smaller levels an organisation's existence becomes very precarious.

A slightly paradoxical consequence of fragmentation and weakness at lower levels of trade union structures was a more prominent role for ČMKOS. It seemed to remain just as visible even while lower levels were fading from view across much of the economy. This continued prominence of ČMKOS leads into a discussion of its influence and of how far that reflects, or conflicts with, the impression left by figures on membership decline.

## Phases of trade union influence

An account of trade union influence in the Czech Republic must focus primarily on ČMKOS. Its strength and influence cannot be measured by a single numerical indicator. Nor can it be treated as a single, undifferentiated whole. It needs to be measured more flexibly in terms of results (policies adopted, wages increased, specific business decisions influenced) and these differed markedly depending on the policy sphere. Unions continued to have a strong voice on employment relations issues, but only fleeting influence on macroeconomic policy issues and very little on privatisation and industrial policies. Social and welfare issues that depend on the state budget are more difficult to assess. Trade unions have been vocal. They have not directly influenced any particular issue, but they may have had a significant indirect influence in holding the neo-liberal direction in check.

Methods used to influence policy decisions changed and developed over time. The initial hope had been that working through a formal tripartite structure would bring influence across employment relations, economic and social issues. This soon faded (Myant *et al.*, 2000). Trade unions, primarily ČMKOS, then developed methods combining lobbying – of MPs and sometimes also of ministries – with mobilisation of opinion through demonstrations and occasionally strikes.

With this their view of the centrality of tripartite bodies shifted. They were no longer seen as the core of a corporatist system but rather as one possible platform from which to influence government and to find allies. Indeed, trade unions were most effective on a policy issue when they could both show strong feeling among their members and use tripartite structures to show agreement with employers. These points are amplified below by following trade union influence through different periods of post-1989 Czech development.

The story in other CEECs would have much in common with that in the Czech Republic. Economic and social changes were broadly similar. However, a great deal depended on the specifics of national politics – which party was in power and with how secure a parliamentary majority – and on the ability of a trade union centre to find the most effective tactics in the different contexts.

## 1. Extraordinary politics, 1989–1992

Leszek Balcerowicz, the Polish Minister of Finance who formulated that country's transition strategy after 1989, used this term to describe the early period in post-communist Poland during which he saw an opportunity for a small and determined elite to impose changes that would have faced massive opposition in a mature democracy (Balcerowicz, 1995). The emphasis here is different from that of much political science literature which focuses on the development and consolidation of a political system which probably tends towards those more familiar in Western Europe. The merit of Balcerowicz's term is that the emphasis is on the massive changes that could take place and how these were made possible by the political system that did exist immediately after 1989. Understanding what happened therefore implies the need for more specification of the nature of the new elite and its thinking.

The post-communist Czechoslovak elite found its first voice through members of the new parliaments (following speedy co-options and then elections in June 1990) and in governments. It was internally differentiated, but more around broad philosophical issues and generalised interpretations of the failings of the past than around any understanding of detailed policy issues. Post-communist elites have been studied in some detail (e.g. Eyal *et al*, 1999), but more from a sociological perspective than in terms of implicit political programmes. For present purposes the following three points serve as a summary (cf Myant and Drahokoupil, 2014);

* the new elite had no experience of 'normal' policy making. They owed their prestige and trust to some record of opposing the old regime and they were concerned mostly with philosophical and general questions (democracy, market economy, liberal thinking, neo-classical economics).
* they received outside advice from international agencies but this was always adapted to fit with their critique of the communist system. Reforms were very frequently more 'radical', more market oriented and to be implemented more quickly than international agencies suggested.

- necessary changes would lead to losses for some and some opposition, if not social unrest, could be expected. In the worst case this could threaten to reverse the reform process. The conclusion drawn varied between the need for caution and compromise and the need for determination and speed with only minimal social safety nets.

In many areas of policy making, in line with Balcerowicz's characterisation, the new elite faced minimal external constraints, in the sense of opposing or correcting voices from social interests. That was not true where trade unions were concerned. In that (unique) case, there was a serious organisation that could make serious proposals. That was probably more true in Czechoslovakia than in other CEECs due to the unity and coherence of purpose of the unions there. The central point in their emerging thinking was that they supported market-oriented reforms, but looked for strong safeguards against excessive social costs. Some early programmatic documents used the term 'a socially and ecologically oriented market economy' (Myant, 1994: 75) which was seen as close to western European experience. They hoped to achieve it by negotiating protections against the effects of a free market. Indeed, in all spheres conflicts were to be resolved – before they arose if possible – by dialogue and agreement.

The key was to be collective bargaining – at enterprise and sectoral levels – and tripartite representation in line with international experience. The relevant ministers were sympathetic to this while those with a clearly neo-liberal bent were busy with economic policy issues. The legal framework was discussed in the new tripartite body, the RHSD (Rada hospodářské a sociální dohody, Council for Economic and Social Accord, formed in September 1990). There were Czech, Slovak and Czechoslovak bodies, with the federal level most important until the break-up of Czechoslovakia in 1993 after which the Czech and Slovak bodies continued. It should be added that when they emerged these were tripartite largely in name only as employers' organisations were yet to take shape in any meaningful sense.

The outcome, accepting international advice from European and international trade union bodies and from the ILO, removed a number of previous veto powers for trade unions and replaced them with protections against arbitrary dismissal, limits on working time and a legally-guaranteed framework for collective bargaining. Unions retained rights to information and consultation but not to formal participation in management.

Opposition to this degree of union influence came not from employers – there was no employers' voice in this early period – but from MPs from the emerging right who showed their colours in the crucial parliamentary debate in December 1990 (www.psp.cz). Support in parliament came from an emerging left which argued essentially that trade unions had to be given their place so as to limit the risks of social conflict. This could appear a weak argument, but trade unions too had put the view that high levels of legal protection made sense in the difficult transition period after which protection for employees could increasingly be assured through collective agreements (Myant, 1994: 64–8). They threatened a

general strike if the agreements previously reached in the RHSD were not translated into law, but it is unclear whether they could have mobilised their
membership. The vote in parliament was close, but the unions' position was
narrowly accepted. Thus in this policy sphere the voice of outside advice from
international agencies broadly triumphed over domestic advocates of neo-liberal
oriented reforms thanks to the role of trade unions and the latent threat of social
unrest.

Although the fear of major unrest or protests quickly faded, this legal framework largely remained, albeit with many revisions on points of detail. The free
market thinking swept across privatisation policy and influenced changes in
social policy, but made noticeably less headway in the employment relations
sphere after the initial changes of 1990. The key, as made clear in following
sections, was the ability of the trade union side to exert an adequate degree of
influence on an issue that was never of that great an urgency to governments – it
would have minimal effect on the key issue of the state budget – plus their ability to find common ground with important employers' representatives.

This did not apply in the macroeconomic policy sphere which saw a very rapid
rise and fall of trade union hopes of creating a more clearly corporatist framework
for policy making. A start was made for 1991 in the form of a 'General
Agreement'. Unions initially conceived of this as a grand bargain. They would
support economic reforms while the government would prevent an excessive
decline in living standards. In practice, already in 1991, the government failed to
honour promises on indexation of minimum wages and unions lacked the strength
to mount any serious protest (Myant, 1993: 193–6). That was the end of any ideas
of a global collective agreement. General Agreements were signed up to 1994, but
they were too general to mean much. The tripartite was essentially a framework
for consultations, the results of which the government could ignore if it so wished.

The reason for that failure is very clear. Union leaderships could not mobilise
opposition to the governments' policies. Indeed, union leaders themselves were
not united. Some explicitly opposed raising minimum wages, which they saw as
implying reducing pay differentials. Overall, union members held views spanning
the political spectrum but, as in society as a whole, they generally supported the
governments' economic reform policies. That applied both at the political level
and within workplaces where major reorganisations and job losses were met with
acceptance.

Trying to organise strong protests against the government at that point would
have meant isolation from the political mainstream and from much of the unions'
membership. As a leading figure in Czech unions despairingly declared in 1993,
'in our country trade unionists don't behave like trade unionists'. Instead, 'the
great majority of citizens and of trade unionists are content to tolerate the fall in
living standards' (R. Falbr, quoted in Myant, 1994: 59). A lack of interest in
openly opposing governments is broadly confirmed by opinion poll evidence and
by voting behaviour of trade union members.

The two features of a low level of employee militancy alongside a substantial
body of employment law set a relatively permanent feature of Czech employment

relations. As others have argued from different contexts, it became exceptionally dependent on the state (e.g. Kohl and Platzer, 2007). The Labour Code covered an enormous range of employment issues and possible areas of dispute such that trade union representatives referred to the law rather than to the results of local collective agreements to resolve specific disputes. The hope that collective agreements would gradually become more comprehensive and replace the need for laws was never fulfilled. This is similar to experience across CEECs and indeed in much of Western Europe.

## 2. Czech capitalism, 1993–1998

In the first years after the break-up of Czechoslovakia, the Czech Republic was ruled by coalition governments of the right. There were attempts at major changes to labour law, but the employers' side was not interested. Their main representative body was dominated by large industrial enterprises privatised either by the voucher method or by direct sale to rising entrepreneurs. They had no reason to pick a fight with unions who they saw at least partially as allies in supporting the RHSD as a channel of communication with the government. There they raised issues of tax and industrial policy, leaving employment law as a settled issue.

Collective bargaining was beginning to take shape in enterprises and taking a non-conflictual form. Agreements frequently repeated the provisions of labour law without modification and pay demands were explicitly constrained by strict wage control laws in publicly-owned enterprises up to April 1992 and from July 1993 to July 1995. Thus bargaining was pursued because it was seen as the right thing to do rather than because it followed from the need to reach agreement between conflicting parties under pressure from a groundswell of demands. By 1993 some basic organisations were starting to press for bigger pay rises, but the levels were still comfortably affordable.

Conflict between trade unions and the right-wing government was more open, starting from government attempts to amend employment law. The most important was a proposal to ban trade union representation in public administration which was dropped after negotiation (Myant et al., 2000: 729). Evidently, that was not a priority area for the government which was turning its attention to reforming social policy.

That was an important area of conflict that shaped further trade union thinking on methods of political influence. In 1994 ČMKOS opposed government plans for pension reform and used newly-created expertise to propose an alternative based on experience from other countries. No headway could be made through the tripartite RHSD. New tactics were then tried including a petition, a street demonstration and a 15-minute general strike (claiming about 10 percent of the workforce participating). The aim was to influence public opinion and hence MPs. There was some success with the latter: coalition governments with small majorities (later often minimal majorities) meant that lobbying of MPs could bring results. However, on this occasion, the government won the vote in parliament.

There is a clear contrast with the period of 'extraordinary politics'. The dispute over pensions related to quite detailed policy proposals, raising the retirement age in steps. It was not an issue coloured by abstract and philosophical debates. The outcome depended on political parties represented in parliament. They were not tightly disciplined parties, but this was no longer an issue decided by individuals driven by ideology. Many were prepared to listen to trade unions. There was not as yet a distinct business view on this issue and the reform gave little extra role to the private sector.

In response to union opposition to this pension reform, Prime Minister Václav Klaus downgrade the status and remit of the tripartite, limiting it to employment and social issues and clearly defining it as no more than a consultative body. From the trade union point of view little was lost and they made only limited protests. Employers lost more as they had been more active on economic policy issues. Klaus's target, which he referred to several times in this period, was a still further reduction into a bipartite body in which only employers and unions would meet. That would have freed the government completely from the need to consult with social partners, marking a return to the days when the elite could reign undisturbed.

He was soon forced to change his approach (Myant *et al.*, 2000). In 1997, with mounting economic difficulties and its tiny parliamentary majority under threat, the government agreed to resurrect the RHSD in its original form. This was not a response to new trade union demands but rather a pre-emptive move to limit the danger of possible labour unrest. That fear had been resurrected by a five-day strike by railway workers in February 1997, over issues of pay and restructuring, which led to major concessions from the government. Changes in the RHSD were also associated with a more conciliatory approach in general. Moves to introduce a law restricting the right to strike were dropped and a legal provision for compulsory extension of sectoral agreements to non-signatories – a power available to governments but unused after 1995 – became possible again.

The ČMKOS still staged a demonstration (claiming 100,000 participants) calling for a new government and Klaus's government did resign shortly afterwards. It is impossible to say how big a role trade union activity played. It is also unclear what unions would have done had they been ignored. There was talk of a general strike, but that would only have been a token gesture, as in 1994, with no obvious means of follow up had that too been ignored. Somewhat paradoxically, this moment of trade union assertiveness was followed by the departure of the railway workers' union from ČMKOS to form, alongside unions that had no interest in militancy, ASO as a weak confederation that made no demands on its affiliates. The railway workers complained over lack of solidarity during their strike and over the failure of ČMKOS to call for a one-hour general strike in September 1997.

### 3. Social Democrats and inward investment

Elections in 1998 led to a minority Social Democrat government followed by a coalition under that party's domination from 2002 to 2006. Union influence was affected both by political changes and by changes in economic structure.

Trade unions' political influence after 1998 was immediately helped by the government's broad commitment to the principle of social dialogue. This period saw a consolidation of methods and channels of union political influence. The RHSD grew with a substantial apparatus of commissions covering individual sectors and themes. It largely established itself as a permanent feature, fully recognised by subsequent governments, even if they were never obliged to listen to its members' recommendations.

Impending EU membership strengthened the argument that social partnership should be seen as permanent and that reinforced the permanence of the RHSD. It brought some changes to employment law, but these did not amount to a fundamental change as the 1990 framework was close to EU requirements, but any debate over employment law presented an opportunity for advocates of more substantial liberalisation. The government, dominated by Social Democrats, was not interested and nor, for reasons explained below were key employers.

However, in other respects EU accession reinforced a neo-liberal direction as it brought pressures to keep budget deficits under tight limits. These were negotiated in 2002 and included cuts in benefits and some taxes. This time union protests left them isolated. There was no particular reason for any employer to take their side. ČMKOS published a detailed argument against the government's policies, with proposals for achieving budget balance by smaller reductions in taxes on enterprises, higher taxes on top incomes and no cuts in state benefits (Fassmann *et al.*, 2004).

This was important in marking a shift towards providing a basis for a coherent alternative to a neo-liberal direction. However, it did not alter the government's position. Union opposition was then backed by a public demonstration on 13 September 2003 (claimed participation 20,000), but the government did not shift. The issue soon died as good economic growth improved the position of the state budget.

At the same time, changes in economic structure were altering the nature of the employers' voice in two different directions. On the one hand, there was a rising number of successful domestic entrepreneurs and a larger number of high-income individuals in general. That increased the attractiveness of familiar elements of the central European neo-liberal agenda, especially reductions in tax levels on high personal incomes that had been introduced a few years previously. There were also more Czech employers willing to side with right-wing politicians who were clarifying their agenda over employment law changes.

However, the collective employers' voice that was heard through tripartite structures was coming under the strong influence of multinational companies. The 'Czech' capitalists, who controlled major enterprises privatised into domestic ownership in the early and mid 1990s, left the stage after the failure of their business plans (Myant, 2003). Those enterprises either disappeared or were transferred into foreign ownership, joining the growing share of the economy controlled by multinational companies which accounted for 27.6 percent of industrial employment by 2002. The employers' organisations were similarly transformed. The most important employers' body, the SPČR (Svaz průmyslu a dopravy Česká republiky, The Union of Industry and Transport of the Czech Republic) saw the representation of Czech manufacturing employers on its highest body fall from over half in 1996 to zero in 2006 (Confederation of Industry of the Czech Republic, *Directory of Members 1996/7*, Prague, and www.spcr.cz/cz/dynamic/predstavenstvo.php). Membership shifted towards smaller enterprises while manufacturing was represented only by large German multinational companies which could lobby on their own behalf on specific issues that concerned them.

Multinational companies were likely to remain silent or even actively distance themselves from proposals for blanket labour market liberalisation. This followed logically from the position and experiences of those inward investors (Bluhm, 2007; Tholen, 2007). They generally recognised unions when they took over a going manufacturing concern, but the relationship required clarification through some important conflicts in 2001. In the most formative of these, in branches of Siemens and Bosch, unions needed to fight to ensure recognition and acceptance from management. Their principal weapon was publicity which was particularly uncomfortable for major German companies that had to answer accusations in their home country that they were imposing worse conditions in the Czech Republic.

Generally, relatively non-conflictual collective bargaining took shape in manufacturing multinational companies, as in large Czech-owned enterprises, while retailing and other service sectors frequently had no union representation. Wages in the foreign-owned manufacturing companies rose more rapidly than in the economy as a whole – albeit remaining well below western European levels – and trade unions increasingly gained a range of further benefits that went substantially beyond the minimums guaranteed by law.

These workplace relations were important to employers' positions over much of employment law. The perennial themes for some right-wing politicians, backed by some prominent Czech employers, typically included removing protection against arbitrary dismissal and limiting trade union rights over health and safety and over limitations on working hours. However, multinational companies avoided identification with this agenda. They did not need conflict in workplaces, but they did want some changes to allow for more flexibility in working hours and forms of employment, over which Czech law was often quite rigid. Unions could agree to much of this under certain conditions if other fundamentals of employment law remained unchanged. Once major employers – especially the Škoda car manufacturer owned by Volkswagen – declared a lack of interest in radical liberalisation of employment law, the voice of more ideologically-driven radicals was neutralised (Myant, 2010a: 904–5).

## 4. Return to neo-liberalism

In 2006 a right-wing government came to power, albeit with a minimal parliamentary majority, and pursued a systematically neo-liberal agenda (flat tax, higher VAT, cuts in benefits, charges for health care, increasing private role in pension provision, but no major change to employment law). ČMKOS responded with a detailed critique, which the government side ignored. Following internal discussion of tactics, the decision was for a public demonstration (23 June 2007, claimed 35,000 participants), the form of protest that became increasingly important to ČMKOS. There was even a token one-hour general strike during another major protest action in June 2008 aimed against government policies of reform of the social-benefit, tax and health systems with the claim that 900,000 employees participated in one form or another. The number was similar to that claimed in 1994, suggesting considerable ability to mobilise opinion, but the extent of enthusiastic participation cannot be estimated.

The neo-liberal drive was briefly interrupted after the economic crisis hit the Czech Republic at the end of 2008 and the start of 2009. There was a strong impact on collective bargaining in that the union side was soon accepting agreements which in many cases included no wage rises, albeit generally retaining other benefits that had been gained above the legal minimums. When conditions worsened again from 2010 there was frequently a shift towards explicit agreements trading wage restraint for guarantees of employment for a core workforce. This was a time of concern, if not fear, rather than one of determination and conflict. It was also a time of accelerating decline in membership partly because of workplace closures and partly because unions lost members' confidence as they seemed unable to defend employees' conditions.

However, political changes created new openings. The right-wing government fell in March 2009 and was replaced by a caretaker government with support from right and left. This, a government of non-party figures albeit backed by political parties, was much more open to outside opinions. The new, non-party, Prime Minister genuinely did not know how to solve the problems posed by the economic crisis. The RHSD therefore had more potential influence than ever before. This was probably the most important period since 1990 in which discussions between social partners could really have some significance.

However, the government shifted away from concern with an economic stimulus – as pressed for initially from the EU – to assuming that the crisis was being resolved, thanks to an external stimulus, and therefore that the only problem was the rising budget deficit. This was reflected in the budget proposal for 2010 (from September 2009) which included spending cuts in some areas alongside a few promises of higher spending within a previously-agreed stimulus package.

Unions and employers both shared the view that the crisis was still a serious issue and produced an emergency 21-point anti-crisis package in late 2009. After some quite tense arguments, the RHSD accepted an amended version in February 2010, with 38 points and any previous firm commitments watered down. The package included some long-standing demands from the employers' side (less administration and regulation), from both sides together (against tax evasion and corruption), primarily from the union side (including employment-enhancing investment and new housing construction) and some new demands primarily pressed from the union side for measures to stem an anticipated rise in unemployment by support for temporary reductions in working hours.

However, the wording as agreed with the government was characterised by vagueness where possible (not to implement the German *Kurzarbeit* system favoured by unions, but to 'elaborate an analysis': not to 'prepare a programme' for building houses to rent, but to prepare a realistic strategy 'after an analysis of the need'). Implementation followed only on some simple points that the government had included. The package as a whole was forgotten after parliamentary elections in 2010. Even before that, it seems clear that, without some threat of militancy from below, negotiations through the RHSD cannot change government macroeconomic or budget policies.

In 2010 a new right-wing government was elected aiming to reduce the budget deficit by cutting spending. Thus, although not a member of the Eurozone and not facing serious budget deficit problems by international standards, the Czech government took up with enthusiasm the new EU policy of fiscal restraint. Unions representing public sector employees and ČMKOS responded with street demonstrations. Discussions in the RHSD continued as regularly as before, but the government had no need to, and did not, agree to proposals for alternatives from either employers or trade unions. Demonstrations organised by ČMKOS increasingly took up slogans of general opposition to government policy as a whole. Participation also increased, up to claims of 50,000.

ČMKOS also strengthened its intellectual input, producing in 2012 a substantial programmatic document, following on and building from analyses produced over the preceding months and years, which contained an analysis of the economic situation and proposals for the future [launched 2 July 2012, www.cmkos.cz/studie-ekonomicke-analyzy-prognozy/3444-3/vize-cmkos]. These centred on an active anti-crisis plan, keeping the budget deficit to 3 percent of GDP, and raising tax revenues by measures against corruption and tax evasion plus some increases in direct taxation.

Taken together, public demonstrations plus programmatic documents suggest that trade unions were claiming a place at the centre of resistance to the neo-liberal direction of policies, seeking to influence and persuade political parties, other organisations and public opinion. By no means all of the membership were enthusiastic. There were continual divisions between unions in public and private sectors over the value of protests and continual worries over excessive involvement in politics. The ultimate test of its positive impact would be adoption of, or continuing adherence to, these policy directions by political parties and then their subsequent electoral success. Parliamentary elections in October 2013, following the breakdown of the previous right-wing coalition largely precipitated by scandals and abuses of power such that any impact of trade union activities remains unclear, were followed by a coalition in which Social Democrats were the largest force. That promised a period of greater dependence on social dialogue, but the nature of the coalition limited the scope for major changes in state budget policies.

## Conclusion

Czech trade unions have become and remained substantial organisations able to formulate policies and to press their views by mobilising part of their membership in public demonstrations. They changed over the years after 1989 both as a result of changes in society and as a result of changes in their own approach. They lost membership but developed methods of working that gave them a continuing ability to influence at least some policy areas. Piecing together the implications of this for assessing their actual level of influence requires an analysis both of individual policy spheres and of the changes in Czech society and politics that shifted the environment in which unions operated.

The sphere of clearest impact was employment law on which the main union centre retained influence throughout the period. The unions' position was strengthened by unity in union aims, by support from membership and by the lack of any determination from opponents to bring changes. The reasons for this are partly that, albeit for different reasons in different time periods, a number of major employers preferred harmony with trade unions to conflict over an issue that promised them very limited gains. A further reason was that employment law was never that important to governments as, unlike neo-liberal reforms of social services, it did not hold out prospects for reducing state spending. EU accession was not crucial in terms of formal requirements as the western European example had been broadly embodied into employment law changes in 1990. However, a vaguely-defined European social model remained a continual reference point for Czech trade unions to justify a degree of resistance to liberalisation of employment law.

The state budget sphere, meaning public spending and taxation policies, was a clearer test of the trade unions' ability to wield influence. Pressure for reform in a neo-liberal direction strengthened over the years as it acquired a clearer and stronger social base, both in growing numbers of high-income individuals and in growing diversity of the Czech business community. This was strengthened by EU pressure for fiscal restraint. Trade unions remained the largest mass organisations, but they increasingly operated in a political environment alongside business lobby groups and business-related experts.

Attempting to influence the state budget sphere led unions to develop tactics that combined work in tripartite bodies, lobbying MPs and mobilising public opinion. The impact of the first two of these was relatively clear. The impact of public demonstrations is harder to assess, not least because they tended to be staged after other methods had failed. They had no visible impact on right-wing governments, but public demonstrations could still warn a government to be cautious in future. They could also influence public opinion and hence future election results, particularly when backed up by proposals for alternative policies.

Thus Czech trade unions have changed in many respects since 1989. Society and politics are very different from that early period and the trade union reaction to those social changes leaves them, as at the start, ambiguously placed as part of a potentially broad labour movement while also avoiding explicit identification with any particular political party. In some policy spheres their influence is demonstrable while in others it is either absent or impossible to demonstrate with certainty. It is therefore unclear how far they have contributed to making the Czech Republic more resilient than its neighbours to pressures towards a more neo-liberal policy direction.

# Note

1 Estimating the so-called relative wage effect is complicated by the difficulties in controlling for other variables, such as skill levels. Evidence used by some ČMKOS-affiliated unions suggests pay about 5 percent higher where collective bargaining is established (e.g. Souček, 2006).

# References

Avdagic, S. (2005) 'State-labour Relations in East Central Europe: Explaining Variations in Union Effectiveness', *Socio-Economic Review*, 3(1): 25–53.

Balcerowicz, L. (1995) *Socialism, Capitalism, Transformation*, Budapest: Central European University Press.

Bluhm, K. (2007) *Experimentierfeld Ostmitteleuropa? Deutsche Unternehmen in Polen und der Tschechischen Republik*,Wiesbaden: Verlag für Sozialwissenschaften.

Bohle, D. and Greskovits, B. (2006) 'Capitalism without Compromise: Strong Business and Weak Labor in Eastern Europe's New Transnational Industries', *Studies in Comparative International Development*, 41(1): 3–25.

Bohle, D. and Greskovits, B. (2012) *Capitalist Diversity on Europe's Periphery*, Ithaca: Cornell University Press.

Crowley, S. (2004) 'Explaining labor weakness in post-communist Europe: Historical legacies and comparative perspectives', *East European Politics and Societies*, 18(3): 394–492.

Crowley, S. and Ost, D. (eds) (2001) *Workers after Workers' States: Labor and Politics in Postcommunist Eastern Europe*. Lanham, MD: Rowman & Littlefield Publishers.

Eyal, G., Townsley, E. and Szelenyi, I. (1999) *Making Capitalism Without Capitalists: Class Formation And Elite Struggles In Post-Communist Central Europe*, Verso.

Fassmann, M., Pelc, V. and Vintrová, R. (2004) *Mýty, lži a pověry českých reforem veřejných financí*, Prague: Pohledy.

IVVM (Institut pro výzkum veřejného mínění) (1995) *Důvěra občanů v některé instituce*, Research Report 9510, Prague: IVVM.

Kohl, H. and Platzer, H-W. (2007) 'The Role of the State in Central and Eastern European Industrial Relations: The Case of Minimum Wages', *Industrial Relations Journal*, 38(6): 614–635.

Kubicek, P. (2004) *Organized Labor in Postcommunist States: From Solidarity to Infirmity*. Pittsburgh, PA: University of Pittsburgh Press.

Myant, M. (1993) *Transforming Socialist Economies: The Case of Poland and Czechoslovakia*, Aldershot: Edward Elgar.

Myant, M. (1994) 'Czech and Slovak Trade Unions', in M.Waller and Myant (eds), *Parties, Trade Unions and Society in East-Central Europe*. Ilford: Frank Cass, 59–84.

Myant, M. (2003) *The Rise and Fall of Czech Capitalism,* Cheltenham: Edward Elgar.

Myant, M. (2010a) 'Trade Union Influence in the Czech Republic since 1989'. *Czech Sociological Review*, 46(6): 889–911.

Myant, M. (2010b). *Trade Unions in the Czech Republic*. Brussels: European Trade Union Institute.

Myant, M. (2014) 'Economies Undergoing Long Transition: Employment Relations in Central and Eastern Europe', in A. Wilkinson, G. Wood, and R. Deeg, *Oxford Handbook of Employment Relations: Comparative Employment Systems*, Oxford: Oxford University Press, pp. 359–384.

Myant, M. and Drahokoupil, J. (2014) 'The road to a distinct system? The development of the welfare state in the Czech Republic', in Voráček,E. and Zudová-Lešková, Z. (eds), *Theory and Practice of the Social State in Twentieth Century Europe*, Prague: Institute of History, Czech Academy of Sciences.

Myant, M., Slocock, B. and Smith, S. (2000) 'Tripartism in the Czech and Slovak Republics', *Europe-Asia Studies* 52(4): 723–739.

Ost, D. (2005) *The Defeat of Solidarity: Anger and Politics in Postcommunist Europe*, Ithaca: Cornell University Press.

Ost, D. and Crowley, S. (2001) 'Introduction: The Surprise of Labor Weakness in Postcommunist Society', in Crowley and Ost (eds), *Workers after Workers' States: Labor and Politics in Postcommunist Eastern Europe*. Lanham, MD: Rowman & Littlefield, pp. 1–12.

Souček, J. (2006) 'Kampaň na podporu kolektivního vyjednávání podnikových kolektivních smluv na rok 2007', *Kovák*, 27, 25 August, http://archiv.oskovo.cz/kovak/2006/PDF/kovak27.pdf [Accessed 4 April 2016].

Stanojevic, M. (2007) 'Trade Unions in Slovenia', in Phelan, C. (ed.), *Trade Union Revitalisation: Trends and Prospects in 34 Countries*. Oxford: Peter Lang, pp. 347–362.

Tholen, J. (2007) *Labour Relations in Central Europe: The Implications of Multinationals' Money*. Aldershot: Ashgate.

# 10 Building and reshaping social dialogue in the CEECs

## From formal Europeanization to new dependencies in Bulgaria and Romania

*Violaine Delteil and Vassil Kirov*

## 1. Introduction

Just after the political changes of 1989, the Central and East European Countries (CEECs) undertook a vast programme of reforms as part of the transition from planned to market economics and from totalitarian government to democracy. This "great transformation" involved serious political risks, including the thorny "transition dilemma" (Bohle and Greskovitz, 2006) of pursuing reforms with high social costs while building democracy. Far from being secondary, the establishment of bodies for social dialogue, actively encouraged by the International Labour Organisation (ILO) and involving new and reformed union and employer organisations, has in fact been as a valuable lever for promoting social peace and providing political legitimacy to governments. From the early years of transition, most countries opted for tripartism, setting up frameworks to structure collective bargaining at the sector and company level. The start of accession negotiations to the European Union (EU), at the end of the 1990s, and especially the adoption of the *acquis communautaire* provided a new instrument for promoting institutional convergence with this central component of the European social model (ESM).

The construction of a new system of industrial relations (IR) took place within the delicate context of the transition to democracy and the difficult international reintegration of poorly competitive economies. It involved new actors in specific roles and strategies that were not easily comparable with those in Western Europe and which only partly achieved the hoped-for process of Europeanization. Europeanization does exist formally, but in practice, real convergence is quite strongly qualified in terms of the functioning of structures and their regulatory capacities.

At the end of the 1990s and in the early 2000s, several voices identified the limits of a form of "façade tripartism" or indeed an "illusionary corporatism" (Ost, 2000). In many sectors, branch level regulation was an "empty shell". Collective bargaining at company level, which developed strongly in the early 1990s, especially in state enterprises, has declined steadily. With hindsight, social dialogue at all levels has mainly acted to maintain social peace (Petkov, 2015), providing bargaining coverage and employee representation in a small share of companies.

This qualified assessment confirms the limited power of the EU to structure IR, which has run progressively into two major obstacles: i) the resistance and reinterpretation of exogenous rules by local actors, whose original strategies (aimed especially at institutional or political survival) were often far from consolidating community social regulation; and ii) the ambivalence of European governance, whose flexible rules on IR are sometimes contradicted by the mandatory rules favouring economic competitiveness (Meardi, 2007), and which increasingly supports the neoliberal agenda of international institutions and foreign investors.

The outbreak of the crisis in 2007 has hit the economies of the region hard, affecting IR at several levels: tripartism has often been reactivated, but is increasingly instrumental and limited to being a tool for political communication (Bernaciak, 2013; Myant, Chapter 9). Collective bargaining regulation has been variously challenged.

Bulgaria and Romania joined the EU in 2007. In many ways, they have been emblematic of the limits of Europeanization in IR, due to endogenous and exogenous dependencies. These range from: path dependency, that goes back to their Communist inheritance as well as their relatively late and chaotic transition which eroded the regulatory powers of public authorities; to new external dependencies shaped by markets, multinational companies (MNCs) and international institutions (led by the EU). Bulgaria and Romania are paragons of "dependent capitalism" associated with "weak states" (Bohle and Greskovitz, 2012), illustrated by poorly competitive and weakly regulatory economies, and even nurtured by the "low road" Europeanization which the Commission has more evidently supported during the crisis.

This chapter aims to complement the literature which is almost exclusively focused on Central Europe (Ost, 2000; Toth, 2001; Crowley, 2004; Myant 2010). It is based on a comparative study of these two South-East European countries, drawing on numerous interviews conducted over the last two decades. Alongside the specificities of the individual paths taken by Bulgaria and Romania, the chapter highlights the common traits of their more "peripheral" capitalism, compared to Central Europe. This includes: i. the extensive, and apparently paradoxical use of tripartism until the crisis, which contrasts with its progressive marginalisation in Central Europe; and ii. the particularly marked and persistent deficit in regulation at all levels (i.e. the macro, meso and decentralised levels). This research confirms the limits of European convergence.

The chapter focuses on the modalities of the Europeanization process in IR and its limitations. It begins with a brief review of the literature (Section 2), which is followed by an analysis of the recomposition of IR since the early days of the transition (Section 3). Section 4 extends this to the last crisis. The last section concludes with a twofold interpretation of the observed limits of "low road" Europeanization.

## 2. The limits of institutional convergence in "dependent capitalisms"

This section reviews the contemporary literature, and examines the power of the EU to structure IR in Eastern Europe. It is not exhaustive, but concentrates on contributions which inform our own hypothesis and analysis.

### 2.1 The very selective transfer of the EU industrial relations model

Research summarising the social Europeanization of the CEECs stresses the ambivalent impact of the EU on the national social models of Eastern Europe and the limits of convergence (Vaughan-Whitehead, 2003; Meardi, 2007; Contrepois *et al.*, 2011).

The relativity of "top-down" Europeanization conducted by the EU follows three principal factors. It refers primarily to the limits of the structuring power of "hard law" (EU Directives), and even more so of "soft law" (guidelines, recommendations, good practice, etc.). The hard law has imposed new forms of protection on the new Member States, and in some cases has blocked attempts at deregulation: for example, in Romania, where first employers and then governments tried to raise the legal working time to 60 hours per week in 2005. Usually, however, the broad room for interpretation left to the transposition of directives has limited harmonisation to a minimum. Lastly, in some cases, the acquis communautaire has actually allowed legislation to roll back social policy and restrict union rights, as concerning the Directive on employee representation in several countries in the region (Meardi, Chapter 7). Not surprisingly, soft law has had limited influence in supporting the convergence of standards, procedures or practices, such as in correcting the subordinate place accorded to social partners in the governance of "national plans for employment" (Meardi, 2007), or even in disciplining governments for complying with negotiated social pacts. More surely, soft law has participated in diffusing new cognitive schemes, by which the new instrumental interpretation of social dialogue by the EU underpins the function of such dialogue as a "tool for carrying out change" (Maggy-Germain, 2007).

Secondly, and in a corollary manner, "top-down" Europeanization is also running into the (implicit) limits of the European project concerning institutional convergence. This lack of resolve is borne out by the fact that injunctions to comply with EU practices by the CEECs have been revised downwards. This follows the implicit contract which gives the new Member States greater institutional permissiveness in order to guarantee their attractiveness and competitiveness, and at the same time offers great opportunities for foreign direct investment coming from the older Member States (Pilat, 2007). An indicator of this tacit agreement is the fact that the malfunctioning of social dialogue identified by the Commission in regular pre-accession reports never constituted a reason for blocking negotiations or imposing sanctions, as was the case in other fields.[1]

The political project linking EU enlargement and liberal globalisation is also reflected in the asymmetric governance of the EU, whereby economic regulation, armed with strict standards, has indirectly induced competition between European territories and social models, especially given gaps left by indicative social regulation (Meardi, 2007).

Lastly, Europeanization is also running up against institutional or cultural resistance by influential domestic actors who are faced with imported institutions which are neither internalised nor desired by them. East European tripartism was actively encouraged by the ILO (Aro and Repo, 1997), and then the EU. But it is a clear illustration of the distortion or "conversion" (Thelen, 1999) of exogenous standards. This tripartism has been taking place in a context and with an original set of actors that have no equivalent in Western Europe. It has become a kind of "illusionary corporatism" (Ost, 2000/2010), or "communication corporatism" (Bernaciak, 2013), a formal corporatism with a high instrumental value, in which the goals of political legitimacy tend to override regulatory objectives (Delteil, 2016).

EU structural funds are rarely mentioned in the analysis of social Europeanization, but they have also played a significant role (even if indirectly) in influencing the revision of IR systems. The fact that access to European funds is conditional to the participation of social partners in the management of programmes has been a powerful incentive for unions to be involved in social partnership, at all levels of government. Yet, as cooperation among social partners is mainly directed towards employment policy (the fight against discrimination, informal labour etc.), which is generally an area of consensus and highly time-consuming, union efforts are diverted away from pursuing industrial action (Petkov, 2015; Delteil, 2016).

Despite the limits of "top-down" Europeanization, the forces promoting a "bottom-up" approach have had little influence. In Western European MNCs, the project of establishing minimum standards in human resource policies within companies has only very selectively favoured a transfer of employment rules to East European subsidiaries: firms generally seek to exploit the institutional or informal permissiveness of host countries to obtain competitive advantage (Contrepois *et al.*, 2011).

On the other hand, membership by Eastern European unions of European or international union organisations has tended to lead to the acculturation of those "new" union actors, without however leading to the sustainable structuring of transnational union cooperation. Within firms, both in- and outside European works councils, cooperation has remained limited to a few MNCs, led by major car and energy companies (Delteil and Dieuaide, 2010). East European employee representatives (unionised and independent) have generally been fairly passive at the different levels of the European social dialogue (Kirov, 2015; Safta-Zecheria, 2015).

## 2.2 *"Dependent capitalisms" and "weak states"*

Bulgaria and Romania joined the EU in 2007, three years after the countries of Central Europe, and clearly showed the large "distance" of their social models vis-à-vis the "European social model". This stands out in two characteristics of

Bulgarian and Romanian capitalisms which differ from the other CEECs. The first relates to the "semi-peripheral" (Bohle and Greskovitz, 2012) or "dependent" (King, 2007; Nölke and Vliegenhart, 2009) nature of capitalism in the Balkans. Both countries are indeed marked by a more peripheral (and later) integration into EU trade networks and the global value chains controlled by Western multinationals, compared to their Central European neighbours.[2] Further specificities relate the greater dependence on foreign capital flows subject also to a larger volatility, as confirmed during the crisis. Lastly, these economies have been structurally under supervision by supranational institutions since the 1990s: either via a Currency Board as in Bulgaria which was set up under the influence of the International Monetary Fund (IMF) in 1997, or through repeated financial assistance programmes in Romania, the last one providing implicit support and expertise for an unprecedented offensive by centre-right forces to dismantle labour and social dialogue legislation in 2011 (Delteil and Banarescu, 2013).

The second characteristic relates to the weakness of public authorities and hence "weak States" (Bohle and Greskovitz, 2012), which are defined by the authors as specificities of the Balkans. "Weak States" are characterised by the scarcity of financial and cognitive resources and the incapacity of States in mediating interests, disciplining capital, filtering the demands of elites and the power of lobbies and even by weaknesses in guaranting respect for laws. Administrative and cognitive weaknesses are far from being secondary and contribute to external dependency. They enhance the need to turn to outside expertise, and open up channels of influence to international and private organisations (foreign investors and chambers of commerce, as well as to domestic oligarchic-style companies). These affect public agendas and reforms. Poor arbitration capacities across interests and the lack of correction of imbalances by public authorities also shape tripartism. "Weak States" relay "strong governmental power" in negotiations with social partners, as a limiting result the possibilities of more balanced regulation that could be seen as more-or-less legitimate (Delteil, 2016). Furthermore, "weak States" also limit the institutional complementarities likely to support economic performance and in fact provide scope for: the expansion of the informal economy, collusion of business and politics, corruption, as well as the capture of resources by private actors and organised crime, all of which in turn weaken the State and reduce its resources structurally.[3]

## 2.3 The original positioning and weaknesses of social partners

The theoretical debate on Central and Eastern Europe has largely examined the strengths and weaknesses of social partners, especially unions.

Unionisation rates (or membership of employer organisations) provide an initial indicator. They began to fall at the start of the transition, declining from levels of nearly 100 percent throughout Eastern Europe to rates now found in Anglo-Saxon countries. Within the CEECs, Romania and to a lesser extent Bulgaria stand out in having fairly high union membership: 33 percent and 20 percent respectively.[4] Romania's situation has even been consolidated in the last

10 years, linked to a slight rise in unionisation supported by (pre-electoral) job creation in the public sector in 2007 (see Table 10.1). Recent data, however, confirm lower membership in 2012, in both countries.[5]

Yet a union audience only translates very imperfectly into the ability to influence politics (Borisov and Clarke, 2006; Meardi, 2007). This is especially true in the CEECs, and this picture also is also linked upstream to the limited capacity of unions to organise and represent employee interests within companies (Crowley and Ost, 2001; Ost, 2001/2010). The failure by unions to play their role fully is undoubtedly also a consequence of the previous regime and anti-communist dissidence, and reflects forcefully the heuristic power of the "path dependency" approach. The rejuvenated unions and those created *ad hoc*, some of which (like Podkrepa in Bulgaria) contributed to establishing politically liberal forces, have unanimously accepted the risky game of cooperative tripartism. They have *de facto* condoned reforms weakening social policies, in the name of "social partnership", recalling their preference of cooperation instead of open conflict (Spasova, 2015).

These specific features along with unions' low organisational and cognitive resources explain low unionisation rates, and more generally the limited investment on the ground and lack of industrial action. This observation has been radicalised by the expression of "labour quiescence" (Crowley and Ost, 2001), which in our opinion is biased by analysis that was centred first on Poland, marked by the early conversion of Solidarity into a political force.

In contrast, the debated impact of the concentration or fragmentation of unions on their influence has not led to unanimity in the literature. Comparisons have significantly qualified Crowley's thesis (2004: 412) concerning the link between

*Table 10.1* Trade union membership figures, 2003–2012

|          |             | 2003      | 2008      | 2012      |
|----------|-------------|-----------|-----------|-----------|
| Bulgaria | CITUB       | 393,191   | 328,232   | 275,762   |
|          | CL Podkrepa | 106,309   | 91,738    | 88,329    |
|          | Promyana    | 58,613    | 50,000    | n.a.      |
|          | Others      | 10,000    | 6,000     | n.a.      |
|          | Total       | 568,113   | 475,970   | 364,091   |
| Romania  | CNSLR Fratia | 800,000  | 800,000   | 306,486   |
|          | Cartel Alfa | 325,000   | 400,000   | 301,785   |
|          | BNS         | 375,000   | 375,000   | 245,527   |
|          | CSDR        | 345,000   | 345,000   | n.a.      |
|          | CSN Meridian | 170,000  | 170,000   | 320,204   |
|          | Others      | 20,000    | 30,000    | n.a.      |
|          | Total       | 2,035,000 | 2,120,000 | 1,174,002 |

Source: www.eurofound.europa.eu/sites/default/files/ef_files/docs/eiro/tn0904019s/tn0904019s.pdf and www.eurofound.europa.eu/observatories/eurwork/comparative-information/national-contributions/romania/romania-industrial-relations-profile.

fragmentation and union weakness. In some cases, the hegemonic position of a union, as in Slovenia, the Czech Republic or Slovakia, provides relatively more power to a bi-polar model than that found in Poland or Bulgaria. But other examples as found in Romania, which combined high union fragmentation with relatively strong political influence of unions prior to the crisis, suggest a more multi-causal approach should be mobilized. Part of the explanation concerns the level of union politisation or the force of politico-union coalitions which some authors view as implicit channels of influence that are often more effective than tripartism (Delteil, 2016), whereas others view these primarily as a force for delegitimising unions (Glassner, 2013).

Institutional rules also play a determining role in framing and limiting the right to strike, while government measures may render protest action useless (Varga and Freyberg-Inan, 2014). Economic factors (crises, unemployment but also migration) should not be forgotten, as they have participated in neutralising much union negotiating power. Lastly, the external dependence of East European types of capitalism is reinforced by employment opportunities in Western Europe which have strengthened *exit* strategies at the expense of *voice* (Meardi, 2012).

Another indicator of unionisation can be found in the low number of strikes or other industrial action, which merits underlining. Though the data are too poor to make comparisons, figures on industrial conflicts (especially working days lost to strikes) confirm the continous fall of industrial action in the region.

The number of days lost in strikes and other conflicts was relatively high at the start of the transition in the CEECs (Ekiert and Kubik, 1998), but action was concentrated in certain sectors (Bafoil, 2006:442–443): the public sector (especially education and health), transport, and mining (as in Romania). The fall-off in action is very clear in Romania. According to the ILO, there were 85 strikes in 1999, 8 in 2005 and only 2 in 2006.[6] The crisis has only marginally and sporadically led to more conflict, concentrated at the national level and so to the detriment of action in companies. According to estimates by Bulgaria IR Profile (Eurofound), only 6 strikes were recorded between 2011 and 2013.[7]

Lastly, the (relative) weakness of unions is to be associated with the weak coordination of IR systems, resulting especially from a deficit of regulation at the branch level. In a majority of CEECs, branch committees have largely remained "empty shells", indicating clearly the unsuccessly spread of the European social model, and incidently the EU priority placed on macro (tripartism) and micro (company) social dialogue.

Along with the scarcity of mechanisms for extending collective bargaining agreements (or their lack of application), this finding explains the weakness and erosion of the share of employees covered by collective agreements. The CEECs stand well below the average of the old Member States.[8] In Bulgaria, collective agreements covered 40 percent of employees in 2002, 30 percent in 2008 and 25 percent in 2012–2013.[9] The retrenchment in Romania came later and was more brutal, linked to the dismantling of the Code for Social Dialogue (see Section 3), with coverage collapsing from 82.5 percent before the crisis to 35–40 percent in 2012–2013. But these results must be analysed: in Bulgaria for example, many sectoral agreements provide very few clauses compared to the minimums set out in the Labour Code.[10]

Upstream, such weak regulation also reflects the singularity of the employer organisations and its positioning in the IR system. Employer organisations which did not exist under the former regime, do not play the role attributed to them in West European economies. They are reticent about being involved in social dialogue, especially in negotiations, and in general refuse to be affiliated with sectoral federations. While "avoiding" social dialogue, employer organisations in Eastern Europe are by contrast strongly engaged in lobbying, seeking to influence politics directly or through informal channels. This strategy of avoiding regulatory bodies is also shared by foreign direct investors who prefer to benefit from the institutional permissiveness of the region, and their ability to lobby States. Employers' strategy of withdrawal is important to the impoverishment of sectoral regulation. More generally, it also reduces the empowerment capacities of unions and employers to act as counterveiling forces in the face of governments' instrumentalisation of tripartism.

## 3. The originality of industrial relation models up to 2007

The gap between IR models in Western and Eastern Europe stems less from the nature of formal rules than from the specific roles played by the parties involved (States, employer organisations and unions). It also follows from imbalances in power in a socio-political context that has marked the long transition and integration process into Europe by these post-socialist states. These realities are borne out clearly by Bulgaria and Romania, and highlight the specificities of tripartism and IR at company level.

### 3.1 The recomposition of actors based on original roles and strategies

The unions bring together several organisations including: former unions like the Confederation of Independent Trade Unions in Bulgaria (CITUB), which has tried to free itself of Communist Party control since the early 1990s (Kirov, 2005) or the CNSLR-Frăţia in Romania, as well as new protest unions such as the CL "Podkrepa" in Bulgaria or Cartel Alfa in Romania. However, while Bulgaria has been characterised by a bipolar union scene since the transition, the union landscape in Romania is far more fragmented, with five confederations: CNSLR-Frăţia, BNS, CSDR, CNS Cartel Alfa and Meridian each with a considerable number of affiliated federations.

For Bulgaria, the specificity of CL Podkrepa needs to be emphasized, as the union was a co-founder and active partner in the Union of Democratic Forces (SDS), a liberal organisation. For the CITUB, the situation is even more complex. According to surveys by the ISTUR in 2000, the new decade saw 40 percent of this union's members vote for the Bulgarian Socialist Party, and another 40 percent vote for the SDS. Such political preferences and the commitments of the unions to a strategy of neutrality help explain their support for cooperation in social dialogue. It must also be recalled that until the early 2000s, the CITUB promoted the view that MNCs were beneficial in transferring the ESM, and were more virtuous than domestic companies. The union's view was changed later (ISTUR, 2008).

If the unions have managed to preserve as certain strength in terms of membership, despite the fall in unionisation rates, their legitimacy is nevertheless declining. This is true for their political and electoral legitimacy (*input legitimacy*)[11] which has been battered by politisation, corporatism and even the corruption of certain organisations.[12] It is also true for results (*output legitimacy*), which have been tarnished by the cautioning of unpopular reforms promoted via tripartism.

As elsewhere in the region, employers are poorly structured and "avoid" engagement. They often refuse to follow negotiation practices, especially at the sectoral level. There has been a proliferation of employer organisations in both countries. During the 1990s in Bulgaria, the Bulgarian Chamber of Commerce (BIA) and the Bulgarian Chamber of Commerce and Industrie (BCCI) were joined by two organisations representing SMEs. Subsequently, the Bulgarian Confederation of Employers and Industrialists (CEIB) and the Association of Bulgarian Industrial Capital (ACIB) emerged, drawing together privatisation funds and large companies. In Romania, the number of national employer organisations which had become representative, signing parties to national collective agreements rose from 5 in 2001 to 13 in 2008.

### 3.2 Intermittent and instrumental tripartism

Tripartite social dialogue was precocious in Bulgaria, and late in Romania. It has been stamped by the hegemonic power of government, and the weak autonomy and influence of social partners. Tripartism has been activated when political needs dictate, in order to legitimate reforms that are socially sensitive, and/or to neutralise forces of potential protest. Tripartism has moreover been characterised by intermittent use, interrupted frequently by the return to government unilateralism (Kirov, 2005).

Compared to the other CEECs, however, such tripartism is less of a facade. This can be explained by the conjunction of two factors: firstly, political volatility, which tends to delegitimise politics, pushing the government to find another source of legitimacy in enlarged (tripartite) governance, ameanable to share responsibility for painful reforms. Secondly, the "weak State" and its weak regulation capacity. This hinders the applicability of reforms and limits *de facto* the risk run by government, employer groups and unions in committing themselves to concerted social negotiations.

In Bulgaria, tripartism took off in the 1990s, with the creation of a first tripartite body, named the National Commission for the Coordination of Interests (NCCI). In August 1990, the government, the unions and the employers signed an Accord to resolve urgent social problems, stemming from the economic crisis. On 18 January 1991 (on the eve of shock reforms), an agreement ensuring industrial peace was signed. On 13 June 1991, an agreement to pursue the application of economic reforms and to preserve social peace was signed. It contained three chapters relating to stabilisation, employment, income and social security, restructuring and privatisation.

This institutionalisation of tripartism may be viewed as the result of two main factors: on the one hand, the strong electoral volatility which until the 1996–97 crisis encouraged governments to share their responsibility for reforms, along with social partners (Bernaciak, 2013); and on the other hand, the strategies of the two main union confederations which associate a legitimation strategy constructed via their participation in the "social partnership", and the desire for emancipation from actors linked to the communist past, as illustrated by the CITUB (Kirov, 2005). Breaking this link deprives the unions of informal contacts in politics and means that formal connections have to be activated.

Though the unions are favourable towards cooperation, consultation is nevertheless conflictual. On several occasions they have protested against government action by withdrawing from tripartism (in 1994 and for longer in 1996), or by rejecting the tripartite pact put forward by the Socialists who returned to power in 1995. The financial crisis in 1996–1997 and supervision by the IMF and the World Bank via the Currency Board changed the whole situation, by encouraging the government to seek support for its austerity programme from the social partners. Following this strategy, the latter entered several agreements in 1997: the "Memorandum for priority joint activities" put forward by the Union of Democratic Forces under external pressure (the agreement launched the first major privatisation programme), the "Charter for Social Cooperation" which aimed to ensure industrial peace during this phase of accelerated reforms and privatisation, and to provide social partners with the guarantee of participating in the revision of legislation.

As of 1997, tripartism intensified further, reflecting a "real partnership" nationally, according to the social partners (Kirov, 2005). It showed itself especially in the preparation of social reforms. The social partners were also active in working groups putting forward amendments to the Labour Code (revisions in 2001). This legislation is considered to be balanced in terms of labour flexibility and workers' protection. In Bulgaria, the subsequent period was characterised by the failure of negotiations in signing the collective bargaining agreement of 2002. This was followed by a revival of social dialogue relating to the necessity of making labour legislation conform to the *acquis communautaire* (finalised in 2006), and organising the management of structural funds. The renewed social dialogue led to the signing of a "social pact" in 1997, aimed at preparing EU membership and supporting growth. The pact led to a proliferation of tripartite commissions connected with efforts to absorb structural funds. These commissions emerged "at all levels" of government (central, regional and local), and operated on the basis of minimalist consultation.

In Romania, tripartism was not established before its first, late political transition, and then led to an ambitious and painful programme of reforms in 1997 and 2000. Romania also oscillated between the signing of agreements and breakdowns in tripartism. The tripartite agreement was challenged by the Cartel Alfa union in 2000 (with support from the EU, which exceptionally criticised the modalities of negotiation). This was followed by the signing of social pacts in 2001 and 2002 concerning wages, before a new impasse was reached in 2004, and subsequently the new "social pact for stability" signed the same year.

A long-running battle over the Labour Code began in 2003. It too illustrated the way the tripartite structure was overtaken in the negotiation of reforms, by a wider economic game which included explicitly the intervention of external forces. This reform aimed at deregulating the labour market, drawing on arguments of EU harmonisation, and it pitted two opposing forces against each other. On the one hand, strong union resistence which benefited from support by the leftwing of the Social Democratic Party, and by a majority of domestic employer organisations, which represented major companies receiving direct or indirect support from public authorities (Trif, 2008). On the other hand, outside actors (the IMF, World Bank, the American Chamber of Commerce, etc.) put new and ever greater pressure on the public policy debate. The social forces won this battle, but as soon as the ink was dry on the signed agreement, the outside actors launched a new offensive, making a series of calls for deregulation. This was rapidly picked up by a neoliberal coalition of SME entrepreneurs and conservatives (Ban, 2013: 24). In the process, the IMF used the financial assistance agreement signed with Romania in 2004 to include labour market deregulation in its loan conditions, prior to mandating the World Bank to formulate legislative proposals and to pressing the government to adopt these by the end of the Standby agreement. Along similar lines, the Council of Foreign Investors lobbied for the obligation of employers to negotiate with unions representing workers to be dropped from the new Labour Code (Trif, 2014: 3). When the new conservative government came to power in 2005, it initially gave assurances to the international lenders, before these promises were challenged by union mobilisation which obliged the government to negotiate a new Labour Code that was relatively favourable to workers in 2006 (Pilat, 2007). Tripartism therefore only confirmed reforms that were discussed and negotiated outside the arena of social dialogue.

After these years of intermittent tripartism, and during the euphoria of strong growth and EU membership, Romanian and Bulgarian tripartism led to the signing of longer term social pacts (2007–2010), oriented towards EU harmonisation and support for growth and competitiveness.

Tripartism has thus been facilitated by EU promotion, which took over from the ILO. But in its East European version (excepting Slovenia), it remains different from the models and experiences identified in Western Europe since the 1980s.[13] It can be distinguished from the "neo-corporatism" of Scandinavian countries, based on the autonomy and strength of the social partners, and which has led to relatively balanced regulations centred on flexicurity (associated with wage discipline). It is also different from the tripartism found in Ireland and Italy in the 1990s and which aimed at fiscal discipline and/or qualification for Economic and Monetary Union (Avdagic *et al.*, 2011).

The functionality of tripartism is more directly political in the CEECs, less assured in its regulatory capacity and less favourable to social forces. It can be associated with an extreme version of "demobilised macro-corporatism" (Baccaro and Howell, 2010), used to define South-West European tripartism. The East European one is characterised by strong governmental intervention, less cooperation on behalf of employers, and often less powerful influence by unions.

Upstream, the singularity of tripartism in the CEECs is inseparable from the existence of "weak States", which do not provide unions with the same guarantees that their demands are taken into account in the arbitration of public policies. It is also marked by the structural weakness of union legitimacy and a lack of resources, encouraging unions to take part in tripartism and "social partnership" at the cost of industrial action. As a result, the IR systems in Bulgaria and Romania continue to differ clearly from Slovenia, which remained the unique example of neo-corporatism in the CEECs.

### 3.3 Sectoral and company level social dialogue: the formal transfer and deviations from the European model

Another difference of the Western and Eastern IR systems concerns sectoral social dialogue, defined as the real "weakest link" (Ghellab and Vaughan-Whitehead, 2003). Here, as well as at company level, an examination of the formal criteria of IR systems shows up several types of malfunctioning linked to the coverage and content of collective labour agreements (CLAs) and sectoral tripartite cooperation.

In Romania, a high share of employees was covered by collective agreements, up until the reform of the Code on Social Dialogue in 2011. But this coverage was high only from a formal point of view, which did not prevent there being a deficit in the regulation of concrete practices in a certain number of sectors (Trif, 2014). As Trif has claimed (2014), it was hard to impose the application of CLAs even before the crisis, and even sometimes labour law, especially concerning low-wage workers.

In Bulgaria, certain sectors (the public sector, education, health and heavy, privatised industries) are covered by CLAs (at branch and firm level). But they are often minimalist, merely "cut-and-paste" versions of the Labour Code. Other sectors that are important in terms of employment, such as hotels and catering etc., are not covered by CLAs. The importance of the informal economy and informal practices in both countries are powerful vectors of deregulation in a certain number of sectors and firms, because these practices strip collective agreements of their real usefulness.[14] The actual application of collective agreements at branch and company level is also problematic.

In contrast to sectoral regulation which is often lacking, it is important to mention the clear rise of sectoral tripartism. In both Bulgaria and Romania, this manifests itself by the creation of consultative councils under the supervision of various ministries. As of the 2000s, it is possible to identify more than 80 tripartite sectoral bodies, whose activity is limited to consultations and is often "intermittent" and mainly activated by ministries as laws are put forward.

For its part, collective negotiation at company level was reactivated in the early 1990s. It covers a wide range of issues, including employment conditions, levels of pay, health and safety, training, the exercise of union activities and so on. The unions have had to acquire negotiation skills which did not exist previously, and have indeed accumulated considerable experience in this area since the middle of the 1990s.

The State often intervenes in such company compromises, during privatisations, and imposes employment guarantees in certain cases, under pressure from the unions. But these promises only generally apply to a fraction of jobs. In Romania, for example, where State intervention has been clearer than in Bulgaria, privatisation contracts have often allowed two thirds of jobs to be cut, through the use of significant compensation for voluntary departures (as in the case, for example, of GDF and Dacia; see Delteil and Dieuaide, 2010). Moreover, repeated promises to save companies made by governments are very relative and contingent on strong political and economic instability leading States to give up previous commitments.

Lastly, company level practices especially highlight the limits of the Europeanization of employment rules, be it over health and safety conditions, working time, the use of social dialogue, or employee representation which was especially emblematic of differences in legal obligations.

This is illustrated in Bulgaria for example, where Europeanization of employees' representation was long postponed, especially by unions, due to fears of competition, hostile policies and intervention by employers. It finally took shape in the Labour Code of 2006 (when Directive 2002/14/CE was transposed into national law, shortly before entry into the Union). However, the possibility for employee representatives with information consultation rights to be elected is not obligatory (Kirov, 2011). As a result, the application of EU legislation on information and consultation remains limited in Bulgaria. Studies show that after nearly five years of the law being in place, only 10 percent of companies actually have elected employee representatives (Mihaylova and Mikova, 2011).

In Romania, Directive 2002/14/EC was adopted by Law 476/2006.[15] It came into force on 1 January 2007, when the country joined the EU. According to Eurofound analyses, the execution of this legislation has been hard at company level. So even if the law stipulates that information and consulation are obligatory, it does not provide for application mechanisms, and so it remains a missed opportunity, as is the case in Bulgaria. The Directive on European works councils for its part obliges representatives to be designated in the East European subsidiaries of MNCs, though this does not lead to real union leverage for these new representatives. They were initially discrete and sometimes even close to local management, and had limited impact on a "managerial social dialogue" that is largely orchestrated by management (Delteil and Dieuaide, 2010).

## 4. Crisis, the acceleration of reforms, the reassertion of tripartism as a means for legitimising reforms and deregulation

The crisis which began in 2008–2009 has badly affected both countries. At the start of the crisis, political leaders in both countries and especially Bulgaria argued that their economies could resist the imported crisis. But economic dependency rapidly undermined this assumption and pushed both countries into a prolonged economic stagnation. In 2009, GDP fell by 6.6 percent in Romania and by 5.5 percent in Bulgaria, before returning to very low growth in the following years. This led to a rise in unemployment, which was especially strong in Bulgaria (the rate of unemployment rose from 5.6 percent in 2008 to 12.4 percent in 2012) and to renewed macroeconomic tensions in Romania (the budget deficit expanded to 9 percent of GDP in 2009). As a result the country had to accept supervision by the international institutions.

The crisis modified the balance of power, at two levels, reinforcing the pressure of external forces domestically, which in turn strengthened neoliberal forces acting on the countries' social situation. External pressure was enhanced also by the influence of active financial and political actors. In terms of financial assistance, the EU, IMF and World Bank henceforth acted together to impose significant conditions concerning structural reforms. In addition, the EU was able to use two further levers to influence policy in these countries: it menaced to freeze structural funds (implemented partially in Bulgaria as of 2008, and again in 2013), and it menaced to delay access to the Schengen area until now. This has been a particularly powerful lever to use with governments that had made full EU membership a top-ranking electoral promise. As of 2011, the new European governance, organised on the basis of the EU semester, also became a means for expressing increasingly-powerful, specific recommendations,[16] notably with respect to labour market flexibility and the tight control over wage growth, including that of minimum wages.

This external influence on the internal political and social game has also benefited from a new explicit convergence agenda, as the EU has now adopted the neoliberal creed of other international institutions (IMF and World Bank, etc.). It in turn has been supplemented by the increasingly pressing and explicit demands of foreign chambers of commerce.

The external influences, however, were only able to prosper under the auspices of a neoliberal revision of domestic agendas by local politicians, which was facilitated in return by the instrumentalisation of external constraints. This revision expressed itself in the voluntary signing of a "Euro Plus Pact" in 2011 by both countries, which has enhanced the tight monitoring of supranational bodies at the national level.[17]

The increasing intervention by external forces has an ambivalent impact on the domestic governance of dependent capitalisms, closely tied up with weak States. On the one hand, it reinforces the coordination capacities of public authorities, albeit in a specific mode, namely that of the external coordination of fiscal discipline, monitored by experts from the EU and other international institutions (IMF, World Bank, etc.). To some extent, this outside supervision has met with a degree of ascent from public opinion, which views outside control as a means for tackling clientelism and corruption at the pinnacle of government. This incidently explains why Europhilia has resisted to the shock imposed by the crisis in Bulgaria and Romania, in contrast to trends observed in the majority of CEECs and in the Southern EU countries which have been hit hardest by the neoliberal policies imposed by the EU and other institutions.

On the other hand, these external pressures have now converged in a normative manner and have actively participated in the introduction of neoliberal reforms, leading to a reinforcement of the minimalist and competitive dimension of the social State, and to a brutal shift to the deregulation of IR in Romania. This has been orchestrated by a centre-right government, and led to a revision of the Labour Code and the social dialogue Code in 2011. Romania's reforms also sealed the unpicking of inter-professional collective bargaining, the scrapping of the extension mechanism for branch agreements, the tightening of criteria allowing unions to set up in companies (now a minimum of 15 persons working in the same company are required to set up a union branch, compared previously to 15 persons in the same profession, but in different firms), and the criteria of union representativeness which open up the right to collective negotiations at firm level (a union must now represent at least 50 percent of employees compared to a third previously). Lastly, union representativeness has been completedly overhauled across new economic sectors, replacing the existing sectoral organisations, etc.

Concerning labour law, the reforms have incorporated the recommendations of the American Chamber of Commerce word-for-word, revealing explicitly the power of lobbying by MNCs, based on a whole arsenal of legal expertise.[18]

This phase of radical reform was also accompanied by unparalleled union protest. Tripartism was not bypassed purely and simply, as elsewhere in the region. Instead it was activated and controlled by government so that its instrumental and weakly regulatory dimension was reinforced. Consultation won out over negotiation, with time accorded to the latter often being reduced so that actors were caught short, while the social pacts of the crisis were successively overridden (Delteil, 2016). Far from intervening to help the unions, the EU provided tacit support for legislative changes, even when these tweaked Community law.

In response, the Romanian unions asked for support from the ILO, whose "Technical Memoranda" have identified breaches of Community standards, putting pressure on political actors to correct legislation. This Victor Ponta promised on coming to power in 2012, but it has not materialised.

In Bulgaria, and in contrast to Romania, the reforms have been more parametric than paradigmatic. The crisis has above all confirmed the orientation in favour of fiscal austerity, wage moderation and competitive tax cutting.

The crisis in Bulgaria has also led to a reactivation of tripartism much more clearly than in Romania (Bernaciak, 2013), proof indeed that the shift to austerity has not only been favoured by consultation but also constitutes a necessary condition for concerted practices. In April 2010 after much discussion, the government and social partners in Bulgaria agreed to 59 measures to fight the crisis. In the wake of this agreement, two national, bipartite agreements were signed in November 2010 for: i) home workers (linked to Bulgaria's ratification of ILO Convention No 177 on homeworking passed in 1996); and ii) on tele-working (the implementation of the agreement between European social partners on distance working of the 16 July 2002). These agreements are a concrete expression of a new autonomisation strategy by the social partners, which can be compared directly with government attacks on tripartism.

While tripartism was indeed mobilised to validate anti-crisis measures, it was in fact quickly bypassed by the political authorities. This was first done with the forced introduction of a measure revising payment of the first three days of sick leave in 2010. It occurred again in 2011 with the decision to override the "social pact" negotiated on retirement, which raised the age of retirement in an unilateral manner. These two measures led the unions to withdraw from the National Council for Tripartite Cooperation roundtable temporarily, and to hold demonstrations and threaten strike action (Delteil, 2013).

As of November 2014, in the wake of the creation of the second Borissov government and a failure of a bank, the tripartite social dialogue was reactivated after intense debate over the minimum wage and pension reform. The employer organisations went to court to challenge the government's decision to raise the minimum wage. Nevertheless, the executive confirmed its decision by Decree, in May 2015. In the same month, after much debate, a compromise was reached between the government and the social partners relating to pension reform.[19]

The crisis and the opening hostilities between the unions and governments had led the unions to redefine their strategies and forms of industrial action. The unions have moved to asserting themselves more strongly as "forces for proposals", participating actively in the definition of social pacts to manage the crisis. Moreover, they are more extensively searching for outside support, beginning with ILO "guardianship", which is an indicator that transnational union action is still embryonic.

Yet this strategic revision has little weight when it comes to gaining negotiation power and influence in the socio-political game, in a context in which domestic neoliberal forces benefit from external economic dependency.

Unionism is having trouble finding its second wind, in the face of declining membership due to job destruction, and a persistently discredited image with the public fed by serial allegations of corruption (Trif, 2014). In particular, unions are struggling to obtain renewed support in societal movements, and in stronger popular protest. They are also having trouble plugging the gap between their demands (centred on the social model) and the concerns of citizens which are mainly oriented towards local environmental struggles, and the fight against endemic corruption at the pinnacle of the State. The union discours has indeed evolved since the start of the crisis, becoming increasing anti-neoliberal, especially in Bulgaria where liberalism has historically found support amoung unions themselves. But it should be noted that unions have still not dropped their reactionary position on environmental issues.

The crisis has also had important consequences on the influence of sectoral and company-level regulation. In Romania, following deregulation, the number of collective bargaining agreements per branch collapsed, leading to a sharp fall in the rate of employee coverage (hardly 20 percent in 2012, compared to 80 percent beforehand). There was also a marked decline in company agreements (down from 7,732 in 2008 to 4,209 in 2012). In Bulgaria, following a small rise between 2008 and 2012 (1,493 to 1,616 for company CLAs), both sectoral and company agreements fell.

From many points of view, these two countries appear (along with the Baltic States) to have radicalised the decentralisation process found in the region (Bernaciak, 2015). In contrast to the Visegrad countries (apart from Hungary), collective regulation remains more tenuous, is more often bypassed by companies, and is less often enlarged to new issues, such as employment protection (in exchange for wage concessions). This observation illuminates once more the disciplinary limits "weak States" face, as they are unable to orient governments towards defining new regulations and opposing the spread of managerial unilateralism.

## 5. Conclusion: default Europeanization and/or "low road" Europeanization in Bulgaria and Romania

At the end of this chapter, it is right to examine the meaning of this great transformation which has not spared the field of industrial relations as has been shown here. This long run movement corroborates the existence of a specific form of "dependent capitalism" and the idea that capitalisms are diverse. The chapter also provides lessons concerning the nature and very relative scope of the Europeanization process.

As paragons of the "dependent capitalism" model, Bulgaria and Romania first and foremost illustrate the impact of historical legacies, as well as of peripheral European integration. They demonstrate singular characteristics which run from being "weak States" that are permeable to private interests with weak regulatory powers, through to the significance of informal practices. Together these are the fruits of path dependency and the recent economic pressures induced by peripheral integration of their economies into international markets and supply chains. They also follow from the victory of neoliberalism against the backdrop of power relationships which are very persistently unfavourable to employees and their representatives. The field of IR is directly affected by this patchwork of circumstances, be it the "tripartism of political legitimation", the sectoral regulatory deficit, the importance of informal regulations at company level, or the original upstream positioning of actors in this field. These include: employer organisations which "avoid" regulation in favour of lobbying; governments seeking to instrumentalise the social dialogue; union organisations that have a higher propensity to take risky bets on tripartite cooperation; social partnership "at all levels"; and a managerial social dialogue. This defensive strategy reflects the institutional crisis of unions. It allows unions to have a role in decision-making initially, giving them "input legitimacy", and more recently facilitating their access to European funds. This strategy has undoubtedly become more risky since the crisis, as unpopular but "necessary" reforms risk further tarnishing the "output legitimacy" of the unions, placing them back in the "trap" of the early days of the transition (Petkov, 2015).

The unions are aware of this risk, and that of losing more ground and credit to other social movements. They have significantly updated their cooperation strategies, in favour of more expert and offensive actions, mobilising new modes of action. These range from demands to use bipartism in Bulgaria (thus sealing the autonomisation of the social partners vis-à-vis government), or the recourse in Romania to ILO expertise as a tool for pressuring government.

In many ways, the singularities of East-European dependent capitalisms reflect Mediterranean capitalism but more radically. This concerns the deficit of the State as regulator and the share of the informal sector, or the use of tripartism as "extra-parliamentary support for reforms" (Avdagic *et al.*, 2011: 9; see also Baccaro and Simoni, 2008), against backdrop of external pressures. Social forces have only been partially able to obstruct measures of pay and social deregulation. However, unions have been able to retain a power of veto, and so have blocked the use of instrumental tripartism (strongly promoted by the European Commission).

Secondly, the observation here that Europeanization has been minimal raises several complementary interpretations.

This may reflect the limits of a "bottom-up" Europeanization, resulting from low support or resistence by local actors to EU standards. It is strongly illustrated by the two countries studied here, where resistance follows from a culture of social relations in which informality if not illegality are widespread (and intensifying since the crisis) or in certain cases from political-economic alliances (connected to the transnational business community) seeking to preserve institutional permissiveness as a source of competitiveness.

This observation may also reflect the absence of voluntarism in the EU to promote a top-down convergence in the systems and practices of East European IR. This point is supported by a patchwork of indicators if not proofs: the dropping of all allusions to the "European social model"; the weakening of conditionalities concerning the adoption of the *acquis communautaire* in IR; more recently, the absence of intervention by the EU over practices bypassing or avoiding social dialogue by a majority of East European governments – a silence which is all the more remarkable during this time of crisis and which compares with the strong injunctions issued by the EU to the Mediterranean economies; the continuing silence of the European Commission (where the DG Ecofin has consolidated its normative superiority over the DG Employment) in the face of the non-conformity of East European legislation with respect to EU standards, as in Romania.

Lastly, such minimal Europeanization can also be interpreted in another way, which is more complementary than contradictory to the above. Instead of the Europeanization of social dialogue being defective, Europeanization is itself now leading towards a model of social dialogue that is becoming more neoliberal. This new model results from a paradigm shift at three levels, which trends in IR within the "dependent capitalisms" appear to exemplify. On the one hand, social dialogue has been largely transformed, with consultation now playing a key role, at the expense of negotiation and regulatory objectives. On the other hand, cooperation and "social partnership" has removed all space left to conflict (between actors with distinct, if not antagonistic, interests), and to any consideration of the structuring role played by the expression of social demands and the search for compromises. Finally, by reflecting an EU rule (the "protocol on social policy" adopted in 1993), a social dialogue procedure "in the shadow of the law" re-establishes the constraint of a return to governmental unilateralism in case bipartite or tripartite negotiations fail.

The positioning of the Commission clarifies this shift in interpretation, which tends to reduce tripartism to a "consultative forum on public policies",[20] and social dialogue to being a simple instrument of "partnership for change",[21] a "flexible adaptation method, which is effective and non-conflictual as a means of overcoming obstacles to modernisation".[22]

In this paradigm, "dependent capitalisms" are maybe not so much resistant territories vis-à-vis EU standards, than long-lasting laboratories for a renovated model of industrial relations that are more compatible with neoliberal globalisation. This would constitute a complementary drift in the European project away from "social democracy" which is not without risks when prospering together with authoritarian populism, social anomie and strong economic dependency.

## Notes

1   For Bulgaria see the 2003 report http://ec.europa.eu/enlargement/archives/pdf/ key_documents/2003/rr_bg_final_fr.pdf
2   It should be noted that Romania's manufacturing industry is far more integrated into global value chains, due to varying orientations and levels of FDI in both countries (Ban, 2013). This results in a higher technological content of its exports, compared to Bulgaria, which is more locked into low cost production for its domestic market (energy and construction).
3   Again, the two countries differ on this: Bulgaria's corruption is mainly dominated by oligarchic companies (such as Multigroup in the 1990s, or more recently the KTB bank), whereas in Romania corruption is led by politicians and parties.
4   Compared to 12 percent in Poland and Hungary and about 10 percent in the Baltic States: www.worker-participation.eu.
5   Different sources such as Eurofound, Visser (www.uva-aias.net/208) and Laborsta of the ILO (http://laborsta.ilo.org/) give different unionisation rates and other indicators, such as coverage of collective bargaining agreements.
6   ILO, 2008, http://laborsta.ilo.org/STP/guest
7   ILO data is not available for Bulgaria.
8   25 percent in Poland, between 14 percent and 18 percent in Slovakia and 15 percent in Lithuania.
9   ICTWSS database (Visser, 2015).
10  See for example the collective agreements by branch, at www.nipa.bg
11  The expressions "input legitimacy" and "output legitimacy" have been taken from Scharpf, F. (1999).
12  During the 1990s, there was an explicit and very temporary compromise between unions and governments, which led to the postponement rather than the concerted

definition of ambitious reforms. One example is the role played by Podkrepa in the nomination of managers in companies that were still state-owned. The implicit compromises of economic and political elites around the capture of public resources were enhanced in some cases during privatisation, via the support and complicity of unions concerning the de-capitalisation practices orchestrated by management. In exchange, they obtained guarantees to maintain jobs and ensure firm survival (often with the help of indebtedness).

13　The situation in Slovenia is original, as macro-corporatism is based on a strongly-organised employer movement (as company affiliation is obligatory), and a unified union movement which is relatively strong and characterised both by social demo-cratic values and a protest culture which is favourable to achieving compromises and guarantees that negotiated agreements are implemented (Bohle and Greskovitz, 2012).

14　According to Hazans (2011), in 2008–2009, informal workers accounted for 13.2 percent of employees in Bulgaria and 11.8 percent in Romania (compared to only 6–7 percent of informal "salaried workers").

15　www.eurofound.europa.eu/observatories/eurwork/comparative-information/national-contributions/romania/romania-the-impact-of-the-information-and-consultation-directive

16　http://ec.europa.eu/europe2020/europe-2020-in-your-country/bulgaria/country-specific-recommendations/index_en.htm.　www.imf.org/external/country/rou/index.htm?type=23

17　For Bulgaria, this fiscal supervision supports the introduction of a "Financial Stability Pact" which was voted by Parliament in 2010, and which seeks to cap government spending at 40 percent of GDP, as well as limit public deficits to 2 percent and debt to 40 percent of GDP.

18　See in particular the White Papers of the Council of Foreign Investors (2007 and 2009), and the recommendations of the American Chamber of Commerce to the government in early 2009. As part of the Bill on the new Labour Code, these two asso-ciations have claimed that they were assisted by a team of 30 experts (http://m.amcham.ro/index.html/articles?articleID=618).

19　www.dnevnik.bg/bulgaria/2015/05/20/2536684_socialnite_partnyori_dogovoriha_vdiganeto_na_vuzrastta

20　European Commission (2014), Industrial Relations in Europe, p. 72.

21　Commission Européenne (2005), « Restructurations et emploi. Anticiper et accom-pagner les restructurations pour développer l'emploi : le rôle de l'Union Européenne », COM (2005), 31 mars, p. 13.

22　Communication de la Commission européenne, COM (2002) 341 final du 26.6.2002.

# References

Avdagic, S., Rhodes, M. and Visser, J. (eds) (2011) *Social Pacts in Europe: Emergence, Evolution, and Institutionalization*, Oxford University Press.

Baccaro, L. and Simoni, M. (2008) 'Policy concertation in Europe: understanding govern-ment choice', *Comparative Political Studies*, 41(10): 1323–1348.

Baccaro, L. and Howell, C. (2010) 'Institutional Change in European Industrial Relations: Reformulating the Case for Neoliberal Convergence', Conference paper. Council for European Studies, Seventeenth International Conference, Montreal, 15–17 April 2010.

Ban, C. (2013) From Cocktail to Dependence: Revisiting the Foundations of Dependent Market Economies, March 13, http://papers.ssrn.com/sol3/papers.cfm?abstract_id= 2233056 [Accessed 4 April 2016].

Bernaciak, M. (2013) 'Social Dialogue revival or 'PR Corporatism' Negotiating anti-crisis measures in Poland and Bulgaria', *Transfer* 19(2): 239–251.

Bernaciak, M. (2015) 'All roads lead to decentralization? Collective bargaining trends and prospects in Central and Eastern Europe', *Transfer* 21(3): 373–381.

Bohle, D. and Greskovits, B. (2006) 'Capitalism without compromise: strong business and weak labor in Eastern Europe's new transnational industries', *Studies in Comparative International Development* 41(1): 3–25.

Bohle, D. and Greskovits, B. (2012) *Capitalist Diversity on Europe's Periphery*. Ithaca and London: Cornell University Press.

Contrepois, S., Delteil, V., Dieuaide, P. and Jefferys, S. (eds) (2011) *Globalising Employment Relations*, London: Palgrave.

Crouch, C. (2004) *Post-Democracy*, Cambridge, Polity Press.

Crowley, S. (2004) 'Explaining labor weakness in post-Communist Europe: historical legacies and comparative perspective', *East European Politics and Societies* 18(3): 394–429.

Crowley, S. and Ost, D. (eds) (2001) *Workers after Workers' States. Labor and Politics in Postcommunist Eastern Europe*, Lanham: Rowman & Littlefield, 2001.

Delteil, V. and Dieuaide, P. (2010) 'Comités d'entreprise européens et européanisation des RP dans l'UE élargie : résultats d'enquête auprès de huit firmes multinationales françaises', *Travail et Emploi*, No.123, juillet-septembre, pp. 39–51.

Delteil, V. (2013) 'Bulgarie : Feu le tigre des Balkans, de l'impasse économique à la crise politique', *Chroniques internationales de l'IRES*, No.140 : 3–15.

Delteil, V. and Banarescu, M. (2013) 'Roumanie : Le modèle social sous la pression des bailleurs de fond : les syndicats à la recherche de nouvelles tutelles', *Chroniques internationales de l'IRES*, No.143: 133–151.

Delteil, V. (2016) 'The Tripartism of Political Legitimation or the (Post-) Democratic Face of Dependent Capitalisms: the Case of Bulgaria and Romania', https://halshs.archives-ouvertes.fr/halshs-01152979/document [Accessed 4 April 2016].

Ghellab, Y. and Vaughan-Whitehead, D. (eds) (2003) *Sectoral Social Dialogue in Future EU Member States: the Weakest Link*, International Labour Office – European Commission, Budapest, 2003.

Glassner V. (2013) 'Central and eastern European industrial relations in the crisis: national divergence and path-dependent change', *Transfer*, 19(2): 155–169.

Iankova, E. (1997) *Social Partnership After the Cold War: The Transformative Corporatismon Post-Communist Europe*, Ph.D. dissertation, Cornell University.

Kirov, V. (2015) 'The Europeanization of the Bulgarian trade union movement: achievements and challenges', in Landgraf, C. and Pleines, H. (eds) '*Europeanization of Trade Unions in EU member states of the Eastern Enlargement*', IbidemVerlag, Hannover, pp. 161–180.

Kirov, V. (2012) 'Evaluation of the operation and effects of information and consultation directives in the EU/EEA countries. National Report Bulgaria', prepared for the European Commission, DG for Employment, Social Affairs and Inclusion.

Kirov, V. (2003) 'Bulgaria: a still Undeveloped Component of Industrial Relations', in Ghellab, Y. and Vaughan-Whitehead, D. (eds) '*Sectoral Social Dialogue in Future EU Member States: the Weakest Link*', International Labour Office, Budapest, 2003, pp. 77–104.

Kirov, V. (2005) 'Facing EU Accession: Bulgarian Trade Unions at the Crossroads' in Dimitrova, D. and Vilokx, J. (eds) *Trade Unions Strategies in Central and Easter Europe: Towards Decent Work'*, ILO, Budapest, pp. 111–152.

Maggi-Germain, N. (2007) 'Sur le dialogue social', *Droit Social*, No.7/8, juillet-août.

Mihaylova, T. and Mikova, V. (2011) *Analysis of the study for the situation and the results of the establisghlent of I&C system,* Sofia, ISTUR, Non published report.

Myant, M. and Drahokoupil, J. (2012) 'International integration, varieties of capitalism, and resilience to crisis in transition economies', *Europe–Asia Studies* 64(1): 1–33.

Nölke, A. and Vliegenthart, A. (2009) 'Enlarging the Varieties of Capitalism: The Emergence of Dependent Market Economies in East Central Europe', *World Politics* 61(4): 670–702.

Ost, D. (2000/2010) 'Illusory Corporatism in Eastern Europe: Neoliberal Tripartism and Postcommunist Class Identities', *Politics and Society,* December 2000, 28(4): 503–530; reprinted in Warsaw Forum of Economic Sociology 1:2, Autumn 2010: 91–122.

Ost, D. (2011) "Illusory Corporatism Ten Years Later", Warsaw Forum of Economic Sociology, Spring 2011, 2(3): 19–49.

Petkov, K., (2015) Les nouveaux mouvements syndicaux et sociaux en Europe de l'Est, *Les mondes du travail*, No.15, pp. 45–64.

Safta–Zecheria, L. (2015) 'European Governance and the Romanian Cartel Alfa Trade Union Confederation', in Landgraf, C. and Pleines, H. (eds) *'Europeanization of Trade Unions in EU member states of the Eastern Enlargement'*, IbidemVerlag, Hannover, pp. 277–294.

Scharpf, F. (1999) *Governing in Europe: effective and democratic?* Oxford University Press, Oxford.

Spasova, S. (2015), *Professionnalisation à travers la socialisation internationale et les "usages de l'Europe"*. Le cas des organisations syndicales en Bulgarie, KNSB et KT Podkrepa, après 1989. Thèse de doctorat, Université Libre de Bruxelles.

Thelen K. (1999) 'Historical Institutionalism in Comparative Politics', *The Annual Review of Political Science*, 2: 369–404.

Tóth A. (2001) 'The failure of social-democratic unionism in Hungary' in: Crowley, S. and Ost, D. (eds) *'Workers After Workers' States: Labor and Politics in Postcommunist Eastern Europe'*, Lanham, MD: Rowman and Littlefield, pp. 37–58.

Trif, A. (2014) *'Austerity and collective bargaining in Romania'*, National Report: Romania, Dublin City University and European Commission, November, p. 44.

Trif, A. (2008) 'Opportunities and Challenges of EU Accession: Industrial Relations in Romania', *European Journal of Industrial Relations* 14(4): 461–478.

Varga, M. (2013) 'Refocusing studies of post-communist trade unions', *European Journal of Industrial Relations*, 19(2): 109–125.

# 11 Expansion of higher education and graduate employability

## Data and insights from Central and Eastern Europe

*Petya Ilieva-Trichkova and Pepka Boyadjieva*[1]

## Introduction

Since the fall of communism in 1989, Central and Eastern European countries (CEECs) have experienced a radical change in their economic model, given their transition from planned to market economy (Delteil and Kirov, Chapter 10; Makó and Illéssy, Chapter 5). The accession to the European Union (EU) has become a priority. During this process, hardly any social sphere was left unaffected, including higher education (HE). The EU instrument for the development of a coherent and comprehensive strategy in education was defined as an Open Method of Co-ordination, which should draw on tools organized as "mutual learning processes" (Council of the EU, 2002). Introduced in the Lisbon strategy, this soft law way of policy was used by the EU to press CEECs to converge with EU objectives. However, although the principle of subsidiarity prevented the EU's direct involvement in HE policy of different countries,[2] the real processes of transformation of HE systems in CEECs have been developed, not only based on learning, dissemination and harmonization, but also through imposition[3] (Dale, 1999; Tomusk, 2004; Boyadjieva, 2007).

The three main drivers of Europeanization in HE, which have gradually turned to some degree into imperatives, have been the Bologna process, the EU benchmarks, and the EU programmes and funds. The Bologna process was launched in 1999 as a joint initiative of 29 countries, aiming at creating a common European Higher Education Area by 2010. Gradually the Bologna Process was taken over by the EU and the European Commission as their own higher education policy (Tomusk, 2004: 77–78). The setting up of benchmarks by the European Commission is a very important instrument for imposing changes in HE in all European countries, CEECs included. Thus, in 2010, a special benchmark, as part of the Europe 2020 strategy, was introduced. According to this benchmark, the share of the population aged 30–34 having completed tertiary education should increase to at least 40 per cent by 2020 (European Commission, 2010). For the CEECs, this target is more pressing than for the other European countries because they have to overcome their lagging in the development of HE, inherited from the communist regimes.

At the same time, the issue of enhancing the employability of graduates has been recognized as one of the tools to reach the Europe 2020 strategy goal of becoming a smart, sustainable, and inclusive economy. According to the new EU 2020 benchmark on graduate employability, introduced in 2012, the share of employed graduates (20–34 year olds) with upper-secondary or tertiary education should be at least 82 per cent. In 2012, the New Members States are the countries with rates below the EU average (Eurydice, 2013: 46). A strong impetus for modernisation and Europeanization of HE in the post-communist period comes from different EU programmes (for example TEMPUS and its successor – HE Capacity Building) and Structural Funds. Some donor agencies (World Bank, national governments of some Western countries through bilateral aid programmes, and private foundations, such as the Soros Foundation) have also influenced HE development in CEECs (Halász, 2015).[4]

Within this context, the important question is how the process of Europeanization in HE – and more concretely its emphasis on expansion of HE – influences graduate employability in different post-communist countries. Despite the common legacies, the CEECs represent quite diverse models of capitalism (Bohle and Greskovits, 2012). That is why it is worth studying how these different types of capitalism interact with the expansion of HE to create opportunities for graduate employment. There are important large-scale comparative studies on graduate employment in Europe. However, only few or none of the CEECs have been included in these studies (for example Schomburg and Teichler, 2006; Allen and van der Velden, 2011). Being part of comparative studies allows us to better understand the transformation processes and its results in CEECs. This is why the present chapter tries to fill this gap, by focusing on employment opportunities of tertiary graduates in nine CEECs (Bulgaria, Croatia, the Czech Republic, Estonia, Hungary, Lithuania, Poland, Slovakia, and Slovenia). It aims at exploring graduate employability in the context of HE expansion. More specifically, the chapter addresses the following research questions *Does graduate employability differ in CEECs adhering to different types of capitalism?* and *What are the factors which influence employability of HE graduates in CEECs?*

The chapter continues with a literature review. On the basis of presentation of the main approaches to graduate employability and countries' 'institutional packages', we outline our theoretical considerations and assumptions. Then we briefly discuss HE expansion in CEECs and present our methodology. We proceed with our results and a discussion of our main findings. The final part provides concluding remarks.

## Literature review and theoretical considerations

Although the concept of employability is widely used, there is generally no unanimity about its meaning (Gazier, 1998; Tomlinson, 2012). Following Tholen's study (2013) and further developing his ideas, we distinguish two distinct strands of literature on graduate employability: *mainstream* and *alternative*.

## Mainstream view of graduate employability

The mainstream view, which is supported by the majority of policy-makers, media and research contributions, emphasizes the extent to which the individual can adapt to the labour market (LM) demands, and subsequently invest in improving skills, knowledge or other characteristics. This line of reasoning is grounded in the *human capital theory*. In fact, the human capital perspective (Schultz, 1961; Mincer, 1958; Becker, 1993) has exerted a great influence on the contemporary development of HE and the rise of knowledge-economy discourse. It implies that education is a form of investment in individual human capital and that the increase of a person's stock of education, interpreted as a form of capital, may be perceived as a key to economic growth. A common feature of the literature devoted to the human capital perspective is that it focuses on the productive potential of human beings and closely relates employability to the idea that the individual can act as their own entrepreneur. Therefore, the individual makes decisions and is responsible for the reallocation of their resources in line with the economic incentive, taking into account the potential risks and uncertainties, and responds to the demand for skills. Given this, employability becomes the measure of how well the individual had succeeded in providing a match between their human capital profile and LM demands (Thijssen *et al.*, 2008; Tholen, 2013). Overall, this mainstream view implies that the LM is made up of individual actors who independently respond to LM opportunities and incentives.

## Alternative view of graduate employability

The alternative view pays more attention to the macro-structural elements in explaining graduate employability. It takes into account the extent to which employability is structured by inequalities and opportunity, and that it is not dependent only on an individual's human capital. More specifically, it regards employability as "relational, contextual and, most importantly, conflictual" (Tholen, 2013: 5). Brown *et al.* (2004) point out that all policy statements on employability have failed to grasp that employability possesses not only an absolute dimension but also a relative one. They define the employability of individuals as: *the relative chances of getting and maintaining different kinds of employment*[5] (Brown *et al.*, 2004: 25). This line of reasoning is grounded in the *job competition model* (Thurow, 1975), *positional theory* (Hirsch, 1976), developed by economists, but also in the *credentialist theory* (Collins, 1979) within sociology. As Hirsch puts it: "[t]he value to me of my education depends not only on how much I have but also on how much the man ahead of me in the job line has" (Hirsch, 1976: 3). Collins (1979) observes that education becomes more costly and promises less of a payoff for given levels of credentials than previously; hence students, and those who pay their bills, are relatively less willing to make the investment. He focuses on 'credentialism', or the increased requirements for higher level positions, used by more advantaged individuals to further their status. According to the *credentialist theory,* the rapid expansion of educational qualifications, faster than the number of jobs, has led to 'credential inflation'.

Overall, according to this alternative literature, LM behaviour is heterogeneous, contingent upon people's identities, roles, class, ethnicity and gender but also the (institutional, social, economic or political) structures, values, and/or discursive forces (Tholen, 2013). Thus, in contrast to the mainstream view, the alternative one claims that individual employability depends, among other things, on the employability of others and how graduates act.

### Bridging different views of graduate employability

In a comparative study on graduate employability in Great Britain and the Netherlands, Tholen (2013) attempts to bridge the two aspects of employability – the micro and the macro ones – in a comprehensive manner which integrates agency and structure, in order to fully understand labour-market behaviour. Tholen's study show that the relation between jobs, education, rewards and skills may be understood in different ways in different countries. Thus, his study demonstrated that the interaction and interpretation of the particular characteristics of the LM and educational structure lead to distinct intersubjective ways of dealing with employability and participating in the competition for graduate jobs.

Our main theoretical assumption is in line with this combined perspective. We share the view that graduate employability can be fully comprehended only by simultaneously taking into account both individual action and the effects of structures. More specifically, we assume that employability refers to *graduates' abilities to find employment* and that these abilities have two sides: *agency-related and structure-related*. The *agency-related side* is connected with graduates' knowledge, skills, attitudes, identities, and values, whereas the *structure-related* one refers to the more general social conditions and the position of graduates on the LM. The *structure-related* side reflects the state of the LM, which depends on the development of the economy, the adopted regulations in the LM, and finally, the state of HE (incl. structure of HE institutions, level of massification and structure of graduate body). The *structure-related side* of employability is very important if we do not want to fall into the trap of 'blaming the victim'. Employability is *embedded* in the wider social and institutional context of a given society that is nationally-specific, even when it is subject to common trends, such as HE expansion. Having in mind the heterogeneity of the LM conditions and the diversity of perspectives for personal development and rewards which different jobs offer, we further assume that employability relates not simply to graduates' abilities to find employment but to *graduates' abilities to find employment of specific quality* (regarding payment, required level of education and career opportunities) (Boyadjieva and Ilieva-Trichkova, 2015).

In order to capture the structure-related side of employability and the embeddedness of employability in the wider social context of a given society, we proceed with discussion of the institutional context of the post-communist countries.

## The country-specific institutional 'packages' in CEECs

As Saar and Bjørn (2013: 63) have recently convincingly argued, there has been a trend towards comprehensive approaches that view institutional contexts in different countries as multi-dimensional and highly interactive, forming country-specific institutional 'packages'. Regarding post-communist countries, some authors assume that they comprise a homogenous group often referred to as transition countries – a group which followed a common path-dependency. Thus, Eyal, Szelenyi and Townsley (1998) propose that CEECs followed a specific form of capitalism, which is not known in other countries, called 'capitalism without capitalists'. Later on, others claim that the model of capitalism followed by these countries can be classified as 'dependent market economy' (Nölke and Vliegenthart, 2009). The main feature of this form of economy is the fundamental dependence on investment decisions by transnational companies. This type of capitalism gains comparative advantage due to skilled, but cheap labour, the transfer of technological innovations within transnational enterprises, and the provision of capital via foreign direct investments.

However, Bohle and Greskovits (2007, 2012) argue that the post-communist countries are rather heterogeneous. More specifically, they distinguish three types of capitalism in CEECs: *neoliberal, embedded neoliberalism* and *neocorporatist*. According to their typology, Estonia and Lithuania can be classified as neoliberal economies, the Czech Republic, Hungary, Poland, and Slovakia – as embedded neoliberal and Slovenia – as a neocorporatist one. Bulgaria represents a special case, as it has acquired only some of the features (but not all, and not in a homogeneous manner) of the neoliberal regime, whereas Croatia has acquired some of the feature of embedded neoliberalism.

In fact, the link between capitalism and the developed system of HE has not been explicitly discussed in any of the models which focus on the varieties of capitalism in CEECs. Nölke and Vliegenthart (2009: 687) analyse the education and training systems in CEECs, and emphasize that one of the specificities of dependent capitalism is that the existing vocational skills are sufficient, and major investment to upgrade skills would endanger the cost advantages of these countries. However, they do not refer explicitly to HE. In the typologies of education and training systems and of skills formation systems, Saar and Bjørn (2013: 54–70) outline some important features of education and training systems in different institutional models. But they too do not point specifically to the development of HE. With the present analysis, we intend to firmly raise the question of the place of the developed HE system as an important part of a given country's specific 'institutional package'.

Based on the above literature review and the outlined theoretical considerations, we argue that *graduates' employability is embedded into national and institutional contexts*. In other words, graduate employability depends not only on the individual factors (acquired level of education, type of acquired HE degree, gender, social background), but also on structural and institutional factors, such as the size and the structure of graduate body, the state of the economy and on the

LM in a given country. Furthermore, we expect that the influence of HE expansion on graduates' employability is nationally-specific.

## Brief overview of higher education development in CEECs

It is well-known that in all countries that found themselves under Soviet influence after the Second World War the field of HE was strongly politicized and elitist and similar policies were employed in it (in particular, in regulating access to HE) (see Connelly, 2000). But the different national social-political and academic environments predetermined the difference in the procedures and criteria used in implementing these policies, and the different results of the policies. For instance, the class-based admission quotas in access to HE were abolished in Hungary in the 1970s (Szelényi and Aschaffenburg, 1993) while in Bulgaria they were retained until 1989 (Boyadjieva, 2013). As a result of the Europeanization process after 1989, the main carrier of which has been the Bologna process, the following significant innovations were introduced in all CEECs, qualitatively changing their character (EACEA/Eurydice 2010, 2012): i) emergence of the private sector in HE. ii) introduction of new structural elements, such as the three-cycle degree system (Bachelor's, Master's and PhD degrees), the credit system and university quality assurance systems. iii) restoration of university autonomy and academic freedom. iv) encouragement of mobility of students and staff. In all CEECs the expansion of HE has led to a transformation of their HE systems from elitist and unified to mass and diversified ones. However, regarding diversification and liberalization of HE here studied countries fall into three groups: Poland and Estonia have introduced very liberal rules for establishing new higher education institutions (HEIs); Slovakia has stuck to more conservative legislation; whereas Bulgaria, Hungary and Slovenia have followed a more balanced policy (Boyadjieva, 2007; Kwiek, 2013a; Simonová and Antonowicz, 2006; Slantcheva and Levy, 2007).

HE expansion in CEECs is an important feature of the context in which graduate employability occurs and depends on. In line with the worldwide trend (Schofer and Meyer, 2005) and the EU recommendations, HE has been expanding in all nine countries examined. The collapse of communism in 1989 created specific settings for this expansion. It was followed by a series of HE reforms which were, to a great extent, driven by the political and economic opening and liberalization taking place in these countries (Cerych, 1997). Furthermore, expansion took place in a context of underfunding of old public institutions and the emergence of new private institutions, opening their doors to hundreds of thousands of new students (Barr, 2005; Kwiek, 2013b). In fact, the existence of some of the private HEIs became possible due to foreign investors who thus transferred Western-European and American views about HE and its curricula to CEECs.

Despite the general trend of expansion, the countries differ in terms of the speed of expansion. Thus, Slovakia is the country with the highest growth in the absolute annual number of graduates per 1000 population for the period between 2000 and 2008 – 14.1 per cent per year, followed by the Czech Republic with 11.1

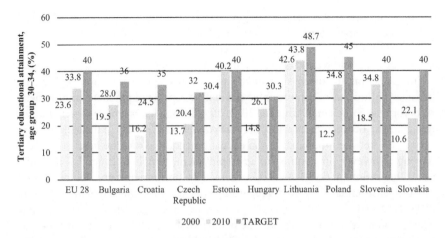

*Figure 11.1* Tertiary educational attainment, age group 30–34, in nine CEECs, in %

Note: Data for EU 28 and Croatia for 2000 refer to 2002, because it is the first year for which data for them are available.

Source: Eurostat (EU LFS). Online data code: t2020_41 (data extracted June 2016), calculated by Eurostat.

per cent growth. In Bulgaria and Hungary this share is the lowest – respectively 2.0 and 0.7 per cent. For all other countries, the growth achieved for this period is higher than the EU 27 average of about 4.5 per cent per year (European commission working staff document, 2011: 66). In terms of the national Europe 2020 targets for tertiary educational attainment in the age group 30–34 (Figure 11.1), in 2010, only Estonia met its national target of 40 per cent. The country with the highest share of graduates in 2010 was Lithuania (43.8 per cent). In the same year, Hungary and Slovenia were very close to their national targets and are the countries in which the percentage of graduates in the 30–34 age group almost doubled between 2000 and 2010. Notwithstanding the high speed of expansion in the period between 2000 and 2008, in 2010 Slovakia had the lowest share of graduates aged 30–34, at 22.1 per cent. The increase in the share of HE graduates in this age interval in Poland was almost threefold. Whereas in 2000, this proportion was only 12.5 per cent, in 2010 it amounted to 34.8 per cent. In Bulgaria and Croatia, the expansion was relatively modest. In 2010, in Bulgaria, 27.7 per cent of people aged 30–34 had a HE degree, compared to 19.5 per cent in 2000. For Croatia this growth was respectively from 16.2 per cent to 24.5 per cent.

## Methodology

The analysis is based on data from the European Social Survey (ESS) 2010, and from the official statistics. The ESS is representative of all persons aged 15 and over, resident within private households, for the populations of the participant countries. The analytical sample we used consists of 2086 individuals. The sample includes all respondents, aged 25–64, with a tertiary degree and who belong to the labour force (LF)[6] in the selected nine countries.

We differentiate *two* aspects of graduate employability: *vertical mismatch* and *unemployment,* and we focus in particular on the first one, since it has been under-estimated within the discussion and measurement of graduate employability, and because it allows us to capture some qualitative aspects of graduate employment.[7] According to Støren and Arnesen (2011: 199–240), whereas *unemployment* refers to a graduate being without a job, the *vertical mismatch* refers to the lack of corre-spondence between the level of the education acquired and the level required in the job. However, in contrast to unemployment, which is generally measured according to international standards, there is no uniform and undisputable typol-ogy or measurement framework regarding education-job mismatch (see Quintini, 2011; ILO, 2014). In this chapter we use a normative approach for its assessment. The reason for that is twofold. On the one hand, we wanted to use as many objec-tive measures as possible. On the other hand, this approach was the preferable approach in some recent reports (for example European Commission, 2012). Thus, the vertical (education-job) mismatch is measured as the percentage of graduates who were in paid work in the last 7 days, and whose occupation is not in the first three categories of the International Standard Classification of Occupations (ISCO) 88com and who belong to the LF. More specifically, ISCO 1, 2 and 3 are categories of occupations usually requiring tertiary qualifications. ISCO 1 refers to Legislators, senior officials and managers, ISCO 2 to Professionals, whereas ISCO 3 refers to Technicians and associate professionals. Therefore, HE graduates who are employed in some of the other categories, ISCO 4–9, are classified as vertically mismatched. We measure unemployment as the percentage of HE graduates who are either unemployed or actively looking for a job within the LF in the last 7 days.

We use descriptive statistics, bivariate associations and logistic regression for the data analysis. At descriptive level, we explored the extent to which this phenome-non is spread among HE graduates who live in these nine countries. Then, we explored the relationship between the vertical education-job mismatch and the level of HE expansion. To account for the expansion we used two measures:

1. Percentage of population with tertiary education attainment, 15–64, as of 2010.
2. Per cent change of tertiary students in the period 1998 and 2010.

Next, two logistic regression models were estimated (Models 1 & 2). The *dependent* variable in both models indicates if a graduate is vertically mismatched or not. In the first model we added, as an *independent* variable, a variable distinguishing all nine countries to explore the chances of graduates from all nine countries being vertically mismatched. In the second model we added personal characteristics of graduates. Thus, Model 2 includes a dummy variable indicating the gender of the individuals (0 male, 1 female). We also control for parental education status (0 no higher education; 1 at least one parent with higher education), age (25–34, 35–44, 45–54 and 55–64), and the duration of tertiary programmes. It was important because, in the context of the Bologna process, HE has become much more heterogeneous. We distinguish three types of tertiary programmes in accordance to their duration: short, medium and long. Short duration refers to ISCED[8] 5A, short and ISCED 5B, short; medium – to ISCED 5A, Bachelor; long – to ISCED 5A, Master and ISCED 6, Doctor. They are grouped in two categories. In the first one we add short and medium duration, whereas in the second group only the programmes with long duration.

## Results

### Descriptive statistics

Figure 11.2 illustrates the incidence of vertical mismatch and the unemployment among graduates (aged 25–64) who are part of the LF, by country for 2010. Overall, the results reveal that graduate employability varies by country when we measure it with these two measures. We find the Visegrad countries with the lowest share of graduate unemployment. Furthermore, Poland and Hungary had an incidence of vertical mismatch of less than 10 per cent. These results suggest that, despite the expansion of HE in these countries, the embedded neoliberal model which they followed influenced graduate employability positively. The Czech and Slovak Republics, which also adhere to the embedded neoliberal model, have much higher vertical education-job mismatch, but lower rates on both indicators in comparison to the other studied CEECs. This suggests that Poland and Hungary have a more *inclusive* (less differentiated) form of labour integration among all the Visegrad countries.

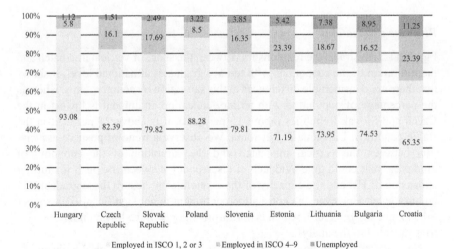

*Figure 11.2* Distribution of people (aged 25–64) with tertiary education (ISCED 5–6) in the LF, employed in ISCO 1, 2 or 3, in ISCO 4–9 and unemployed in nine CEECs, 2010, in %

Source: ESS, 2010 (own calculations), weighted data (dweight).

At the other end of the spectrum, Croatia and Bulgaria have the highest shares of graduate unemployment among all nine CEECs. Despite that, it seems that Bulgaria exhibits more similarities with the Baltic countries than Croatia, although it has a higher share of graduate unemployment compared to Estonia and Lithuania which, according to Bohle and Greskovits's classification (2012), follow a purely neoliberal model of economy, and which have quite similar levels of education-job mismatch among graduates. In the middle we could place Slovenia, which, according to the above-mentioned classification, has a neo-corporatist economy. Slovakia has a similar level of education-job mismatch to the one which we saw in the neo-corporatist Slovenian economy. However, the data show that the level of education-job mismatch among graduates, both in terms of level and structure of this mismatch, is very similar to the one observed in Slovakia, which has an embedded neoliberal model.

In our view, the country differences in graduate employability might be related to the differences in the capacity of the economies to create opportunities for graduate employment, which is most probably due to their specificities as dependent economies. Thus, some countries might have provided a better match between supply of qualified LF and demand, whereas in others, this link is not so straightforward. Another explanation has to do with the effects of the economic crisis, which did not hit all countries equally, and uneven recovery patterns. It might be the case that HE graduates had to take jobs which were below their level of education, in order to escape from unemployment. Overall, the results reveal that vertical mismatch is a more widely-spread phenomenon in comparison to unemployment among the highly-educated people in all nine countries.

### *Bivariate associations*

Figure 11.3 illustrates the relationship between the share of vertical mismatch and the saturation of the economies with tertiary graduates at national level. It shows that there are considerable differences in this saturation by country. Thus, whereas the percentage of population with tertiary education attainment is lowest in the Czech and Slovak Republics (about 15 per cent), it is above 25 per cent in the Baltic countries: Lithuania and Estonia. We observe a trend of positive association between the vertical mismatch and the saturation of the economy of graduates, that could give evidence of discrepancy between the push for further expansion of HE and the capacity of the economies to absorb these graduates at country level. However, the correlation coefficient is not significant (Pearson's r =0.340, not sig. $p < 0.05$), which is not surprising, given the low number of countries included in the analysis.

Next, we evaluated how the HE expansion, measured through the change of tertiary students in a given country in the period between 1998 and 2010, influences the share of vertical mismatch. We did so by calculating the bivariate association between the proportion of increase of the number of students and the share of people with HE, 25–64, employed in ISCO 4–9. The correlation analysis

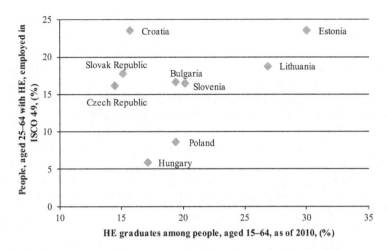

*Figure 11.3* Scatterplot of the vertical education-job mismatch among HE graduates, 25–64, in the LF in 2010 against percentage of population, 15–64, with tertiary education, as of 2010, (%)

Note: N (countries) = 9.

Source: ESS, 2010 (own calculations), weighted data (dweight) and Eurostat (EU LFS). Online data code: edat_lfse_03 (data extracted June 2016); data on the population, 15-64, with tertiary education (ISCED 5-8).

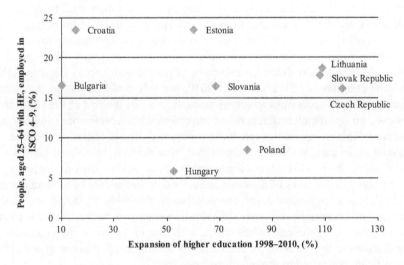

*Figure 11.4* Scatterplot of the vertical education-job mismatch among HE graduates, 25–64, in the LF in 2010 against expansion of HE (1998–2010), (%)

Note: N (countries) = 9. Due to lack of data for the period 1998–2002, the % for expansion for Croatia is calculated for the period between 2003 and 2010.

Source: ESS, 2010 (own calculations), weighted data (dweight) & Eurostat. Online data code: educ_enrl5 (data extracted June 2016); data on tertiary students (ISCED 5-6), (own calculations).

reveals a very weak negative relationship between these two variables (Pearson's r = – 0.127, not significant at $p < 0.05$).

Overall, the analysis of the bivariate associations between the vertical mismatch and the supply side of HE (measured via the saturation of HE graduates within the economy and the expansion of HE in a given country), has not provided a convincing answer for a relationship between the level of vertical education-job mismatch among HE graduates and the supply of HE in the studied nine CEECs. In other words, the HE expansion itself is not a sufficient determinant in explaining vertical education job mismatch that could be interpreted by other factors, like the type of the economy and its capacity to create jobs for qualified LF. Another potential factor might be the level of differentiation of HE in these countries, which could lead to problems with the signalling value[9] of the tertiary degrees to employers.

### *Logistic regression analyses*

In order to shed more light on the potential factors which determine the chances of graduates to be vertically mismatched, we continue our analysis with a presentation of the estimates of the logistic regression models (Table 11.1). Two different models are employed.

The country differences in the odds of being vertically mismatched among HE graduates are shown in Model 1. Estonia – a country with a neoliberal 'institutional package' – serves as a reference category for a comparison. The estimates in Model 1 reveal that graduates from Poland, Hungary and the Slovak Republic, which all adhere to an embedded neoliberal model, have significantly lower odds of being vertically mismatched than their Estonian counterparts. They are also among the countries with the lowest shares of people with tertiary degrees in the whole population, aged 15–64, as of 2010, but this could be due to the better capacity of their economies to create graduate jobs. In the rest of the countries, however, no significant differences in comparison with the reference category are observed. This suggests that graduates' employability is indeed embedded in national social context. Model 2 shows that, after the individual level factors are added, these coefficients remain consistent to a great extent. The only differences are observed in the cases of Slovenia and Slovakia. In the case of Slovenia, after controlling for individual-level characteristics, the odds of being vertically mismatched become significantly different in comparison to the reference country. In contrast, in the case of Slovakia, after the inclusion of individual-level characteristics, the odds of being vertically mismatched become statistically insignificant compared to the reference category.

Model 2 estimates reveal that gender has no effect, given the other covariates. Age also seem to have a minor effect. Nevertheless, people aged 35–44 are less likely to experience vertical mismatch, adjusting for the other variables. Model 2 also shows that having a high socioeconomic background decreases the likelihood of being vertically mismatched. Finally, the type of tertiary degree *does* matter. Specifically, the estimates derived from Model 2 reveal that graduates

*Table 11.1* Logistic regression coefficients from two models estimating the vertical mismatch among graduates (25–64) who are in the LF in nine countries

| Country ref.: Estonia | Model 1 e(b) | Model 2 e(b) |
|---|---|---|
| Bulgaria | 0.746 (0.516,1.078) | 0.878 (0.600,1.283) |
| Hungary | 0.168** (0.085,0.335) | 0.137** (0.069,0.273) |
| Poland | 0.277** (0.171,0.450) | 0.332** (0.202,0.547) |
| Slovenia | 0.730 (0.481,1.109) | 0.487** (0.316,0.751) |
| Slovak Republic | 0.577* (0.364,0.914) | 0.782 (0.481,1.271) |
| Czech Republic | 0.642 (0.400,1.030) | 0.740 (0.451,1.214) |
| Croatia | 0.961 (0.631,1.462) | 0.970 (0.622,1.514) |
| Lithuania | 1.095 (0.757,1.584) | 0.985 (0.672,1.445) |
| *Gender ref:. male* | | |
| Female | | 0.907 (0.717,1.149) |
| *Age ref.: 25–34* | | |
| 35–44 | | 0.673* (0.496,0.911) |
| 45–54 | | 0.816 (0.601,1.108) |
| 55–64 | | 0.801 (0.566,1.133) |
| *Soc. background ref.: none of the parents with HE* | | |
| At least one parent with HE | | 0.655** (0.509,0.844) |
| *Type of tertiary programme ref.: with short & medium duration* | | |
| With long duration | | 0.388** (0.303,0.498) |
| Constant | 0.362** (0.280,0.469) | 0.844 (0.581,1.226) |
| Wald chi2 | 60.810** | 149.651** |
| Pseudo R-squared | 0.0368 | 0.0759 |

Notes: e(b) – exponentiated coefficients. Confidence intervals in parentheses. Robust standard errors are included in the models.
Significance: *p<0.05, **p<0.01, (n=2086).

Source: ESS, 2010 (own calculations).

who studied in long tertiary programmes, such as Master's and PhD, are less likely to experience vertical education-job mismatch than those who studied in tertiary programmes of shorter durations.

Finally, Figure 11.5 displays the vertical mismatch probabilities based on the full multivariate logistic regression which we estimated (Model 2). It reveals the probability of being vertically mismatched vs. being in a job which requires HE, after controlling for gender, age, socioeconomic background and type of tertiary programme. More specifically, whereas the predicted probability of being employed in ISCO 4–9 in Hungary, Poland and Slovenia is below 20 per cent, it is between 21 and 25 per cent in the Slovak and Czech Republics and Bulgaria, and is at the same level (26 per cent) in Estonia, Croatia and Lithuania. Overall, these results suggest that the probability of HE graduates being vertically mismatched is higher in countries with neoliberal 'institutional packages'.

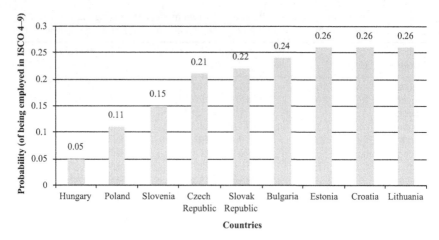

*Figure 11.5* Probability of being vertically mismatched in nine CEECs

Note: All estimates are significant at p<0.01.

Source: ESS, 2010 (own calculations), (n=2086)

## Discussion of the results

Our comparative study of employment opportunities of tertiary graduates in nine CEECs identified that, although unemployment is not so widely spread among HE graduates, they are exposed to other forms of risk such as being employed in a job which is not commensurate with their level of education. Further analysis of different aspects of quality of graduate employment such as payment, training, and type of contract, as well as the incidence of horizontal mismatch, would reveal a broader perspective on graduate employability.

We also observed considerable country differences in graduate employability. In our view, it has to do with the fact that there are country-specific 'institutional packages' in each country. This means that the state of the economy and the social policy in a given country are not independent factors, but they influence each other and form specific 'institutional packages' in each country and, in this way, they influence graduate employability. Thus, it seems that countries with embedded neoliberalism, and especially Poland and Hungary, provide better institutional packages for a lower vertical mismatch and lower unemployment among HE graduates compared to the neo-corporatist Slovenia, the neoliberal countries (Lithuania and Estonia), and especially compared to the two countries which do not follow a clear model of economy according to Bohle and Greskovits (2012): Bulgaria and Croatia. Our finding that, in addition to similarities, there are differences in graduate employability between countries which adhere to identical models of economy in CEECs suggests that the existing classifications of CEECs, even the most differentiated ones as in the Bohle and Greskovits's (2012) scheme, need to be further elaborated, taking into account the specificity of institutional development of education/HE and its linkages with employment and welfare systems. Obviously, since education/HE is a relatively autonomous sphere,[10] the specificity of the HE system and its development in each one of the countries (part of this specificity derives from HE legacies from the communist past and part of it has been formed during the transformation process after 1989) should also be included in country-specific 'institutional packages' which determine graduate employability. Thus, we found grounds to suggest that the four Visegrád Countries – the Czech Republic, Hungary, Poland, and Slovakia – should be further differentiated, and that Balkan countries could form one or two additional patterns.

Overall, the empirical results have demonstrated that the *influence of HE expansion on graduates' employability is embedded into national and institutional contexts*. This finding is consistent with the conclusion that "while common trends are evident across national context, the HE–labour market relationship is also subject to national variability" (Tomlinson, 2012: 408). Our results are also in line with Štefánik and Horvát (2015), who provide evidence about differences in private returns of expanded tertiary education in the labour markets of different countries. Obviously, the HE expansion has created new conditions and challenges for graduates' employability. However, our analysis does not allow us to draw the conclusion that the expansion itself automatically creates problems in graduate employability. The chapter provides evidence that this relationship is mediated through the state and structure of the economy in each country. Graduates' employability also depends on the structure of the graduate body and how it matches the LM demands. More specifically, graduates' chances of being vertically mismatched vary by HE degrees. Therefore, graduates' employability is not only embedded into a national context, but it is also identity-specific. By revealing that the chances of graduates being vertically mismatched vary significantly between different HE degrees, our analysis is in line with the conclusion from a recent comparative study on school-to-work transitions, which covers a wide range of CEECs, (Kogan *et al.,* 2011) that treating tertiary graduates as a homogenous group on the LM is not appropriate in expanded and diversified education systems. That is why it is worth investigating, in future research, how HE expansion in CEECs influences employability of graduates of different tertiary programmes (fields of study).

In our view, the problems that graduates currently experience on the LM may be viewed as a sign that, in the context of HE expansion, HE has characteristics of a "positional good". It means that the value of education one has on the LM depends on how much education other people have. Our analyses also show a significant effect of the socioeconomic background of graduates. So, given the higher supply of HE, people with lower socioeconomic background are in a worse position in the graduate jobs queue. The fact that high socioeconomic background serves as a safety net, and decreases graduates' odds of being vertically mismatched, could be interpreted as a sign of the important role of personal networks and informal relations alongside, or independent of, the role of official employment offices in mediating labour demand and labour supply. It might also be a reflection of the evolution of the skills required in the knowledge-based economies (less standardized, and related more to capacities of adaptability and critical thinking). Further studies are needed to show whether this result is specific for CEECs or whether it is also valid for more economically-developed countries with a stable democratic order.

## Conclusion

Following the worldwide trend of educational expansion, and influenced by the processes of Europeanization and globalization after the fall of socialism in 1989, HE systems in Central and Eastern Europe have transformed from elitist to mass ones (UNESCO, 2009). To a great extent, the massification of higher education in CEECs has been a catching-up process with the Western countries. Against this background, the chapter has studied how the expansion of HE in nine CEECs, as part of their Europeanization, has influenced graduate employability. It shows that the impact of HE expansion was moderated by the peculiarities of the type of capitalism which CEECs have adopted in their transition to a market economy, namely the specific forms of dependent capitalism. Thus, the chapter contributes to the discussion on varieties of capitalism and the essence of dependent capitalism. Nölke and Vliegenthart (2009: 678) argue that foreign capital and investors in CEECs, which are a key factor in dependent capitalism, are not "in favour of a generous public education system or of their own substantial investment into their labour force". Further analyses are needed in order to show how the policies of transnational companies to invest mainly in semi-standardized goods affect HE development and graduate employability in different CEECs.

One of the main limits of the Europeanization in the sphere of HE is that, despite the political rhetoric, it has been realized mainly as a "top-down" policy, and mechanisms of learning and harmonization have been often replaced by the mechanism of imposition. The EU policies were not designed in a way that acknowledges the specificity of the LM in different CEECs countries and that, due to this specificity, they could have uneven effects. However, it is not the same to have 40 per cent of people aged 30–34 years with HE, as is the EU benchmark, in a developed country with a stable economy, and the same share in a transforming country with a neo-liberal economy, or in a transforming country which has not yet built its economic model.

The need to gain competitive advantages globally and the decline of job openings brought the problem of rising unemployment to the fore. Thus, fostering employability of people became high on the European agenda. However, the EU benchmark on employability has been defined in very narrow terms and misses important dimensions of employability which, as our study has shown, are worth considering. The chapter has demonstrated that, by looking at both sides of employability – the agency-related and structure-related ones, we can better reveal its nationally-specific institutional embeddedness. Furthermore, by taking into account the qualitative aspects of employability, the chapter shows that employment rate is important, but not sufficient, measure of employability. This is why it should be complemented by additional measures such as qualification mismatch, career perspectives, etc. In this sense, the expansion of HE needs to be supported by increasing the quality of HE, and this should go hand-in-hand with fostering the capacity of the economies to create graduate jobs. Otherwise, it may lead to broken promises from education and growing frustration among people with tertiary degrees. There are already indications of that, which in many cases translate into a brain-drain[11] of highly-qualified people from CEECs to Western Europe or North America.

In the context of knowledge-based economies and a world-wide trend of expansion of HE, the development of a country's HE system becomes a key element of its 'institutional package'. Benefits from tertiary education are no longer privileges of the wealthy elites, but are open to a wider range of the popu-lace in these societies. HE has moved to its mass era and this expansion is expected to continue in the next decades. That is why contemporary societies cannot be fully understood without taking into account their HE systems. Bearing this in mind, there is a need for the classifications of the models of capitalism to be further elaborated, by paying more attention to the specificity of HE develop-ment and placing it as an important element, closely related with the other elements (especially the type of economy and economic specialisation), in the countries' 'institutional packages'.

## Notes

1   The authors have made equal contributions.
2   Article 149 of the EU Amsterdam Treaty (1999) states that "the Council...shall adopt incentive measures (in the sphere of education), excluding any harmonization of the laws and regulations of the member States".
3   The mechanisms through which national educational polices are effected could be compared on different dimensions (Dale, 1999). For instance, whereas learning, dissemination and harmonization are voluntary processes, based on mutual learning and cooperation, imposition is a compulsory process, initiated by external authorities.
4   Regarding the influence of external resources on educational reforms in CEECs, Birzea (2008: 110) argues that this influence "was so great that some countries (e.g. Romania and Bulgaria) even ran the risk of educational policies becoming incoherent, owing to their excessive dependence on external donors".
5   Italics in the original text.
6   We define the labour force as people who, in the last 7 days, report being in paid work or are unemployed and are actively looking for a job.
7   In this chapter we do not cover the issue of wages. One of the limitations of the ESS data is that they refer to household income as a whole, and do not allow us to specif-ically distinguish graduate income. There are studies which have shed light on the issue of wages. For example, a study using meta-analysis, by including approximately 50 wage estimates, has shown that overeducated individuals earn less than they would earn at a job requiring their schooling, but more than their just-educated work colleagues (Rubb, 2003). Moreover, our recent study, using Bulgaria as a case study, has explored the income of graduates as an important aspect of graduate employabil-ity (Boyadjieva and Ilieva-Trichkova, 2015).
8   International Standard Classification of Education, version 2011.

9   Attendance at some types of HEIs or programmes may "signal" ability to employers (Spence, 1973), whether or not they do, in fact, impart skills more efficiently than other types of schools.
10  The idea of education as a relatively autonomous sphere/field is well-established in sociology of education (see for example Bourdieu, 1988).
11  The brain drain is a widely-researched phenomenon. A recent study shows that migration among the highly-qualified workers from Central and South-eastern Europe is currently extensive to the Western parts of the EU (see for instance Nedeljkovic, 2014). The emigration rates among the tertiary-educated tend to increase in the period between 1990 and 2010 in Bulgaria, the Czech Republic, Hungary, Poland, Romania, Slovakia and Slovenia, with the highest increase in Bulgaria, where the increase was eightfold (from 1.53 per cent to 12.22 per cent). As of 2010, the emigration rate among the tertiary-educated is highest in Romania – 20.36 per cent and lowest in Slovenia (9.59 per cent). For Bulgaria, the Czech Republic, Hungary, Poland and Slovakia, this rate is between 10 and 15 per cent (For more details see Brücker *et al.*, 2013).

## Acknowledgements

The authors acknowledge the support of the Project 'Negotiating early job-insecurity and labour market exclusion in Europe', funded from the European Union's Horizon 2020 research and innovation programme, under grant agreement No 649395, and the support of the National Research Council (NCN) through its MAESTRO grant DEC-2011/02/A/HS6/00183 (2012–2017). We would like to thank editors of the book for their valuable comments on an earlier version of this chapter.

## Databases

ESS Round 5: European Social Survey Round 5 Data (2010). Data file edition 3.2. Norwegian Social Science Data Services, Norway – Data Archive and distributor of ESS data.

## References

Allen, J. and van der Velden, R. (eds) (2011) *The flexible Professional in the Knowledge Society: New challenges for higher education*, Dordrecht: Springer.
Barr, N. (ed.) (2005) *Labor Markets and Social Policy in Central and Eastern Europe: The Accession and Beyond*, Washington, DC: World Bank.
Becker, G. (1993) *Human Capital: A Theoretical and Empirical Analysis with Special Reference to Education*, 3rd edn. London: The University of Chicago Press.
Birzea, C. (2008) Back to Europe and the second transition in Central Eastern Europe, *OrbisScholae*, 2(2): 105–113.
Bohle, D. and Greskovits, B. (2007) 'Neoliberalism, Embedded Neoliberalism and Neocorporatism: Towards Transitional Capitalism in Central-Eastern Europe', *West European Politics,* 30(3): 443–466.
Bohle, D. and Greskovits, B. (2012) *Capitalist Diversity on Europe's Periphery*, Ithaca: Cornell University Press.
Bourdieu, P. (1988) *Homo Academicus,* Stanford: University Press.

Boyadjieva, P. (2007) 'Diversity Matters: A Lesson from a Post-Communist Country', in G. Krucken, Ch. Castor, A. Kosmutzky and M. Torka (eds) *Towards a Multiversity? Universities between Global Trends and National Traditions*, (pp. 108–131). Transaction Publishers.

Boyadjieva, P. (2013) 'Admission Policies as a Mechanism for Social Engineering: The Case of the Bulgarian Communist Regime', *Comparative Education Review*, 57(3): 503–526.

Boyadjieva, P. and Ilieva-Trichkova, P. (2015) 'Institutional Diversity and Graduate Employability: The Bulgarian Case', in R. Pritchard, M. Klumpp and U. Teichler (eds) *Diversity and Excellence in Higher Education: Can the Challenges be Reconciled?* (pp. 153–171). Rotterdam: Sense Publishers.

Brown, P., Hesketh, A. and Williams, S. (2004) *The Mismanagement of Talent. Employability and Jobs in the Knowledge Economy*, Oxford: University Press.

Brücker H., Capuano, S. and Marfouk, A. (2013) Education, gender and international migration: insights from a panel-dataset 1980–2010, mimeo. Online available: www.iab.de/en/daten/iab-brain-drain-data.aspx#Contents [Accessed 4 April 2016].

Cerych, L. (1997) 'Educational Reforms in Central and Eastern Europe: Processes and Outcomes', *European Journal of Education*, 32(1): 75–96.

Collins, R. (1979) *The Credential Society: A Historical Sociology of Education and Stratification*, New York: Academic Press.

Connelly, J. (2000) *Captive University. The Sovietization of East Germany, Czech, and Polish Higher Education, 1945–1956*. Chapel Hill and London: University of North Carolina Press.

Council of the European Union (2002) Detailed Work Programme on the Follow-up of the Objectives of Education and Training Systems in Europe. 6365/02.

Dale, R. (1999) 'Specifying Globalization Effects on National Policy: A Focus on the Mechanisms', *Journal of Education Policy*, 14(1): 1–17.

EACEA/Eurydice (2010) *Focus on Higher Education in Europe 2010: The Impact of the Bologna Process*. Brussels: Education, Audiovisual and Culture Executive Agency.

EACEA/Eurydice (2012) *The European Higher Education Area in 2012: Bologna Process Implementation Report*. Brussels: Education, Audiovisual and Culture Executive Agency.

European Commission (2010) *Communication from the Commission. EUROPE 2020: A strategy for smart, sustainable and inclusive growth*. Brussels, 3.3.2010 COM(2010) 2020.

European Commission (2012) *EU Youth Report*. Luxembourg: Office for Official Publications of the European Communities.

European commission working staff document (2011) *Progress towards the common European Objectives in Education and Training. Indicators and benchmarks 2010/2011*. www.cedefop.europa.eu/en/news-and-press/news/progress-towards-common-european-objectives-education-and-training-2010–2011 [Accessed 4 April 2016].

Eurydice (2013) *Education and Training in Europe 2020: Responses from the EU Member States*, Brussels: Education, Audiovisual and Culture Executive Agency.

Gazier, B. (1998) Employability – 'Definitions and trends', in B. Gazier (ed.) *Employability: Concepts and policies* (pp. 37–71), Berlin: European Employment Observatory.

Halász, G. (2015) 'Education and Social Transformation in Central and Eastern Europe', *European Journal of Education*, 50(3): 350–371.

Hirsch, F. (1976) *Social Limits to Growth*. Cambridge, Massachusetts: Harvard University Press.

ILO (2014) *Skills mismatch in Europe: statistics brief,* Geneva: International Labour Office, Department of Statistics.

Kogan, I., Noelke, C. and Gebel, M. (eds) (2011) *Making the Transition: Education and labour Market Entry in Central and Eastern Europe*, California: Stanford University Press.

Kwiek, M. (2013a) 'From System Expansion to System Contraction. Access to Higher Education in Poland', *Comparative Education Review,* 57(3): 553–576.

Kwiek, M. (2013b) *Knowledge Production in European Universities: States, Markets, and Academic Entrepreneurialism,* Frankfurt am Main: Peter Lang.

Mincer, J. (1958) 'Investment in Human Capital and Personal Income', *Journal of Political Economy*, 66(4): 281–302.

Nedeljkovic, V. (2014) Brain Drain in the European Union: Facts and Figures. Rethink Education Working Paper, No. 4. Online available: www.bridgingeurope.net/ uploads/8/1/7/1/8171506/wp4_rethink_edu_braindrain_nedeljkovic.pdf [Accessed 4 April 2016].

Nölke, A. and Vliegenthart A. (2009) 'Enlarging the Varieties of Capitalism. The Emergence of Dependent Market Economies in East Central Europe', *World Politics* 61(4): 670–702.

Quintini, G. (2011) *Over-Qualified or Under-Skilled: A Review of Existing Literature*, OECD Social, Employment and Migration Working Papers, No 121, OECD Publishing. Online available: www.oecd-ilibrary.org/social-issues-migration-health/over-qualified-or-under-skilled_5kg58j9d7b6d-en [Accessed 4 April 2016].

Ray, L., Eyal, G., Szelényi, I. and Townsley, E. (1998) 'Introduction' in *Making Capitalism Without Capitalists: Class Formation and Elite Struggles in Post-communist Central Europe*, 1–16. London: Verso.

Rubb, S. (2003) 'Overeducation: a short or long run phenomenon for individuals?', *Economics of Education Review,* 22: 389–394.

Saar, E., and Ure, B. O. (2013) 'Lifelong Learning Systems: Overview and Extension of Different Typologies', in E. Saar, B. O. Ure and J. Holford (eds) *Building European Lifelong Learning Society: The Enduring Role of National Characteristics*, London: Edward Elgar Publishing Ltd.

Schofer, E. and Meyer, J.W. (2005) 'The worldwide expansion of higher education in the twentieth century', *American Sociological Review*, 70(6): 898–920.

Schomburg, H. and Teichler, U. (2006) *Higher Education and Graduate Employment in Europe: Results from graduate surveys from twelve countries*, Dordrecht: Springer.

Schultz, T. W. (1961) 'Investment in Human Capital'. *The American Economic Review*, 51(1): 1–17.

Simonová, N. and Antonowicz, D. (2006) 'Czech and Polish Higher Education – from Bureaucracy to Market Competition', *Czech Sociological Review,* 42(3): 517–36.

Slantcheva, S. and Levy, D. (2007) (eds) *Private Higher Education in Post-Communist Europe: In Search of Legitimacy*. New York: Palgrave Macmillan.

Spence, M. (1973) 'Job Market Signaling', *The Quarterly Journal of Economics*, 87(3): 355–374.

Støren, L. A. and Arnesen, C. Å. (2011) 'Winners and Losers', in J. Allen and R. Van der Velden (eds), *The Flexible Professional in the Knowledge Society New Challenges for Higher Education*, Dordrecht: Springer, 199–240.

Štefánik, M. and Horvát, P. (2015) 'Is tertiary education expansion observable in private returns to education? (Evidence for Middle and Eastern European Countries)', *European Educational Research Journal*, 14(5): 418–429.

Szelényi, S. and Aschaffenburg, K. (1993) 'Inequalities in Educational Opportunity in Hungary', in Y. Shavit and H.-P. Blossfeld (eds) *Persistent Inequality. Changing Educational Attainment in Thirteen Countries*, Boulder: Westview Press.

Teichler, U. (ed.) (2007) *Careers of University Graduates. Views and Experiences in Comparative Perspectives,* Higher Education Dynamics, V. 17 Dordrecht: Springer.

Thijssen, J., Van der Heijden, B. and Rocco, T. (2008) 'Toward the Employability-Link Model: Current Employment Transition to Future Employment Perspectives', *Human Resource Development Review,* 7(2): 165–183.

Tholen, G. (2013) 'What can research into graduate employability tell us about agency structure?' *British Journal of Sociology of Education*, 1–20.

Thurow, L. (1975) *Generating Inequality*, New York: Basic Books.

Tomlinson, M. (2012) 'Graduate Employability: A Review of Conceptual and Empirical Themes', *Higher Education Policy,* 25: 407–31.

Tomusk, V. (2004) 'Three Bolognas and a Pizza Pie: Notes on Institutionalization of the European Higher Education System', *International Studies in Sociology of Education*, 14(1): 75–95.

UNESCO (2009) *Trends in Global Higher Education: Tracking an Academic Revolution. A Report Prepared for the UNESCO 2009 World Conference on Higher Education*, by Altbach, P.G., Reisberg, L. and Rumbley, L.E. http://unesdoc.unesco.org/images/0018/001831/183168e.pdf [Accessed 4 April 2016].

# 12 Between commitment and indifference

## Trade unions, young workers and the expansion of precarious employment in Poland

*Adam Mrozowicki, Mateusz Karolak and Agata Krasowska*

### Introduction

The Polish labour market has undergone deep changes over the past fifteen years related to the development of flexible, and oftentimes precarious, employment. Even though the expansion of atypical employment has also been observed in other Central and Eastern European (CEE) countries (Kahancová and Martišková, 2014), Poland remains a "frontrunner" in terms of the share of temporary employees. Between 2000 and 2014, it rose from 5.6 per cent to 28.3 per cent for employees aged 15–64, and from 14.2 per cent to 71.2 per cent in the case of young workers (15–24). At the same time (2000–2014), in other Visegrád countries which fall into the same type of embedded neoliberal regimes (Bohle and Greskovits, 2012) or dependent market economies (Nölke and Vliegenthart, 2009), the share of temporary employees (in the age category 15–64) increased considerably less: in Hungary from 5.6 to 10.8 per cent; in the Czech Republic from 7.2 to 9.7 per cent; and in Slovakia from 4 per cent to 8.8 per cent (Eurostat LFS). Moreover, as estimated by the Central Statistical Office of Poland (GUS, 2015), 1.4 million of the temporary employees work solely on what are called 'civil-law contracts,'[1] which are the least secure and stable form of the employment and the among most popular type of employment contract used for hiring young people.

Workers with all types of temporary employment contracts are underprivileged in terms of wages and protection against dismissals, and they experience a higher risk of poverty, economic deprivation and financial exclusion as compared to permanent employees (Kiersztyn, 2012). Additionally, those with civil law contracts and the self-employed are excluded from the regulatory protection and rights guaranteed by the Labour Code. Taking into account the most common denominators of precarious work (Rodgers, 1989; Kalleberg, 2009), such as low wages, limited or no social security entitlements, low job security and a limited voice in employment relations, we can objectively call them 'precarious workers'.

This chapter explores the expansion of precarious employment in Poland and the responses to it by the Polish government, trade unions, and the young workers affected. In the first part of the chapter, we discuss the interplay of internal (domestic) and external (European and global) factors which underlie the precarisation of employment in Poland. We argue that the combination of measures aimed at economic restructuring, combating unemployment, and adjusting Poland's regulations to the European Union requirements, together with the responses of various domestic actors (including trade unions), led to the creation of a dual labour market. Some categories of workers, including young people, women and elderly employees, have been systematically pushed into underprivileged positions. In an attempt to improve their situation, in the mid-2000s workers, and young workers in particular, opted in mass for an "exit" strategy through migration (Meardi, 2012). However, in the wake of the economic slowdown in 2008–2009, counter-movements against the precarisation of workers began to be more visible in the public sphere. The issue of workers' precariousness became one of the core topics of union mobilisation. As a result, these 'atypical' forms of employment became widely described in the public and media discourse as "junk jobs" performed by "the precariat". This helped politically frame worker discontent. The greater union focus on precarious employees is also visible in other CEE countries (Greskovits, 2015; Kahancová, 2015; Mrozowicki *et al.*, 2013), being one of the indicators of the "end of patience" in the region (Beissinger and Sasse, 2014).

While the Polish trade union efforts were partially successful, as reflected in recent (2014–15) legislative reforms regarding temporary contracts and civil law contracts the direction of the future changes will depend to a large extent on the strength of organised labour. This in turn depends on, *inter alia*, the ability of Polish trade unions to attract young workers, who work predominantly on non-standard employment contracts. Therefore in the second part of this chapter we analyse the attitudes of non-unionised young precarious workers in the service sector toward trade unions, based on biographical research conducted in 2013 in Poland. We identify the frictions between young workers' life strategies and their perception of trade unions, as well as the potential opportunities for the revival of the latter.

## Three waves of precarisation in Poland: external and internal factors

Even though it is unquestionable that precarious employment also existed in state socialism (see for instance Mach *et al.*, 1994), the level of job security became an important new factor differentiating between the labour market core and peripheries in Poland after 1989. Three waves of this process can be distinguished. Firstly, in the immediate wake of the systemic transformation in the 1990s; secondly in the late 1990s and the first half of the 2000s, in the context of the Poland's accession to the EU; and thirdly, between 2009–2015, as a result of the Polish government's response to the economic crisis. Below we briefly discuss each of these "waves" and the particular responses by the government and the young workers affected.

## Market dreams and economic hardships: the first wave of precarisation in the 1990s

Unlike in some other CEE countries, most notably Slovenia, the transition from a planned to a market economy following the systemic transformation in Poland in 1989 was explicitly based on the idea of "shock therapy", co-designed by American and Polish economists and implemented by Leszek Balcerowicz, the Minister of Finances in the first non-communist government. Micro-economic liberalisation, macro-economic stabilisation, and deep economic restructuring (involving the privatisation of state-owned companies) were prescribed as the way to achieve accelerated growth, based on the imitation of the "well-tested" solutions of Anglo-Saxon liberal market economies (Hardy, 2009; Jasiecki, 2014). As a result of the privatisation and restructuring of the state-owned enterprises unemployment, officially inexistent in 1989, grew to 16.4 per cent in 1994. In the period 1989–1993, average real wages declined by around 29 per cent (Kieżun, 2012: 131). Unemployment and the attendant risk of permanent joblessness, increasingly limited access to unemployment benefits, and diminishing wages became the main sources of this first wave of precarisation.

The "myth of the market" (Kolarska-Bobińska, 1998) as a panacea for the troubles of the state socialist societies served as the justification for the neoliberal reforms of the late 1980s and early 1990s. The clash of this myth with the reality of economic hardship resulted in ambivalent workers' attitudes, helping to shape their consciousness. On one hand, sociologists noted the individualisation of workers' life strategies and their individual 'privatisation', marked by their retreat from the public sphere and increasing focus on private/family lives (Ziółkowski, 2006). On the other hand, despite the erosion of trade unionism, workers' protests in some of the key restructured economic sectors in early 1990s did contribute to some changes in social and economic policy, which had an impact on the mechanisms of precarisation.

Firstly, the idea of searching for "compromises between market transformation and social cohesion" led to the emergence of the "embedded neoliberal economy" in Poland and other Visegrád countries (Bohle and Greskovits, 2012). These "pensioners' welfare states" (ibidem: 152) focused on passive labour market policies to soften the consequences of the harsh economic reforms, mainly via early retirement schemes and increasingly selective welfare policies. The "offer" for young workers, in turn, consisted of the promise of upward mobility through entrepreneurship and higher education, but their labour market needs were not dealt with systematically by policy-makers in early 1990s (Kozek, 2012: 230–232).

Secondly, the first wave of precarisation became closely linked with employers' strategies developed in the course of restructuring, privatisation, and the development of the new private sector. New labour market peripheries began to emerge out of those affected by the unstable and low-paid employment conditions in the weakly unionised private sector (Gardawski, 2001).

Thirdly, labour market segmentation became reinforced by trade union weakness. Workers' protests in the early 1990s led to the creation in 1994 of a Tripartite Commission on Social and Economic Affairs, requiring consultations between trade unions, employers, and government representatives with respect to social policies and minimum wages, with the goal of maintaining "social peace". However, the growing reluctance of successive governments and employer organisations to engage in this tripartite and sectoral social dialogue, together with diminishing union membership and its mobilisation capacities, soon rendered this Polish tripartism "illusory" (Ost, 2011). In addition, trade unions had already begun to lose their legitimacy in workers' eyes, since as at least some of them, most notably NSZZ Solidarność, came out in support of the painful market reforms (Mrozowicki and Van Hootegem, 2008).

## *Flexible employment and the second wave of precarisation (late 1990s–2008)*

As observed by Drahokoupil and Myant (2015: 329), despite the increasing risks of job loss as a result of restructuring, the CEE countries' workers continued to enjoy a relatively high level of *formal* employment protection by labour legislation in the 1990s. In this context, the flexibilisation of employment became a new dimension, resulting in the creation of a 'dual labour market' in the 2000s. Together with the already-mentioned factors, three additional important developments took place, including 1) a general shift in the Polish political economy in late 1990s/early 2000s, related to the attempts to attract foreign direct investment; 2) measures adopted to fight the unprecedented high levels of unemployment in early 2000s; and 3) the ambiguous (and sometimes unintended) consequences of the adjustment of Polish legislation and labour market policies to the 'hard' and 'soft' requirements accompanying accession to European Union (Meardi, Chapter 7).

A few years after the systemic transition and following the unsuccessful attempts to build a national capitalism Poland, similarly to the other Visegrád countries, shifted towards an economy based on foreign direct investments, which were supposed to build on its complex of plants and manufacturing legacy from state socialism (Bohle and Greskovits, 2012; Jasiecki, 2014; Hardy, 2009). As argued by Nölke and Vliegenthart (2009: 672), the relatively low labour costs and medium level of labour market flexibility became important features of the "dependent market economies", whose comparative advantages were said to be "based on institutional complementarities between skilled, but cheap, labour, the transfer of technological innovations within transnational enterprises, and the provision of capital via foreign direct investment (FDI)".

As pointed out in this volume by Drahokoupil and Myant (Chapter 3), the pressure of multinational corporations (MNCs) to change labour legislation in the CEE countries was rather modest compared to that of domestic business. However, it can be argued that the accumulated structural power of the MNCs had an indirect impact on the labour and fiscal policies (Bohle and Greskovits, 2012: 168–169). In order to attract foreign capital, the CEE policy makers began to compete to provide "business friendly" policies and conditions. In Poland, the law on special economic zones (SEZs) was introduced as early as in 1994, creating a framework for tax incentives for both domestic and foreign businesses. Arguably, the SEZs were more than just neo-liberal "exceptions" and played a key role in determining new, flexible labour regimes (Mrozowicki and Maciejewska, 2013).

The main changes in the Polish labour law were introduced in 2002–2003, at the peak of Poland's highest unemployment rate after 1989, which rose from 10.2 per cent in 1998 to 20 per cent in 2002, including 39.6 per cent among those aged 15–24 (Eurostat LFS). This rapid unemployment growth was mainly the result of the economic slowdown and the second wave of privatisation. Importantly, the restructuring of some sectors, for instance, steelworks and shipyards, were also among the conditions imposed on Poland's accession to the European Union.[2] In this context it was observed that "the issue of liberalising restrictive provisions in the Labour Code which, according to employers, have prevented the creation of new jobs, has become especially urgent" (Czarzasty, 2002).

The employers' expectations of flexible employment legislation overlapped with the adjustment of labour law to the European Union requirements. The role of the EU has been somewhat ambivalent. On one hand, the intended movement towards the convergence of the European Social Model implied the introduction of some worker-friendly policies, including non-discrimination principles, rather favourable formal regulations of temporary agency work, and some new (albeit not always effective) institutions of employment relations, such as works councils and European Works Councils. On the other hand, the implementation of the EU *acquis communautaire* was "slow and rather patchy" (Drahokoupil and Myant, 2015: 332), and intertwined with pressures from internal actors.

The most telling example is the regulation of fixed-term employment contracts. As a result of employers' pressure, the 2002 amendment to the Labour Code suspended – until Poland's accession to the EU in 2004 – the restrictions regarding the maximum permissible number of consecutive temporary employment contracts (Czarzasty, 2002). This contributed to a significant growth in the number of such contracts. While in the year 2000 only 5.6 per cent of all employees were employed on fixed-term contracts, in 2004 that number already rose to 22.4 per cent (Eurostat LFS). After 2004, as a result of the adjustment of Polish law to Directive EC 99/70, a third consecutive fixed-term contract concluded with the same employer had to become a permanent, open-ended contract. However, despite trade union opposition, no maximum duration of fixed term contracts was introduced and short notice periods (only two weeks) were retained. By 2007, over 28 per cent of employees had such a temporary contract, sometimes concluded for many years.

Speaking more generally, the loopholes in the legislation and the problems with law enforcement, arising from the weakness of trade unions, cumbersome labour court proceedings, and the limited sanctioning power granted to Labour

Inspectorates, made it possible to bypass even the more favourable legislation. For instance, although the Act on Temporary Agency Work (2003) stipulated that TAWs should be employed on temporary employment contracts, it did not preclude their employment on civil-law contracts. Consequently, the share of TAWs with civil-law contracts has been growing: from 38 per cent of all TAWs in 2005 to 44 per cent in 2014 (MPiPS, 2015). Similarly, even though in 2002 a new paragraph precluding the replacement of employment contracts with civil law contracts was added to the Labour Code, the civil-law employment has continued to boom, especially in the period after the beginning of the global recession in 2008.[3]

This new wave of precarisation disproportionally affected young people, whose entry into the labour market came to be shaped by the experience of temporary employment and low-paid and unpaid traineeships and voluntary work, partially resulting from the labour market policies applied to this group of workers. The collective experience of young workers during this period of time was reflected in their migration. As indicated by Meardi (2012), the mass exodus abroad following the EU enlargement in 2004 can be interpreted as a form of "exit" strategy (in Hirschman's sense) of workers discontented with their labour market situation. While in 2002 there were 450,000 Poles living in the EU countries, just five years later, in 2007, the number reached almost 1.9 million (GUS, 2013). People aged 15–34 accounted for almost 50 percent of all post-accession migrants. In addition, the Polish 'post-accession' migrants were better educated than both those who stayed behind in Poland as well as the 'pre-accession' migrants (Kaczmarczyk, 2012: 178). This latter phenomenon indicated exhaustion of the strategy of occupational advancement through university education in the semi-peripheral, "dependent market economy" of Poland.

Simultaneously, the second wave of precarisation was accompanied by the emergence of trade union organising in the private sector, growing union mobilisation in the public sector, and the emergence of new, younger and proactive union activists in newly-established union organisations (cf. Krzywdzinski, 2010; Kubisa and Ostrowski, 2014; Mrozowicki and Van Hootegem, 2010). Migration abroad, together with the improved economic situation after 2004, strengthened the bargaining power of workers and contributed to the eruption of strikes in 2006–2008, with the total number in 2008 (12,765) being higher than in the early 1990s.

### *Global economic recession and the third wave of precarisation (2008–2015)*

The most recent 'third' wave of precarisation occurred as an aftermath of the financial crisis of 2008. Even though the Polish economy was not impacted by the crisis as much as the economies of other EU countries, nevertheless preventive measures aimed at limiting the expected job and financial losses were put forth by employers' organisations and trade unions in the Tripartite Commission and proposed to the government in Spring 2009. The government decided to introduce mostly those policies which would increase labour flexibility without strengthening labour protection. The 2009 Act on Alleviation of the Effects of the Economic Crisis on Employees and Entrepreneurs (the so-called "Anti-crisis Act") allowed the employers to conclude unlimited numbers of fixed term contracts as long as the total period of employment did not exceed 24 months. Moreover, the Act extended the reference period for calculating working time from 4 to 12 months, and included the option of flexible working hours (24-hour work cycle) (Czarzasty, 2009). Other measures aimed at increasing flexibility included the amendment of the 2010 regulations governing temporary agency work, which removed the six-month prohibition of employment of temporary workers by an employer who imposed collective dismissals and the extension of the maximum length of employment by temporary work agencies from 12 to 18 months.

Although the crisis period was treated as an exceptional situation and the Anti-crisis Act was in force only until the end of 2011, the measures for the flexibilisation of working time were permanently inscribed into the Labour Code during its revision in 2013. This took place despite the fierce union opposition, which resulted in their withdrawal from the Tripartite Commission in June 2013. While the share of temporary employees in total employment grew only slightly in the 15–64 age category (from 26.4 per cent in 2009 to 28.3 per cent in 2014), it rose significantly among the youngest (15–24 years old) employees, from 62.8 per cent in 2008 to 71.2 per cent in 2014. The reintroduction of the Labour Code limits on the number of consecutive fixed-term contracts in 2011 might have also stimulated employers' interest in civil law contracts. The estimated number of people with whom a civil law contract was concluded and who were not employed based on an employment contract elsewhere grew from 546,700 in 2010 to 1,400,000 in 2013 (GUS, 2015).[4]

Once again the EU's role in these developments is ambiguous. According to Drahokoupil and Myant (2015: 339), the EU agenda (and recommendations) following the economic crisis reflected a "belief that problems with competitiveness and employment levels were linked to high wages and high employee protection." The European Commission (EC) pressure became stronger in the context of a new method of economic governance, the "European Semester", which was introduced in 2010 to coordinate national-level economic policies in the EU in three areas: structural reforms, fiscal policies, and the prevention of excessive macroeconomic imbalances. Although the EC officially disapproves of the dualisation of labour market in Poland, in its most recent (2015) recommendations it suggested that

> Rigid dismissal provisions, long judicial proceedings and other burdens placed on employers encourage the use of fixed-term and non-standard employment contracts. Furthermore, the perceived high cost of contracts covered by the labour code leads to excessive use of civil law contracts (*umowy cywilno-prawne*), which are attractive to employers due to the associated lower social security contributions.
>
> (European Commission, 2015)

Thus, the EC essentially approves the concept of addressing labour market segmentation by further flexibilising employment and lowering employment costs and reducing the "other burdens" placed on employers, rather than by increasing protection for those in vulnerable employment. This EC agenda is obviously convergent with the stance of employers, and in contrast to the approach of trade unions to the issue of "junk", temporary, and civil-law contracts. This is further discussed below.

## Trade unions and precarious employment: towards a countermovement?

As argued and documented elsewhere (Czarzasty and Mrozowicki, 2014; Mrozowicki *et al.*, 2013; Trappmann, 2011), trade unions in Poland and some other CEE countries were not particularly focused on non-standard employment until the mid 2000s.[5] In Poland, the legal barriers to the unionisation of precarious employees included a narrow definition of those eligible as "employees" (i.e. those with employment contracts), under the Trade Union Act, to join and establish trade unions. This excluded those with civil-law contracts and the self-employed from union membership (Czarzasty and Mrozowicki, 2014). In addition, due to the very low (15–25 per cent) coverage of collective agreements and the virtual absence of sectoral level agreements, the legal possibility to represent non-standard workers through collective bargaining was (and so far still is) very rarely used. Comparative research on Poland, Romania, Estonia and Slovenia shows that unions tend to consider the organising of temporary employees as a resource-intensive endeavour in which the returns (in terms of membership gains) are limited (Mrozowicki, 2014: 311). Anti-union employer strategies, workers' fear of job loss, distrust of unions, and limited knowledge of workers' rights – in particular among young people – are other factors which make workers reluctant to join trade unions even if legally they may do so.

However, the spectacular growth of non-standard employment contributed to a rise in the relevance of trade unions' agendas in Poland by the end of the first decade of the 2000s. The protracted crisis in the national level social dialogue with the government after 2009, marked by the stalemate in tripartite consultations on minimum wage and labour market legislation in 2009–2013 and the subsequent withdrawal of trade unions from the Tripartite Commission in June 2013, as well as the limited scope of collective bargaining at the sectoral level, forced unions to search for new forms of expressions of discontent. These included public and media campaigns, street protests, and pressure to change legislation. Notably, the shift from traditional approaches, based on collective bargaining and social dialogue, to more innovative ones was also observed in other countries in the region, in many cases coinciding with other forms of citizens' mobilisation outside the workplace (Greskovits, 2015; Kahancová, 2015). The issue whether this variety of union strategies against the expansion of precarious employment might be interpreted as a "countermovement" against the unleashed expansion of the market forces is an open question, requiring more detailed comparative and historical research (Polanyi, 2001 [1944]). In any case they clearly denote a transformation of union focus and tactics.

In Poland, the first step was to bring the terms "junk contracts" (*umowy śmieciowe*) and precariat (*prekariat*) into the media, public and mainstream political discourse (in that order). The term "junk contracts", specific to Poland, refers mainly to the civil-law contracts, overused by the employers and depriving workers of their rights such us minimum wage, paid holiday, and health and pension insurance. The term was firstly used in the mid-2000s by the activists of the anarcho-syndicalist All Poland Trade Union Workers' Initiative (OZZ IP). Thanks to personal contacts between union activists and supporters, it made its way to the mainstream All-Poland Alliance of Trade Unions (OPZZ) and NSZZ Solidarność. It was made popular through union campaigns and entered the mainstream political discourse in the early 2010s' decade. While the notion of 'precariat' is, in turn, less common in the Polish union and political discourses, the situation is rapidly changing, partially as a result of the well-publicised debates following the publication of the Polish edition of *The Precariat* by Guy Standing (2014), and a book on the precariat by Jarosław Urbański (2014). For instance, in explaining the unexpected results of the Polish Presidential Elections in 2015 (which were won by Andrzej Duda, the right-wing conservative candidate of the Law and Justice (PiS) party, with the anti-establishment, right-wing populist candidate, Paweł Kukiz, getting unexpected 20.8 per cent of votes) media explanations included "the anger of the precariat" (Pawlicka, 2015).

New narrative resources have helped trade unions to frame the problems of precarious workers. In 2008, the Youth Commission of OPZZ indicated that jobs offered to young people are often of worse quality, including fixed-term contracts and lower wages. The campaign "Commission Contract Generation" against unpaid labour and misusing civil law contracts was launched by the Trade Union Forum (FZZ) in 2011, in cooperation with the Democratic Student Alliance (DZS) (Trawinska, 2011). In 2012, the "Sisyphus" campaign was carried out by NSZZ Solidarność against the expansion of "junk contracts", spreading information about the disadvantaged situation of those with civil-law contracts on the streets, on the internet, and in spots in the major national media. The issue of "junk contracts" was featured during the anti-austerity protests and union demonstrations in 2011–15. For instance, in their campaign against the extension of the retirement age to 67, the unions pointed to the problem of workers with civil-law contracts, who are not included in the pension system at all due to the nature of their employment. The demand to counteract the extensive use of "junk contracts" was also formulated in the first general strike in Poland since 1989, in the Upper Silesia region in 2013, and in the "Days of protests" organized by all three national trade union confederations in September 2013. The combined unions' initiative to fix the minimum wage at 50 per cent of the national average wage also tackled the problem of precarious workers. An important role in the campaigns was also played by the demands to counteract the precarisation of work in the public sector, voiced, for instance, during the nurses' and midwives' protests in 2011.

Notably, many of these campaigns involved union cooperation with non-union actors. For instance, the precarisation of women's work became an important theme of *Manifas*, the demonstrations by women's movements which in the early 2000s were joined by trade unions (including the All-Poland Trade Union of Nurses and Midwives and OPZZ). During the hundred-thousand-strong anti-government demonstration "Awake Poland!" (in September 2012), NSZZ Solidarność was supported by the main right-wing political party, Law and Justice (PiS), and in circles related to the Catholic "Radio Maryja". The linkages between Solidarność and PiS, which are officially downplayed by the union, in fact became stronger with Solidarność's support for PiS candidates in the presidential and parliamentary elections in 2015.[6] This broadening of the field of action is also visible in the case of radical unions (such as Workers' Initiative) and those political forces which consciously attempt to mobilise precarious workers. In May 2015, Workers' Initiative co-organised a campaign and demonstration called "We, the Precariat". In the course of the parliamentary election campaign in Autumn 2015, a new political party *Razem* (Together) emerged, which called itself the party of the precariat. It drew on the experiences of the Spanish *Podemos* and established informal links with trade unions as well. In the October 2015 elections it managed to get 3.62 per cent votes. Although this did not give it parliamentary seats, it did secured state funding for it until the next elections.

Besides campaigns and street demonstrations, trade unions are also experimenting with various approaches to the trade union organisation of non-standard employees. As a result of its international cooperation and the incorporation of Anglo-Saxon organising models, NSZZ Solidarność targeted atypical employees in its trade union organising campaigns developed since the late 1990s. More often however their problems were locally addressed by large company and inter-company trade unions. For instance, the activities of some inter-company union organisations of NSZZ Solidarność and Workers' Initiative in some multinational companies (such as Volkswagen, GM Opel and, more recently, Amazon) included membership campaigns aimed at temporary agency workers (Mrozowicki and Maciejewska, 2015). In Volkswagen plants, as a result of the implementation of the Charter on Temporary Agency Work negotiated by the VW World Works Council in 2012, temporary agency workers can constitute no more than 5 percent of all staff. Some trade unions (such as Workers' Initiative, Confederation of Labour OPZZ and the Nationwide Trade Union of Midwives OZZP) began to organise the self-employed and unemployed. The Workers' Initiative and the Confederation of Labour OPZZ have also experimented with "milieu union committees". Similarly to community unions in the UK and Japan, they involve all workers regardless of their employment status (in the form of peer-support groups) and are considered the basis for establishing inter-company trade union organisations in the future (ibidem). However, the effects of these activities are still limited.

Finally, and perhaps most importantly, the Polish trade unions, similarly to their CEE counterparts (Kahancová, 2015), have become very active in applying legal pressure at the national, and increasingly at the international, levels to improve the situation of precarious workers by changing labour law. As noted by Greskovits (2015: 281), the EU and international labour legislation has allowed them to "frame their demands in European labour rights terms and use such regulations to externalize domestic conflicts." In 2012, NSZZ Solidarność formulated a proposal to reform the legislation on temporary agency work by, *inter alia*, equalising the status of those employed by temporary work agencies using civil-law contracts with other temporary employees. In the same year, the union lodged a complaint with the European Commission claiming the improper application of Council Directive 99/70/EC in Poland, in particular with respect to abuses arising from successive fixed-term employment contracts. This complaint was acknowledged by the EC in December 2013, an acknowledgment which indicated several areas of concern with regard to the regulation of temporary employment in Poland (Surdykowska, 2014). This was followed by a joint proposal of Solidarność, OPZZ and FZZ to change the Labour Code. In September 2015, the new Social Dialogue Council (SDC) Act came into force. It is a result of a compromise proposal made by social partners following the protracted boycott of the Tripartite Commission by trade unions. Consequently the SDC, endowed with broader prerogatives and resources, will replace the Tripartite Commission. The outcomes of its work with respect to policies regarding the precarisation of employment in Poland remain to be seen.

The initial political responses to trade union campaigns have been limited. However, the increasing pressure of public opinion in the context of the approaching parliamentary and presidential elections in 2015, as well as the positive responses of international institutions (European Commission, International Labour Organisation – ILO) to union complaints, led the liberal government of the Civic Platform to implement a series of legislative reforms in 2014–2015. In 2014, legal changes were introduced establishing obligatory social security contributions (to be paid by employers) on all freelance contracts up to the level of minimum wage, starting in 2016. Following the 2014 changes in the public procurement law, the contracting authority (public institutions) can make use of the social clause and give preference to a bidder who employs workers on full-time and open-ended contracts. In 2015, amendments to Labour Code were introduced which limit the number of consecutive temporary employment contracts with the same employer to three, and their maximum length to 36 months. In 2012, as a result of a complaint lodged with the ILO by NSZZ Solidarność in 2011, the ILO advised the Polish government to change its labour legislation so that all workers, including the self-employed and those with civil-law contracts, can join trade unions. In June 2015, following a case filed by OPZZ, the Constitutional Court of Poland deemed the limitation of union membership to hired employees unconstitutional. As a result of both legal campaigns, legislative changes have to be made which will enable the self-employed and workers with civil law contracts to join unions (Czarzasty, 2015).

Nevertheless, despite the variety of innovative approaches used, union membership among young people remains very low. According to the most recent surveys, there were only four per cent of union members in the age category

18–24, and 10 per cent age category 25–34 (Feliksiak, 2014). At the same time, however, the support voiced by young workers (aged 18–24) for the claim that union activities are good for the country is among the highest in the entire working population (44 per cent in 2014, ibidem). In addressing this apparent contradiction, below we provide a brief summary of the results of a qualitative study on non-unionised young workers in Wrocław, a large city in southwest Poland, in which we attempted to understand the dynamics of workers' biographical orientations to the emergent counter-movements.

## Life strategies of young precarious workers: a fragmented basis of counter-movements?

The existing research on the social consciousness and identities of precarious workers in Poland indicates a tendency to question the differences between the situation of those in permanent and temporary employment (Poławski, 2012), to overlook the negative aspects of flexibility (in particular by the middle-classes) (Gdula, 2014), and to frame individual experiences in terms of market discourses (Desperak, 2015). These observations can be interpreted in terms of the so-called "normalisation of precariousness", understood as a social and biographical process through which flexible employment becomes a regular part of occupational careers. In order to understand this process, and the social and biographical limits in creating a potential for counter-movements, the research carried out in Wrocław was aimed at exploring the experiences and life strategies of young precarious workers. It made use of biographical narrative interviews as designed by Fritz Schütze (1983). The fieldwork took place in 2013. In cooperation with sociology students at the University of Wrocław, we collected 24 biographical narrative interviews with workers younger than 30 years old. They were employed using various types of flexible work contracts (self-employed and employed using civil-law contracts), in both low-skilled and high-skilled services.[7]

Cross-case comparisons and data coding followed the guidelines of the grounded theory methodology, including open coding to generate categories and selective coding to build relationships between them (Charmaz, 2006). We were particularly interested in the issue of when (and if) non-standard employment becomes a *problem* for the respondents. Searching for traces of precarious workers' collective agency, we also asked how and to what extent solutions to this problem can be linked to the emergent trade unions' activities against "junk jobs". In interpreting the results, it should be kept in mind that the reported results have their methodological limitations. The case presented is based on a sample of highly-educated flexible workers in a relatively large, developing city. While the generic nature of the categories emerged makes their theoretical generalisation possible, the determination of their statistical distribution in the population of young workers in Poland generally would require further research.

Data analysis made it possible to reconstruct two contrasting types of life strategies connected with the ways in which the respondents addressed their employment situations; the "market-liberal" type, and the "reformist" type

(Mrozowicki *et al.*, 2015). In between these were the narratives of those who saw their non-standard and temporary employment in terms of a "transitory" situation, framed mostly in instrumental and pragmatic terms, as a way of earning money and achieving goals beyond work. In our earlier articles, we called this a "withdrawn" type, to denote their lack of knowledge about trade union activities combined with their rejection of protests and limited interest and belief in any kind of collective action (ibidem: 136). In the following paragraphs, however, we will focus solely on the "market-liberal" and "reformist" types, as they most clearly indicate the scope of the "normalisation" of precariousness and the emergent counter-narratives to it, some of which critically address the current trade union strategies.

The market-liberal type of life strategy is linked with the post-Fordist discourses of resourcefulness, self-confident individualism, life-long learning, and entrepreneurship (Strzelecki, 2012). It is related to the ideal of upward occupational mobility, based on the accumulation of resources, experiences, and skills. It was typical of those who combined sought-after skills and workplace bargaining power with the biographical experiences of successful occupational advancement. Their belief in the power of the market – in which the most resourceful always win – goes together with their questioning the need for collective action. Union protests against "junk contracts" are dismissed as "infantile" (Przemysław), rooted in socialism, "tilting at windmills" and ignoring the forces of globalisation (Agnieszka), and therefore potentially dangerous as they would only increase unemployment and lead to a "second Greece" (Mirosław). The experiences of the upward socially mobile reinforce the stereotypical visions of the labour market, which would work smoothly on its own if only states and unions would not intervene.

Even though some traces of market individualism could be found in the majority of collected narratives, it was only in the "market-liberal" type that the disadvantages of unstable employment were consistently downplayed. In the other cases we could observe the emergence of various biographical problems and tensions related to precarious jobs, including, *inter alia*, limits on access to credit and public health care, the negative impact of flexibility on family and social life, as well as the lack of individual control over working time. Yet the translation of biographical problems into collective frames of reference requires a specific set of narrative resources which provide "values, shared understandings, stories and ideologies" (Levesque and Murray, 2010: 339) allowing for the expression of individual discontent in collective terms. It is in this context that we observed the emergence of the "reformist" type. It was most typical of the narratives of those employed in the cultural sectors and linked with various "alternative milieus" (e.g. squatters movement, LGBT movement, vegan milieu). However, some of its elements also emerged in other cases (except for the "market-liberal" type) in which some references were made to the union discourse of "junk jobs". Within the "reformist" type, only a limited number of informants supported unions without any reservations. More often they saw them in quite critical terms, as a "bunch of old farts" who do not care about young people (Kamila), fighting only for people with "long term and stable contracts" (Urszula), living with "the myth of Solidarność" (Ada), or being "bureaucratically powerless" (Arkadiusz). Simultaneously however, they viewed social campaigns against the expansion of "junk contracts" as necessary. For Ada, a freelance translator linked with the LGBT movement, union protests against "junk jobs" are worth supporting as an expression of "people's discontent with what's going on in the labour market", even if they might "end up with some populism and some far right". Maria, working in a left-wing cafe, thinks that people in Poland "scream too little" against their employment situation and therefore supports union campaigns, even though she admits to having limited knowledge about trade unionism. In these and other narratives, the "reformist" approach combines criticism of the bureaucracy of Fordist institutions, including trade unions, with opposition to the injustice of post-Fordist precariousness. Arguably, the emergence of this type of viewpoint is both a warning signal and an opportunity for trade unions, the latter because it coincides, at least to some extent, with their new tactics to tackle the problem of precarious work.

## Conclusions

This chapter has explored the mechanisms underlying the development of precarious work in Poland and trade union responses to it. Firstly, we claim that the combination of internal (domestic) and external (international and transnational) conditions have contributed to three waves of precarisation of work, as a result of which young people have found themselves in a disadvantaged segment of the labour market. Secondly, we suggested that following the gradual exhaustion of market-individualistic workers' strategies (such as entrepreneurship and investments in higher education) and the mass "exit" abroad (through migration), the space for collective resistance against non-standard employment began to emerge. This new opportunity structure is reflected in the increasingly experimental trade union strategies, which have begun to bring about tangible effects for the situation of precarious workers.

Our analysis confirms the observation of Greskovits (2015: 283) that in studying the new forms and spaces of collective resistance, more attention should be given to activities in which workers and unions act as "angry citizens" seeking out new forms of expression of their discontent. These new forms can include legal pressure at the national and international levels, formation of labour-citizens coalitions, and mass media and awareness-raising campaigns. New union tactics clearly reflect the fact that under the new conditions the traditional union tools, such as tripartite social dialogue, sectoral level collective agreements and workplace mobilisation, become increasingly difficult to implement. The reasons for these difficulties are multiple, including the reluctance of some CEE governments and employers to negotiate with trade unions, the transnational and the EU pressure for employment flexibility, and the expansion of non-standard employment which undermines workers' attachment to their workplaces. It is in this context that the CEE countries, including Polish trade unions, have had to continue their involvement in organisational experiments and new coalitions with social movements and political forces.

However, as argued by Richard Hyman (1999: 108), "building collective solidarity is in part a question of organizational capacity, but more fundamentally it is part of a battle of ideas". The analysis of the narratives of young precarious workers in Wrocław indicates that the Polish trade unions have still a lot of ideological and organisational work ahead of them if they are to convince young workers that they also represent *their* interests. The most general description of our informants' attitudes toward union-led mobilisation against "junk contracts" would be ambivalence. It might be sufficient for "primitive rebels" (Hobsbawm, 1959; Standing, 2011) against "the leftist, liberal or conservative governments' policies of marketization and austerity" and against the attempts to "seek remedy from populist, nationalist or other anti-systemic newcomers to the electoral arena (Ost, 2005)" (Greskovits, 2015: 282). Yet, in order to remain independent economic and political actors, CEE unions cannot rely on the outburst of collective anger. Paraphrasing the observation by Ost (2005), they have to be able to combine new tools with their capabilities to frame workers collective interests in economic terms. The extent to which Polish trade unions are really capable of and, most importantly, willing to develop such inclusive frames for new solidarities remains an open question.

## Acknowledgement

The authors wish to thank the FP7-PEOPLE-2012-ITN programme "Changing Employment" ("The changing nature of employment in Europe in the context of challenges, threats and opportunities for employees and employers"), project no. 31732 for supporting their collaboration in the preparation and writing of this article. In particular, the work of Mateusz Karolak was financially supported by the aforementioned programme.

## Notes

1   The term "civil law contracts" refers to various types of employment contracts which are not covered by the Labour Code and instead are regulated only by the Civil Code. The major forms of the civil law contracts are the freelance contract (*umowa zlecenie*) and specific task contract (*umowa o dzieło*). In both cases no minimum wage applies, they provide no protection against dismissal and, until recently (2015), they excluded workers from trade union membership. Moreover the employers ordering the execution of a specific task are not obliged to cover costs of employees' social security contributions, including social, health and pension insurance.
2   As argued by Trappmann, the elimination of 1.7 million jobs between 1998 and 2002 "resulted from the restructuring of those economic sectors that were supposed to be made profitable as a condition for EU accession" (Trappmann, 2011: 9).
3   Even though no systematic data is available, civil-law employment was very popular in the 1990s in Poland. Until the reform of the Labour Code in 1997, social security contributions did not need to be paid on any kind of civil-law contracts. The reforms enacted in 1997–98 made these contributions obligatory on freelance/specific task contracts.

4    Unfortunately there is no comparable data for the pre-2010 period from the Central Statistical Office.
5    The significant exceptions were their opposition against bogus self-employment and, obviously, their ongoing focus on increasing wages.
6    NSZZ Solidarność officially loosened its links with political parties following the defeat of Solidarity Electoral Action (AWS) in 2001, which contributed to a greater focus on its trade union role. However, its ever closer cooperation with the Law and Justice Party began to be visible since the mid 2000s.
7    This included, among others, (low-skilled) cleaning activities, work in restaurants/pubs, call centres, as well as (high-skilled) cultural, teaching and IT services.

# References

Beissinger, M. and Sasse, G. (2014) 'An end to "Patience"? The great recession and economic protest in eastern Europe', in Bartels, L. and Bermeo, N. (eds) *Mass politics in tough times: opinions, votes and protest in the great recession*, Oxford University Press, pp. 334–370.

Bohle, D. and Greskovits, B. (2012) *Capitalist diversity on Europe's periphery*. Ithaca and London: Cornell University Press.

Charmaz, K. (2006) *Constructing Grounded Theory. A Practical Guide Through Qualitative Analysis*. London: Sage.

Czarzasty, J. (2002) *Amended labour code adopted*, EurWork. Dublin, available at: www.eurofound.europa.eu//observatories/eurwork/articles/amended-labour-code-adopted [Accessed 4 April 2016].

Czarzasty, J. (2009) *Mixed reaction to anti-crisis legislation*, EurWork online, available at: www.eurofound.europa.eu/observatories/eurwork/articles/mixed-reaction-to-anti-crisis-legislation [Accessed 4 April 2016].

Czarzasty, J. (2015) *Poland: New law to grant self-employed the right to join a union*, EurWork online, available at: www.eurofound.europa.eu/observatories/eurwork/articles/labour-market-industrial-relations-law-and-regulation-business/poland-new-law-to-grant-self-employed-the-right-to-join-a-union [Accessed 4 April 2016].

Czarzasty, J. and Mrozowicki, A. (2014) *Union organising in Poland and in CEE: experiences, trends, alternatives*. Warszawa: FES.

Desperak, I. (2015) 'Precarisation of work in precarious world', *Forum Socjologiczne*, Special Issue (forthcomming).

Drahokoupil, J. and Myant, M. (2015) 'Labour's legal resources after 2004: the role of the European Union', *Transfer: European Review of Labour and Research*, 21(3) 327–341.

European Commission (2015) Council Recommendation on the 2015 National Reform Programme of Poland and delivering a Council opinion on the 2015 Convergence Programme of Poland, European Commission, 13.05.2015, available at: http://ec.europa.eu/europe2020/pdf/csr2015/csr2015_poland_en.pdf [Accessed on 4 April 2016].

Feliksiak, M. (2014) *Związki zawodowe i prawa pracownicze*, Report no. 106/2014, Warszawa: CBOS.

Greskovits, B. (2015) 'Ten years of enlargement and the forces of labour in Central and Eastern Europe', *Transfer: European Review of Labour and Research*, 21(3): 269–284.

Hobsbawm, E. J. (1959) *Primitive Rebels: Studies in Archaic Forms of Social Movement in the 19th and 20th Centuries*, Manchester: Manchester University Press.

Hyman, R. (1999) 'Imagined solidarities: can trade unions resist globalization? in Globalization and Labour Relations, Leisink, P. (ed.). Cheltenham: Edward Elgar, pp. 94–115.

Gardawski, J. (2001) *Powracająca klasa. Sektor prywatny w III Rzeczypospolitej.* Warszawa: Wydawnictwo IFiS PAN.

Gdula, M. (2014) 'Klasa średnia i doświadczenie elastyczności', *Polityka społeczna* 5–6, pp. 40–45.

GUS (2013) *Migracje Zagraniczne Ludności. Narodowy Spis Powszechny Ludności I Mieszkań 2011.* Warszawa.

GUS (2015) *Wybrane zagadnienia rynku pracy*, available at: http://stat.gov.pl/obszary-tematyczne/rynek-pracy/pracujacy-zatrudnieni-wynagrodzenia-koszty-pracy/wybrane-zagadnienia-rynku-pracy-dane-za-2013-rok-,9,2.html, [Accessed 4 April 2016].

Hardy, J. (2009) *Poland's New Capitalism*, London: Pluto Press.

Jasiecki, K. (2014) 'Institutional transformation and business leaders of the new foreign-led capitalism in Poland. In *'Business leaders and new varieties of capitalism in post-communist Europe'*, in K. Bluhm, B. Martens, and V. Trappmann (ed.). Routledge, pp. 23–57.

Kaczmarczyk, P. (2012) 'Labour market impacts of post-accession migration from Poland', In *Free movement of workers and labour market adjustment. Recent experiences from OECD countries and the European Union*, Paris: OECD, pp. 173–196.

Kahancová, M. and Martišková, M. (2014) *Bargaining for social rights: reducing precariousness and labour market segmentation through collective bargaining and Social dialogue.* Slovak contribution to the BARSORI project, updated version.

Kahancová, M. (2015) 'Central and Eastern European trade unions after the EU enlargement: successes and failures for capacity building', *Transfer: European Review of Labour and Research*, 21(3): 343–357.

Kalleberg, A. (2009) 'Precarious work, insecure workers: employment relations in transition', *American Sociological Review* 74(1): 1–22.

Kiersztyn, A. (2012) 'Analiza ekonomicznych konsekwencji zatrudnienia na czas określony dla jednostek i gospodarstw domowych', In: M. Bednarski,K. W. Frieske (eds) *Zatrudnienie na czas określony w polskiej gospodarce. Społeczne i ekonomiczne konsekwencje zjawiska.* Warszawa: IPiSS, pp. 93–121.

Kieżun, W. (2012) *Patologie transformacji*, Warszawa, Poltext.

Kolarska-Bobińska, L. (1998) 'Egalitaryzm i interesy grupowe w procesie zmian ustrojowych', In: W. Adamski (ed.). *Polacy '95. Aktorzy i klienci transformacji.* Warszawa: Wydawnictwo IFIS PAN.

Kozek, W. (2013) *Rynek pracy. Perspektywa instytucjonalna*, Warszawa, Wydawnictwo UW.

Krzywdzinski, M. (2010) 'Organizing employees in Central and Eastern Europe: the approach of Solidarność', *European Journal of Industrial Relations*, 16(3): 277–292.

Kubisa, J. and Ostrowski, P. (2014) 'Młodzi w związkach zawodowych. Rewitalizacja czy reprodukcja?' In: Czarzasty, J. and Mrozowicki, A. (eds) *Organizowanie związków zawodowych w Europie. Badania i praktyka*, Warszawa: Scholar, pp. 71–92.

Levesque, C. and Murray, G. (2010) 'Understanding union power: resources and capabilities for renewing union capacity', *Transfer: European Review of Labour and Research*, 16: 333–50.

Mach, B. W., Mayer, K. U., and Pohoski, M. (1994) 'Job changes in the Federal-Republic-of-Germany and Poland – a longitudinal assessment of the impact of welfare-capitalist and state-socialist labor-market segmentation', *European Sociological Review*, 10(1): 1–28.

Maciejewska, M. and Mrozowicki, A. (2015) PRECARIR project. Poland: Country report. PART II, unpublished report draft. September 2015.

Meardi, G. (2012) *Social failures of EU enlargement. A case of workers voting with their feet.* New York: Routledge.

MPiPS (2015) *Informacja o działalności agencji zatrudnienia w 2014 r.* Ministry of Labour and Social Policy, Warszawa.

Mrozowicki, A. and Van Hootegem, G. (2008) 'Unionism and workers' strategies in capitalist transformation: the Polish case reconsidered', *European Journal of Industrial Relations*, 14(2): 197–216.

Mrozowicki, A., Bajuk-Sencar, T. and Roosalu, T. (2013) 'Precarious work in the retail sector in Estonia, Poland and Slovenia: trade union responses in a time of economic crisis', *Transfer: European Journal of Labour and Research*, 19(2): 263–274.

Mrozowicki, A. (2014) 'Varieties of trade union organizing in Central and Eastern Europe: a comparison of the retail and automotive sectors', *European Journal of Industrial Relations* 20(4): 297–315.

Mrozowicki, A. and Maciejewska, M. (2013) 'Conflicts at work in Poland's new capitalism: worker resistance in a flexible work regime'. In: G. Gall. (ed.). *New forms and expressions of conflict at work.* Houndmills: Palgrave, pp. 191–211.

Mrozowicki, A., Krasowska, A. and Karolak, M. (2015) 'Stop the junk contracts' Young workers and trade union mobilisation against precarious employment in Poland'. In: A. Hodder, L. Kretsos (eds) *Young workers and trade unions. A global view.* Basingstoke: Palgrave Macmillan, pp. 123–141.

Nölke, A. and Vliegenthart, A. (2009) 'Enlarging the varieties of capitalism: the emergence of dependent market economies in East Central Europe', *World Politics*, 61(4): 670–702.

Ost, D. (2011) 'Illusory corporatism' Ten Years Later. *Warsaw Forum of Economic Sociology* 2(1): 20–49.

Pawlicka, A. (2015) Gniew prekariatu. Interview with Agata Bielik-Robson, Newsweek online, available at: www.newsweek.pl/co-wybory-mowia-o-polakach-rozmowa-z-agata-bielik-robson,artykuly,364100,1,z.html [Accessed 4 April 2016].

Polanyi, K. (1944) *The Great Transformation.* New York: Farrar & Rinehart.

Poławski, P. (2012) 'Precarious generation on the Polish labour market', *Polityka Społeczna* (English Edition), 1: 15–22.

Rodgers, G. (1989) 'Precarious jobs in Western Europe. The state of the debate'. In: G. Rodgers, J. Rodgers (eds) *Precarious jobs in labour market regulation. The growth of atypical employment in Western Europe*, Geneva: International Institute for Labour Studies, pp. 1–16.

Schütze, F. (1983) Biographieforschung und narratives Interview, *Neue Praxis*, 3: 283–293.

Standing, G. (2011) *The Precariat. The new dangerous class.* London: Bloomsbury Academic.

Surdykowska, B. (2014) *Fixed-term contract regulation under EU scrutiny.* EurWORK online, available at www.eurofound.europa.eu/eiro/2014/01/articles/pl1401029i.htm, [Accessed 4 April 2016].

Trappmann, V. (2011) 'Precarious employment in Poland – a legacy of transition or an effect of European integration ? Overview of the labour market in Poland'. *EMECON* 1, pp. 1–22.

Trawinska, M. (2011) *Unions and students act to help young workers.* EurWORK online, available at www.eurofound.europa.eu/eiro/2011/06/articles/pl1106039i.htm, [Accessed 4 April 2016].

Urbański, J. (2014) *Prekariat i nowa walka klas*. Warszawa, Instytut Wydawniczy Książka i Prasa.

Ziółkowski, M. (2006) 'Zmiany systemu wartości', In: J. Wasilewski (ed.) *Współczesne społeczeństwo polskie. Dynamika zmian*. Warszawa: Wydawnictwo Naukowe Scholar. pp. 145–174.

# Index